0055385

D0897800

PHICINC 99

Communication Incompetencies

A *Theory of Training Oral Performance Behavior*

Gerald M. Phillips

With Contributions by
Lynne Kelly and Rebecca B. Rubin

Southern Illinois University Press
Carbondale and Edwardsville

Library of Congress Cataloging-in-Publication Data

Phillips, Gerald M.
    Communication incompetencies : a theory of training oral
performance behavior / Gerald M. Phillips with contributions by
Lynne Kelly and Rebecca B. Rubin.
        p.   cm.
    Includes bibliographical references.

    1. Bashfulness. 2. Oral communication. 3. Behavior modification.
4. Speech—Study and teaching. 5. Pennsylvania State University.
Reticence Program. I. Kelly, Lynne. II. Rubin, Rebecca B.
III. Title.
    BF575.B3P45   1991
    153.6—dc20   90-9827
    ISBN 0-8093-1459-2   CIP

The paper used in this publication meets the minimum requirements of American National Standard for Information Sciences—Permanence of Paper for Printed Library Materials, ANSI ZX39.48–1984. ∞

Contents

Preface

The Pennsylvania State University Reticence Program conducted its first class in 1965. Since then, the program has grown into the oldest and largest of its kind in the country. It has served nearly five thousand students in its twenty-five years of existence. As far as we know, it is the oldest and largest program in the country for modification of the performance behavior of shy people.

The program is based on a common syllabus used in all sections. Every instructor makes the same assignments, conducts office conferences similarly, uses the same criteria and method of critique, and has essentially the same outcome. Most students both approve of the course and give evidence of improvement. There have been few dramatic "recoveries" or "major breakthroughs." Successful instruction proceeds in small increments.

A consistent offering was a major component of the program from the very start. We believed at the begining that the personal influence of the instructor must be kept to a minimum. The important thing was to find a technology of instruction that facilitated improvement for everyone but above all did no harm. We agreed that any changes made would be agreed on collectively and adopted by everyone.

Over the years, there were a number of changes. What started essentially as an exercise in sensitivity training became a highly formalized process of behavior modification largely through the contributions of innovators like Tim Hopf, Kent Sokoloff, Lynne Kelly, Nancy Metzger, and Cynthia Begnal. My question as director and teacher in this program was, What was working? I had to make the decisions about what was to be added and what kept.

It is very hard for a teacher to detach from the emotional connections made with the students in order to do research on what happens during the teaching process. To step back and look at the students as units of study requires a kind of dehumanization. But, after all, we teach students in classes. We do not and cannot sit on logs with them and make erudite dialogue. This is especially true in the teaching of oral performance behavior. This process, once called "teaching speech," requires that each student have an audience. It also means that the teacher, whatever concern he or she might have about individual differences, must generalize a pedagogy. Students must have a common text and common assignments; the teacher lectures to the whole group, and the grading system must be consistent. There is very little time for consideration of individual differences.

Most of the time anyway, attention to individual differences means playing favorites or honoring diminished responsibility in somewhat the same fashion that the insanity plea excuses criminals from punishment but takes up a lot of court time. The argument for honoring individual differences is compelling because it is humanistic, but there are no data to support it other than anecdotes and claims by individual teachers, whose act of claiming marks them as self-proclaimed exemptions from the obligations of their own art.

In the final crunch, teaching must be consistent. There must be a method designed to accomplish goals, and there ought to be a way of assessing whether the goals are met. In most cases, this means examinations. But there is no formal examination available for measuring success in improving oral performance behavior. Athletes can be measured by whether they win or lose. Cooking students can be measured by how palatable their preparations are. Winemakers submit their products to competitions. But in the speech classroom, evaluation is done by the same individual who sought to "improve" the student. Clearly, objectivity is lacking in the process.

And so in 1974, when Nancy Metzger discovered that the effects of instruction in the PSU Reticence Program seemed to last at least a year, and Susan Oerkvitz came to essentially the same conclusion with students going back as far as seven years, it became important to discover what there was in the method that worked.

This started my fifteen-year quest to discover what was working in the program. It was time to understand how inept, hesitant, fearful speakers became competent after a brief fifteen-week instructional experience.

The process was not miraculous. If anything, it was slow and tedious. Students labored in order to produce meticulous outlines. Teachers sat attentively by the hour responding to rehearsals of speeches they were about to hear in the classroom. The class required more hours from both teachers and students than the other speech classes, and the grading curve was considerably lower. Yet, the students consistently rated the course as one of the best they ever had. Perhaps this was a miracle.

But nobody in the teaching profession talks about miracles, not if they have a brain in their head. Educational innovations come and go. We have had new math and the phonic reading system. And in communication we have gone through a great many panacea programs from Delsarte to the "motivated sequence." Furthermore, there is a tendency among speech educators to make claims and to avoid testing their innovations.

Modesty of claims is of paramount importance. We argued the course was effective because students said it was. We thought we saw improvement, but we were as likely to be biased as any speech instructors. The Oerkvitz and Metzger studies, however, suggested rather strongly that we were making real changes. A recent, as yet unpublished, study by Lynne Kelly, Robert L. Duran, and John Stewart at the University of Hartford confirms the conclusions that the program of instruction brought about genuine changes.

In the early days of the Reticence Program, the dedicated instructional staff made the same kind of outlandish claims for their pedagogy as any young instructors might be expected to make. But the genuine claim that can be made about the Reticence Program was that its pedagogy was "instructor free." That is, any speech instructor of average competence or better could take the standard syllabus, and if they followed instructions to the letter, they could have a successful outcome. As measured by student evaluations, no instructor in the Reticence Program was ever evaluated by the students below the 80th percentile, while instructors in other sections averaged about 50 percent. Talented and brilliant instructors in other sections often achieved a high outcome, but no other *instructional style* seemed consistently effective.

My conclusion was that the method itself represented a technology of performance improved that needed to be studied. It was simple enough. We taught composition and delivery. We proceeded through preparation, rehearsal, performance, and criticism. We did this again and again. Our adaptation to individual differences was to encourage the students to set their own goals and consequently generate their own specific performance assignments.

Our goal was to leave the students with a set of heuristics they could use to help them cope with speech performances in their business and professional careers. And what Susan Oerkvitz discovered was that most of them, approximately 80 percent, did exactly that. They remembered the steps they learned in the Reticence Program and were still using them *seven years after the fact*.

The empirical evidence led me on a quest for a theory of performance modification. Among the questions that had to be answered were, What is teachable, and what methodology most effective in teaching it? These questions presumed, in essence, that speech teaching was an enterprise about which theory could be generated from which hypotheses could be derived and tested.

This book represents my theory of performance modification. The Kelly, Duran, and Stewart study suggested that the methodology worked best with the students with the most serious problems. The lack of literature on results of teaching methodologies applied to oral performance modification leaves a large gap. We do not know whether teaching speech does any good for the ordinary student, but we have good reason to believe that students with communication problems benefit from a formal process of instruction. In this book, I justify the pedagogy of the Penn State Reticence Program and extract from it a theory of modification of incompetent oral performance.

And of course, it is an argument, a theory. The hypotheses must be generated and formal tests conducted not only for problem speakers but for the ordinary students in the ordinary speech classes. Does instruction do any good? It is an intriguing question.

This book tops off a long and productive career. At the moment this manuscript was completed I was celebrating the start of my fortieth year in the classroom and the completion of my thirty-fifth book. I have taught public speaking and group discussion on all levels; I have taught interpersonal theory, communication theory, rhetorical theory, theory of research, gender role in communication, organizational communication, among other things. I have written texts in virtually every basic area of speech communication. Throughout all this, my attention has always been on the quiet, withdrawn, nonparticipating student. I have been supported by a great many people in these endeavors.

Thanks especially to Laura Muir whose thesis first caught my concern back in 1960 and to Carroll Arnold whose political intervention made it possible for the first course to be offered in 1965. Samuel Osipow, then head of the PSU Division of Counseling provided support by producing the original class, a group of students ready to drop out of school rather than take the basic speech course.

The original group of teachers included Tim Hopf (now at Washington State University), Larry Steward (now at Portland State), and Douglas Pedersen and David Butt who are still at Penn State. Herman Cohen and Kathryn DeBoer, both members of the PSU faculty, supported the program by regularly teaching sections. In addition, several graduate student instructors contributed greatly through their theses and dissertations. These included Kathleen Domenig, David Sours, Lynne Kelly, Susan Oerkvitz, Nancy Metzger, Bruce McKinney, Lynne Grutzeck, and Barbara Streibel. There was a long list of instructors including Walt Matreyek, Dolores Rafter, Robert Harrison, Kent Sokoloff, Kathleen Kougl, Susan Ackerman-Ross, Susan Stone-Applbaum, Peter and Susan Glaser, Michael DeMasi, Paul Friedman, Jerry Zolten, Marie Bartlett-Stagl, Jan Turner, Susan Sorenson, John Gardner, Molly Wertheimer, Mary-Linda Merriam, Mary Mino, Joy Dunbar, Jim Dupree, Larry Albert, Beverly Romberger, Patti Thomas, and Roger Pace. Jim Keaten and Jim Dolhon are teaching it today. I hope I have not excluded anyone.

Kent Sokoloff deserves special acknowledgment for his collaboration with me in some of the most important research. Lynne Kelly has continued this research on her own and has recently made some consequential contributions, especially in chapter 2 of this volume. Currently, the program is being directed by Cynthia Begnal; James Keaten and Jim Dolhon are presently teaching sections.

My thanks also to those who labored through earlier drafts of this manuscript; Rod Hart, who shredded it; Lynne Kelly, who helped me put it back together; Cynthia Begnal and Mary McComb, who critiqued it in its final form. And of course, to Kenney Withers, Director of the Southern Illinois University Press, who let me put it together as I thought it. It is now an agenda. Replies and arguments are welcome.

My gratitude is boundless to Lynne Kelly for her contributed chapter and to Rebecca Rubin for her invaluable Appendix. I am especially grateful to Dennis Gouran, who helped me materially through a very challenging chapter 11 and who read and commented on the manuscript at an early stage. I am equally grateful to Herman Cohen, who talked through many of the more difficult concepts with me virtually every night through the writing of this manuscript.

The challenge to the speech profession is this: I declare that it is our mission to study the performance of oral communication and learn how to modify it. Communication itself is the property of all disciplines. It is the performance of it that is the special concern of the field called "Speech Communication." This book is offered as a first step on a repetition of the journey to discover a theory of how we can modify the way we speak begun more than two thousand years ago by Aristotle, his teachers, his contemporaries, and his followers.

1

Understanding Communication Problems

One of the essentials of being human is the requirement to share both space and time with others. We humans use talk to make the process of sharing orderly. We organize our lives and our societies by talking with one another. When people are unwilling or unable to talk well, their ability to make things come out "right" is impaired. In the simplest possible terms, making it come out "right" is the universal social goal.

The purpose of performance instruction is to change the student's natural oral communication behavior in order to facilitate accomplishment of social goals. It has a genuine narcissistic appeal. Each human is a rhetor seeking to influence the thought and conduct of everyone else (the audience). The competitive nature of the process is ameliorated by the necessity to work in groups in order to sustain such essential processes as nurturing neonates, educating the young, re-creating and procreating, and providing for the common defense. Oral communication is the link connecting the participants in these group processes as well. Rhetoric, thus, is much more than simply standing on a platform and addressing an audience. It is the art of using oral discourse to make things come out "right" in all social situations.

When people cannot do well at oral performance, they are very likely not to do well as humans. For at least five decades, a small community of scholars within the field of speech communication and an even smaller group in clinical psychology have studied people defined as oral communication-impaired but not speech defective. Their efforts have been addressed at people identified by various nouns, for example, shy people, communication apprehensives, stage-fright victims, among others. The labels assigned to inept oral communicators tended to identify various aspects of personality: diffident, timid, cowardly, anxious, and so on.

A major university press has recently been publishing a series of books, each of which carries the title, *The Rhetoric of . . . [Something or Other]*. The use of "rhetoric" in this fashion requires a prepositional phrase somewhat like "the art of . . ." or the "discipline of . . ." An art, according to a current dictionary (Random House, 1987), refers to "the principles or methods governing any craft or branch of learning," for example, the art of speaking, while a discipline is defined as "a branch of instruction or learning," for example, the discipline of rhetoric, which is the art of something or other having to do with speaking.

The same dictionary lists the following possible definitions for the word *rhetoric*. The paraphrasing is mine:

1. Undue use of exaggeration
2. Art or science of specialized literary uses of language
3. The study of the effective use of language
4. The ability to use language effectively
5. The art of prose as opposed to verse
6. The art of making persuasive speeches; oratory
7. The art of influencing the thought and conduct of an audience
8. A work on rhetoric

Note the use of "art of" in four of the eight possible definitions. What could "the rhetoric of . . ." refer to? Could it be the principles and methods of using language in a given discipline or by some person? The seventh definition above describes the normal social situation of ordinary human beings all of the time.

During the past twenty-five years the Penn State Reticence Program has provided training for nearly five thousand inept communicators. Those who taught in the program attempted to avoid pejorative labels as they concentrated on developing an effective pedagogy for modification of oral performance. The program was originally designed for people who were apprehensive about communication. Because it focused almost exclusively on inept behaviors, however, it grew into a program that accommodated to the needs of a wide variety of people. Since the focus was on specific inept behaviors, labels became relatively unimportant. The neutral term *reticence* was selected because it did not carry pejorative connotations.

THE BACKGROUND OF THE RETICENCE PROGRAM

The Reticence Program was based on the early work in stage fright summed up by Clevenger (1959). Concern about fear of public performance was, by the 1970s, generalized to all communication situations. McCroskey,[1] especially, applied the concept "communication apprehension" to a wide range of social situations.

While the main emphasis of research was focused on generating theoretical explanations of communication anxiety and its effects on social behavior, a few educators devoted their efforts to development of programs designed to modify inept social behavior in whatever form it presented.

For example, the original group of students in the Reticence Program included the following: Joseph, an entomology major whose fear of social interaction made him appear almost mute; Louise, an elementary-school teacher, whose fear of speaking to adults made her break out in hives anytime she was required to speak at the PTA; Levi, an angry young man, whose hostile tone of voice alienated virtually everyone to whom he tried to speak; Laura, once "cute," now overweight, who had learned to "shrink" into the background to avoid contact with others; Harvey, an architect, whose stuttering was so bad he could not make the mandatory oral project demonstration required for him to graduate.

The original group of eighteen students were selected for the program by the Division of Psychological Counseling, who chose them because their inability to pass a required course in public speaking kept them from graduating. The diversity of the group convinced the instructors, first, that if there was a general cause of inept communication, they did not know it, and second, some kind of individualized instruction was required to meet the individual needs of the students. The paradox was that clinical treatment was not possible, or even desirable. Thus, it was necessary to devise a general program based on individualization. Examination of various theories purporting to explain social ineptitude

1. James McCroskey is the most prolific author in the field of speech communication. For a good view of his contributions we suggest his 1970, 1977, 1982b, and 1984 publications and McCroskey and Richmond, 1982b.

provided a varied menu of possible explanations. While many of the theories focused on "shyness" or "communication apprehension," all took note of the fact that whatever caused it, the problem itself was the inability of individuals to perform effectively in social situations.

THEORIES OF INEPT SOCIAL BEHAVIOR

Psychological Theories

Shyness. Most psychologists lump people with social communication problems into a category called "shy." Zimbardo (1977) and Pilkonis (1986) focus on shyness as as a social neurosis. Buss (1986) defines shyness as "discomfort, inhibition, and awkwardness in social situations." A definition like this is hard to deal with. Does it mean that anyone who is awkward is shy? Boors are often awkward. So are people from other cultures. "Awkward" is a pejorative social judgment. Steve, one of the original "R-Program" students developed disabling stage fright during his valedictory address in high school when he discovered he was unzipped. Thereafter, he tugged at his fly whenever he spoke to others. Levi, on the other hand, would often gesture so widely that he would knock objects off the table. The behavioral indicators of awkwardness cover a wide range, and definitions of awkwardness do not apply to all situations. Similar criticism can be applied to "discomfort" and "inhibition." Both are internal processes. They can be described but not observed. The work of those who concentrated on shyness as a psychological problem is characterized by attention to internal dynamics, with little description of the behaviors regarded as disabling. Thus, the explanation seemed to demand a clinical solution.

Buss (1986) summed up the psychological consensus by explaining that shyness may be a genetic trait like fearfulness, low sociability, or lack of physical attractiveness. But factors like lack of experience, low self-esteem, and public self-consciousness could also account for inept social behavior. People are not universally shy. They are different in one situation than in another. And so the dialectic between state and trait became a theoretical preoccupation.

To those interested in improving social behavior, however, the complex theoretical explanations offered little help. It was not clear whether awkwardness was genetic or whether people could learn to be awkward. Physical appearance seemed to play some role, but there does not seem to be a formal universal definition of what was appealing and what was not. Regardless of etiology, it seemed that people were socially inept in different ways in different situations. To apply the label "shy" to all of them appeared to beg the question. Actually, "shyness" is a reification, an adjective turned into a noun. People who perform awkwardly in public situations are sometimes called "shy." They are sometimes called "klutzie." Sometimes they are comedians and are paid well to perform awkwardly in public. As we do with so many psychological terms, we turn a useful adjective into a noun, for example, depressed into depressive. "Shy," a description, becomes "shyness," a state of being. We literally bring a state or condition into being without ever defining its invariant evidences and symptoms. Once it exists, we deal with it as if it was real.

Anxiety. Anxiety is an important component of psychological explanations of shyness. Theorists seem to associate shyness and social anxiety tacitly, but the implications are unclear. Does it mean people who are anxious and fearful about social encounters are shy, or does it mean that people who call themselves shy are, therefore, anxious? Is anxiety a sine qua non of shyness? Furthermore, anxiety is variously defined. Is a person anxious who reports himself anxious, or is there some objective state that can be invariably labeled "anxious"? And of course, the state versus trait argument goes on unabated.

Whether anxiety comes from genetic or social influences, it has an unmistakable effect on both willingness and ability to communicate. However, it is not clear whether altering the way shy people feel about their social interaction has any effect on their behavior. The underlying clinical assumption is when shy people are no longer anxious, their behavior will change and they will no longer be shy. The assumption has not been extensively tested. Nor is it clear that social anxiety invariably impedes social performance. Thus, studies of anxiety and apprehension take on a life of their own, often divorced from social performance behavior.

In his public lectures James McCroskey often offers as an example of how anxiety works, the case of the basketball player who clutches at the free-throw line because he fears failure. When anxiety is removed, the basketball player regains his former skill. Simple enough. However, if a person who could never sink free throws was anxious about it, removal of the anxiety would not confer the skill he never had. If his survival depended on basket shooting, it would be necessary for him to learn how to do it. Anxiety could impede both learning a skill and performing it, but success would be contingent on learning the skill.

The successful basketball player legitimately believes he can sink baskets because he has already done so. Each basket he sinks reinforces his belief that he can do it. On the other hand, if an inept player believed he was skillful, it would have no effect on his skill. Neither the skill nor the belief can exist apart from each other. The analogy holds for social skill. Successful communicators believe they can do well because they have done well. They are not anxious because they are confident. This is an intriguing tautology; confidence is the absence of anxiety. Those who avoid social contact because they are fearful, because they know they are inept must (1) learn how to try, (2) try, (3) have some success. At that point they can be disabused of their anxiety. Merely removing the anxiety would not make them skillful. A few people may be so anxious they may have to control their anxiety even to begin learning.

As a further example, consider the "think system" used by Professor Harold Hill with the River City Boys' Band.[2] The system works well in a musical. A parallel is Norman Vincent Peale's "you can, if you think you can." The facetious among us can think of a number of activities to which this would not apply. Most of us are notorious wishful thinkers. It is comforting, albeit unrealistic, to believe you can do anything you want to do.

Attempts to measure anxiety about communication have had limited pedagogical application. In 1970 McCroskey introduced the PRCA, a scale designed to measure "communication apprehension." We will consider the theoretical underpinnings of this scale in chapter 10. The PRCA consisted of a number of statements about nervousness in various social situations. Respondents answered based on their own impressions. The test was not given at a time when they faced the situations. Consequently it does not measure what they do when they are in the situations. What it does not take into account is the behavior available to people at given times in given places. Social repertoires make a difference. A person might be anxious in one situation simply because he lacks the technique to manage it. Another person might be anxious in the same situation because she had tried and failed on a previous occasion. The

2. Meredith Willson's musical comedy *The Music Man* may not have been intended as an indictment of "self-esteem" based therapies, but underneath the delicious fantasy lies the clear message that "you can if you think you can" only happens in Fantasyland.

fact that neither situations nor people are constants tends to vitiate the explanatory power of theories of communication apprehension.

Furthermore, there are some serious questions that can be raised about the words "anxiety" and "apprehension" to label feelings associated with social performance. "Tension" might be more appropriate, since such feelings are not necessarily harmful. In fact, it is questionable whether skillful performance can be achieved by anyone who does not feel some tension. Furthermore, if it is presumed that feelings are relevant at all, we have a genuine problem specifying what we are talking about. There is no way to measure subjective events or conditions. When they are made public either as confessions or responses to questionnaires, they produce nominal categories manageable in statistical analysis, but they do not, in any way, represent or describe the feelings that purportedly provide the bases for the responses.

Stage fright. Stage fright has been an object of concern for more than sixty years. Shy people are especially fearful of social situations, but many of them seem to perform quite well in public. Zimbardo (1977), in fact, makes quite a point about various celebrities he met who confessed to being shy. Whether this was merely "name-dropping" or presentation of evidence is moot. It is clear that fear of speaking in public is different from anxiety about social contact. Steve (the memory of whose unzipped fly hampered him on the public platform) had no trouble at all at social gatherings. Louise (who broke out in hives) despaired of being able to follow the rules for effective public speaking, although she was positively charming at cocktail parties.

Public speaking requires formal compliance with obligations of form, content, and presentation. The utterance must be prepared in advance, rehearsed, and delivered flawlessly. Public speaking appears to evoke a special kind of fear in most people. An apocryphal survey purports to show that people under forty report they fear giving a speech more than death itself. If this is not true it ought to be, because generations of public-school teachers offer testimony to the trepidation with which most of their students face their first public experiences.

It may not be so much the act of performing as the thought that someone is watching them that bothers stage-fright sufferers. They anticipate that someone will think critical thoughts about them and maybe even express them. They are particularly afraid that someone will notice their nonfluencies and nervous mannerisms.

The impact of these worries on behavior is hard to assess. Clearly, in some cases, physiological responses to social situations imperil the speaker. Sensations from increased adrenalin flow cause them to take flight or freeze, or worse, blunder into counterproductive action. It may well be that the sensation that makes one speaker ineffective helps another succeed. It all depends on how the speaker interprets what he or she feels. Interpretation is a function of perception of the social world.

In sum, the psychological approach to the study of communication does not appear to offer much to a pedagogy of oral performance behavior. Regardless of the etiology of the disability, it is necessary for people to perform socially. Since the connection between learning about and learning how has not been formally established, the founders of the Reticence Program elected to concentrate on modification of performance behavior in particular contexts. This unapologetic "state" approach appears to be the only option for the teacher.

Theories Based on Social Interaction

The nature of interaction. Human interaction consists of performance and evaluation. We talk to others, observe how they behave, listen to them talk, and then make decisions about whether or how to deal with them. Effective communicators know this and respond accordingly. They control their acts to appeal to those whose approval they seek. They defend themselves against those they regard as hostile and ignore those they classify as irrelevant.

Everyone, regardless of how effective they are, invariably feels moments of concern about the possibility that they have forgotten a crucial fastener or mispronounced a word. They wonder what people are thinking about them, whether they are laughing at them or getting angry with them. Skilled communicators use these worries to anticipate what may come next and adapt to it. But everyone has a few social situations to which they cannot adjust. One way to distinguish inept from skilled communicators is in the number and variety of situations they cannot manage.

Social interaction means a surrender of privacy. Shy people, for example, report they are sensitive to messages from their own bodies. They describe physical sensations that accompany their attempts at socialization. They also report that they are aware of fears of embarrassment and the possibility of disapproval. The external signs of these feelings are excessive concern with physical appearance. They check zippers and buttons, nervously tug at their skirts, twist their hair, try to make themselves obscure. They often regard themselves as too fat or too thin, awkward, and ungainly. Their preoccupation with physical appearance and activities like coughing, sneezing, sweating, or breaking wind keeps them in a constant state of discomfort when they are with others. To minimize their discomfort, they may avoid or withdraw entirely from social situations. Many of them report they believe others can read their inner feelings and that their behavior gives away too much of what they think. They feel that whatever they say, they will reveal themselves too much, give away important secrets, make themselves vulnerable.

Communication ineptitude, a function of labeling. It is customary to label people according to the way they play their social roles. People, once labeled, tend to display the behaviors associated with the label. Carol Warren (1982) explains the process by describing how people judged in a courtroom to be insane take on after the fact the characteristics associated with the category into which they have been put. Essentially, this describes the decision system most of us use when we interact with others.

In ordinary socialization we tend to label the people with whom we associate. We may call them "charming," "popular," "confident," or "outspoken" or make references to a "good personality." We discriminate between types of personalities by using synonyms. An "outgoing" person can also be "pushy," for example. Synonyms for labels assigned to the same behaviors can be positive, negative, or neutral.

There are few neutral synonyms for shyness. Consider: timid, diffident, frightened, bashful, skittish, timorous, scared, shamefaced, verecund. The most positive synonyms are "diffident" and "reserved." There are no simple words for "verbal nonfluency," "awkward and disjointed flow of ideas," "averted gaze or lack of eye contact," or "inappropriate gestures and facial expressions." In fact, we do not have a language appropriate for the social criticism of communication performance. Consequently, we tend to apply labels that apply to global personality. Shy people, for example, tend to regard any labels assigned them as pejorative. This has obvious effects on reputation and self-esteem not to speak of the constraints it imposes on social interactions. The labels, originally for observed social behaviors, become global personality evaluations and obscure the original behaviors. It is relatively easy to modify simple communication behaviors in a classroom but changing a whole personality is a virtually impossible clinical task.

Consider how the hostile words children use on each other affect their behavior. Overweight children called "fatty" can be driven to anorexia; bespectacled children called "four-eyes" can be pushed to depression; the obnoxious references to girls whose breasts develop early may motivate them to sexual precocity. If one has the name, why not the game. It is hard to be a deviant. Wimps and nerds (labels often assigned to shy people) have a hard time surviving socially.

The few positive references assigned to shyness are often used by shy people as rationales for sustaining their behavior. Shy adults, for example, may be called "good listeners." They are nice to have around. From the standpoint of the shy person, it is easier to find someone who approves the behavior and develop a relationship than attempt to modify the behaviors that led to the label. Shy people cannot be faulted for not taking risks. By avoiding conversation, shy people spare themselves from the ridicule associated with social gaffes.

Management of intimate relationships. The problem of changing the label is most serious in intimate relationships. When people relate closely to one another, they must negotiate and bargain for direction and control of the relationship. The popular view of intimacy disseminated by Watzlawick and his colleagues (1967) is that there are two kinds of relationships; symmetrical and complementary. In symmetrical relationships, intimate couples share decision making and control. In complementary relationships one partner leads, the other follows. Shy people, according to this formulation, would become submissive partners in complementary relationships. What might we call the dominant partner, who might also be socially inept? Domineering? Authoritarian? These labels also do not contain cues to the behaviors that motivate their assignment.

The complementary/symmetrical dichotomy is not quite as simple as theorists would like to believe, however. For one thing, genuine shared control is hard to achieve in any relationship. In typical relationships partners divide up responsibility so that each controls particular aspects of it. The arrangements are sometimes negotiated. Often, one partner is more powerful than the other and simply assumes control. But arrangements are always subject to modification. Skillful talk is required to sustain equity in an intimate relationship. People who are not able to adjust their discourse to meet the requirements of various social situations are labeled. The label, in turn, contributes to their reputation and impairs the possibilities of success in subsequent social engagements.

People are labeled at the outset of the relationship and play the assigned role so long as the relationship exists.

Self-esteem. Self-esteem is an elusive concept. It refers to the notion that the way people evaluate themselves affects their social behavior. Presumably, people with high self-esteem are willing to take risks because they believe they can succeed. People with low self-esteem anticipate failure and take few chances. The phrase is tautological, however. It is not clear whether we ascribe low self-esteem to people we think perform ineptly, or we respond to people who claim low self-esteem by regarding any of their behavior as inept. The association between low self-esteem and shyness is frequently made, but it is not clear which causes which.

Popular conceptions of self-esteem are often convoluted. Abraham Maslow (1954), for example, identifies levels of motivation ranging from survival to actualization. As people achieve each level, they supposedly become more confident and have higher self-esteem. In this paradigm, high self-esteem comes from success. Those who lose consistently have low self-esteem. Because they have often failed, they predict failure for themselves in subsequent endeavors. Alfred Adler (Ansbacher, 1936) describes people who are motivated to act in order to overcome their adversities, but it appears that most people surrender to them. At least, this appears to be the case with those called "shy."

It is easy to misunderstand the concept "self-esteem." It is possible, for example, to think of "self" as a real location inside the human, a homunculus with the capability of deciding and directing. The problem with homuncular theories, however, is that each requires another homunculus theory *ad infinitum.* Operationally, self is a situational judgment made by a human about his or her prognosis for success in a given social situation. Low self-esteem for a shy person might be a judgment that a particular social situation was one in which silence or nonparticipation was potentially the most productive course of action. Thus, when therapists suggest that a shy person can become more effective by acquiring high self-esteem, an important step is missing. If self-esteem has any viability as a concept, it must depend on a memory of successful acts. A person who believes his inept behavior is skillful presents himself as a complete social klutz.

It became clear very early in the Reticence Program that effective performance depended to a large extent on what individuals were able to see themselves doing. Levi, for example, saw himself as a victim. Other people would get angry and impatient with him. He responded by taking the bull by the horns and greeting them with hostility. It is the old "self-fulfilling prophecy" cliché, but quite appropriate, since the labels we accept about ourselves tend to govern the way we present ourselves to others.

Marginality. Klutziness is not a trivial matter. People are rejected if they cannot meet the norms of social behavior in a given group. The term *marginal* is used to describe people who seek to be accommodated in a new social setting but play so badly they are not accepted by the members. They either do not know the rules or follow them awkwardly. They are somewhat like pledges in a fraternity house. Often they overdo what they think they should do, but mostly, they hang back and watch. Many, like immigrants, for example, never learn to play well and remain marginal throughout their lives.

The case of the immigrant is important. Around the turn of the century, European ethnics, barred by language disparities from full participation in the mainstream Anglo-Saxon society, formed their own social groups (Ceska Sin, Ancient Order of Hibernians, Sons of Italy, B'Nai B'Rith) in which they could acquire status. These local ethnic organizations were characterized by high expressiveness and often volatile speaking. They served as buffers against the social rejections experienced in the main society, where people were disqualified if they talked funny. It was, however, relatively easy to make repairs. The sons and daughters of the immigrants learned general American English, or the regional dialect of choice, and were thus able to enter the mainstream (although some Golembiewski's had to become Gilberts in the process).

Furthermore, it is, theoretically, fairly easy to deal with representatives of other ethnic groups because we expect them to act differently. We expect the people in our own social groups to act as we do and we are uncomfortable when they do not. Shy people learn that they are safe so long as they follow the prevailing etiquette. They try to be neutral. To avoid klutzy behavior, they do not behave at all. The operating rules for shy people who wish to be included, if not necessarily accepted, are listen silently, do not interrupt, and nod as if you understand.

But all of us must enter new groups. It is virtually impossible to avoid it. Marriage means joining our spouse's family; a new job means adjusting to unfamiliar social rules; a new neighborhood means arranging interaction with the people next door; new friends mean unfamiliar socialization. Those who cannot modify their behavior to fit the requirements remain marginal, silent, nonparticipants.

Many people seem to think that merely wanting to be a member of a new group means automatic acceptance. They resent it when they are not taken in. They feel they are entitled. (The concept of entitlement that will recur in several iterations in this book is very important.) However, in order to get the privileges of membership, one must pay the dues. You may get to use the country club golf course by paying the greens fee, but to be accepted as a member you must not only pay the initiation fee but also be able to walk and talk like a member.

People who claim to be part of a group expect the respect and friendship of the other members. But most people are naturally suspicious of newcomers. They do not accept new people as members until they act sufficiently like members so that no one is uncomfortable around them. Member talk is reserved for members. People who act strangely hamper member talk and generate antagonism. Shy people learn that their silence allows them to be around in most places even if they are generally invisible to others. Klutzes attempt to retain the communication behavior of other groups and sometimes even demand that members of the new group adjust to them. It simply does not happen. Even when people are forced by law to be together, they do not necessarily interact socially because of it.

A cognitive theory. Aaron Beck's (1976) book on the treatment of depression is based on the premise that, in order to improve, a patient must understand both her own life situation and the world in which she lives. Philosophically speaking, people live in worlds created out of their own experience. When they encounter new situations, they draw on the memory of similar situations they have experienced in the past. Some people, however, appear to have trouble finding appropriate analogies. They may not have experience in situations that serve as precedents, or they may erroneously ascribe reasons for their success or failure. They may not even understand how communication is used in social life or be able to make an appropriate selection of a strategy to use. Because of this intellectual confusion, they may refrain from social participation or restrict themselves to simple and safe responses.

One of the premises on which the Reticence Program was built was that rational selection of social options depends on memory of skillful activity. By training people in social skills, they are provided with an active repertoire of social choices from which they can choose when necessary. This view is analogous to the rational-emotive therapy of Albert Ellis (1983), which depends on the theory that underlying beliefs affect a person's social choices. If the individual does not see the "world" accurately, he or she might make ineffective or inappropriate choices.

The premise seems reasonable, Shy people, for example, consistently display social misorientations. Many, for example, will argue that "small talk is unimportant and unnecessary" and excuse themselves from it accordingly. As a result, they are unable to perform the rituals necessary to initiate relationships. In their own defense, shy people argue that they do not wish to relate to people who are so shallow they would depend on small talk. They make the whole issue sound like a major moral crisis. Most people, however, understand the nature of phatic communion as a form of safe investigation of the qualifications of others and an important preliminary ritual in social connecting.

The cognitive dimension is important, for it is possible to modify what people know and believe about socialization. It also supports the argument that shyness is not a disease. It is normal for people to assess themselves and decide to change their behavior in order to improve. Those who take Dale Carnegie (1964) courses or attend classes at a university, as well as those who join Toastmasters and similar support groups, have made their decision as a result of an assessment of their own behavior. Conceptual understanding is often necessary as a basis for specific training in behavior change.

An Economic Explanation

There is an economic flavor to shy behavior. Tim Hopf, one of the first instructors in the Penn State Reticence Program, once commented that a shy person is one for whom the projected loss from participation outweighs the possibility of gain. Hopf argued that people examine social situations and decide whether or not it would be useful to participate. This implies a kind of cost-benefit analysis based on a person's assessment of his own capabilities.

This fits Bitzer's (1968) model of the "Rhetorical Situation" in which a person feels urgent about participation in a given social setting and prepares and delivers discourse designed to modify the situation in a desired direction. How people assess their personal urgency to participate depends on their evaluation of their personal capability in that case, which in turn depends on their general view of their personal capability. With apologies to Bitzer, the economic significance of the concept cannot be underestimated. People will decide what it is possible to gain or lose depending on their past record in similar situations. Their perception of their own ability interacts with their estimate of what is at stake in a given case and directly influences their decision about whether to participate and, if so, in what way. Shy people display a general tendency to overestimate what they can lose and to underestimate their ability to gain.

Of all the inept communicators, shy people are particularly skillful at using predictions of inevitable failure as an excuse for not participating at all. This also gives them 100 percent success in foretelling the future. They do not gain because they do not participate, and they know it. They console themselves with the knowledge that had they participated, they would have lost. Most inept communicators learn who they "are" and what they can do. They often talk about their inherent tendencies to be the way they are. They cling to the notion that "good speakers are born, not made." Unfortunately, trait theory is an explanation, not an excuse. Regardless of tendencies and propensities, salubrious modifications can be made to accomodate to particular states. Once their potential listeners accommodate to their ineptitude, they ask little of them and that is usually exactly what they get.

A Freudian theory. When we try to combine psychological, social, and economic explanations, we end up with something like a Freudian model that presumes people strive to achieve a pleasure principle. The way they explain their success or failure to themselves constrains the social choices they make. Each person has a different pleasure formula. Those who are socially resourceful appear to have many ways to achieve pleasure. Those with restricted repertoires tend to confine themselves to a few safe objectives.

Freud created two fictions, the ego ideal and the superego (Hall, 1954). The ego ideal represents goals based on observation of others. The superego restrains behavior through conscience. Both exert pressure on the individual, superego to restrain us from getting involved in things that would generate guilt, and ego ideal to motivate activities designed to achieve pleasure.

There is a very simple dialectical balance in this theory. The outer self can go about acting, run amok if it chooses, with full encouragement of inner self, if and only if (1) it succeeds in getting what inner self wants, and (2) it does so without making inner self feel guilty. Alternatively, ego must be gratified by its behavior. The evaluation of gratification is done by superego. Thus ego would be outer self and superego inner self. But Freud's theories include the element of id, the biological self. This enables us to consider genetic propensities and organic malfunctions in a theory of shy behavior. A shy person (1) may have a genetic tendency toward the condition; (2) may have a physical disability; (3) may have had unpleasant social experiences; (4) may lack instruction on how to behave; (5) may feel guilty about the possibility of failure; (6) may be afraid of social participation; (7) may model his or her behavior on that of other shy people. The integrated shy personality would be a human literally contented with less, unmotivated to seek more, resigned to a particular niche in life.

As reasonable as it may sound, Freudian theory, like so many theories is mostly fanciful and cannot be documented empirically. Real self does not exist on an anatomy chart and there is no ledger sheet in the brain. Physiologists cannot locate id, ego, and superego. All of these terms are abstractions that help us explain what we observe, but they are not amenable to direct observation or experimental control.

The most important feature of the Freudian model is that people do not react directly to social events. Sensory data of social experience are received, classified, sorted, and stored in memory. It is to memory of experience that people react.

But memory is an exclusive possession of an individual. It cannot be investigated directly. In fact, we do not have accurate indexes of what we can remember. Sometimes we are amazed by what we have stored away, and when we remember some obscure past event, it is hard to tell how accurate it is. Furthermore, memory can be processed so we always face the problem of accuracy. We can modify what we have stored and a good deal of what we remember deviates from the actual events. Thus, in attempting to understand any human communication problem, we must attend to its overt features, the part that can be studied empirically. This is all we can subject to scientific scrutiny.

A *rhetorical suggestion.* At some point, all explanations of inept communication behavior converge on the relationship of what people believe about themselves and the effect it has on their behavior. People act in the world, get information about the results of their action, and store it to use on subsequent occasions. We learn to socialize by socializing. We learn in our homes how to deal with particular types of authority figures (parents or their surrogates), and we carry our knowledge into social living. We adapt it to include relationships with teachers and policemen. We accommodate to power claims of our peers and superordinates and we control our subordinates. Eventually we take a place in a smaller society; a new family, a friendship, a clique, a group, a club, or a gang. We adapt social learning to our position in the workplace. For example, our attitude toward our supervisor on the job is a function of (though not necessarily an isomorphism of) our relationship with our parents. Some of us learn that parental authority is responsible and reliable and use what we learned about it to ingratiate ourselves with other parental types like municipal court judges and district supervisors. Others learn that parental authority is not reliable and use it as a guide to what not to do when we encounter authority figures.

Eventually we generate our own social rules. These may include etiquette, table manners, group norms, group problem-solving agendas, protocols for interviewing or negotiating, synchronous moves for forming intimate relationships, and methods of fighting and resolving conflict. We learn how to manage in a particular family or child-rearing unit, and we also learn how to observe other social groups so we can participate in them. Our genetic heritage as well as the social conditions in which we live affects our acculturation. Furthermore, our view of our own capabilities and human possibilities in general shapes our sense of facility in moving from group to group. This adds up to the notion that we could alter our social position and label, if we could learn to follow new personal rules of behavior.

This point of view, synthesized out of all of the various explanations for inept communication provides the basis for the Penn State Reticence Program. It has great potential for explaining problems in communication performance. It can also serve as a basis for instruction and training. In the following chapter by Lynne Kelly, we will show how it has been applied in the Penn State Reticence Program to improving communication performance. In the chapters to follow we will generate a theory of how people can be trained to achieve performance competence.

2

The Penn State University
Reticence Program

By Lynne Kelly

BACKGROUND

Researchers and theorists have been preoccupied for half a century with people who report they are fearful about social communication, for example: systematic desensitization (McCroskey, 1972), cognitive restructuring (Fremouw & Scott, 1979), visualization (Ayres & Hopf, 1987), and rhetoritherapy (Phillips, 1977). However, the discussion has been very much like that of the weather; people don't seem to be doing much about it. A recent survey revealed there are very few special programs operated by speech communication departments at colleges and universities (Hoffmann & Sprague, 1982).

The Penn State Reticence Program has been in continuous operation since 1965. It originated in the work of Laura Muir (1964) who noticed that a great many people came to her speech clinic who did not have a standard impairment. They were simply poor communicators. The name "reticence" was coined to describe these people who communicated little, and awkwardly when they did.

The original group of students enrolled in the Penn State Reticence Program were about to leave school because they believed they could not cope with the course in public speaking required for graduation. The students in the early years of the Reticence Program received generous doses of unconditional positive regard and individualized training. The program quickly adapted to the needs of its clientele and became performance-centered. Founded on the educational philosophy

18

of Robert Mager (1972), the pedagogy became a program of individualized performance modification based on certain standard principles. The term *rhetoritherapy* was coined, tongue in cheek, by Phillips (1977) as the name for the special skills training approach used in the Reticence Program. As defined by Phillips and Sokoloff (1979), rhetoritherapy is "a form of systematic, individualized instruction directed at improving speech performance in mundane, task, and social situations" (p. 389). The rationale for this method has been provided elsewhere (Cohen, 1980; Phillips, 1977, 1986; Phillips & Metzger, 1973; Phillips & Sokoloff, 1979).

While the Reticence Program is specifically designed to serve college students, its pedagogy has been tested in both elementary and secondary classrooms. From 1968 to 1971, extensive pedagogical experimentation was conducted under Title III of the Elementary and Secondary Education Act. Programs were generated in Alameda County, California, and Area J of Central Pennsylvania, the purpose of which was to test rhetoritherapy as a pedagogical prescription. The program was further tested clinically in a program of group counseling and training, offered to more than three hundred clients from 1970 to 1975.

OPERATIONS

Recruiting Students for the Program

Students enter the Reticence Program from various sections of the required speech course. At the Pennsylvania State University, students can choose one of three performance options: public speaking, group discussion, or speech criticism. There is also a special honors section. The Reticence Program is not listed in the course schedule. The only way into the program is to register for one of the three options. Because the course is required for graduation, even the most severely hampered individuals will enroll.

On the first day of class, students are given a handout that describes the special option. It lists seven possible problems:

1. Difficulty asking and answering questions in class
2. Avoiding speaking to professors and authority figures
3. Apprehension about job interviews and communication on the job
4. Inability to do committee work or participate in groups
5. Difficulty meeting strangers and initiating friendships
6. Manifest signs of stagefright
7. Self-diagnosed shyness

Students are told that if they feel they have any of the seven problems, they may go to an interview and apply for admission to the special sections. Those who inquire are interviewed by one of the special section instructors. The purpose of the interview is to ascertain whether the student needs the special services offered in the option.

During the interviews, students are asked to describe their problems. The interviewers watch carefully for signs of inept communication. Most students who come in are apprehensive about the interviews. They fear being assigned to a remedial course. It is, therefore, important to avoid the stigma of remediation in promoting the option. Emphasis should be on the skills a student can acquire in the class. Words like *shyness* or *apprehension* are inappropriate. For one thing, they are laden with pejorative connotations. For another, the course is not directed at psychological conditions. It is designed to alter performance behavior.

The program is dependent on a speech-course requirement. Those most in need do not enroll in voluntary programs. In fact, they tend to avoid communication training altogether. Even so, it is not possible, ethical, or desirable to attempt to force individuals to enroll under any circumstances. The option itself is driven by the premise that successful instruction is based on a voluntary therapeutic alliance between instructors and students. Studies indicate that those who volunteer into the Reticence Program represent a range of problems and score higher on measures of communication apprehension, shyness, and social reticence than students enrolled in regular sections (Kelly & Duran, 1988) and display clearly distinguishing variations in vocal performance (Rekart & Begnal, 1989).

The Screening Interview

The objective of the screening interview is to enroll only students who need the program. Regular speech performance classes are generally quite successful in handling ordinary discomfort about public speaking. Furthermore, no speech course can be expected to remedy serious ineptitude in socialization. There are special courses provided for speakers for whom English is a second language. What the interviews are designed to pick up are reports of impairments in any of the seven situations mentioned in the course handout. The interviews usually take less than fifteen minutes.

Students often report global kinds of problems indicative of trait. Most can also specify particular situations that are especially troublesome.

Interviewers are trained to take the focus off personality and fix attention on situations. Some students report they are quite all right in most social situations but fear public speaking. It is up to the interviewer to find out whether the fear is abnormal or whether they are merely displaying the apprehension common to most students about platform appearances.

Students who experience occasional situational difficulties and who express a normal fear of public speaking are encouraged to return to their regular speech classes. Because there are a limited number of instructors available for special training, enrollment must be restricted to those who can benefit most from the instruction.

The benefits of instruction in regular speech performance classes must also be considered. There is considerable disagreement on the value of such courses. Many major institutions, such as Harvard, Yale, MIT, California-Berkeley, Southern California, Amherst, and Dartmouth, either do not offer speech training or have terminated it. There are no studies demonstrating that students improve performance as a result of instruction in public speaking, for example. Efforts to train students in interpersonal communication have been generally unsuccessful. They have mostly become preoccupied with sensitivity and assertiveness training and have not taken hold in major universities. Furthermore, few elementary and secondary schools offer general training in oral performance.

It is hard to explain why speech performance training did not take hold in American education, although there is considerably more of it in America than in foreign countries. Europeans express dismay, in fact, at the American practice of training college students to speak and write their native language. It may be that speech training has been rejected because there is no evidence that it does any good. Another explanation may be that speech competency is taken for granted. Generally speaking, we do not ascribe social failure to incompetency at oral discourse. We ascribe it to personality. We often see inept oral discourse as an indicator of deficiencies in personality or character.

The pedagogy in the Reticence Program has been demonstrated effective, at least at improving performance in the seven crucial social situations enumerated in the advertising. Individual assessments are made by comparing papers written by each student at the beginning and end of the course. These papers are reports of the students' assessments of whether or not they have improved outside of class. Instructors compare the reports with their observations of improvement in class exercises.

Virtually all students are able to point to some gain confirmed by instructor observation. Furthermore, two studies by Oerkvitz (1975) and Metzger (1974) documented the lasting effective of training. What follows is a description of a common procedure used by all instructors. The student is greeted and seated. The interviewer introduces herself and waits to see if the student does the same. Most students will introduce themselves, but the most reticent do not. If the student does not offer information, the interviewer asks him to state his name. The interviewer then asks the student why he came for the interview. The answer usually refers to one of the items on the handout (see below).

Announcement Handout for Penn State Reticence Program
Option D is an emphasis of Speech Communication 100 established to assist students who have special communication needs. It is designed to work directly on specific problems in communication within academic and social settings. In Option D, students are expected to set individual goals to accomplish communication tasks which they have heretofore been reluctant to try and unable to do. Check the following kinds of communicative concerns:

1. You may have difficulty asking questions in class and participating in class discussions. You may be reluctant to strike up acquaintances with classmates.

2. You may shy away from speaking to professors after class and avoid office conferences.

3. You may feel apprehensive at employment interviews and uncertain about how to communicate on the job with your boss and fellow employees.

4. You may be uneasy about committee work and feel that you don't contribute your fair share in group problem-solving discussions.

5. You may have difficulty meeting strangers and opening up new friendships. In social situations, you may find yourself a non-participant on the fringe of the group.

6. You may be unusually troubled, feel physically ill, shake, or sweat when you have to present formal reports in public situations.

7. You may experience difficulty with shyness. If you feel any or all of these communication concerns are yours and if you wish to work specifically on solving them, you are eligible for an interview for Option D. IF YOU ARE IN DOUBT ABOUT WHETHER OR NOT YOU HAVE SPECIAL COMMUNICATION NEEDS, COME FOR THE INTERVIEW. There is no obligation to enter Option D; it is entirely voluntary. However, you cannot enroll in Option D without an interview.
Interviews are confidential and will be conducted in(Building Name)

any time between 9:00 a.m. and 4:00 p.m. on Thursday (date) and Friday (date), and between 9:00 a.m. and noon on Monday (date). The interviewer will discuss your communicative needs with you, and the two of you will decide whether or not Option D can be useful to you. If you elect to enter Option D, your transfer will be automatic; you will not need to go through a drop-add procedure.

The interviewer goes through the handout with the student, asking him or her to identify which of the concerns he or she feels. The interviewer also probes a sense of the breadth and depth of a student's communication problems. For example, if the student reports difficulty carrying on social conversation, the interviewer will ask questions about with whom this is a problem and in what types of situations. She is trying to determine if the problem is fairly generalized or situation specific. Probing further, the interviewer asks what kinds of difficulties the student experiences during social conversation. Does he have trouble initiating, maintaining, or terminating social conversation? The probing provides information about the nature and extent of the student's problems. It is important to note that no personal questions are asked. Interviewers define their roles as diagnosticians of communication behavior problems. When students offer information about their feelings, interviewers ignore it and press on with the protocol. If students express emotional concerns, these are minimized. Concentration in the interview is on problems in performing necessary speech tasks.

When the protocol is completed the interviewer describes the program to the student. The description emphasizes that the course is designed for people who have some of the seven concerns. The interviewer makes the point that the course is not an escape from an unpleasant situation represented by the required speech class. On the contrary, the student will be required to confront communication situations both in and out of class.

Following the description of the program, students are encouraged to ask questions. Typical questions include, "How will I be graded?" and "Is this more work than a regular speech class?" The interviewer explains that in addition to exams and a group project, students are graded on the number of communication goals they complete in and out of class, and that papers are required before and after attempting each goal. It is important to call students' attention to goal setting. It emphasizes to them that they will be rewarded for their communication accomplishments.

Some students who show up at the interviews are not appropriate for the program because they do not experience difficulties communicating. They have a variety of reasons for coming: curiosity, they don't like their instructor; they are looking for an "easy A"; they have a friend in the course; and so on. It is easy for an interviewer to recognize these people because of the way they approach the interview. They come into the interview office, announce that they are there to find out about the special program, and introduce themselves. Those who truly need the program tend to hang around outside the office and wait to be invited in.

Interviews with ineligible students are fairly simple. They generally-report nervousness about public speaking. They do not seem to be able to point to specific situations that trouble them, nor can they give accurate descriptions of the "trouble." They are usually quite fluent in whatever they say. At that point, the interviewer explains what the program is about and why the student is not an appropriate candidate. The interviewer explains that fear of public speaking is quite common, and that courses in public speaking are usually quite successful in overcoming it.

The screening interview is a standardized procedure designed to select appropriate students for the special instruction provided. A study by Sours (1979) supports the validity of the screening interview procedure. He compared interviewers' evaluations of students, presenting behavior with initial evaluations made by classroom instructors, and found they agreed. In essence, the screening process is designed to discover whether students display state or trait difficulties and the extent to which their communication problems interfered with management of important social situations.

Training Instructors

Instructors must be experienced at teaching speech performance courses. They should not be clinicians. The course operates in a relatively formal performance mode. The considerable individual contact between students and instructors is confined to preparation for speech experiences and evaluation of performance. Instructors are discouraged from doing anything approximating personal counseling.

Potential instructors serve an internship in which they assist an experienced teacher for a semester of observation that includes participation in screening interviews and some instructional activities like reading student papers, monitoring goal situations, and conducting demonstration classes. In essence, the trainee observes every aspect of teaching in the program and participates to some degree. Trainees meet briefly once a week with the instructor they are assisting to discuss pedagogical issues and get their questions answered.

The decision about eligibility depends on how well the trainee met the obligations of the internship. A second consideration is the trainee's motivation to teach in the program. The trainer must take into account the trainee's commitment to teaching the course. A number of people find it very difficult to work with noncommunicative students. They become impatient and demanding. Rhetoritherapy must be administered in a low-key fashion. Finally, it is important that instructors be firm enough to demand completion of all the work. Students are quick to take advantage of any opportunity not to perform.

THE PROGRAM OF INSTRUCTION

Course Content and Organization

A standard syllabus is used by all instructors to maintain much consistency across sections. Class sections are restricted to approximately twenty students, although in practice, students with problems continue to turn up throughout the semester and are added. Classroom instruction is confined to teaching of performance skills encompassing seven rhetorical subprocesses. These include identification of situations amenable to modification through talk, selection of audiences for talk, setting communication goals, analysis of audience and situation, adjusting ideas and language to meet audience needs, adapting delivery to meet audience needs, assessment of personal effectiveness. Course content is divided into nine units.

1. *Basic communication principles.* Emphasis in this unit is on cognitive restructuring. Students are taught about how they can influence the outcome of social situations through effective communication. They are introduced to basic concepts about performance based on communication theory and social rhetoric. Instruction is applied to the assignment to write an analysis of their communication performance in social situations.

2. *Goal analysis.* The procedures for goal analysis are derived from the work of Robert Mager (1972). Instruction is designed to help students acquire three skills: (1) the ability to define clearly personal performance goals; (2) the ability to list criteria that would indicate successful goal

accomplishment; and (3) the ability to plan and rehearse communication behaviors to accomplish a specific rhetorical goal. Ability at goal analysis is essential to accomplishment of the subsequent assignments in the course.

Students are directed to phrase goals in performance terms. They often set unrealistic goals for themselves, for example, "I will carry on a conversation with a stranger and we will become friends." A more realistic goal would be, "I will approach a stranger and carry on a three-minute conversation." Unrealistic or "fuzzy" goals set people up for failure. ,

The next skill, the ability to list criteria that indicate successful goal achievement, is also extremely important. Students have a tendency to evaluate themselves in terms of how they felt about their communication, rather than the effectiveness of their behavior. If, for example, a student gave a speech judged by the instructor and the audience to be very good, but the student felt nervous, she might assume that the speech had been a total failure. Students are taught to identify behaviors that would indicate they had successfully communicated. For example, "My listener looked at me directly while I talked," rather than "I felt I impressed him."

The final goal analysis skill is the ability to prepare to accomplish a communication goal. Students are provided with a form (see below) designed to help them plan for a communication experience. Most students appear to believe that good speakers are born with a special talent, they do not recognize the importance of preparation. Students are taught to make written plans of how they will prepare for, initiate, carry out, and end discourse to accomplish their communication goals.

Goal Analysis Preparation Sheet

STEP ONE: State your end goal in a single sentence. (Be sure to include who your audience will be and how long it will last.)

STEP TWO: List your criteria for success of this goal. Describe the performances that you would have to see happen in order to agree that the goal had been accomplished. "I will know that I have accomplished my goal when I have done the following:"

STEP THREE: Give details of the goal:

    a. When will you attempt the goal?

    b. Where will you attempt the goal?

    c. What is it that you want to accomplish by talking to this person?

    d. Why did you select this person to talk to?

    e. Is there anything special you must do because of the communication context?

    f. Is there anything special you should avoid because of the communication context?

STEP FOUR: Preparation and practice:
    a. List the activities necessary to prepare and practice.
    b. Describe how you will start your goal.
    c. Describe how you will progress with your goal. What behaviors will you engage in as you carry out your goal?
    d. How will you end your goal?
STEP FIVE: Try to account for possible outcomes of your goal.
    a. What's one possible positive response you could get? What will you do if you get it?
    b. What's one negative response you could get? What will you do if you get it?
    c. What's the most likely response you will get? What will you do if you get it?
    d. If something goes wrong, when would it be your fault? The other person's fault? The fault of circumstances?

Upon completion of a goal, the students write a report describing in detail what happened when they tried to accomplish their goal.

Goal Report Format Sheet

STEP ONE: State your end goal.
STEP TWO: Describe what happened when you tried to carry out the goal.
    a. How did you begin?
    b. How did you proceed from there?
    c. How did the audience react?
    d. How did you adjust to audience response?
    e. How did you end your goal?
STEP THREE: Evaluate your success.
    a. How do you think it went? Were you successful? Why or why not?
    b. If you were unsuccessful, was it your fault, the fault of the other, or the fault of circumstances? (Explain)
    c. Did you achieve all of the performances that you had listed as criteria for success? Which ones did you achieve?
    d. Would you do anything differently if you were to do the goal again? Are there any specific performances you would like to improve? How do you intend to improve them?
STEP FOUR: Are there any additional comments you would like to make?

Writing the plan and the report helps focus students on the details of communication performance. They have unlimited access to the instructor during the planning process. Instructors are charged with

guiding students to behavior-based statements on both their plan and
their report.

3. *Audience and situation analysis.* To assist in the development of
a communication goal plan, students are trained to use a set of heuristics
to conduct an audience and situation analysis. Through the use of
these heuristics, students can examine important variables in potential
communication situations such as time of day, time available, the
physical setting, social norms, relationship(s) to the other(s) involved,
possible goals of the other(s), and appropriateness of the goal for the
particular audience.

4. *Social conversation.* Discussion of in-class social experiences is
used to teach students fundamentals of effective social conversation.
Students use audience and situation analysis to help them determine
whom to approach for conversation and how to initiate and end interaction. Techniques such as follow-up questions, open-ended questions,
the use of situational cues, and so forth, are taught to help students
maintain conversations. A simulated party is often given in class at the
end of this unit to provide students with an opportunity to practice their
conversation skills. Various guests are invited, refreshments are served,
and students are assigned to open and carry on conversations with three
people they had not previously met. After the guests leave, the instructor
leads the class in a discussion of their experiences, such as how they
initiated conversations, what topics they discussed, and how they ended
interactions.

5. *Class participation.* In this unit audience and situation analysis,
as well as thorough preparation, is once again stressed. Students are
taught to observe norms for participation in a particular class, to observe
typical teacher responses, to be prepared by completing all reading and
other assignments, and to jot down questions and opinions they have.

6. *Organizing ideas (structuring).* Students are taught a method of
organizing ideas called structuring (Phillips & Zolten, 1976; Zolten &
Phillips, 1985). The method is an alternative to traditional outlining
and includes seven formal patterns of arrangement for ideas. Each of
these seven structural patterns has a visual diagram representing the
particular relationship expressed among the ideas. The student selects
the structure that best fits the relationship among points to be discussed
and physically or mentally draws the diagram. Although the method
was originally designed for organizing public speeches, it can be applied
to talk in any situation. Students are taught to use the method in any

situation where they will be giving extended comments such as in class participation or job interviews.

7. *Job interviewing and résumé writing.* Students are provided with materials and information that resemble what would be taught in a regular course that dealt with this topic. They are taught to conduct a self-analysis to decide what their goals, skills, and interests are, and so forth. They are taught how to prepare a résumé and how to prepare to answer typical interview questions. This unit ends with mock interviews held during class time. Students who elect to participate in the interviews prepare a résumé and present themselves for an interview. Several interviewers (faculty members, community business people, graduate students conduct the interviews and advise students on possible changes in their performance behavior.

8. *Small-group communication.* Instruction differs from standard training in group performance behavior in the emphasis placed on making consistent contributions to discussion. Instructors emphasize that remaining quiet deprives the group of the ideas of those who do not speak and the entire group loses out. The teacher emphasizes that the advantage to having people work in groups is that there are more ideas generated, more perspectives, and more resources to draw upon, none of which occur if members withhold their ideas and opinions. Students are placed in groups of four or five to complete a brief in-class task as well as a group project. Topics involve some aspect of course content. For example, groups have reviewed textbooks for the course and designed packages of materials for teaching course units.

9. *Public speaking.* The last content area given specific attention is public speaking. The concept of public speaking as "extended conversation" (Winans, 1931, 1938) is emphasized to combat some of the misconceptions these students have about what a public speech is supposed to be like. They have a tendency to be so wrapped up in their emotions about the act that it has no real meaning as a communication event. The last thing they seem to worry about is the content of what they will say. Instructors try to persuade students to be more message-centered and less self-centered. For this reason, students are trained to be attentive to their audience and to be familiar enough with their topics so they can adapt to what they see. Although they are prepared through structuring, they are required to perform with brief notes. Extempore and impromptu modes of delivery are encouraged.

Lecture material focuses on choosing a residual message, identifying a main point, analyzing the audience and situation, generating and organizing ideas (using structuring), incorporating forms of support, and using visual aids. This material is similar to material covered in a regular public speaking course.

Before students present their first full-length speech in front of the entire class, they are required to rehearse with the instructor. Although this is very time-consuming, it appears to be a very effective technique. First, it gives the students a chance to rehearse with a "live" audience so they can see how that feels. Second, they receive the instructor's advice as to how they can improve their speeches before they deliver them to the class. Presenting a speech to the course instructor gives most students enough confidence to face the class. In the few cases where students do not feel ready for a large audience, the instructor, with the student's permission, arranges a small audience of three or four students to remain after class for the speech. After that, the student is required to present the speech to the full class. The rehearsals are sufficient to reinforce the confidence required to perform effectively.

There is no oral criticism of speakers. Each speech is followed by applause and a question-and-answer period. After the last speech on a given day, the instructor makes some general comments, all of a positive nature. For example, the teacher might mention that the speakers all presented clearly organized speeches that demonstrated their understanding of structuring. Comments on individual performance are presented in written form and contain both positive comments and suggestions for improvement. Students are invited to see the instructor privately if they wish additional critique and recommendations for improvement. About 90 percent do.

Student Assignments

Throughout the course, students complete a series of assignments designed to help them improve as communicators.

"Self-as-Communicator" paper #1. At the first class session, students are assigned to write a two-page (maximum) paper in which they describe themselves as communicators. They are asked to enumerate what they see to be their strengths as specifically as possible. They are also asked to identify situations in which they have difficulty and behaviors they wish to improve. These papers are not graded. They are used as agendas for individual conferences with the instructor. They are also compared with "Self-as-Communicator" paper #2 to assess the students' perceptions of the progress they made in the course.

Individual conference. The instructor meets with each student for approximately thirty minutes to discuss the Self-as-Communicator Paper. The purpose of the conference is to develop a personalized syllabus of goals the student will seek to accomplish during the course. The instructor helps the student select a simple goal with which to start. It is very important that the student successfully accomplish the first goal. This provides a basis for subsequent success.

Out-of-class goals. Students complete a minimum of three outside the classroom context. Most students complete one or two additional goals. Goals include social ("I will carry on a five-minute conversation with . . ."), group ("I will make a two-minute statement at the next meeting of . . ."), classroom ("I will ask the professor two questions at my next . . . class"), interview ("I will make an appointment with my adviser and ask the following . . ."), and public speaking ("I will present a ten-minute report to my . . . class"). Students plan their strategy with the instructor, rehearse with classmates, and report after they have made the effort.

In-class goals. These include public speeches, group oral presentations, job interviews, or the oral interpretation of literature (although all students must present a minimum of one individual speech). The procedure is the same as for out-of-class goals. Students prepare a goal analysis, receive instructor approval, complete the goal, and write a goal report.

Group project. Students are required to participate in at least two group exercises; one a warm-up project, the other a semester-long project. The group activity is designed to give students an opportunity to practice impromptu and responsive speaking. Unlike the public-speaking assignments, they are not required to rehearse with the instructor. The instructor monitors and critiques some of the sessions. Also, each group is required to present a written document summarizing their work and to present an oral report, as a group, as well.

"Self-as-Communicator" paper #2. At the end of the course, students write a second paper in which they readdress the questions they considered in their first paper. Students describe the changes they have seen in their communication behavior and identify areas in which they need further improvement. These papers are ungraded, and students are informed that they will not be read until after final grades have been

turned in. These papers are compared with the first so that instructors can get an idea of the nature and extent of improvement.

The course must be modified to fit terms and semesters, but it is important to maintain the same assignments and exercises. The tasks the students are required to perform have been carefully studied and their probable outcomes defined. The teaching plan is essentially teacher-free, that is, it does not depend on a particular kind of personality to administer it. In fact, charismatic teachers have a good deal of difficulty implementing the syllabus. The essential premise is that the students must have confidence in the system, which they can take with them when they leave, rather than in any personality.

3

The Problems of Problem Communicators

WHAT ARE COMMUNICATION PROBLEMS?

A quarter century of experience with the Penn State Reticence Program has convinced us that these people are not so very different from those who do not report having problems. In fact, there are very few really effective communicators. Most people limp along as best they can. What distinguishes the people who come to the Reticence Program is their willingness to admit their problem and seek help. We cannot resist the notion (although we cannot document it) that the students enrolled in the program represent Everyman. They are the proper domain for the discipline of speech communication whose mission ought to be the study of conscious oral performance behavior. This moralistic proclamation is, of course, debatable. For our purposes we can keep the peace by confining our remarks to the theory and technique of speech performance pedagogy.

It is not always smart to study a population from a selected sample, in this case, of people who confess to having problems. On the other hand, there is no reason to believe that they differ from the norm in any way other than degree. Thus, we can learn about oral performance behavior by observing their oral performance behavior and extrapolate to people in general.

But the explanation of oral performance behavior is not simple. It requires knowledge from several cognate disciplines, for example,

psychology, which studies the theory, control and modification of conscious mental events and psychoanalysis, which deals with the unconscious. Because oral performance behavior takes place in a social milieu,
those who study it must also be familiar with sociology, anthropology,
economics, and political science. These disciplines inform theories of
why and how people communicate. They are also the source of metaphors useful in explaining communication performance. It is also necessary to understand the physiology of the vocal mechanism. Though
speech, in its fundamental form, is a physiological process. It is especially
important in identifying speech problems to be able to assign difficulties
to psychological, development, social, and physiological processes.

Speech communication theory is not about mental processing or how
society operates. The study of human speech requires explanations of
how humans use discourse to attempt to influence and alter the world
around them. Such study especially emphasizes criticism of performance
for the purpose of finding ways and means to improve it.

Contemporary scholars have argued insistently about whether speech
problems are personality traits or the result of social states (for example,
Andersen, 1987). For the speech teacher, the argument is moot. Even
the person most poorly endowed genetically can be trained to improve.
Thus, speech instruction is fundamentally "state." It is directed toward
facilitating the best possible performance in the given case.

Human life can be divided into two kinds of situations in which oral
communication takes place: the cyclic and the occasional. Biologically
speaking, cyclic events include, but are not confined to, daily matters
like eating, eliminating, intercourse, and sleep. Occasional biological
events include puberty and menopause. Cyclic social events include
recurrent contacts such as people at work, neighbors and friends, family
members, and intimate partners. Occasional events include first meetings and accidental contacts.

Human concern with cyclic acts is to make them tolerable—to satisfy
minimum requirements and to make them interesting—that is, to get
the best one can from them. Occasional events must be safe and profitable. That is, one must try to avoid pain and obtain pleasure. Those
who study oral performance behavior must concentrate on discovering
how people adapt their personal goals to their propensities and limitations
in the social situations they encounter in order to fulfill this "prime
directive."

We have no quarrel with those who study communication from the standpoint of psychology or literary criticism. Their ideas and discoveries are often useful in explaining why and how people perform. However, because our concern is with conscious management of oral performance we gravitate to the art of rhetoric as a source of basic propositions. When oral performance behavior reaches a minimum level for both cyclic and occasional events sufficient to satisfy personal goals within the parameters of social situations, we call it competent. When it does not meet minimum levels, we call it incompetent. (Rebecca Rubin discusses communication competence in the Appendix. For those unfamiliar with the concept, it might be useful reading right now.)

The obligation of the speech performance instructor is to provide a technology of performance change so that those who come for instruction can be helped to achieve the maximum level of performance ability in the situations they encounter as constrained by their genetic inheritance. In order to do this, teaching must be expressly directed at carry-over. Educational experiences are occasional. They are not repeated. To make them effective they must be made to fit the cyclic nature of our lives.

Once we make permanent connections with people, most of what we do is routine. We get up in the morning, make conversation over coffee, leave for work, come home, swap notes, eat dinner, and then move on to the activities of the evening. Occasionally there are quarrels, battles with neighbors, problems with the children.

Most of us lead routine lives at work as well. We manage to routinize the way we handle ordinary phone calls, regular meetings, contacts with colleagues, interviews with the boss. Occasionally we have an exercise in crisis management.

It is relatively simple to adapt social performance to the cyclic and routine social events of our lives. All we need to do is draw on memories of successful encounters yesterday, the day before, and the day before that, and repeat what we found effective. When we are confronted with a change in the behavior of the audience for our acts, however, we must respond accordingly. It is the function of performance instruction to generate a repertoire of behaviors that lead to successful outcomes. When we repeat counterproductive behaviors we can learn to be incompetent. If we are trained to adapt effective behaviors to the mundane communication events of our lives, we become competent.

Some occasional events become routinized and vice versa. Our unexpected contacts can become regular associations. Any routine contact can change suddenly and appear occasional should either of the parties modify their behavior. Thus, the composition of our social rhetoric requires continual synthesis of the general and specific as we adapt to the nature of each situation. To be effective, a person must be able to draw on the memory of successful cyclic experience and apply it to occasional events.

INCOMPETENT ORAL PERFORMANCE

Teachers of speech are mainly interested in bringing oral performance behavior up to some standard of effectiveness. A theory of modification of performance behavior can be constructed either from philosophical speculation or from observation of the ordinary. We prefer the latter. We will generate our theory of rhetorical competence from our consideration of substandard performance and conclude our work by proposing a theory of technology for modifying the oral performance of social rhetoric in a variety of situations. Throughout, we will use the following definition of competent oral discourse:

> *Competent oral discourse is any talk that accomplishes all or part of a social goal without generating undesirable concomitants sufficient to neutralize or outweigh the advantages gained.*

Competence is normally judged by consensus; for a speech behavior to be considered competent, it must be so regarded by the speaker as well as by sophisticated observers.

The sine Qua Non of Inept Communication

A *definition*. Human beings talk to one another in order to accomplish human business. Those who talk skillfully get more of what they seek from others than those who do not. They do it by convincing other people to comply with their wishes; to love, obey, and cooperate with them; to enjoy life with them. Those who are not effective live at best with their goals partially met, anonymous, unaware of why they are not getting what others get out of social living.

Charles Van Riper (Van Riper & Emerick, 1984, p. 34) defined speech disorders as follows: "Speech is abnormal when it deviates so far from the speech of other people that it calls attention to itself, interferes with communication, or causes the speaker or his listeners to be distressed."

Van Riper's definition applies specifically to disorders of voice, articu-

lation, quality, and fluency; normally the province of speech patholo-
gists. However, there is no reason why it cannot be applied to the speech
of ordinary people, many of whose speech deviates so far from the speech
of others that it interferes with communication and causes both speaker
and listeners to be distressed. As to "calling attention to itself," the fact
that we identify people's personalities by their speech makes this point
obvious.

Laura Muir (1964) was the first to identify people who did not have
obvious pathologies but whose speech was a problem for them. She
created the category of "reticence" to subsume these people. Muir's
reticent speakers did not qualify in any category to which Van Riper's
definition applied. Their speech was normal in every physical sense, it
was not effective. Muir characterized these people as "reticent" because
the term did not carry pejorative connotations. Subsequently the word
"shyness" came to refer to a subcategory of speakers who did not participate in social situations. Many reticent speakers do not qualify as "shy,"
at least the way the word is used by contemporary psychologists. "Shyness" is a concept that contains connotations of emotional distress and
psychological disturbance. As Muir defined the word "reticent" it referred to people who did not talk much or who talked ineffectively when
they did.

These problems of definition suggest that we lack a general taxonomy
for nonpathological communication problems. We tend to describe
good speakers with literary adjectives like "compelling" or "magnetic,"
while we ascribe psychological qualities like "introvert" or "low self-
esteem" to poor speakers. But not all speech is literary, and speech
performance and personality are not synonymous. If we wish to modify
speech performance to make it more effective, we must eventually
conceptualize what effective speech performance looks and sounds like
and provide categories of normal performance, deviation from which
constitutes ineptitude worthy of instruction or treatment.

A great many people claim to have problems with social communication. Regardless of how they are named, those problems have both
internal and external components and consequences which can be quite
different for each individual. Thus, we cannot be clear whether there is
any empirical similarity among these people other than their claim to a
label. Lynne Kelly's (1982) research shows that most people cannot
distinguish a person who calls himself or herself shy from one who does
not. On the other hand, Scott Kuehn, in research as yet unpublished,

seems to find a social consensus about how shy people behave. Further-more, Rekart and Begnal (1989) have produced evidence that people who claim to be shy have characteristic vocal patterns measurable by sensitive equipment even when they are not evident to observers.

We cannot assume, however, that individual deviations come from the same source or that they have similar internal effects. Michael Hyde (1980) eloquently argued the case for a phemonenological view of speech problems or, at least, for those associated with anxiety. He declares that because people each live in their own private misery they are unable to share their feelings. They are similar only in the labels they share. This makes concepts like shyness paradoxical. Certain aspects of inept communication behavior can be measured and described. However, its personal impact must be considered in light of the individual's life history and personality. There is no common etiology or treatment, even when people behave similarly or make common claims about their condition.

Behavioral aspects of shyness. Kuehn's preliminary research indicates that shy people are identified and labeled by others because they avoid contact, do not initiate conversation, and show physical signs of distress when they communicate. More specifically, shy people call attention to themselves by talking less and more softly than others, avoiding eye contact, presenting a diffident demeanor, refraining from initiating conversation, and, in general, not appearing to conform to social speech norms. What they do—or more precisely, what they do not do—inter-feres with communication. Because they are unable to achieve their interpersonal goals, they often report feeling anxious in social situations. They also apply labels to themselves, "shy," among others, or "nerd" or "klutz." They sometimes report feeling guilty and angry about their inability to manage socially, and they express resentment at being bul-lied, pitied, regarded as social "wimps."

The degree of reported and visible distress and disability varies from person to person, from time to time, and from situation to situation. Whatever their problem, however, most people called shy are preoccu-pied with the effect they have on other people. They do not necessarily associate their communication behavior with the effects. Rather, they tend to ascribe whatever they see their problems to be either to some defect in their personality or to willful resistance on the part of others.

This posture presents a real problem to teachers, first, because there is no necessary connection between the way people feel and the things they do, and second, because teachers cannot modify personality any-way. The central issue becomes how to focus the attention of the "shy" communicators, or any inept communicator for that matter, on behavior that can be modified.

To put this issue in perspective, consider that there is a great deal that any given person *cannot* do. For example, some people do not ski because they do not know how, some because they never wanted to, and some because they are afraid to. Skillful skiing is not a requirement for social living, however, and so people are not terribly concerned about the problem of "ski shyness." On the other hand, a person who wants desperately to ski but lacks the skill can go voluntarily to a ski instructor. If he subsequently discovers that he fears skiing, he can seek psychological treatment for his "phobia." It is all a matter of individual choice. The obligation to communicate, however, is not as easy to avoid. People must communicate in order to maintain their relationships with others.

Because our focus must be on behaviors, we will, from this point forward, refer to the objects of our discourse as "inept" or "incompetent" communicators. We recognize that a great many of them, if not the majority, qualify for the label "shy." On the other hand, our theory requires us to ignore the psychodynamics inherent in the word "shy." We are, in fact, not diagnosing our students; we are necessarily rejecting the "medical model."

The Medical Model

Humans are enamored with the medical model. We tend to classify our adversities according to it. When we do, it shapes the way we think about our problems. Harrison's *Principles of Internal Medicine* (1974) and Weed (1975) agree that to qualify for the medical model a problem must first have a set of symptoms common to all cases. That is, every case in the category must meet a sine qua non definition. In measles, for example, each case would have sensitivity in the eyes, sore throat, with white spots in the mouth and the presence of a particular infectious organism. There may be individual differences in the severity of the symptoms, but the symptoms define the disease. Unless a problem meets the requirements for the diagnostic category, the treatments of record for the category cannot be considered appropriate.

Second, all cases of a given disorder must have a common etiology. The etiology helps explain the problem and identifies potential treat-ments. For example, fractures from blows to the limbs are treated differently from those resulting from defects in the bone. One of the main objectives of medical research is to refine taxonomies of disease via discovery of differential causes.

Treatment, the third element, depends on both discovery of causes and nature of symptoms. Medical practitioners are constrained by their armamentaria. Some treatments work and some do not. There are government regulations about the use of treatments. Furthermore, each treatment has specific indications and contraindications; side effects are detailed and warnings are issued. For example, antibiotics are specific to particular organisms and are useless unless the proper organisms are both present and involved in the pathological state under treatment.

DSM/III (1982) attempts the same kind of formulation for psychological disorders. Underlying both medical and psychiatric diagnosis is the notion that there are clearly marked disease categories for which treatments are either available or potential. Good practice requires diagnosis followed by appropriate treatment. So rigid is the process that it is legally ossified by definitions of what constitutes malpractice.

Such precision does not exist for incompetent communication. Shy people, for example, do not have common sets of symptoms or etiologies, nor is there a consistently effective treatment. Not one of the major works in clinical psychology or psychiatry refers to shyness or any other communication ineptitude as pathological conditions. Neither the *Encyclopedia of Human Behavior* (Goldenson, 1970) nor the *Encyclopedia of Psychology* (Corsini, 1984) contains entries for shyness. There are no index entries for it in *DSM/III* (1982), and the massive unabridged *Comprehensive Textbook of Psychiatry [CTP/IV]* (1985) contains only four references to shyness, all in a chapter on disorders of childhood and adolescence. These are all incidental references, not main headings referring to specific disorders.

Clearly, shyness is not seen as a pathological category by physicians and psychiatrists. While a few psychologists have opened "shyness clinics," their work is largely humanistic and characterized by a paradoxical process of treating social problems with individual therapy. The only treatments using group contact are found in programs offering humanistic therapy like EST and Gestalt therapy, by certain radical religious sects or by personality improvement systems like Toastmasters and Dale Carnegie. For those, shyness is one of many human conditions addressed by their formulas.

Since there is no nosology for shyness, the problem is identified by labeling. Shy people are either self-diagnosed or called "shy" by others. However, when we examine the details, we often discover shy people have problems similar to those experienced by ordinary people whether they identify them as problems or not. We presume the urgency some people have to be identified as pathological comes from their commitment to the cure promised them by the medical model.

The common feature that unites shy people is that they all believe they have trouble communicating with others. But there are a great many people not displaying any of the behaviors associated with shyness who believe they also have trouble. Because there is little consistency among inept communicators in presentation or etiology, a treatment or instructional program must be addressed to specific problems, not categories. In essence, shyness does not exist until it is brought into existence by a label assigned by the "sufferer" or those with whom he comes in contact. So it is with all the other people who are socially incompetent.

The Presentational Forms of Inept Communication Behavior

Studying and treating inept communication behavior are complicated by the many forms in which it presents. For example, some people are quite aware of their counterproductive behaviors, while others are only vaguely aware that they are not accomplishing what they must in social situations. A few have had communication problems pointed out to them.

Many inept communicators use their self-diagnosis as an excuse to avoid social contact or to explain why they feel awkward in the company of others. They seem to use the label to earn rewards like being excused from social obligations. The self-diagnosis often motivates more skillful socializers to intervene on their behalf. Shyness is generally regarded as an acceptable personal excuse for inept social behavior. So is "stage fright" and aphorisms such as "speakers are born not made," or "some people got it and other people don't." (We use similar excuses to avoid dancing, golfing, or visiting unpleasant relatives.)

When a person has problems called to his or her attention by others, it is usually done in global terms. People do not generally comment on the role of vocal quality, loudness, or grammar. They use reifications like "dull," "uninteresting," "wimpy," "hostile," "aggressive," or "shy." These focus the individual's attention on personality and complicate the process of behavior modification.

Disabling Effects of Incompetent Communication

Despite the fact that we cannot yet provide a definition of communication incompetence, there is no question about the way it affects the
people who claim to suffer from it. Shy people suffer from anxieties,
resentments, and hostilities that impair the quality of the lives they live.
Their ineptitude makes them lonely and bored. Some live in a fantasy
world like Walter Mitty. Others are perpetually frustrated because they
cannot conduct their social lives satisfactorily. Shy people can be fearful,
hostile, apathetic, and depressed. They may be the butt of jokes and the
objects of hostility. Worst of all, they are likely to be ignored.

Understanding shy people begins with a sense of the nature of effective
human socialization. It is impossible to get empathy with the condition
of the inept communicator without understanding what effective communicators are able to get from the social milieu. Not all ineffective
socializers are shy, but the consequences of ineptitude are similar regardless of its nature. Furthermore, inept communication has consequences
for both the individual and society.

Aristotle believed that humans would identify and select truth and
justice from their alternatives, if all ideas were given an equal hearing.
Inept communicators cannot get an equal hearing for their ideas because
they are unwilling or unable to meet the social standards for effective
communication. They are thus disabled and society is deprived of their
contributions.

But it is important to keep in mind that just because inept communicators are socially deprived, they are not necessarily "nice" people. A
great many shy people, for example, harbor serious resentments against
the people who have "put them down." They sulk and pout and sometimes plot revenge. Sometimes they use their shyness as a weapon against
others. Often, they are uninteresting. It is not easy to work with such
people. They do not respond well to instruction. Most of them must be
literally retrained in the simplest of social skills.

This should not be construed as an argument on behalf of the civil
rights of inept communicators, although we strongly believe people have
a right to be left alone if that is their choice. Furthermore, we know that
it is impossible to intrude and attempt to modify the life of any person
if that person does not wish to be modified. Rather, we regard skillful
communication as a matter of personal responsibility and place the
burden for improvement on the individual. In essence, what we offer

here is a theory and technology of pedagogy for performance improvement.

PROBLEMS COMMON TO INEPT SPEAKERS

Inept speakers come in various sizes and shapes with a wide variety of difficulties. They have some features in common, however. We cannot consider these features to be "symptoms" of their problem. Their problem is best described by the communication behaviors associated with it. What we will discuss now is some of the effects inept communication can have on those who suffer from it.

Egocentrism

Most poor speakers are egocentric about it. They often have an exaggerated view of the notice others take of them. In social situations, they may feel they are constantly on display and other people are aware of small details of their appearance and demeanor. Some literally believe that other people could see their knees knocking or hear sounds of impaired digestion associated with their social fears.

Kelly's 1982 studies cast doubt on this. Listeners may be aware of gross deviations in communication behavior on the part of the those who speak to them, but they do not normally spot small behavioral details. They are certainly not aware of what other people feel except by inference from what they see and hear. One reason shy people especially respond inappropriately is because they misinterpret what others are seeing and thinking. Inappropriate social response is commonly a result of inept communication behavior.

Quiet and unaggressive people often complain about the lack of regard others have for them. They may want to have their say or discuss their feelings and their resentments, but they do not know how to get attention, or what to do with it when they get it. They believe they are entitled to consideration, however, and resent others for not giving it.

They cannot be faulted for their egocentrism. We are all narcissistic about our feelings. One of the major problems we all have in communicating with others is the difficulty of explaining how we "really feel." In fact, we may not know, and even if we know, it is virtually impossible to phrase it in language that makes it worthwhile for anyone to listen. Neither our joy nor our pain can ever be fully expressed. Physicians know this; it is simply not possible to understand the personal relationship a patient has with physical pain. It is even more difficult to understand the psychic pain suffered by people whose inept communication disqualifies them from accomplishing important social goals. Thus, people who have always been adept at socialization can never really understand the pain suffered by people who are not.

Misunderstanding Social Situations

Inept communicators tend to misunderstand social situations. They do not understand that people socialize in order to accomplish personal goals. Some assume that trust and affection will automatically be extended to them by everyone. Others tend toward paranoia and expect nothing but hostility from others. Neither understands the role that negotiation plays in social relationships.

For example, a friendship (or marriage) is like a small society. There must be some legislative authority (a way to make common decisions), an executive (a way to carry out decisions), and a judicial system (a way to resolve conflict). The bargaining required to make a friendship or a love affair work is very complicated and especially difficult for those who do not understand the quid pro quo of relationship building. People often express dismay at rejections they suffer from those whose friendship they seek. They also find it difficult to explain what they have to offer to the friendship. This may mean they had nothing to offer (unfortunately, often the case), or they had something to contribute but did not know how to offer it. Even worse, it may mean they did not know they were supposed to offer anything. The belief that relationships are automatic is one of the most seriously disabling beliefs held by inept communicators.

Lack of Awareness of Social Rules

Another important generalization is that inept communicators appear to be baffled by social rules. Either they do not recognize them or they refuse to admit they exist. They carry on their social lives in line with their egocentrism, oblivious to the fact that people who interact with one another are required to follow rules. Because they are unable to conform to standard routines for making requests and offers, negotiating, arguing, and displaying affection, they forfeit their ability to win social rewards.

David Riesman (1950) described three kinds of individuals: tradition directed, inner directed, and other directed. Inner-directed people often sacrificed group membership because they marched to the beat of their own drum. They set their own rules and sometimes attracted others to them. Both tradition- and other-directed people played by the rules, although for different reasons. Inept communicators present an interesting paradox. They are not clear enough in their social convictions to be inner-directed. Their inherent narcissism prevents them from becoming sufficiently other-directed to exchange with others.

In any case, people cannot succeed socially if they are entirely egocentric. They cannot demand compliance from others, and successful social bargaining depends on communication skill. Thus, inept communicators deny themselves the opportunity to act on their own behalf. This does not reduce their egocentrism. It merely increases their frustration and bitterness at not being able to get very much of what they want from others.

Problems in Relationship Building

The logical outcome of social ineptitude is defective relationships. It is hard enough to learn social rules that already exist. A new relationship requires generation of social rules. A great deal of contact and talk are necessary to negotiate a bond that preserves each party's integrity. In one form of defective relationship, one person dominates the other to the point of denial of equity. Such relationships are no accident. They are negotiated by a dominant party telling the other party the way it is going to be. The submissive party takes little part in the process other than to acquiesce. Another form is one in which the parties are only loosely connected. They get along until the relationship is challenged. Then it comes apart. In those relationships, neither party is competent to manage events and resolve conflicts.

Antipathy to Small Talk

Social foreplay is carried out through small talk. Skill at phatic communion is learned by imitation and practice. Inept communicators are often so trapped by their attention to their own problems that they fail to acquire skill at listening to others. It is not possible even to begin relationship formation without learning the basic routines of meeting and greeting. Shy people, especially, are so concerned about their own comfort and convenience that they seem unable to understand the necessity to provide quid pro quo to sustain the transaction of social business. Excessively aggressive communicators concentrate on getting their own way and ignore attempts by others to negotiate. They who are oblivious to social obligations simply blunder through, impressing no one.

Reluctance to Change

Our experience with inept communicators leads us to believe they generally resist instruction. In regular speech classes competent speakers are quite willing to improve. For inept speakers, however, the decision to cooperate with instruction means they must concede their own weakness. Thus, they will often reconcile themselves to learning to live with whatever social contacts they have. Sometimes they will seek panaceas like sensitivity or assertiveness training, which have limited utility because they presume the trainee will function in a social milieu where all others have been similarly trained. When the nostrum does not live up to its promise, it only confirms their notion that they must avoid changing altogether.

Virtually all shy people complain of the discomfort they feel when they attempt to modify their social behavior. They report two problems consistently. First, they find it hard to accept the new image of themselves that emerges as they became more skillful. Second, they point out that their friends seem uncomfortable when they experience the new behaviors. The inevitability of change in personal behavior is a major consideration in training. The comfort concomitant with having a social style that allows predictable outcomes is attractive in comparison with the tension that necessarily accompanies behavior change. It stands to reason that if you've been buffeted around for a long time and begin to fight back, your antagonists might get hostile. It is often more convenient and comfortable to avoid the hostility by simply remaining what you are. The negative synergy that comes about from the relationships in which shy people find themselves militates against their extending the effort that change requires. This often blinds them to their own problems. They will deny their own incompetency and offer the excuse that they can speak effectively anytime they want to (they just haven't wanted to lately).

Awkwardness in Disclosure

Ambiguity about personal disclosure is another important aspect of the social nonconformity characteristic of many inept communicators, especially shy people. In addition to being unable to argue, bargain, and negotiate well, shy people are ambivalent about what they tell others about themselves. Possession of personal information confers power. It is a kind of currency in relationship. We disclose the most to the people to whom we are closest and reserve information from our casual contacts. Shy people tend to get mixed up on both levels. They will often keep their thoughts and feelings concealed from the people with whom they are close, and overdisclose to strangers, often therapists to therapists and teachers. Once given the opportunity to disclose, their words seem like catsup pouring out of the bottle after the block was fixed. Joost Merloo (1964, p. 24) remarked: "I regard skeptically all those who speak with the pathos of seemingly open truth and honesty; behind this tactic there often lies the most perfidious form of hypocrisy, for much confession is a pure strategy to provoke someone else's deepest secrets in exchange for superficial ones."

Response to Charismatics and Authoritarians

Inept speakers are also easy victims of charismatics and authoritarians. Their need for structure seems to impel them to seek predictable relationships. Their tendency to be submissive often leads them into the grasp of dominant personalities. Since they cannot play an adequate role in relationship building, they are concerned about the reliability of others in their lives. The effect seems to be that once shy people develop relationships, they stay with them regardless of what happens. This means they have to ignore changes in order to preserve the image of stability. Finding an authoritarian who will control them provides a kind of security. By being obedient and subservient, they can guarantee themselves a consistent, albeit often painful, social situation. Thus, a great many people are locked into connections with people who use and often abuse them simply because they lack the skills necessary to look out for their own needs.

This pattern suggests a hypothesis that those who fall under the control of charismatics like evangelists or unscrupulous politicians, are likely to be people unable to find security in their other interpersonal relationships. It is possible that shy people may compensate for their lack of satisfaction with interpersonal relationships by attaching themselves to a dominant figure and becoming part of the claque.

Fear of Criticism

Underlying the social difficulties experienced by inept communicators is fear of criticism. It is especially important in the way they view public performance. Those who believe they are going to perform badly will speculate on the consequences. They will be deterred from trying.

In social situations fear of criticism is associated with fear of risk. If you behave badly, people will not like you. If they do not like you, they will not give you what you want. They can punish you. Hypersensitivity to response is a powerful deterrent to action.

What is it that people fear about communication with others? Is it the performance of the act itself? That is, do they fear preparing and saying words? Or is it the reaction from others that concerns them? If it is the reaction of others, what is it that they think others can do to them? In the classroom, for example, people who do not participate usually get a bad grade. But there is always the fear of ridicule from peers. Criticism manifests itself in social interactions in the form of sanctions, rejection, public hostility, denial, and even physical threats from parents, superordinates, and peers.

The question is, Do inept communicators know this? Do they make their decisions about whether to participate or not based on knowledge of the nature of the exchange? Are they more sensitive to possible criticism than those who are more skillful? Could it be that their limited repertoire of possible responses raises the cost of any kind of behavior?

Anticipation of negative response can effectively control what a person says. Children learn that certain topics can irritate or anger their parents. They either avoid them or use them to evoke a response. The ability of the listeners to impose social sanctions places the speaker effectively under their control. The rhetorical view of speaking places heavy emphasis on the listener. The process of discourse is a synthesis of the contributions of the participants. Each speech act must consider a listener and a possible response. The extent to which people are able to differentiate possible responses and estimate the probabilities that one might be more effective than another could account for skill and lack of it. To be a "good" or "effective" speaker, it would seem, requires that the speaker understand the situational possibilities, be able to select ideas, and phrase them in ways that maximize the odds of a desired response. The individual who cannot distinguish an affirming response from a critical one is handicapped.

Not all inept communicators are fearful. Some are oblivious. They appear secure, unperturbed, and unchallenged. They are, in fact, downright dull. Most of us project our personality in the hope of attracting or impressing others. Some inept communicators have already learned they cannot do this.

ANOTHER ATTEMPT AT A DEFINITION OF INEPT
COMMUNICATION BEHAVIOR

The fact that we cannot regard communication ineptitude as a pathology complicates defining it. In chapter 1 we defined competent oral discourse as talk that facilitates goal accomplishment without undesirable concomitants. This is a critic's definition, not a teacher's. A teacher needs an operational definition in order to specify the variables toward the modification of which teaching will be directed.

Shy people make up a large proportion of communication incompetents. They report many different feelings about their disabilities, and when they come for help, they are urgent about having those feelings addressed. They do not display consistent disabling behaviors; there is no standard etiology or nosology for shyness.

To write an operational definition of shyness as a specific case of communication incompetency requires consideration of psychological and social dimensions of the problem, but essentially it demands concentration on behaviors. A shy person will remain shy by designation unless and until shy behaviors are replaced by nonshy behaviors. The important question is, What do shy people *do* that leads others to regard them as shy?

Once we focus on "doing," we can ignore all prior designations. It is no longer important to identify "shy" people. Once we have identified inept behaviors, we can work on modifying them, without labeling the individual at all.

Since social discourse is directed at accomplishing some social goal, every unit of discourse must be situationally locked. The interests of the other participants are crucial in the selection of what to say and how to say it. Social speech is systematic; responsive rather than reactive. In fact, reactive or signal-type speech is usually ineffective. People who do not understand the constraints involved in social speech have a cognitive deficit. Thus, in defining incompetency, we need to discover what the incompetent individual does not know about communication in general. Remedying this deficit will not necessarily alter the way a person speaks, but it will alter his willingness to learn to alter it.

In the next chapter we will examine communication incompetence as a performance problem, with particular emphasis on its rhetorical character. We will begin our inquiry into the question of how specific communication behaviors affect the outcome of social transactions.

4

Etiology of Communication Incompetence

We have now defined our problem as modification of social performance behavior. We have identified some problems in social performance behavior and labeled them "communication incompetence." In so doing, we used the simplest possible definition of competence, that is, a person can perform competently if he or she has been seen to do so. The criterion for teaching is to get students to perform effectively communication behaviors they could not perform prior to instruction. We will not argue whether instruction causes or facilitates the behavior.

ISSUES IN DEVELOPMENT AND ACCULTURATION

Developmental Issues

The teaching of oral performance has largely been based on tradition. Scholars have paid a great deal of attention to philosophical and linguistic issues, and social scientists have done a number of behavioral studies describing how people communicate in various conditions. But there are few formal attempts to study how oral performance skill develops.

In fact, there is very little tangible evidence that methods used by speech teachers actually work. We rely on anecdotal evidence, for example, "Wow, they really improved," but we do not know in what way, or what brought about the perceived improvement.

We believe that children learn to speak by imitating people around them. Most know how to speak in some fashion by the time they enter school. They are given little or no formal instruction in speaking after that. In fact, the schools emphasize reading and writing but ignore speaking and listening. Teachers tacitly assume that their students can speak and listen, and they interpret failure to do so either as a sign of intellectual incompetence or willful disobedience.

Moreover, a great many children are required in the classroom to perform speech tasks for which they have not been trained. "Show and Tell" seems simple enough, but it is actually a formal public speech. To do it well requires either exceptional talent or careful training. Failure at early public performances could have serious consequences for subsequent performances.

If children learn performance mainly by imitation, it raises serious questions about whom they choose to imitate. Children seem to have little trouble learning the norms of primary groups like their families (with some notable exceptions). The problem comes in adapting to new groups. The process of adaptation itself appears to be a skill that children must learn. If their families are isolated and lack skill in adjusting to strangers, the children are likely to be disabled in that regard also.

The paradox in training people in effective social speech is that it is impeded by our cultural mythology. We make quite a "to-do" in our society about how unethical it is to manipulate others. The formalities of training in effective speech appear manipulative. Students must be trained to think about the situation and their listener and adapt according. Most people seem to prefer to believe the prevailing myth that there is some kind of magic in human relationships. People who get along have the right chemistry. Someone who can mobilize loyal support in others has leadership ability or charisma. Good speakers are "born, not made." Little attention is paid to the techniques of communication necessary in building relationships.

To be sure, planning discourse carefully to support social exchanges puts a damper on "romance." But there is support for the notion that people in close relationships face a great many risks in exchanging. While consensual validation, for example, is important in dispelling feelings of isolation, it requires considerable disclosure. There is always a danger when people share secrets. Therefore, it is important that people acquire skill in how to manage it.

As we become aware of the risks involved in social interaction, we may become justifiably suspicious of others. Rarely do we get good advice about how to behave. Because most people are awkward and inept in their interpersonal relations, learning by modeling means that our social errors become habits. Commonly, the exchanging of intimacies is handled by methods tantamount to faith healing. Training programs like sensitivity training, assertiveness, EST, and other formulary systems directed at modifying attitudes, offer magic as a method for building satisfying relationships.

For their part, either children learn to fit in and get along by going along, or they become confrontational and aggressive. Only a few learn the skills of managing relationships well, and we haven't a clue as to how they do it.

Acquisition of skill may well be a function of criticism compatible with Homans' (1975) idea that people will repeat behaviors that are rewarded. We, thus, tend to develop our personalities in Sullivanian[1] fashion. We tend to repeat the behaviors that we think get us desirable responses from others until they become habitual components of our personality.

While criticism is clearly important in the development of our style of discourse, it only works when it comes from a valuable someone. If the critic is someone whose general approval we seek, we tend to respond to criticism. If the critic is irrelevant or we regard him as hostile, we ignore or resist the criticism.

Our definition of criticism includes any responses other people make to our behavior. The way people react to us can be construed as criticism. In general, criticism is a very volatile process. Most people resent it, few know how to respond to it. We are more likely to believe the compliments we are given than take complaints seriously. Furthermore, few critics accompany their negative remarks with suggestions for improvement. Even in the classroom, critical comments are more likely to be admonitions to improve rather than prescriptions for behavior change. When schoolchildren are very incompetent, they are assigned to remediation and appropriately stigmatized. Remediation rarely has anything to do with social living. Speech correction, in particular, must be administered outside of normal social contexts.

1. We urge reading Sullivan thoroughly. His view of interpersonal relationships, although cynical, is clearly behavioral. His works are cited in the references. For a superior review of his thinking and the development of his theories, we recommend Perry, 1982.

Learning to Socialize

Young people appear to learn to behave socially by immersing themselves in a context of other people. It is very hard to tell what they learn from whom, however. Some things, like hairdos and dress, tastes in entertainment and sports, and even preferences in reading, are matters of norms. To find out what to do, they observe the most popular person in the group and imitate. The more subtle problem of how people acquire their communication behaviors is not so easy to solve. Attempts to study how people model their behavior have not produced much of value (Gardner, 1983; Perry, 1985).

There are issues in acculturation that are not easy to explain. For instance, how does a person learn to identify which behaviors are associated with success and which with failure? Some people believe mere membership in the proper group is a sign of success. But how do they identify which group is proper? What criteria do they use to select whom to imitate?

Some young children choose adult-defined goals as signs of success. They struggle to excel in school or athletics, music or art. They plan for college and for careers. They learn to be polite. Often, they pay the price of rejection by peers for acceptance by adults.

And peers are important—Sullivan believes they are crucial to survival in adolescence and young adulthood. As a matter of fact, having close friends is important throughout life. But we know little about how people select their friends and associates. Some associations, of course, are mandatory. We learn to deal with the people who sit next to us in school, or who work at the next desk. But people are relatively free to choose their social companions. And we do not know how they do it. We can observe and describe the process of relationship building, but we do not know what people seek from each other and what they think they can offer to get it.

Moral Development

Lawrence Kohlberg (1981) offered an intriguing model of social development based on acquisition of social values. Although direct measurement of values defies human capability, we commonly assess them by monitoring talk and drawing inferences. While values are reifications, Kohlberg's model specifies some qualities that might be reflected in communication behavior.

Kohlberg states that young people develop socially in stages by acquiring strategies in sequence. First, they learn to avoid punishment, next to gain rewards. These are mostly learned within the family or at school. As socialization broadens, they learn to make exchanges and avoid rejection by their peers. In adulthood some acquire skills that enable them to do their duty, engage in legalistic activity, and act in line with conscience. One way to assess communication competency is to evaluate the role played by discourse in identifying appropriate maturity in value development.

Kohlberg did not associate speech behaviors with these stages, but it seems obvious that to avoid punishment one must argue that he "didn't do it," while to earn the reward he must argue that he "was responsible for this or that." Social exchanges leading to acceptance of friendship are usually the outcome of oral bargaining; avoiding rejection means being able to make one's talk fit the norms. Doing one's duty, making legal argument, and taking moral stands are each reflected in discourse.

The sexist "he" was used in the preceding paragraph because Gilligan (1982) responded to Kohlberg by arguing that women developed differently, especially on the more mature levels. This, she argued, was reflected in the way they argued their case. Men, according to Gilligan appeal to law, precedent, and higher powers, while women defer to relationship and emotional commitment. This argument cannot be resolved here, but it is important to consider that morality is reflected through discourse. How handicapped is the person who cannot accurately represent his or her case under the proper circumstances?

The ultimate social question is how do people socialize? We know little; we believe much. Is it really the case that democratic leadership in which everyone respects everyone else's rights is the best way to run a family or an organization or, for that matter, a love affair? Are authoritarians always wrong? How far can we go with a laissez faire attitude toward our relationships?

Social Awareness

Our work in the Reticence Program taught us that few people are able to cope with the social requirements of large organizations, and even less qualified to handle intimacy. There really are very few people who are genuinely skillful at social communication.

There are also a great many myths that pervade thinking about socialization. Scholars argue about democratic versus authoritarian leadership (Haiman, 1950) and symmetrical versus complementary relationship (Watzlawick et al., 1967), but the fact of the matter is that there is very little information about how a person should communicate in order to modify relationships. In essence, performance is ignored. Considerable influence, however, is ascribed to the magic of "good communication."[2]

True to their narcissistic inclinations, our students thought a lot about what they wanted from others, but it did not seem to occur to them that they had to do something to get it. They would make requests on the grounds that they "wanted" the other person to do it. They had not even become sophisticated enough to think in terms of entitlements.

Nor were they sufficiently considerate even to try to make their speech interesting. Typically, their conversations were replete with nonfluencies, clichés, vocalized pauses, "y'know," and "like, I mean." Even in regular sections of the speech performance course we found few people who appeared skillful at presenting a case, defending a point of view, or sustaining interesting social conversation. Furthermore, most people do poorly asking for help. They have difficulty explaining their problems to people like physicians or counselors, and they lack the ability to get attention from people important in their lives.

Instruction in social communication tends to follow a cognitive default. That is, students learn *about* social situations in detail, with little or no training in performance behaviors designed to accomplish social goals. It seems axiomatic that we can regard virtually everyone as relatively inept at ordinary socialization. They have even more difficulty with crisis situations.

Social Crises

"Adulthood" is that period of life in which humans are in full sail in their vocational and family life. Most people arrive there with limited communication skill. Their "ways" are set. They can communicate adequately in some situations and have learned to avoid those in which they are inept. Most still have not learned to adapt effectively to the stress that comes with changes that will beset them to the end of their lives.

2. Corollary to "good communication" is "quality time." Just as there is no sound advice about what constitutes good communication, there are no criteria for quality time. These are examples of the pervasiveness of clichés in our understanding of interpersonal communication.

Adults are described by personality-related adjectives, for example, "passive," "standoffish," "taciturn," "withdrawn," "depressed," "anxious," "circumspect," "good follower," "team player," "reserved," "prudent," "conservative," "timid," or even "nerdlike." Some are regarded as "snobbish" or "arrogant" because they stand apart from social interaction; others may be designated "aggressive," "pushy," or "arrogant." Few of us escape having an adjective applied to our personality by someone. It is amazing how those adjectives refer mainly to communication behavior.

Most adults experience some serious problems in dealing with others. There are no authoritative estimates of how many adults experience "midlife crisis," but the existence of it is an axiom of adult existence. People do not ask "if" we have had our crisis; the question is more like "have you had it yet?"

The cliché "midlife crisis" has come to refer to any problems people have handling major decisions about social relationships, family life, work, and philosophy of social living. The concept expresses the idea that most people suffer from angst. Some are dissatisfied with aspects of their lives and some despise their lives in general. The crisis is the sense of despair that overcomes them when they believe that there is nothing they can do to alter their situation. It is often reflected in frenetic problem solving, drastic decision making, and making errors that make life even more difficult.

The problems of life do not change. Throughout our lives we deal with issues of friendship, love, status, power, self-image, work, pleasure, and social fit. Adults are often tired and mostly creatures of habit, however, and life changes, common in adulthood, may easily overwhelm them. Few are sufficiently versatile to handle the contingencies of losing a job, divorce, or illness.

What commonly happens is that some adversity compels people to discover they have not developed the social skills they need. The adversity may be chronic or acute. Troubles on the job, for example, may include the nagging, pervasive discontents of boredom and frustration or the traumatizing fear of being fired. Family problems may include discontent with the status quo or the difficulty of resisting new temptations. Health problems can drastically affect our lives. Rarely, however, do we recognize that many of our problems can be addressed by our own efforts. It is easier to ascribe our misery to mysterious forces like Kismet or "that's the way it goes."

The *CTP IV* (pp. 1943–1951) lists several problems that seem to affect most people at midlife:

1. Body changes including simple aging, development of chronic diseases, decline in sexual capability, declining physical attractiveness.
2. Economic problems including stagnation on the job, increasing expenses from the needs of growing children and aging parents, and increasing concern about preparation for retirement and medical emergencies.
3. Reduced options in social roles including, hardening of role specifications (spouse, parent, job title), and fewer opportunities to make interesting social connections. Divorce and widowhood also complicate the social picture.
4. An extensive menu of psychological problems: increased competitiveness, increased fatalism and despair about accomplishments, frenetic efforts to cling to youth, hardening attitude and development of biases.

Physiology is the prime criterion. It dictates feeding time, mating season, and potential conflict for leadership of the pack or herd. Humans are required to go through essentially the same processes. They start with ritualistic social routines (referred to as phatic communion). Simple "Hello, how are you?" "Fine, how are you?" routines indicate safety. Each cultural group then has its procedures for extending contact. The rules of consideration and good manners apply to all participants. People who do not comply are usually shunned and eventually are ejected from the group. All of this is based on the human's urgency to be homeostatic, to know what to expect, to be able to predict the next move with reasonable accuracy. Those who give erratic signals or cannot make sensible prediction are disqualified from effectiveness at doing social business.

Stake

People have different motivations for talking with others. Some stand to gain a great deal if they make a sale or a friend. For most, their ego is at stake. Reputation and status are also important considerations. Generally, people seek information, sentiments, goods, and services from others. They invest emotional and intellectual energy in socialization to the extent they think they can gain from it, but their effectiveness is not necessarily related to the amount of emotional and intellectual energy they expend. Thus, the person who cares the least maintains the greatest control in any social relationship. When people do not understand what they have at stake, they may not perform effectively. If we take an economic view of social conversation, clearly people have a great deal to lose. Losing may not be an infallible sign of rhetorical incompetence, but it is an indicator. When one does not achieve a social goal, it is entirely possible that the cause lay in defective goal setting, composition, or presentation.

PREVAILING SOCIAL NORMS

There are clichés that accurately assert what is appropriate in social discourse. Our reticent students were surprisingly unaware of these commonplaces. They were, in fact, hostile to the idea that they existed. The notion that people could somehow know one another "really" without discourse was very popular with them. One does not need to be an anthropologist, however, to understand some of the basic norms of American social discourse. Incompetent speakers consistently violate these norms.

People ought to look you in the eye when they talk. If they do not, either they have something to hide or they are shy. There is something about eye contact that appears important in mainstream American society, although there are some social segments for whom direct gaze is a sign of arrogance.

We have a great many social superstitions connected with eyes. For example, heavy eyelids signal fatigue or depression. Darting or blinking eyes signal uncertainty or uneasiness. Blank stares indicate vapidity or lack of comprehension. We read warmth, love, and courage in people's eyes and respect people who can look us squarely in the eye.

The belief that eyes represent personality is much like the old superstition that there was a criminal face. There is, of course, no data to support any of these beliefs about eyes, although there is considerable data to support the assertion that people believe these things.

But if there is a consistent meaning assigned to eye behavior, it is incumbent on speakers to manage their behavior so that it evokes the appropriate response from their listeners. It is even useful to attempt to comply with the expectations of others on that score.

A person ought to be able to make small talk. First impressions are important. Once again, we have a situation where there is no evidence to support the myth. Few of us can accurately assess character based on personal appearance. Regardless, we make judgments based on what we see initially. We tend to be suspicious of people who cannot handle the amenities of routine social interaction. Since initial contacts always contain the potential for intensification, small talk provides an opportunity for people to size each other up. Behaviors such as handshakes, inquiries about health and welfare, and opening questions about region of origin (where ya' from?) and employment (whaddya' do?) are critical in the management of the delaying routine necessary to process initial data and make a decision about the desirability of future contact.

A person ought to have an interesting voice. Specialists in communication disorders deal with articulation defects, problems in voice quality, stuttering, and vocalized pauses. There are many reasons why a person may have a speech problem, some of which may be associated with neurological deficiencies or disease, and some of which are associated with social training. People may have dialects or accents; they may imitate the speech of their parents who may not have been very good speakers. However, they are judged on conformity with standards for fluency and quality of voice.

We live in an anchorperson environment. We tend to look askance at people who speak with a rural twang (they are rubes), an accent ("furriners"), a southern drawl (hillbillies), or an urban street dialect (hoods). We expect conformity to general American English pronunciation, and if we do not get it, we assign pejorative labels. We expect blacks and Hispanics to discard their natural form of talk when they are "out in public," although the gracious among us are willing to concede them the luxury to be bidialectal in their own company. (We also expect our rock stars, especially the British ones, to conform to the best standards of black dialect when they sing, otherwise they are not considered "authentic.")

Stutterers and others with voice or articulation disorders are often the butt of jokes. We are also suspicious of those who use vocalized pauses. Too many "and uhs" and "y'knows" mark the speaker as less than mature.

We also respond to quality of voice. Men are supposed to have relatively low voices. High voices signal that you are either an Irish tenor or somewhat less than manly, usually the latter. We expect our movie heroes to have rich baritones. The villains are often selected because their voices sound harsh, raspy, and sneering. Comics often put considerable strain on their voices to make them sound funny by being inappropriate to the role. The classic case is Lou Costello attempting to play a heroic cowboy.

By the same token, we expect our women to speak with slightly higher voices, which are also warm and rich. A female baritone is either seen as a barfly or a wanton woman. The prototype for the seductress was Marlene Dietrich whose whiskey baritone was the sine qua non of her sexuality. Mae West's low voice made it clear that she was not a woman one would bring home to meet mother. And of course, the male with the squeaky voice has been a vaudeville joke for generations.

Vocal variation is a requirement for social success. People are supposed to be able to manage their voices so that they are interesting to others. The judgment about "interesting" is based on both content and manner of discourse. There are social agreements about how voices are to be used. Loudness is for emphasis, softness for confidentiality, high pitch for excitement, and so on. Some skillful speakers can use softness to heighten tension and sustain attention. The voice is supposed to be inflected, but in a natural way. A person who speaks in a monotone is regarded as boring, but for the same reason, excessive variation in voice is regarded as a sign of phoniness. We are impatient with whiny voices and antagonized by those who clip their speech. The idea is to suit the pattern of speaking both to the ideas and to the audience.

This is not easy to do. One of the most difficult things for theatre directors to do is get actors to sound authentic as they inflect their voices. It is very hard to coordinate aspects of pitch, fluency, intensity, and vocal variety with the flow of ideas to convey the impression that it is a consistent natural act. A speaker whose inflections do not coordinate well with the ideas can be evaluated as insincere. Questions, for example, call for a particular kind of inflection at the end of a sentence. Even though the form of the sentence is interrogative, unless the inflection is proper, the discourse may not be regarded as a sentence and consequently will not receive a response.

Awkward nonverbal behavior is regarded as a sign of incompetence. Some people are able to manage gestures and facial expressions so that they support discourse. That is, they may use a gesture to emphasize a point or change facial expression to show how seriously they take a particular idea. The training of an actor exemplifies the ideal of natural social conversation. An effective social communicator is supposed to be able to coordinate ideas, words, expression, articulation, vocal control, and body movement so that the message appears intelligible, coherent, and interesting.

Those who are unable to conform suffer social sanctions. Consider the advertising campaign by a deodorant company in 1987 that featured the slogan "Never let 'em see you sweat!" The idea is that there are "signs" of weakness. Perspiration, blushing, trembling, blinking, shaking, breathlessness, and other involuntary nonverbal expressions are some of those signs. This creates genuine problems for those whose apprehension shows, but they are also clues to internal agitation that may require treatment before performance instruction can be administered.

There are accepted norms for content and process of social discourse. People are supposed to be interesting. They are expected to take their listeners into account. They are cautioned against "shop talk" or making uncompensated personal disclosures. Social norms also impose taboos on potentially controversial or irritating topics (don't talk about politics or religion) as well as various forms of slang and profanity (don't use the "f" word in mixed company). People involved in social interaction are expected to be aware of these norms and observe. Furthermore, they are expected to follow the "rules of procedure," like taking turns, answering questions, staying on the topic, inviting others into the conversation, and so on.

PEDAGOGICAL PROBLEMS

Students are not taught the norms of social speech in school. Occasional elementary teachers include units on "good manners," but for the most part, we simply believe all students come equipped to talk competently.

The beliefs we hold about what constitutes "effective speech" are embodied in what is taught in formal courses mostly in colleges. High schools occasionally offer instruction to students who are already skilled in forensics (including debate and contests in "individual events). Proprietary courses like Dale Carnegie Systems attempt to build confidence through teaching techniques of meeting and greeting, remembering names, soliciting information from others, and speaking in simple thought units. There are also semisocial organizations (like Toastmasters) that attempt to train their members in the art of skillful speaking. For the most part, however, this activity is directed at public speaking.

Standard textbooks on speaking offer information mainly about how to select and develop topics and how to outline and support ideas. They also offer a great deal of folk wisdom about "confidence." Student speakers are advised to analyze their audiences, although the systems provided for doing so are often unrealistic and bigoted. (For example, advice is given about finding demographics of age, gender, race, religion, and socioeconomic level. The unspoken premise is that all people in a given group respond the same way.) There is a little information given about delivery, but since the demise of the elocutionist movement, it is considered excessively sophistic or simplistic to provide vocal training. This, despite the fact that a great many people know how to teach delivery effectively.

The textbooks mainly approach public speaking from a rhetorical point of view. The tradition is to encourage extemporaneous speaking directed at specific audiences. However, a recent study (Young, 1989) demonstrated that despite the lip service given to audience adaptation, there is little or no formal instruction offered in how to do it. This deficiency resonates in the attempts at instruction in interpersonal communication.

Students are given situation-specific advice for interpersonal, group, and organizational communication. In recent years special attention has been given to intimate communication, a clear indication that speech communication pedagogy has been responsive to popular trends. But research has been scarce. The pedagogy of oral performance training is based on rhetorical tradition and belief and simply has not been adapted to interpersonal settings. In fact, it is considered inappropriate and manipulative to teach students to regard their interpersonal partners as "audiences." Because we have not yet identified communication behaviors universally accepted as effective in interpersonal settings, we have avoided training specific behaviors. Rather, interpersonal instruction concentrates on ephemeral topics like authenticity, that is, the urgency to reveal oneself and to disclose appropriately.

It may not be a bad idea to avoid instruction in specific social behaviors. On the other hand, it is probably important to develop the concept of interpersonal audience as a basis for training in interpersonal negotiation and bargaining.

The question of what to modify and how to do it remains relatively moot in the instruction of oral performance behavior, however. We will continue to do it as we have been in the past unless and until we get definitive generalizations about the constituents of effectiveness. This will not come easy, but come it must. Focus on competence, or lack thereof, will help us develop hypotheses to test. The results of our experimentation could lead to a general technology of performance modification.

SPECULATION ON THE CONCEPT "COMPETENCE"

Competent discourse is defined by its effects. We accept as a given that all discourse has some effect, but our question is, to what extent does the discourse accomplish the desired effect. A given speaker may achieve a desirable goal accidentally, but this is more a function of listener preference, not the discourse itself. To be competent, the discourse must be planned and directed at an exigence. It must consist of topics appropriate to the situation and influential with the targeted listener. These topics must function as the basis of the invention process and appear in coordinated and orderly fashion as a set of statements phrased in intelligible and interesting language. The speaker must observe the effect and factor it into the decision about the next move. All of this operates out of a fluid and controlled database in memory. The critical decision about competence is made *in the given case* by comparing the objectives of the speaker with the speaker's perception of what is attained based on observation of overt responses presented by the listener. All of this presumes "normal" operation of physiological and mental systems.

Diminished Competency

There are certain mental and physical conditions that impair competency. These conditions cannot be remedied by modification of rhetorical processes. They require either physiological or psychological intervention. Consider, for example, the condition referred to as stage fright. Stage fright refers to something more than the ordinary tension everyone feels when called on to present in public. It is, in essence, a phobia.

DSM/III (1980) refers to a condition called "social phobia." It is described as follows:

> a persistent, irrational fear of, and compelling desire to avoid, situations in which the individual may be exposed to scrutiny by others. There is also fear that the individual may behave in a manner that will be humiliating or embarrassing. Marked anticipatory anxiety occurs if the individual is confronted with the necessity of entering into such a situation, and he or she therefore attempts to avoid it. The disturbance is a significant source of distress and is recognized by the individual as excessive or unreasonable. It is not due to any other mental disorder. Examples of Social Phobias are fears of speaking or performing in public, using public lavatories, eating in public and writing in the presence of others.

Generally an individual has only one Social Phobia. . . . The disorder is usually chronic and may undergo exacerbation when the anxiety impairs performance of the feared activity. This then leads to increased anxiety, which strengthens the phobic avoidance. . . . Unless the disorder is severe, it is rarely . . . incapacitating.

We assume, however, that the social phobia might not only disable a sufferer in particular situations but might also interfere with the instruction and training required to overcome rhetorical incompetencies. In such cases we could advocate whatever "treatment" appears to be effective. The common wisdom is that systematic desensitization is indicated.

Note should be taken of the fact that there are a great many people who sound coherent, but whose thought processes are sufficiently confused to make them dangerous. Sociopaths, for example, are so identified because their behavior and discourse simply do not take others into account. It is important for people to be aware that others can do them harm and to allow for that possibility as they evaluate the discourse they hear.

Physiological impairments that interfere with speech also diminish competency, although it is entirely possible for people with damaged vocal equipment to be effective within their physical limits. Physiological impairment often only affects the delivery of discourse and may have little or no effect on its composition. For the physically impaired, any solution that overcomes defects in intelligibility is usually sufficient to make the communication process appear normal under the circumstances.

The principle of caveat emptor applies to discourse. It is clear that the qualities of interest and inspiration inherent in any message have little to do with the quality of the message itself. The listener has the obligation to go beyond the sound of the message before deciding on what it means. Speakers seek their own ends. Sometimes they take the listener into account, sometimes they do not. Listeners cannot afford to assume goodwill and altruism. Careful listening and observation of behavior are the only ways to get to a speaker's intentions.

We have omitted in the preceding discussion all consideration of the feelings people have when they participate in the exchange of interpersonal discourse. As we noted at the very beginning of this book, these are the legitimate province of psychology and psychoanalysis from which we can receive instruction. There are people who perform quite competently, yet who feel uneasy about doing it and unsatisfied with what they do. There are others who feel little or nothing, but whose performance is less than competent. For purposes of training, we must consider accompanying feelings as irrelevant unless and until they can be identified as impairments to performance. Then we must confront the question of whether the impairment is best removed by improving performance or modifying feelings. The former appears to be the simplest, technologically speaking, because people who do well but feel bad can repair their feelings on their own time, while those who do poorly but feel well need performance repairs in any case. For those who do poorly and feel badly about it, the path of least resistance seems most rational; assume that once the person is more skillful, he or she will feel better about speaking.

In the following chapter we will demonstrate how the theoretical conceptions of classical rhetorical theory, especially the work of the Greek and Roman philosophers (Aristotle, the Sophists, Cicero, Quintilian) provide a basis for a pedagogy of performance modification. Rhetoric presumes that communication behavior is primarily state related. That is, while each person is born with propensities and tendencies, whatever they are, they must be modified to whatever extent possible in order to provide the individual with versatility sufficient to manage the wide variety of speaking situations with which a person is confronted in a normal life.

5

The Rhetorical Canons as a Basis for Pedagogy

THE BOTTOM LINE IN SOCIAL SPEECH

*T*he problems experienced by inept communicators described in the previous chapters are actually problems for ordinary humans. The reality is that most human beings are somewhat less than effective at social discourse. "Less than effective" could mean:

1. Their speech does not meet standards set by people who are supposed to set standards. They do not satisfy others.
2. Their speech does not meet their own standards. They do not satisfy themselves.
3. They cannot use their speech to accomplish legitimate social objectives.

The folklore about social discourse distracts us from some fundamental realities. The mythology is that people are basically kind and considerate and social norms prevent them from acting decently. All it takes to release the milk of human kindness is authentic discourse directed at a person's "real" self. We believe that we give off emanations, or "vibes" as they are sometimes called, or chemistry. When people "match," they can come together in an authentic relationship.

There is a latent sensuality involved in all this. The fundamental unit for interpersonal study is composed of male and female. The reason men are supposed to pursue money and power and women charm and beauty is so they can attract the sex object of their choice. In fact, there is a possessive pronoun commonly associated with relationship: "my friend," for example, or "my mate."

These myths reflect a kind of universal social narcissism. Most of us believe, although we rarely admit it, that other people should be ready, willing, and able to tend to our needs. But we recognize that there is a quid pro quo—that we must give something to get something. The reticent students we interviewed, however, seemed to reflect quite the opposite. They believed, in their adversity, that someone ought to do something *for them*. In fact, the very thought of negotiation as an element in human relationships frightened them.

The fact that human relationships are mostly about sharing time, space, goods, and attention makes them essentially political. In civilized society we talk in order to persuade others to make exchanges with us from which we benefit. People who are not skilled at speaking are not able to accomplish their legitimate goals.

Social speech is purposive, not casual. It does not just happen spontaneously. As DeLaguna (1963) pointed out, humans learned to speak because they had to. It was the only device they had to organize themselves to compensate for their biophysiological frailties in order to defend against an essentially hostile environment. When social speech calls attention to itself, interferes with communication, or causes the user to be distressed, it can interfere with the accomplishment of social objectives. We have defined competent oral discourse as any talk "that accomplishes all or part of a social goal." Thus, our pedagogical concern is with speech in particular settings. Instruction and training must be directed at modification of discourse as a state, not at the modification or management of a personality trait. Thus, the two main components of social discourse are settings and personal goals.

The Case for a Rhetorical Point of View

Rhetoric defined. It is useful to regard social speech as rhetorical. "Rhetoric," said Aristotle (Cooper, 1932), "is the art of finding in the *given case* all the available means of persuasion" (italics mine). Though most contemporary scholars seem to feel that regarding social discourse as rhetoric may be stretching it a bit, James Winans (1931, 1938) explained public speaking as "enlarged conversation." He may have been hyperbolic in order to make a point. The metaphor is quite apt, however.

Even without Winans' authority, it does not take much to see that people seek the same things from social interaction as public speaking. The orator must gain and hold the attention of the audience. He does this by attending to both form and content of discourse. The successful orator finds a way to adapt his message to the needs and wants of his audience guided by Aristotle's dictum, "The fool tells me his reasons, the wise man persuades me with my own."

The essence of the process of public discourse is exchange. The speaker offers the audience a benefit, if they listen and comply. If the speaker gains attention but does not offer a compelling reason for compliance, the discourse fails. If the speaker offers a potentially effective inducement to which the audience does not listen, the discourse fails. To be effective, the speaker must sustain attention and provide motivation to agree or comply.

Social communication is an exchange of short speeches. When it works, it appears to be governed by an agreement of complicity that requires all of the participants to tender something of social value as a form of exchange. Discourse is used to define the blandishments. It fails when participants fail to make effective offers or choose to reject the offer made by another. A successful interpersonal exchange can be described in economic terms. *Person A wants a behavior from Person B and offers Person B a behavior presumed to be desirable in exchange.*

Complicity. Complicity is a social agreement made by the participants to take turns speaking and listening and to observe constraints on the social situation in order that they might explore for possible exchanges.[1] Formal organizations impose complicity through rules that require people to work together. Governments run by laws about decision making, enforcement, and adjudication.

In private relationships the rules and norms of complicity are the result of consensus among the participants. Tautologically, if friends or lovers do not have ways of legislating, executing, and adjudicating, they were not friends and lovers. There must be fundamental agreements on how to generate new rules and norms to accommodate to changes in the relationship. The process appears to be an infinite regress, but

1. There is nothing new in this. Homans (1975) spells it out in simple, behavioral terms. We understand the Skinnerian and essential Marxist mode we are in when we take an extreme position like this. Remember, our job is not to meet some vague criteria of moral philosophy. We are seeking ways and means to modify discourse to the advantage of the individual. In order to do this we must find explicit components on which we can work. We apologize to both ethicists and dreamers for our hyperrealistic Machiavellianism. It is no accident on our part. We picked it. Our argument will unfold.

somehow it starts when two or more people agree to interact under prevailing social norms and then use them to make personalized adjustments. As long as the parties are able to keep adjusting to one another, they stay related. When one or both can no longer adapt, the relationship deteriorates.

When strangers face each other, they need not talk, but they may. If they choose to talk, complicity begins with an exchange of amenities and up to a point, either party has the power to break off. Once a conversation is started, however, there is a modicum of commitment, at least to share a little time, and thus, there is something at stake. Complicity does not guarantee effective communication, but effective communication cannot exist without it.

Furthermore, complicity implies there is a stake in the transaction. Each party has something to gain or lose. The stake can be very small, like spending some stress-free moments in idle chitchat. There is little to lose except a few boring minutes. Everyone, presumably, knows the rules at this point, although some people find it very difficult to stay within generally accepted social norms. They may bore their listeners, refuse to take turns, respond awkwardly, or stop prematurely.

To continue a social relationship, one partner must make an offer or construe something the other said as an offer. Any offer can be accepted or rejected by either party, or it can be negotiated. Rejection terminates the association; acceptance defines the association on the terms offered. In most cases, the party who receives the offer will make a counteroffer, so what is eventually decided is made up of contributions by both parties. There is a presumption that everyone involved has some responsibility for the success or failure of a social interchange, but inept communication by anyone can interfere with the development of the relationship.

Members of any human social system, from government to dyad, must have common rules and methods for making agreements, carrying them out, resolving disagreements, making exchanges and sharing time and space. The culture of a relationship or organization is defined by memories of the historical and literary record of agreements made and the way they were kept or broken. These artifacts form the norms of the culture.

By regarding a social unit as a small society, we can identify essential topics of discourse and examine them in light of the goals of participating individuals and the context of the social unit which forms the context for discourse. It enables us to describe the nature of the complicity; who is seeking what with what record of effectiveness. It also makes it possible to make recommendations about possible modification of both content and form of social messages exchanged.

Rhetoric is an appropriate basis for understanding the exchange of social discourse because rhetoric is a situationally locked performance art. The person skilled at rhetoric is able to communicate well in a variety of situations. Rhetoric deals with the components of discourse in a rational way and does not require blind faith in forces, the effect of which cannot be observed.

The Canons as a Basis for Social Discourse

The classical "Canons of Rhetoric" (DeVito, 1986, p. 50) specify the components of the communication act: inventing and arranging ideas, choosing and delivering clusters of words, and maintaining in memory a storehouse of ideas and repertoire of behaviors. Content of communication (invention) is a matter of personal choice. It depends on the speaker's analysis of what can be obtained in a situation. The process of composition (disposition, style) guides the preparation of ideas so they are intelligible and interesting to others. Delivery refers to the actual utterance. The process is governed by memory.

This breakdown is not as facile as it looks. The Canons have stood the test of time. They represent a legitimate taxonomy of processes. Instructors can situate their pedagogical strategies in each of the Canons. In general, speech instruction does not propose to alter what a speaker thinks. Rather, it concentrates on effective presentation of ideas. Rhetoric is essentially neutral. The skills requisite to effective rhetoric are available to anyone. The same is true of rhetorical instruction. It focuses on external behavior, the act of speaking, not on the value of the ideas expressed. This does not mean that ideas are not valuable and influential, merely that it is not the province of the speech teacher to train students in what or how to think.

In any given case, speech is constrained by the speaker's physiological abilities, memory, vocabulary, and social situation (among other things). The Canons provide categories to deal with each of the components of the speaking process. We need the categories for diagnostic purposes, that is, if we are to modify social performance, we must be able to identify specific patterns of performance that must be changed. We must be able to provide models of behavior as goals for change. In each case, the Canons provide a convenient way to locate modifiable error in discourse.

The Canons are a fiction. They provide a convenient way of classifying the processes involved in the composition and delivery of discourse. They are based on a premise that discourse is neither mindless nor reflexive. For our part, we presume that discourse must be consciously controlled. It does not "just happen," it is made to happen by the "will" of the speaker (whatever that means).

Will is another artificial concept. For our purposes, it refers to choices made by a speaker in a social situation. For example, a person finds himself in a social situation, decides that it can be modified to his advantage by discourse, and therefore, speaks. The underlying intent, that is, the decision about what is to be accomplished as well as the connection between it and discourse can be a function of both conscious and unconscious mind. The actual manufacture of the discourse and its utterance cannot be anything other than conscious.

We do not propose in this treatise to investigate the concept of "thought." We do propose to examine one result of thought, the act of social discourse. For this purpose, the simplistic formulations of the ancients of discourse into invention, disposition, style, delivery, and memory are a perfectly suitable starting point for an analysis. Whatever liberties we take with the classical concepts are a function of the way we propose to use them, that is, as categorical divisions of types of acts, nothing more.

Invention of Social Discourse

Self-motivation. Social discourse is motivated by a feeling of personal need. A person decides that she can achieve some objective by talking with other people. The process is thoughtful and controlled although its purpose, a function of thinking, may be generated in a number of wondrous and mystical ways. Once our speaker picks her goal and decides it can be accomplished in a particular social situation, there is a formal mental process that governs the selection of sayables, their arrangement, phrasing, and utterance.

The immediate goal may be part of a larger complex of goals, or it may be confined just to the situation. If the speaker wants to be "popular," in the given case she can direct discourse to win signs of approval from the people present. For example, if she finds one individual appealing and wants further contact, she may offer various suggestions about the time, place, and activities of another meeting. Her success would be evaluated externally by whether or not her audience (or target) agrees. The speaker's ideas about what would confirm accomplishment come from experience, real and vicarious, and learning.

Motivation of others. To the extent that the speaker is operating consciously, he understands that he must offer something to the listener in exchange for the desired response. This is the basis for the appeals included in the actual discourse. The speaker must, of course, believe that all this is possible. Speakers who do not have confidence in the outcome often refrain from attempting to seek to accomplish their goals.

The concept of invention is based on the assumption that conscious thought precedes speech. Some popular wisdom has it that speech is automatic and that some people have talent and do well at it while others do not. We have already noted how inept speakers believe that prepared discourse is manipulative.

The concept of rhetorical invention presupposes composition. That is, the speaker thinks through the process and makes a careful selection of ideas to be presented to specific listeners in order to achieve a desired and desirable outcome. This precedes the formal process of composition. The rhetorical view is that any idea can be adapted for effective presentation. By attending to relevant aspects of social situations, speakers can learn to adjust both their ideas and their manner of presentation.

Gaining attention. Implicit in the invention process is the requirement that the speaker seek, gain, and hold attention. Attention is crucial to rhetorical success; social discourse is not like a classroom performance, that is, it cannot be quality graded with a letter. Regardless of the artistic quality of the speaker's words, she is ineffectual unless and until she gains attention. In formal settings like lectures or public speeches some attention can be presumed. The audience would not be there without some motivation. But even with a committed audience, the speaker is obliged to solicit attention and sustain it with interesting talk. In social situations, nothing can be presumed. It is the speaker's job to gain attention from the desired audience and hold it. Some speakers gain instant attention because of their identity and reputation.[2] Most ordinary

2. The question of ethos is very complicated. The boss gets attention as does the dictator and the man with the gun. Fathers and mothers sometimes do. Attractive people do. It is questionable whether ethos qualifies as an artistic proof. The concept of credibility is more useful in considering artistic rhetoric, because there are things ordinary people can be taught to do to make themselves appear credible.

mortals, however, must solicit attention from their listeners and give something valuable to sustain it.

Exerting social influence. Persons are socially effective when they get what they want from others—without unpleasant concomitants. It is a simple cost-benefit process. Each social act presumes a response. If the response is satisfying *and* nothing unfortunate happens in addition, it is an effective act.

Unfortunately, although the process is simple, it is not easy. We have, thus far, been unable to discover a one-to-one correspondence between speech act and response. Thus, social activity is polysynchronous. People are seeking social goals simultaneously, which means they are very likely to be engaged either in social bargaining or social combat.

Social effectiveness can be attained through the use of both artistic and inartistic proofs (Thonssen & Baird, 1948, pp. 59ff.). An audience or listener can be motivated inartistically through extortions, blackmail, bribes, and pitiable behavior. Threats of force, appeals to pity, flattery, and pleading are borderline devices albeit often very effective. Arguments on behalf of a point of view and tenders to legitimate bargains are artistic. They are the stuff of classical rhetoric.

The method of influence a person chooses seems related to his or her social position. Those in subservient positions tend to use inartistic persuasions like cash payments, bribes, wheedling, pleading, whining, cringing, or martyrdom to demonstrate their submission to the dominant partner. Their artistic appeals are generally promises of what they can do for the person with power. Somewhat more sophisticated wimps use sycophancy and related flatteries.

When there is relative parity in social clout and reasonable norms prevailing, people bargain with each other. Bullies and others with disparate power often find it convenient to resort to inartistic means. It is easier to threaten to fire an employee than it is to convince him; simpler to whip a child into submission than to reason with him; and thus, when there is no parity in strength, the divine right of kings accrues to the powerful.

In relationships power is always on the side of the person to whom the relationship is least valuable. Threats of leaving usually motivate servility, cringing, and service above and beyond. In the final analysis exerting power inartistically is very profitable. It would be heartening to declare that bullies always "get theirs" and that blackmailers get caught, but this is rarely the case. Most of us find it very hard to counter inartistic persuasions.

Even the ordinary oral discourse of mundane social relationships contains the potential for inartistic rhetoric. Each person seeks from the other all he or she can get at the lowest possible cost. The issues of social relationship are not easily resolved. Often intimidation, bribery, and blackmail are the most effective methods for a person to get his own way. The person who cannot fight back or argue his or her own case effectively generally pays a higher price for whatever the other person is willing to give.

It would also be romantic and heartwarming to declare that there is, for sure, a mode of discourse calculated to produce perfect relationships. Unfortunately, there is no evidence of this either. In fact, we might be in a "Margaret Mead mode," where we have deluded ourselves sufficiently about the romance of interpersonal relations that we have rendered ourselves incapable of studying the reality.

It is an important premise of this work that inartistic proofs are effective methods of persuasion and legitimate insofar as they help the speaker attain his or her goals without undesirable concomitants. Speech teachers and rhetoricians do not customarily train students in the use of inartistic proofs, however. We assume that the natural processes of acculturation provide sufficient opportunities to develop skill at using them. What happens, of course, is that some people become very skillful at inartistic persuasions, while others do not learn them at all, thus placing themselves at a social disadvantage.

Learning about inartistic persuasions is an important component of instruction in the Penn State Reticence Program. While there are some serious ethical issues raised by the question of whether or not to teach students to be able to intimidate or cajole, it is certainly important for them to know about the possibilities.

The distinction Aristotle makes between artistic and inartistic proofs is that artistic proofs must be composed by the speaker, while inartistic proofs exist in and of themselves. They must be applied rather than invented. It is a matter of having the ability to punch out an enemy and merely deciding whether or not it would be appropriate and effective in the given case; this, as opposed to finding some persuasive verbal argument to motivate compliance from a hostile adversary.

In any case, however, the speaker must choose what form of proof to use. When this is consciously done, it is based on two criteria: (1) Which would be most effective? (2) Which would have the least deleterious side effects? Usually missing is a third criterion, Am I able to do what I set out to do? Many a good plan is ruined by inept execution.

Equitable social partners employ artistic discourse to negotiate a fair distribution of influence and authority. Socialization norms in democratic societies are based on negotiation and bargaining for equity under the assumption that direct confrontation and combat would be too costly for all parties involved. Even the most authoritarian corporate structures maintain some leeway for bargaining, and people who possess skills the corporation values can exchange their services for leeway and perks.

But democracies often sustain themselves with myths about defending the rights of the weak. In fact, the greater part of our social business is done by skillful people through artistic means, and those who lack the ability to participate are handicapped. The bottom line is that truly powerful people have no qualms about employing inartistic methods to get their own way.

People may talk about their rights, but they are rarely defended by others, unless of course a fee is involved. In fact, it is a principle inherent in the rhetorical view that each person is responsible for defending his or her own rights.[3] The only alternative for those who cannot influence others is capitulation or resort to inartistic methods. Thus, it appears that inept speakers are desirable citizens of totalitarian states, servile employees, and docile helpmates.

The invention process. The goal of the invention process is to make discourse influential. Talk must be directed at both the rationality and emotions of listeners. Combs and Snygg (1959, p. 17) said: "However capricious, irrelevant, and irrational his behavior may appear to an

3. The legend of Tisias and Corax sets the tone for the rhetorical canons. It is a simple story emphasizing the idea that each "man [sic]" is responsible for his own defense. Nowhere is this more evident than in social interaction, where there is no formal legal system to defend the rights of the weak. According to the legend, Tisias (or was it Corax?) took speech lessons from Corax (or was it Tisias?). Corax guaranteed that Tisias would be a successful speaker, or there would be no fee. After the lessons, Tisias refused to pay. Corax took him to court alleging that either way he must be paid; if the court decided in his favor he would be paid by their decree, and if the court decided for Tisias, he must still be paid since that would prove Tisias was a successful speaker. Tisias countered by saying if the court decided in his favor, the decree would be that he would not have to pay. If the court decided for Corax, it would prove he was not a successful speaker. So there! From this parable we take the lesson that each person is responsible for his or her own defense—except, of course, in court, where he or she is responsible for hiring the best available mouthpiece for the given case.

outsider, from his point of view *at that instant* his behavior is purposeful, relevant, and pertinent to the situation *as he understands it*. How it appears to others has no bearing upon the causes of his behavior" (italics mine).

Each person has stored in his or her mind memories of experience, evaluations, criteria, and caveats from which to draw information to apply to the given case. Some memories are easy to retrieve and some are tucked away in obscure places. Some are private, unique to the person; some are common social knowledge, clichés, and stereotypes.

To be effective, a speaker must accurately estimate what the listener is thinking of and compose discourse accordingly. This is not easy, nor is it probable that any person will be able to do it effectively. That accounts for the give and take of social conversation, a process in which two or more people seek some kind of compatibility and understanding with one another.

The classical conception of rhetoric identified three main sources of persuasion from which to draw during the invention process. *Ethos* referred to personality authority and reputation. The persuader could rely on being "boss" or "father" or "the man with the gun." He could manipulate what people said about him so that he was revered or feared. It is arguable how ethical this kind of proof really is. Charismatics, warlords, and bullies depend on ethos as their main source of persuasion. It is, of course, possible for a person to develop ethos by speaking skillfully. Even so, it becomes a quality, not an action, and therefore remains inartistic.

Logos refers to logical and rational discourse. It is the language of bargaining, and it works well only when there is relative parity between the parties and equity in the social system. It is often easier to deploy ethical proofs (do this because I am the boss, father, priest, or bigger than you) than try to find reasonable arguments. It may be that Mencken was right when he counseled that no one ever lost a dime betting on the stupidity of the people. Rational discourse requires careful composition by the speaker and careful attention by the listener. When a genuine commitment to exchange this kind of talk does not exist, it often falls on deaf ears—and in any event, attention must be obtained before rational discourse begins.

Pathos is somewhat more potent because it plays on the sentimentality inherent in all of us. Pathetic proofs are the substance of wishful thinking and primal fear. In a sense, they could be construed as inartistic because they are generally hyperbolic. Pathos calls for expression. It is generally conveyed by paralinguistic cues, facial expressions, body movements, tears, vocal tone, and so on. The emotional tone of discourse is synthesized into the words. It is a job of acting and can, of course, be stylized to fit the situation.

The speaker synthesizes his persona and expression with the delivery of his statements. Presumably, he is in control of what he does, but in fact, social discourse is often a matter of trial and error. A public speaker can take time to think through each idea and adapt it appropriately. When to threaten, when to beg, when to offer quid pro quo, depends on perception of the situation for which the public speaker can carefully prepare. The social speaker, on the other hand, must be responsive. It is like a Markov Chain; each remark is contingent on the preceding remark. The give and take of conversation allows two or more people to seek social goals simultaneously and cooperatively. It also gives them the opportunity to fight if they choose to do so. The response to each bit of talk is factored into subsequent statements until the contact terminates or some relationship is formed. We can regard social discourse as negotiation for some common basis of understanding that confers a common meaning on actions jointly taken.

The process seeks to reconcile differences in understanding. Because idiosyncratic meanings can be so easily misunderstood, it usually takes a good deal of time to negotiate meanings. One major theory of language development offered by DeLaguna (1963) argued that humans developed the ability to speak because they needed a way to organize themselves against predators, the elements, and social threats. Chomsky (1965, 1975) argues that it arises from physiology. The Bible regards it as a gift from God that can be taken away as a punishment, as it was at the Tower of Babel. Whatever the source, social speech is the method by which humans organize in order to generate collective efforts on their own behalf. The distinction between artistic and inartistic discourse appears bogus in this light. Humans do what they have to do in order to get what they have to get. And hardly anyone gets it all![4]

Disposition of Social Discourse

Tactical processing. Living a life is a strategic process. It is implemented by tactics. Invention is the process of selecting tactics; disposition is the process of putting them in order. Traditionally, we think of

---

4. Facetious as it may sound, the Peter Principle seems to prevail in social discourse. It is not a question of the rich getting richer. It appears that each person develops social problems on his or her level.

discourse as a sequence of ideas. For our purposes, "tactics" is an appropriate word to describe our verbal and physical "moves" on the social chessboard. When people relate to each other socially, they sometimes talk, sometimes act. Together, these form the tactics selected to implement a strategic plan.

When a person speaks or writes formally, the ideas come out insequence. Whether the sequence is intelligible to a listener or reader is moot. There is some kind of order in the arrangement of the symbols of discourse.

Communicative tactics are linear. It is not possible for a person to say two words simultaneously, but acts can be accompanied by gestures, facial expressions, and physical movements. Composition of discourse consists of selecting tactics and putting them in order. Performance is the actual utterances and/or actions.

The goal of the disposition process. Disposition is the process of tactical planning humans do to make the results of their thinking coherent to, and effective with, others. Listeners will only respond to what they understand in the terms they understand it. The monosyllables and random-appearing vocalizations that characterize inept speech are not persuasive because they convey no information to the listener. Even a threat badly delivered is unimpressive.[5]

In evaluating the effectiveness of discourse, intent is the measure of success. It is ephemeral to measure success in terms of personal gratification. It is useful, on the other hand, to measure it in terms of listener response. If the listener does what the speaker expects, then the discourse is effective. If not, there is an error. It is our argument that *disposition is the crucial element in the composition process where error is most likely to be made and easiest to identify.* For example, a speaker's intent may be entirely virtuous and the proposal mutually advantageous, but unless the listener understands what the speaker wants, there is no possibility of accomplishment. Disposition is the process by which ideas are made intelligible. Thus, invented ideas must be processed before they are put into words. Disposition is the interface between idea and delivery. It organizes the ideas and controls the phrasing.

5. In the movie *Take the Money and Run*, Woody Allen, as an inept bank robber, had a good deal of difficulty with a bank teller because his note read, "I have a gub." The ensuing discussion of what a "gub" was effectively foiled the robbery. In essence, a rhetorical view obligates the speaker or writer to make sense. While there is a small body of advice to listeners and an overwhelming amount of advice to readers, the actual onus lies on the person seeking to achieve a social goal through communication.

The process of disposition consists of selecting potentially effective ideas and arranging them into a sequence that appears sensible to the listener. The ideas must also be supported with materials that would make them convincing and interesting. In the following chapter we will introduce a theory of disposition based on the premise that there are a limited number of arrangement patterns from which a speaker can choose. Analysis of the disposition of tactics represents a linchpin of criticism that itself is the process fundamental to pedagogy.

The requirement to organize discourse is not an imposition; it is a social imperative. Unorganized speech can influence accidentally, but it is more likely confuse or bore. The clichés born of sensitivity training that imply listeners are responsible for finding out what speakers mean are unrealistic and impossible of accomplishment. To be effective, discourse cannot be exclusively for the convenience of the speaker. It must be directed against particular abilities and commitments of listeners.

Coherence, however, is not the only criterion of successful speaking. People are not attracted to oral discourse only because they can understand it. It must be appealing. They must have confidence in the speaker and believe that they can get something of value by listening to him. Discourse is a promise. The speaker makes an offer and the listener wants to find out if anything good will happen, if he accepts it. The listener cannot respond to what he or she cannot understand. On the other hand, the listener must believe in the speaker and what he says.

There is nothing to prevent speakers from defrauding their listeners with false promises or manipulate them with counterfeit appeals. The ancient rhetoricians wrote of the "good man [sic] who speaks well." The idea of good is hard to define. Ethical discourse, it would seem, consists of talk that interests the listener and also contains useful and relevant sentiments and information. Ethics are important in context, but they are not appropriate standards for competent rhetoric. In the final crunch, discourse that appeals to a listener and motivates him or her to respond in ways the speaker desires can be considered effective.

Presentational Issues in the Canons

Style. Style refers to the process of coding ideas into language. It continues the process of sequencing ideas down to the sentence or word level. Style refers to the artistry of formal composition, for example word choice and arrangement.

The classical philosophers studied formal oratory and consequently were very concerned about word choice. For centuries since, rhetoric has been associated with literary style. In fact, in universities, rhetoric has become the province of teachers of written composition.

Our main concern is with social discourse, which is hardly literary. Thus, we are concerned only with the simplest message requirements. Once ideas have been put into coherent order, they must be organized into statements. Actually, the composition of paragraphs and sentences follows essentially the same process of structural formatting that controls the tactical deployment of the entire statement. The chief requirements are (1) that the words used by the speaker exist in the vocabularies of the listeners with meanings similar to those in the vocabulary of the speaker; (2) that words refer to images with which listeners are familiar and evoke emotions compatible with those of the speaker; (3) that words be arranged according to some common understanding of grammar. Beyond that, we are not concerned with the literary aspects of composition. Social conversation is largely made up of words that are ordinary and mundane.

Delivery. In written prose, the words must motivate interest by themselves. There is no human to claim attention. In oral discourse speakers can sustain interest by managing both what they say and how they say it. Speakers can modify fluency, pronunciation, loudness, pitch, emphasis, and inflection in order to gain attention. Speakers can also use eye contact, gestures, facial expression, and body movements to attract listeners and sustain their attention.

The speaker can build his credibility (or ethos) by delivering discourse in an appealing way. In fact, when we "size people up," what we are really doing is listening to what they say and watching the way they say it. Speakers who are generally well known use their delivery to declare their identity (like the president of the United States or a skillful comic). Ordinary speakers must establish their skill and competency by speaking well. A speaker who looks good and sounds good is generally regarded as good. In fact, we will tend to accept falsehoods fatuously if they are well spoken, and reject accurate statements if they are mumbled. In that sense, social performance is a job of acting. You simply cannot detect whether a person is telling the truth merely by evaluating delivery.

Since we make many important social decisions at first meeting, it is hard to overestimate the importance of delivery in the rhetorical process. People are often stigmatized with a label representing a defective personality because they perform discourse poorly. It may have nothing whatever to do with their goals, their moral character, or their intentions toward their listeners.

Actually, there are so few good speakers we rarely have to bother considering the impact of effective discourse. Most social conversation is poorly delivered and most people appear awkward and inept much of the time. Although the television medium sets high standards for fluency, articulation, and vocal variety in anchorpersons, much dramatic performance is done in vernacular and presents a perfectly ordinary model for emulation.

For millennia, rulers and priests were trained in the art of delivering discourse well. They and their advisers knew that the sound of the human voice has the power to alienate or attract. Even today, special attention is given to delivery in political campaigns. Despite the obvious need for training, however, most school programs purporting to teach oral discourse concentrate on composition and ignore delivery. They offer training for debaters and actors and remedial training for speech defectives, but they ignore the needs of students for training in the ordinary discourse required in the classroom. As a result there are a great many people who simply cannot speak well. Whatever their composition skills, their rhetoric is ineffective because they cannot get and sustain attention with their delivery.

The fact that there is little training offered in delivery of ordinary discourse does not detract from its importance. The best ideas carefully composed are ineffective when they are not delivered well. There are a few people whose position or reputation gives them special status to whom people will listen regardless of how inept their delivery is (for example, the boss). But major figures like former Secretary of State George Schultz appear unremarkable because their delivery is so dull. Most of us must face the prospect that what people think of us is largely determined by our speech delivery and that we are probably not effective enough to win very many friends with it.

Memory

Memory is the fifth Canon. We will deal with it in depth in a later chapter. We regard the ability to store information accurately and retrieve it when necessary an essential element of skillful rhetoric. When we speak, we choose our ideas from what we have in memory. We depend on memory of experience for heuristics of organization and adaptation. Our memory of success or failure guides our choice of when or whether to speak. Thus, accurate and detailed memory is an essential component of competence at discourse.

But the process itself lies beyond the present comprehension even of the most mature scientists. Artificial intelligence provides a model with which we can study memory and how it operates, but it is not at all clear that there is a real analogy between machine and human intelligence. We simply do not know enough about how human memory works to simulate it perfectly on a computer.

If we take a pure behaviorist posture toward discourse, however, we must concede that there is a linear connection between stimuli and the choice of the words we use in social discourse. Though we do not understand it completely, we know enough to be able to modify the way people compose and utter discourse. In fact, the attempt to apply a pure behaviorist formulation would confront us with the paradox of infinite regress because we would have to explain the cause of attempting to find the cause. But even without concrete scientific evidence of behavioral links, we must believe we have at least some choice in what we store in memory and what and how we retrieve.

By using artificial intelligence as a model for our pedagogical understanding, we can at least isolate the main influences on composition of discourse and discover what is teachable. We look now at the orderly aspects of human discourse, such as the social influences that motivate people to speak, their statements of goals, and the way they put ideas in order and speak them.

Using a metaphor of calculus, we will argue that irregularities can be understood by continuous and sequential factoring of regularities. We will eventually have an unexplained residual. To the teacher, this is irrelevant. Our task is to discover how to modify discourse in order to make it more effective, and we can do this with the knowledge we have presently at hand.

The quality of "know-nothingism" in all of this is warranted by the fact that we must devise technology only with what we know. Wishful thinking, mysticism, and reliance on past norms have no demonstrated efficacy. Our premise is that we can work with the orderly processes of spoken rhetoric. We can diagnose ineptitude by identifying errors in composition and delivery. These two of the five Canons are the most obvious, easiest to explain, and amenable to the kind of tinkering requisite to the construction of an effective pedagogy of social discourse.

RHETORIC AS ORDERLY PROCESS

The Requisite of Formality

If we took a pure behaviorist posture toward discourse, we would have to concede that humans have no choice in what they do. If we opt for this point of view, we are caught in the infinite regress of accounting for all behavior, including our own in terms of internal and external environmental causation. If on the other hand, we choose to explain the nature of discourse with the concept "choice," we would find ourselves trapped in an infinite homuncular regress where we must account for the choices made by each source of choice. For the moment, we will accept Gazzinaga's (1985) explanation of a modular brain that justifies choice by pointing to the areas of the brain where choices are obviously made. We know there is a biological process and we know people make choices. Our instructional plan starts with the choice and does not include the process of choice making; that is, we leave it to the individual to decide whether to talk and what to seek with talk. Our instruction deals only with the preparation and utterance of talk.

We start with the assumption that discourse is a formal process. The physical acts required for thoughtful speech are so complicated that they require conscious mediation to coordinate brain, lungs, larynx, lips, tongue, and the resonators to produce intelligible speech sounds. Consider what happens when a person receives a communication from another and replies to it. Sally talks. Bob hears, interprets, and decides whether and what to reply. If Bob decides to reply, he composes and delivers discourse that Sally hears and responds to in a fashion similar to Bob. Each monitors his or her behavior and that of the other. They hypothesize about the effect their words will have on the other and adjust their remarks accordingly through a kind of calculus of discourse designed to achieve the hypothesized effect.

Limitations on the teaching process. We use discourse to accomplish the human goals of preservation of the species, security, stimulation, territory, and self-identification (Wilson, 1978). Most people have neither the skill nor the moral deficiency required to take complete control of others. Therefore, they must exchange. The idea is to offer something for something. "Oblige me and help with something in my life and I will do the same for you."

This process is built into the basic structures of society through constitutions and legal systems that enable us to make requests and resolve the disputes that arise from conflicting requests. On the job the rules are quite explicit. A person has a list of duties to perform. Someone is designated to supervise and evaluate the work. When duties require collaboration, someone must coordinate. When things do not come off well, those responsible are fired.

Our private lives also require collaboration. Although friendships and families are not normally run by explicit rules, successful ones have logical structures. In general, we are required to communicate to arrange collaborations for the good of the order through which we attain our personal goals as well.

The process is simple but not easy. One person talks, another responds; this is multiplied by the permutations of all the people involved and amplified by the intensity each feels about the matter at hand. The process is simple in that it is rulebound but difficult to understand because of all the possibilities. Participants are often too involved in their own motives to be aware of what is going on; observers are usually not party to the subtle details.

In order to participate effectively, individuals must have sufficient experience from which to extract choices about what to say, to whom, and for what purpose. In addition, communicators must have a mental database of words and phrases that can be connected and spoken in order to implement those decisions. Everything in the process must be applied to the given case. It is concentration on the given case that makes rhetoric so appropriate for examining human social discourse. It is, after all, the art of finding *in the given case ALL* the available means of persuasion.

"All" is a slippery word. The best most of us can do is remember some generalizations and personal experiences. When we want to get a message to another person, we find a category into which the person fits and apply a generalization that fits our listener. In a few cases, we are aware of some specifics about the person and we can use them. But they are also generalizations (about the person not stereotypes). Then we think about what we want, what the other person might want, what the rules are about, what we have to say and can and cannot say. We remember some experiences we had in situations we think were similar, and we estimate how well we did in each of those cases. If we control what we get from our information systems sufficiently to organize our ideas and say the words in an interesting fashion, *and* if the other person is listening, we may manage to accomplish some part of our communication goal. But all of this goes on very rapidly. And we always make mistakes.

Furthermore, any communication encounter is potentially endless. It consists of message and reply, message and reply until the parties are satisfied or break off contact. It is a kind of calculus of social connection. Since no encounter is perfect, each imperfection provides an exigence for a subsequent encounter.

What this adds up to is too much for any teacher to do. If we consider that discourse starts in the mind and ends with the assessment of effect, the teacher who seeks to modify communication is required to be psychiatrist, critic, stage director, literary editor, and lexicographer, among other things. Our question is where to place the focus of instruction. In a sense of triage, the teacher of communication performance behavior must focus on what is most easily modifiable. We have identified these areas as composition and delivery. There are some cognitive issues we must also deal with.

Cognitive Issues

Dual perspective. Dual perspective refers to the ability we have to understand others in terms of our own experience. We do not know anyone else's pain, for example. Therefore, when someone tells us they are having pain we locate the meaning in our own experience. Is it "root canal" pain, "my mate left me" pain, or the angst of "what does it all mean?" We associate what the person says with our own memories and project on the other person the way we felt in circumstances we think were similar. But we cannot remember the pain itself; we can only remember how we reacted to it. Because our capacity to interpret is idiosyncratic, the chance of mutual understanding is very slim.

Dual perspective provides us with the ability to learn vicariously. We need not experience a situation directly to learn about it. Much formal education is offered as vicarious experience in the hope we will be able to apply it when we encounter similar situations in our lives. When we speak to others we use our experience, real and vicarious, to help us decide what to do and say. When we use it well, we are able to adapt to their propensities and needs in order to strike an effective social bargain.

Adaptation and audience analysis are easy to talk about but difficult to perform. Detailed information about the listener is helpful only if the speaker is able to use it in deciding on what to say. When we confine our information to demographic categories like age or gender we are likely to slip into bigoted or stereotypical thinking. In analyzing listeners, it is imperative to concentrate on specifics that can be addressed in discourse.

It is relatively simple to spot a listener's reactions to what we say, but it is difficult to figure out what they mean and adjust to them. Since there is no formal code of response behavior, effectiveness depends on our ability to use previous experience to facilitate adaptation of our words to the given situation. Our dual perspective helps us to adjust the content of our message on the spot so that it is appropriate to the particular listener or audience. In essence, we stereotype and attempt to associate each new experience with our stereotypes. If we tried to take each situation as completely unique, we would be schizophrenic.

Predicting reactions. Humans tend to be homeostatic. To improve the odds of living predictable lives, we have generated social routines to regularize our daily social relationships. In our private lives, we attempt to establish routines that reassure us about where we fit and that those we love share the feeling.

When we say "Hello, how are you?" to someone, we anticipate that their response will be one of several acceptable options for which we are prepared. When we do not get the response we expect, it interferes with our next move. Therefore, we tend to avoid people who do not respond in predictable ways. The interchanges subsumed under the heading "phatic communion" exist so that we can confirm that we live in familiar surroundings. Our personal relationships follow a Holiday Inn pattern; we do not welcome surprises. In fact, when events interfere with the normal routines of an intimate relationship, the whole relationship is both compromised and challenged.

Social discourse can be studied as an exchange of behaviors. We specify a behavior we want from another person and then speak in ways we believe will get it. When we do not get the result we anticipated, we are discouraged. When we call the shot correctly, we are encouraged. Thus, our skill at social discourse is partially a function of learning by a process of self-imposed operant conditioning. We actually decide what rewards and punishes us. If we are skillful enough, we can get partial success with each contact. The behaviorist model breaks down when we consider that each person can decide on the nature of the reward. The human decision process refutes the direct linear causation essential to a behaviorist theory. But it makes the process rhetorical, which, as we have noted, has its own regularities. We could "rhetoricalize" Skinner's formulation by saying "operant conditioning is the art of finding in any given case the most effective reinforcer." This, then, permits the regularity of the behaviorist explanation while allowing for the idiosyncrasy of individual response.

Motivation. We humans cherish romantic notions like "love at first sight," "vibes," or "chemistry," but if we seek to change behavior, we must assume that it is relatively predictable. Predictability in socialization depends on whether the speaker understands the social tactics the listener is using. Presumably, the listener is giving information about what he or she wants to the speaker, who, in turn, can make a request and an offer to exchange. Appropriate decisions about what might motivate others depends on understanding human motivation in general.

The most obvious source of information about how people behave is stereotypes about categories of people. "Audience analysis" is commonly taught to beginning public speakers, based on the notion that there are truisms about "women," "college students," "senior citizens," and other categories. Aristotle offered similar advice in *The Rhetoric*. The problem with dealing in stereotypes is that they are very much like astrological predictions. They are premised on the notion that all people respond to one or more of the common appeals; getting rich, becoming famous, finding love, gaining influence, being safe and healthy, and feeling good about themselves. The idea is to find precisely what it is that motivates the listener in the given case. The speaker who discovers what a relevant listener really wants can appeal to that motive. That is what Aristotle meant when he said, "The fool tells me his reasons, the wise man persuades me with my own."

The catch is that we never know exactly how someone will react to us. Our expectations from others are actually hypotheses about the effect our behavior will have on others. These hypotheses must be tested in action. If we make an error, we must recognize it, acknowledge it, take it into account, and adjust to it. Most often, we do not analyze our social failure—we merely muddle on.

In the initial stages of social contact, success often depends on luck. We happen to say something that addresses the other person's needs, and they do the same for us. Most of the people we meet make little or no impression on us, nor we on them. After a while, we can predict some of the responses of the people with whom we have regular contact, sometimes with uncanny accuracy. Our effectiveness at doing this depends on memory. Normally, we do not concentrate on social events and often our memory provides us with inexact information.

In the final analysis social discourse is more than simple operant conditioning. The capacity to interpret and ascribe motives to others complicates the process far beyond simple stimulus response. We can never really know what the other person is doing inside his or her mind. All we have to interpret is what we can see and hear. Jules Masserman's (1966) experiments with neurotic cats is a case in point. When Masserman conditioned cats to avoid eating by giving them electric shocks, there was a sizable minority that not only resisted conditioning but learned to enjoy pain. There was no way of knowing in advance which cats would interpret the shock as a signal to avoid food and which would interpret it as pleasurable because it was associated with food. So it is that humans respond variously to similar stimuli.

Use of proofs. Proofs are promises. Speakers offer information, opinion, or recommendations for action in the hope that listeners will exchange with them by complying with their requests. An important aspect of proof is what the listener thinks of the speaker. "Do it, believe it, know it, because I say so" can be very influential if the listener thinks the speaker is a good, wise, caring, or impressive person, or is fluent and interesting, or has the power to reward or punish.

Personal entitlements are also persuasive. When a speaker claims to be entitled to a response, the listener will comply provided he or she believes the rules by which the speaker makes the claim. Entitlements work because people believe they must provide what others are entitled to in order to get what they are entitled to.

It is not easy to think up reasons for people to learn, believe, or do things the way you want. Most prefer to learn, believe, and do as they want. The old east Tennessee proverb, "everyone wants local option and unlimited income," applies to everyone. Simple economics says that most people will get others to do as much as possible for them and give as little as possible in return. This is a dim but necessary view of human nature. When people understand it, they sometimes are willing to negotiate and bargain for mutual benefit. But mostly, they simply deplore it and go on demanding their own way.

Most people do not seem consciously aware they are negotiating. The "sensitivity" movement of the late sixties showed that a great many people preferred to believe that relationships were formed and sustained by some mysterious personal force and that people were obliged to be interested in their innermost thoughts and feelings. The work of G. C. Homans (1975) and Kenneth Burke (1969a, 1969b) among others, contradict this belief. Human dialogue is essentially Machiavellian. We use words to manipulate others. Social discourse is responsive and bisynchronous.

Power. The social situation is complicated by the resources and power people possess. In most cases, social discourse represents a juxtaposition of people with more and less power. The powerful person has rewards and punishments to offer the weaker person. The weaker person, on the other hand, must find something to offer the powerful person in exchange for granting the request. It could be ingratiation, flattery, affection, obsequious cringing, information, loyalty, or whatever. Some powerful people find it appealing to have others cringe before them and beg. They are often willing to provide excessive payoffs for it. Others enjoy meting out punishment or manipulating resources. This cynical and combative model enables us to regard social discourse as both tactical and strategic. Parents, politicians, strawbosses, and generals are intimidating. Children, foot soldiers, employees, and ordinary citizens generally are not. The beneficence of the powerful can be sought through supplication, which is inartistic, or compliance, which is prudent, or through rhetoric designed to persuade them that acting in a particular way would be to their advantage. Powerful people often need only to promise to gain compliance from their subordinates, who, for their part, must rely on all forms of artistic and inartistic proofs. However, powerful people must sustain support, for they depend on their followers for survival. Followers and leaders have something to exchange.

It is important to understand the nature of rhetorical power. The kind that comes at the barrel of a gun, from vast sums of money, or from tears is inartistic. But it still requires planning and takes effort to execute. The gunman has to know whom to threaten. It is clearly counterproductive to face down someone with a faster draw. The wheedler and whiner has to know who is annoyed by clawing a blackboard. Inartistic rhetoric is not actually inartistic. And, incidentally, the person with the gun has to be skillful enough to take off the safety catch before firing.

But the thing about inartistic rhetoric is that it requires no quid pro quo. The demand is made and the threat, whine, or oath is offered. If done well, compliance is virtually automatic; if done badly, retribution. The nagging problem is that inartistic persuasion is not reliable. It requires constant vigilance to be effective at it. For example, compliance obtained by whining is tenuous. When the complying party tires of feeling guilty, he or she can cut the cord and end the relationship. Compliance obtained by extortion generates rebellion or the kind of compliance characteristic of Good Soldier Schweik. Furthermore, the cost of sustaining dominance is exorbitant. Sometimes dominants love their power so much they alter their life-style to maintain the allegiance of their followers. Power attained by bribery is costly. Payments must continually be made. At the first default, power ends.

Those who use an artistic rhetoric of power seek affirmation that they are entitled. Appointed or elected officials can be confirmed by assurance that they have earned or deserve their position. This assurance is usually delivered by skillful performance of tasks and expressions of gratitude and flattery by those over whom power is exerted. Politicians can be cajoled by the promise of a vote. Those who have the power to reward can be appealed to by performance of rewardable acts; those who can punish can be placated by avoiding transgressions. In fact, it is not the actions that hold the appeal; it is the talk about the actions that is convincing. The relationship between leader and followers can be appropriately balanced through the use of artistic rhetoric.

Emotion is also a source of power. People who can make the situation more pleasant by manipulation of discourse are welcome, sometimes even when they cannot perform their tasks very well. Social popularity may appear frivolous, but it is important to social survival. Unbroken grimness can generate tension so great that people cannot function well. People who are socially skillful command both respect and attention. While they may not automatically move into positions of power and authority, they are properly postured to be effective in their efforts to influence others.

It not customary for people to acknowledge their awareness of the volitional aspects of rhetoric. Most seem to want to deny the political nature of their social behavior. They express the idealistic belief that people are spontaneous altruists. Oscar Wilde commented that if you find yourself in a world where the virtuous are rewarded and the evil are punished, you are living in a novel. Many people seem to live their lives as if they were characters in a novel, their behavior controlled by some omnipotent author who could make things come out right. They appeal to Whomever is in control for resolution of their problems. They want to share their emotions, for they believe them to be effective persuasions. They do not want to believe that what they feel is premeditated and used as a strategy to gain compliance from others. There is something to be said for "empathy." When people exchange discourse to the point where they feel compatible with one another, they can anticipate and manage threatening and harmful events.

This basic "knowledge" represents *mutatis mutandis*, the cognitions of social rhetoric. The knowledge must be imparted, although its use by any particular person is unpredictable. The diagnosis of "faulty cognition" results in instruction in, but not necessarily in modification of, performance behavior. To conclude this chapter, we must look at the Canons once more, to examine the nature of the errors that can be made in each component.

Identification of Error

Some errors can be corrected easily. Some cannot. Some are amenable to the ministrations of a teacher. Some are not. Once again we face an intriguing problem of triage. Of all the possible errors a person can make in social discourse, which are most productive to treat? Using the Canons, we can isolate some possible errors.

Errors in invention. What if the speaker cannot figure out what can be accomplished in social situations? We can regard this as *exigent incompetence.* The notion of exigence is complicated. It requires considerable cognitive modification. Furthermore, it is questionable whether anyone knows what to do about a person who cannot identify legitimate communication goals. We can instruct people in how to set goals, but changing the way they choose them requires a considerable modification of life-style. At the moment, we can relegate exigential error to the cognitive pile. We can talk about it for the enrichment of our clientele and our own gratification (to display our grasp of theory).

What if the speaker cannot think up something that will make a difference? We can consider this *topical incompetence.* This actually is a problem for the whole educational system. One of the more fascinating discoveries made by Begnal (1983) was that reticent people were very dull. They lacked information; they were not well informed or well read. They literally had nothing to talk about. So many people suffer from this disability that it makes one wonder what the education system is in place for. But topical enrichment is hardly the province of the speech teacher. We can draw a map showing the location of the library and urge students to attempt to read books or watch television news broadcasts, but teaching substantive information about anything but human discourse is not within the province or capability of those whose mission it is to modify social discourse.

What if the speaker cannot select ideas that will appeal to listeners? We can identify this as *audience incompetence*. Understanding human beings is a matter of experience and acculturation. A little training in psychology doesn't hurt either. Speech teachers can augment all of this by providing training in elocution. We can teach people how to generate an expression of wonder on their listener's face by managing the language well. And this is about as far as we can go. We can refer students to the standard works on motive. We can urge them to read and understand Kenneth Burke, although it is not clear that understanding Burke makes one whit of difference in how well people appeal to the motives of others, let alone understand how others manipulate them through motivational appeals.

Errors in disposition. What if the speaker cannot arrange ideas so they make sense? Talk must be orderly to be intelligible. Save for a few specialists in stream of consciousness, disorderly discourse has little appeal. Associative talk tends to confuse social relationships. It is essentially egocentric and while the speaker may have a goal in mind, it is not a viable tactic. Once the decisions have been made about (1) goals for discourse, (2) target for discourse, and (3) what ideas to say, the process of composition is quite formal. As we will point out in the next chapter, there are only a few ways in which discourse can be put together. A kind of grammar applies to the body of discourse exactly as it applies to the paragraphs and sentences of which discourse is composed. When juxtaposition of ideas is unintelligible to a listener, it is called *structural incompetence*.

While there is little a teacher can do to fill a speaker's mind with ideas and words, there is a great deal that can be done to get whatever ideas and words that exist into a structure that makes sense and has appeal to a listener.

Errors in style. What if the speaker cannot think up ways to word ideas or lacks sufficient vocabulary to do so? We can refer to this as *grammatic incompetence* or *vocabulary incompetence*. Both are remediable. Grammatic incompetence is actually a problem in organization. Vocabulary can be built by subject matter training. Neither lies precisely within the province of the speech teacher.

Errors in delivery. What if the speaker cannot say words intelligibly and in an interesting fashion? We can refer to this as *presentational incompetence.* This, more than any other of the behaviors embedded in the Canons is amenable to modification. In fact, the discipline of speech communication was preoccupied for years with elocution. Much of the trend toward philosophy and social science now characteristic of the research in the discipline came as a reaction to overemphasis of training in delivery.

Our experience with the Reticence Program demonstrates that most students need training in delivery. A survey of five thousand students enrolled in a basis speech performance course (conducted in 1986 and repeated in 1987) demonstrated that the vast majority expect to be trained in presentation techniques including intonation, gesture, movements, vocal control, and related skills. Training in delivery is not the province of this book, but we refer our readers to the work of David Alan Stern of Hollywood, California (1982, 1983). Dr. Stern has produced a series of training tapes and related documentation and exercises in the following areas:

1. Vocal Relaxation
2. Breathing for Speech
3. Voice without Tension
4. Speech without Tension
5. Full Cavity Resonance
6. Special Resonance Problems
7. Pitch Variety and Intonation
8. Variety in Pitch and Stress: Articulatory Energy
9, 10. American Vowels and Diphthongs
11, 12. American Consonants and Clusters
13, 14. Applied Skills for Speech Making and Lecturing
15, 16. Applied Skills for Acting
17, 18. Applied Skills for Broadcasting
19, 20. Applied Skills for Voice and Diction Teachers

In addition, Stern has produced training systems in speaking American English without regional dialects, removal of foreign dialects, and elevated or classical American diction. There are a number of other systems for training voice and diction. As we develop a theory and technology for improvement of social discourse we advocate that it be associated with some form of delivery training system and supplemented with academic areas.

Memory problems. What if the speaker cannot receive, store, and retrieve information relevant to the rhetorical process (*memory incompe-*

tence)? We will discuss the role of memory in our chapter on artificial intelligence. Memory, of course, is the foundation for the data process requisite to the composition and delivery of social discourse. It is, however, a process that has, thus far, defied pedagogy.

What if the speaker cannot monitor his own behavior and that of his listeners *(feedback incompetence)?* Training in delivery often includes specific methods of observing audience behavior and modifying discourse accordingly. We will discuss the process of utilizing feedback in the final chapter of this book.

By specifying incompetence as errors in speaker behavior, we can focus on specific activities that can be modified and devise ways and means by which they can be modified. This represents the fundamental premise in this behaviorist approach to a pedagogy of social discourse. In the next chapter, we will deal specifically with *disposition* as we present a formal system for organizing ideas and tactics to make them intelligible and appealing to listeners.

6

What Is Teachable: The Pedagogy of Social Discourse

PEDAGOGICAL TRIAGE

*I*n this chapter we will apply triage to the pedagogy of oral discourse as we discover what communication behaviors are most teachable. We are restricting ourselves to performance modification. We will deal with the affective and cognitive dimensions *only* as necessary to support training behavior change. In essence, we are seeking a technology of performance modification.

Traditional pedagogical theory divides instruction into cognitive, affective, and psychomotor or behavioral. Quite clearly, any system of behavior modification requires supporting information, and of course, the "attitude" must be right for instruction to be successful. We assume some instruction in cognition and modification of affect is a requisite for teaching of any kind. Our main concern is with the difficult task of modifying communication behavior. Only two of the five canons provide behavioral substance that is directly teachable within the natural purview of the speech teacher.

Memory, for example, cannot be taught directly, although every academic discipline fusses about it. Effective use of memory is an important criterion for success in any academic enterprise. The speech student can be guided and advised about what to try to remember, but the act of remembering is the source of performance not part of the process. It is, thus, presumptuous and often counterproductive for the teacher of performance behavior to attempt to train memory.

It is reasonable, however, to advise students about what to look for in memory (and, for that matter, in the library) in order to support the ideas they wish to speak about. Furthermore, in order to adapt to audience response, speakers must refer to previous social experience. But this is part of training in delivery. The interaction between audience response and selection of reaction is part of the acting trade, easily adaptable to the training of the ordinary speaker.

Invention tempts the teacher. Invention, in essence, is thinking and for centuries it has been *ignis fatuous* for academics. Can students be taught to think? John Dewey (1935) apparently thought so. So did many others. For generations students were trained in Latin and geometry, which presumably taught them how to think. (They were probably also fed fish, which everyone knew was "brain food.") But it was like the weather; hardly anyone did anything about it.

In recent years rhetoricians have found euphemisms for thinking. Those tempted by psychology teach "intrapersonal" communication, while those involved in the computer metaphor use the phrase "data processing." Artificial intelligence has actually provided a coherent way to deal with the relationship between what is stored in memory, how it gets there, and how it is retrieved. Contemporary linguistics provides a great deal of information on how it is coded into symbols.

We take the position that the artificial intelligence metaphor is useful in performance pedagogy. We will use it as a basis for our theory of instruction as well as a fundamental tool in instructional technology. In this chapter we will look especially at the canon of disposition to show how a simple artificial intelligence system justifies the use of criticism of structure as a basis for training social communication behavior.

In essence, the common conception of communication is to "think" about discourse, discover things to say in memory, and then encode them into words. These three components cover invention, style, and memory. Style represents a link between the other two canons, disposition and delivery, because words must be linked in an appropriate order. In fact, this fundamental premise underlies the Chomskyan linguistics. Orderly procedure is the keystone of cognitive science. Memory operates in orderly fashion; thinking proceeds according to some ineluctable logic; ideas are turned into discourse by juxtaposing symbols according

to a common system. All three of these components have been fundamentals in the academic system for millennia.

The trivium of rhetoric, logic, and grammar referred to processes
of thought. When the ancients began to function as public-speaking
teachers, they found themselves burdened with the necessity of teaching
everything there was to teach in order to provide the fundamentals for
the real teachables in the speech process, connecting ideas and saying
them in sequence. Hence, Quintilian's *Institutes of Oratory* (1987)
became a manifesto for a whole university.

Basically, it is unreasonable for a discipline to presume itself to be a
"master discipline." Teachers of speech proclaimed themselves to be
rhetoricians and their mission to teach the "art of finding in the given
case all the available means of persuasion." Eventually, however, it
became clear that they had to be logicians and grammarians as well,
because the persuasive appeals had to be organized and phrased appropriately. Continually faced with paradoxes like this, those who purported
to teach oral discourse found themselves trapped either in the overspecia-
lization of the Sophists or the universality of the philosophers, neither
of which ever developed a pedagogical canon as effective as, say, teaching
reading by the phonics method or teaching cursive script through Spen-
cerian exercises. In a sense, in fact, some of instruction in oral discourse
was a good deal like Professor Harold Hill's "think system" in *The
Music Man*; if you understand the fundamentals of rhetorical theory,
performance will take care of itself. Unfortunately, there is no evidence
to support this claim.

On the other hand, we had elocutionists who believed sincerely that
the Spanish plain was rain-soaked despite meteorological data to the
contrary. But the failure of the pedagogical overdose referred to as the
"elocution movement" does not necessarily mean that it is evil to teach
delivery skills. In fact, the speech-teaching profession has abandoned
the traditional core of its pedagogy. Today, there is no discipline that
claims to teach people to say their lines extemporaneously. In fact, the
skills of social speech are abandoned at the theoretical level. Only rarely
is the connection made between the formalities of public speaking and
the apparent spontaneity of social discourse.

It would be good if we could teach everything, but the question of
what *can be* taught within the boundaries of a modest discipline specializ-
ing in performance behavior is very important. Above all, we know that

people's vocal delivery can be modified through simple exercises, practice, and coaching. The works of Stanislavski (1989), among others, make it clear that actors can be trained to deliver lines to fit a directorial scheme. The work of David Alan Stern (1988) demonstrates that the individual components of vocal delivery can each be managed. Voice, pitch, fluency, volume, intonation, and even dialect can be controlled by imitation and the simple kinesics applicable to the vocal parts. Those who train delivery must work within limits. Actors must possess "talent" whatever that is, and ordinary mortals must work within the biological limits imposed by the nature of the lungs and larynxes. But, by and large, should a person wish to modify his or her vocal delivery, it can be done.

If people have something to say, they can be trained to be interesting when they say it if, and only if, they are motivated to change. The complicated relationships required to bring about a change will be discussed in the next chapter. Now we turn to the problem of training people to put ideas and persuasive tactics in order so they might have a coherent presentation. *Coherence and interest represent the two most likely candidates to pass instructional triage.*

PROGRAMMING STRUCTURE

It is easy to oversimplify the process of modifying speech performance behavior and it is important for the teacher to do so. There is so much going on that is inaccessible to pedagogical efforts, that to concentrate on the whole process is to sacrifice the doable. Performance modification is not a matter of inspiration. Overcoming anxiety, developing self-esteem, or understanding communication theory has little to do with behavior. The first step in a pedagogical technology is to teach students to get whatever information they have into coherent order for presentation to a selected audience. The second step is to train them to use their vocal equipment, face, and body to present it in an interested fashion. The teaching process actually starts with the speaker's goal and the topics she chooses to include in her presentation.

We do not minimize the importance of the invention process nor disparage those who teach about it. It is important for potential speakers to know that they must set social goals that can realistically be accomplished through discourse. This requires them to have something to talk about. Once they have goals, it is even possible to teach how to phrase them so they can guide composition of remarks. The instructional system of the Reticence Program (see chap. 2) is based on simple steps:

1. Speaker sets behavioral goal for personal performance.
2. Speaker specifies criteria by which to assess whether the goal has been accomplished.
3. Speaker arranges the ideas to be spoken.
4. Speaker practices and rehearses the statement.
5. Speaker speaks and evaluates the response.

Step 3 is the crucial area in instruction. In step 3, the speaker not only arranges ideas into sequences but arranges subsequences, down to the sentence level. In a formal public speech, the speaker can literally compose a document (although the extemporaneous mode of delivery is encouraged). Once this has been done, the speaker has a script that can be "produced" by a teacher-critic who can work intensively on the utterance itself.

The Interface of Invention and Disposition

We defined incompetent oral discourse as any talk that failed to accomplish a social goal, or that accomplished it but brought undesirable concomitants sufficient to outweigh the advantages gained. We pointed out in the previous chapter, that of the processes classically associated with rhetoric, only disposition and delivery seemed amenable to modification within the purview of the field of speech communication. There is an apocryphal quotation, ". . . rhetoric is queen of all the sciences, for having no subject matter of her own, is yet master of all." This presumptuous statement seems to make rhetoric the core of all intellectual training. The idea is good for the ego but dismaying to the teacher. We have, therefore, decided to focus on disposition and delivery, accepting the idea that invention and style are tied together in memory, and that portion of style essentially grammatical is associated with disposition.

Two-thirds of the undergraduate students enrolled in a basic speech course (covering public speaking and group discussion), included in the study cited earlier, listed three main goals in instruction.

1. Skill at organizing ideas
2. Presentational skill
3. Overcoming performance anxiety

A similarly large proportion objected to cognitive training in history and philosophy of communication. While student wants are not necessarily appropriate justifications for content of instruction, it is important to note that they feel deficiencies in these areas. Furthermore, as we will emphasize later, complicity between student and teacher is essential to successful instruction. Students are more likely to collaborate in achieving their goals than in working on goals imposed on them by their teachers.

Just prior to the moment of utterance, the speaker must put his ideas in some kind of order. At this point, what the speaker has are topics he has decided are useful in discourse. The classical rhetoricians referred to these as *topoi* and used a metaphor of space or location, that is, a topic is a place where a particular kind of idea is stored. There are general topics, or issues that apply to all cases (good and bad, expensive and inexpensive, and so on) and topics specific to the case (surgery or medical treatment, bunt or swing away, etc.). One useful cognitive science explanation is that thought is the result of parallel distributed processing in the brain (Jackson, 1985, p. 410). A virtual infinity of processes go on all at once from which the speaker, in some fashion, chooses those he regards as relevant. There has actually been some progress in simulating this kind of mental processing, but *in vivo* it cannot be observed. We can only infer what goes on by observing artifacts like electroencephalograms or monitoring oral and written discourse.

As varied as thought can be, it is rule bound. It must be sequential in time and space (Eccles & Robinson, 1984, p. 107). A speaker can say only one word at a time. A writer must put the words in some kind of order on the page. Whether or not a listener or reader understands depends on the order imposed by the speaker. The most difficult problem in the theoretical process is the explanation of what happens between input (thought) and output (speech) (Churchland, 1986, p. 410).

Insofar as we know, the process of translating thought into speech takes place in the Wernicke's and Broca's areas of the brain. In Wernicke's area, thought is compiled and organized for processing (Gazzaniga, 1985, p. 154), while the Broca's area controls the actual phrasing and output (Churchland, pp. 159–160).

The organizing rubric for discourse is the objective the discourse is designed to accomplish. We have discussed in chapter 2 how important it is that speakers set goals for their own performance rather than attempt to evaluate their success based exclusively on random response to discourse given by a listener. Most of us cannot avoid expressive discourse that has personal gratification as its objective. However, this kind of discourse can only be effective by accident. Most social discourse is rhetorical, directed at satisfying a social exigence (Bitzer, 1968).

Our pedagogical question: *What modifications can be made in perfor-*

mance behavior that raises the probabilities of a speaker achieving his or her social goal? We cannot train people in memory systems or to "think" any more than any other discipline. The organized use of language has to do with vocabulary, storage, retrieval, and the sensitive insights about which words fit which ideas. However, once the ideas reach consciousness and are phrased into words, we can teach how to put them in order and say them effectively.

We know a great deal about errors in delivery. Starkweather (1983), VanRiper and Emerick (1984), and Boone (1987), among others, give us more than we can handle about how to identify and correct errors in delivery. The vast literature of theatrical performance provides a rich resource for training skillful performance. It remains only to encourage teachers to learn about delivery and how to train it.

The critical problem in instruction seems to lie with organization of ideas and tactics, the literal structuring of the message. More specifically, the task is to find ways to detect errors in organization of discourse and train speakers to remedy them. We start instruction *after* the speaker has responded to the exigence, set goals, and select ideas to present. Our concern is with how the speaker arranges his thoughts and strategies into presentational order so that they are appealing and compelling to the mind of the listener.

The process of training students to structure and present oral discourse depends on the fragile process of criticism. When a critic evaluates the structure of discourse, she must ascertain whether the order in which statements are presented conforms to standards for presentation. The critic can give both moral and technological advice. Moral advice would be, "You ought to be more clear in your outline." Technological advice would require the critic to specify a model that mandates an order for the units of discourse. Moral advice is largely based on personal and vicarious experience as well as shared lore and wisdom. Technological advice depends on formal standards based on research findings for its generalizations. When one receives moral advice, one has choices (the euphemism for which is one does not know precisely what to do). When one receives technological advice, one should know exactly what to do.

THE AVAILABLE STRUCTURES FOR DISCOURSE

The process of structuring starts with specification of a speech purpose or residual message (Phillips & Zolten, 1976) phrased in a single simple sentence in the traditional fashion, for example:

I want to tell my friends why we ought to see *The Mikado* instead of *Frankenstein*.
I want to explain the differences between various breeds of dogs.
I want to explain how to make a paper airplane.
I want to tell you how Cancun looks.
I want to give reasons why they should support my candidate.
I want to give reasons why I should get the promotion.
I want to speculate on what it all means.

The importance of these topics is irrelevant as is their relevance. We assume that most of what people say is unimportant, individually and cosmically. Still, if it is said for a purpose, it can be evaluated as successful or unsuccessful.

Structure is initially imposed between the decision on the purpose of discourse and the selection of the ideas and tactics to be presented. Before the topic is phrased in words, some pattern of connections must be established to guide the speaker in the order of presentation, that is, the sequence in which sentences are to be uttered. In essence, this is a "blueprint" of a speech.

Traditional courses in public speaking teach students to make conscious blueprints of their speeches through the use of outlines.[1] Such planning is not encouraged in social discourse. In fact, the mythology argues that people ought to be "spontaneous" in their social presentations.

During the heyday of the sensitivity-training movement, this meant relatively uncontrolled blurting of "whatever" regardless of the difficulty it may cause. The concept of *negative spontaneity* (Murray, Phillips, & Truby, 1969) argues the contrary. Negative spontaneity is defined as "knowing that you can injure the other party by what you say and consciously refraining from doing so." In operation, such concepts as manners, tact, diplomacy, and consideration are regarded as the hallmarks of civilized people. They cannot be accomplished without thinking about the situation and planning accordingly.

In fact, organization is a sine qua non of intelligibility. We hypothesize that the better the organization, the greater the intelligibility. Now

1. But what is usually missing is instruction in how to write an outline. Our survey of five thousand speech students indicated that nearly three-fourths of them comply with the outline assignment by writing the speech first and generating the outline from the speech, actually a form of busy work. The process of structuring, which we discuss here, is literally the process by which an outline is constructed. It precedes the act of composition, whether the task is a formal public speech, a written composition, or social discourse.

we have the problem of defining the word *better*. In the sense we use it here, *better* refers to improvement of continuity of thought to conform to prototypical patterns known to be clear, accompanied by lack of digressiveness in presentation. That is, we assume that there are some fundamental orders that can be imposed on discourse; they exist in pure form; and we can critique the order of a unit of discourse based on the extent to which it conforms to the pure order.

Sondel (1958) introduced a simple system for structuring messages in her "Field Theory of Communication" (pp. 171ff.). She argues that verbal patterns are abstracted from real patterns in the world. Thinking, she says, "is to make a verbal pattern consciously" (p. 180). The process of discourse commences with a summary composed of "formators," words that create a framework or pattern into which the components or contents of discourse can be fitted. Relying on traditional logical forms, she offers seven basic forms (p. 185): time, space, conjunction, disjunction, analogy, cause-effect, and means to end, concluding with the statement, "this is, of course, not an exhaustive list." Using this as a basis we turn to Simon (1982), who states that the act of imposition of order is a fundamental process in thought; an artificial intelligence bringing the products of thought under control.

This point cannot be overemphasized. Thought itself, according to Simon, is artificial. It is a process of imposing order on what is otherwise a chaotic process. In the simplest and starkest possible terms, we do not know what a human is thinking until some report is made. Intelligence could be defined not so much in terms of mental data processing but in the quality of what is reported. This, in fact, represents the essence of the whole educational and vocational system. We assess intelligence *ad hoc* based on what people say and do. Whatever one might think of the concept "competence," the only way to observe and assess it is to observe and assess its artifacts, thought and action.

A simple blueprint of a building will show the number of stories, the shape of the rooms, location of doors and windows, and so on. Details can be added later like location of plumbing, electrical fixtures. The final product may include specifications of composition, wallboard, plaster, paper, paint colors, and so on. The blueprint can be as simple or as detailed as is necessary. The initial builder needs one kind of plan, the decorator another. The landscape architect may have entirely different requirements. The plan is devised to suit the occasion.

The same process goes on in composition of discourse. A speech structure is, literally, a detailed drawing of the speech's structural plan. The number of basic structures is limited. Essentially, they are "sets," that is, they express the whole of a unit of composition; they exclude what does not fit, and internally, they divide the material into logical subsets, exactly as the blueprint specifies what is to be included in the building and where it is to be. The blueprint specifies relative size of the compartments and in refined form details the contents of the rooms. It excludes everything that does not belong or fit. We believe that all compositions can be similarly blueprinted, that we can draw a diagram of the components of the discourse and specify the contents of the components in the order in which they are to be presented. *In fact, we argue that without such planning, discourse cannot be made, orally or in writing.* The problem is that sometimes, when the speaker is not paying attention, the plans are hasty, distorted, poorly drawn, insufficiently detailed, or simply wrong. When this happens, the speaker makes errors in discourse.

By using the concept of "mathematical set" as a fundamental unit, the structure of most messages can be conveniently expressed in visual diagrams. This is not quite the same as Korzybski's (1933) map-territory analogy. Korzybski believed in the impossible ideal—that language and the things it represented would have a perfect one-to-one correspondence. Our goal is merely to train speakers to devise plans for the utterance of discourse, using as a guide the speaker's goals and the audience's propensities. The structural design of discourse is a guide to the speaker. It is modifiable based on response from the audience. Following Sondel's lead, we commence with three basic sets:

1. The sequence inherent in narrative and instruction (that is, history or how to perform some task). The units follow a time sequence. One *must* precede the other in proper order.

2. The sequence inherent in description (that is, these are the qualities of . . .). The units each represent an attribute of some thing, event, concept, person, condition, and so on. This set is appropriate for definition (among other things).

3. The sequence inherent in taxonomy (that is, these are the components of, or these are the requirements for membership in the category). The units represent "kinds of things." This set enables us to bring things that are alike together but acknowledge variations in nonessential qualities.

These three units represent the blocks out of which more complicated structures can be built. In essence, all composition is a process of connecting sets in some kind of order or sequence. The planning for a formal speech, for example, culminates in an outline that guides the speaker through the utterance of his text. In a written composition it is the plan on which the written statement is based. In social discourse it is more the arrangement of tactics including oral remarks, and it allows for immediate adjustment based on response.

FUNDAMENTALS OF STRUCTURING

The General Principles

The are some basic propositions that underlie the development of a structural set.

The set must be inclusive of the message. Whatever message the speaker intends, the listener can only respond to the message he receives. Although some people claim they can "read between the lines" (or "hear between the phonemes"), people can only respond to what they hear or think they hear. We concede the importance of delivery; that the impact of any utterance can be modified in subtle ways by paralinguistic cues. The essential cognitive content of the message, however, is constrained by whatever meanings are evoked in the listener by the words uttered. The more the speaker exerts control over what she says, the more likely it is the listener will hear what she intends. Understanding is not a matter of change or accident. When a listener understands what a speaker has said, it is usually because of something the speaker did in planning her utterance.

This tautology means the words mean whatever *the* words mean. Elements of delivery can then be consciously managed to constrain further the listener's understanding. It is an error when a speaker transmits an incomplete message or a message containing irrelevancies and digressions.

The components of the set must be mutually exclusive. Overlapping categories create confusion. The composer of discourse must divide the composition into discrete units deployed inductively or deductively. Units like introductions and conclusions are ornamentations and not part of the structural process. However, they have a structure of their own.

The guide to the overall structure is the residual message, the one key idea the speaker wants the listener to remember when all else is forgotten. This sets up the plan for the whole message and its components, each of which can then be structured into its components, and so on, down to the sentence level.

There are a limited number of patterns that can be used. Patterns that do not conform to social logic are errors. Social logic refers to the organization patterns people understand (cf. Sondel). Linguists and grammarians have provided rules for the construction of sentences. These rules are inherently social, that is, they describe how people arrange sentences and how they understand them; they are not prescriptions before the fact to which writers and speakers must adhere.

The subsets may be necessarily sequential. If they are not inherently sequential, the speaker must decide on a sequence.[2] The nature of the set often determines the order in which ideas are presented. For example, when the set presents instructions for performing a task, the components *must* be sequential. When the set describes the qualities, characteristics, or attributes of something, the components can come in the order preferred by the speaker. The speaker, however, tries to follow some rational pattern like important to unimportant, large to small, beautiful to ugly, and so on.

Each subset may take a form different from that of the whole set. For example, if the set designation is a simple classification like "types and uses of dogs," the subset "uses" might include training dogs to do work, which could consist of necessarily sequential steps in training, while the second subset could be a simple classification into descriptions of various breeds.

The Basic Structures

Sondel (1958) identified seven working structures. These were adapted into three one-sided (basic) structures and four two-sided structures by Zolten and Phillips (1985). Time, classification, and space (description) are the basic structures. The four two-sided structures (anal-

2. Someone once commented, "time is nature's way of making sure everything doesn't happen at once." Another communication is "in communication nothing never happens." These are both good ideas. A speaker cannot utter two statements at once. They must come one at a time. If the speaker reverses logical order, then the listener is confused. Furthermore, if the listener is listening at all, he will get some impression. If the speaker pauses, hesitates, stammers, blocks, repeats, or utters nonsense, stares into space, or dances a hornpipe, the listener will get an impression and react to it. The idea is to arrange discourse so the speaker has maximum control over what happens and little is left to chance.

ogy, contrast, cause-effect, and problem-solution) are actually combinations of the basic structures. The two-sided structures can be divided into subtypes. Cause-effect, for example, can also include functional connections, actuarial projection, or correlation. Analogy can include simple comparison, criticism, and metaphor.

Problem-solution actually becomes a subset of the broader category, "argument." The list of structures that follows does not presume to be exhaustive. It represents those identified through examination of a variety of types of discourse, including formal speeches and social conversation.

CLASSIFICATION, or TAXONOMY, is the simplest structure. It merely identifies the members of a set. It is governed by the following rules:

1. The whole structure is all-inclusive of the group.
2. Each division is mutually exclusive (discrete).
3. Each member of the group must meet the sine qua non for membership.
4. Each subdivision must have its own sine qua non that does not violate any element of the sine qua non for the group.
5. For presentation purposes, members must be relatively equivalent.
6. When the taxonomy includes proportions it is called **DEMOGRAPHY.**

DEFINITION (SINE QUA NON) is a variation specifing the qualities that entitle group membership.

1. The qualities must be exclusive to the members of the set and not of any other set.
2. Members may belong to other sets because of other qualities.
3. No unit may be admitted as member if devoid of any quality included in the qualifications.
4. Qualities must be denotative regarding category membership.
5. The subsets are additive. The main set is inclusive.

The structure is diagrammed as follows:

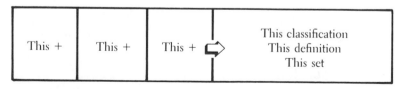

DESCRIPTION is a simple structure made up of characteristics or features possessed by a given entity, concept, location, and so on. It conforms to the following rules:

1. Characteristics include sensory features—appearance, sound, feel, taste, smell—as well as impressions, feelings, attitudes, and so on.

2. Qualities may be denotative or connotative.

3. Features can be included for identification purposes.

4. Features can be included to impress.

5. The presumption is that "etc." follows the last subset, indicating that qualities and features can be added.

6. The speaker has the option to arrange the components into some kind of rational order and to follow the plan.

The structure diagrams as follows:

Appearance		Utility		Location		Etc.
Color	Sound	Recreation	Business	Habitat	Dispersion	

STRUCTURE is a set made up of parts and their connections. It is, essentially, an analog, like a map or formal blueprint.

1. This can be definition or description. Each part is a feature in taxonomy.

2. Parts must equal the whole unit.

3. Parts must be discrete.

4. Connections must be identified (as in articulation of paragraphs, for example).

5. There is a natural order. The parts must be in specified order.

The set diagrams as follows:

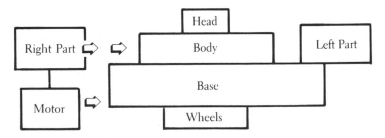

The parts of the diagram are analogs to the thing it represents.

TIME, CHRONOLOGY, INSTRUCTION is a set in which the components are time units.

1. Historical time units must be identified by argument for their utility (comprehension or argument.)

2. Instruction units must follow the rule of necessary precedence (cf. PERT in Phillips, 1973).

The set diagrams as follows:

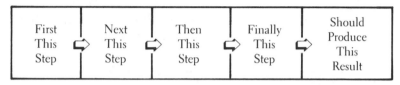

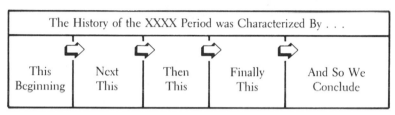

Complex structures are constructed by juxtaposing simple structures.

COMPARISON OR CONTRAST is a two-dimensional juxtaposition of sets on which a calculus of residuals is performed and the result judged (similar, different). When the comparison is simple/complex or familiar/unfamiliar it is called **ANALOGY**. When it is fanciful, it is called **METAPHOR**. This is the diagram:

This Set	This Set	This Set	
=	=	=	Comparison Analogy
This Set	This Set	This Set	

This Set	This Set	This Set	
not =	not =	not =	Contrast
this set	this set	this set	

CRITICISM is a specialized form in which a comparison is made to preset standards. There is an equation in which the components of the standards are compared to the components of the object of criticism and an assessment made (good/bad, effective/ineffective, and so on). The following rules apply.

1. The components of the standards must be defended on the criterion of relevancy and cogency (that is, x, y, z = bad; a, b, c = good. Because object has x, y, b therefore, it tends to be bad, and so on). In essence, the criticism structure positions three classification structures side by side, leading to a final classification that is the estimate or assessment of the criticism. This is the diagram:

This Standard A	Is Met by A′	Contradicted by X	On Balance We Conclude about A, A′, or X
This Standard B	Is Met by B′	Contradicted by Y	On Balance We Conclude about B, B′, Or Y
This Standard C	Is Met by C	Contradicted by Z	On Balance We Conclude about C, C′, or Z

There are a variety of structures drawn from statistical formulations.

SIGN refers to apparently coincidental and usual connections, as X appears and Y appears. It is not clear in this relationship whether X and Y are themselves connected or appear connected because of their actual connection with some nonevident third variable.

CORRELATION represents some sort of connection between X and Y: As X appears, Y appears; as X disappears, Y disappears. **REGRESSION** calculates the formula for the proportions of the connection. **ACTUARIAL PROJECTION** purports to predict future occurrences through examination of connections. The arrangement of variables presumed in this structure can also be **FUNCTIONAL**, that is, the modification of one connected variable brings about change in the other variable in ways that are mathematically describable.

CAUSAL RELATIONSHIP essentially represents the scientific method. It can refer to ascription of cause from examination of data or test of cause through experimentation.

The model for these connections appears the same. The connector words are modified accordingly.

This. . .	This. . .	This. . .
▼	▼	▼
occurs with	occurs with	occurs with
▼	▼	▼
THIS	THIS	THIS

This. . .	This. . .	This. . .
▼	▼	▼
changes with	changes with	changes with
▼	▼	▼
THIS	THIS	THIS

This. . .	This. . .	This. . .
▼	▼	▼
causes	causes	causes
▼	▼	▼
THIS	THIS	THIS

ARGUMENT is an arrangement of sets designed to induce conviction or assent according to the following rules (recognizable as the stock forensic issues):

1. NEED set: Is there a reason to modify the status quo?
2. PLAN set: Here is a proposal for modifications.
3. PRACTICALITY set: Each of the components in 2 is feasible.
4. DESIRABILITY set: Each component will remedy a problem in 1 without undesirable concomitants.
5. REFUTATION set: A direct contradiction, e.g. there is no need, the plan will not work, the plan will bring undesirable concomitants.

In each case, the structure proceeds through enthymemic (because) and exemplar (example) connections, for example:

I. There is a need, because
    A. The citizens are complaining, for example
    B. The costs are excessive, for example
    C. Etc. . . .
II. Here is a plan, for example
    A. Component 1 consists of, for example
    B. Component 2 consists of, for example
III. The plan will work, because
    A. We can afford it, for example
    B. We can administer it, for example
IV. The plan is desirable, because
    A. It will stop the citizens from complaining, for example
    B. It will cut the costs, for example

The general diagram appears as follows:

The Need Consists of		The Plan Consists of	It Will Work Because	It Will Bring No Evils
This Condition X	This Impairment X'	Component X'' to Meet X and/or X'	Removes Condition X Impairment X'	Worse Than X or X'
This Condition Y	This Impairment Y'	Component Y''' to Meet Y and/or Y'	Removes Condition Y Impairment Y'	Worse Than Y or Y'

The person seeking to refute the argument uses the same structure but may negate any block, as: This condition =/=/> (does not) lead to this impairment or this component =/=/> (will not) remove this impairment or removing this impairment =\=\> (will not) lead to this desirable result.

There also appears to be a variant of the argument structure based on admonition or exhortation. This structure approximates the "cohortative" tense in Semitic languages. It synthesizes three main structures around the obligations inherent in any moralistic admonition, "you should; you ought to." There are three obvious heuristic questions that arise from admonition:

1. What should I do?
2. Why should I do it?
3. How should I do it?

This is a variant argumentative form with (2) serving as need, (1) serving as plan, and (3) serving as the practicality argument. The last component, that is, salubrious outcome is left unargued with the implied answer "because I said so" or "because it will please me," or "because it is the word of God or the law."

No structure is pure. In a time structure, for example, the main categories are arranged in necessary/precedent order, but each unit can contain material grouped according to another structure (Zolten & Phillips, 1985).

Structural Fundamentals: An Artificial Intelligence Solution

The logic of the structural argument can be tested by demonstrating that a computer is capable of organizing English sentences in coherent fashion. If the computer can do this, it demonstrates that there are cues in social language that permit the imposition of order in a consistent fashion.

Korzybski (1933) remarked, "all knowledge is knowledge of structure." People tend to make sense of things by putting them in order. This truism enables us to manage concepts like grammar and government. Composition is no exception to the tendency of humans to impose order on what they see and hear.

Listeners cannot record information as fast as speakers can say it. To increase their odds of success, speakers must impose order on their remarks so that listeners can get the "gist" (Hirsch, 1988) of what is being said. Gist is order and is imposed by structure. When a listener does not understand the words, he or she can get some sense by examining the structural relationship of the words. Thus, "She was twonkey" may make no sense, but the listener notes the pronoun and verb and presumes that "twonkey" is a quality or a class. Unfortunately, the quality of synonymy sometimes confuses the issue and requires the listener to reduce what he hears to whatever language he has available. The structure, meanwhile, remains intact. The same is true for homographs like "fast," meaning "a person runs rapidly" or "a color does not run at all." The cliché is that the "context" determines the meaning, but the context is actually the larger structure into which the smaller structure fits. Context is not a random juxtaposition of stimuli. As we will point out in the final chapter, humans make order out of the chaos of social interaction. Whatever order the human imposes represents the context for his utterances. Thus, attention to fundamental structures provides a basis for reduction of language to a limited number of nouns, verbs, and connectors that provide cues to their arrangement.

We hypothesize that **all** intelligible simple English sentences can be reduced to seven basic formulas (give or take the formulas not yet discovered):

1. The components of X are A, B, and C.
2. The qualities of X are A, B, and C.
3. To accomplish X do 1, 2, and 3 in that order.
   The events from X to Y are 1, 2, and 3 in that order.
4. X is similar to Y in the following respects: 1, 2, 3 . . .
5. X is different from Y in the following respects: 1, 2, 3 . . .
6. X occurs when Y occurs.
   X changes as Y changes.
   X causes Y.
7. The problem X can be remedied by Y.

The hypothesis can be tested by attempting reductions on naturally occurring simple sentences such as those written on ordinary outlines for public speeches produced by freshman and sophomore students. If virtually all sentences can be reduced to one of the basic forms, or if nonreducible residuals contain the features of an unanticipated form, it is possible to move to the next step of programming.

This would consist of using a cyborg concept, that is, making a human into a database and enforcing the requirements of the structures on his or her composition process. The advantage of the cyborg process is that it solves one of the major barriers to an effective expert system, that is, the use of a formal database such as a dictionary or thesaurus as a source of information. The human is a data storage and retrieval system and generally responsive to directive questions. Theoretically, the expert system takes an initial speech purpose statement from the database, presents the basic alternatives in menu form. The database selects the most appropriate structural form, rephrases the statement accordingly, and then responds to directions through the process of building the structural outline of the composition.

Introduction to the Programming Problem: The Grevitz

The question is, Can a computer be "trained" to orient itself to a set of sentences relevant to some common issue or idea and, regardless of the order in which the sentences are presented, arrange them into a formal structure? This would be somewhat like the problem confronted by the student who returns from the library with a set of 3-by-5-inch note cards, trying to arrange them into the outline of a composition.

For the past twenty years, we have used such an exercise to teach students the principles of forming structures as a preliminary to outlining. (See the *Instructors' Manual* to Zolten & Phillips [1985] for the original problem.) The Grevitz exercise gives the students a list of sixty-two random statements, each relevant to a central theme (residual message or speech purpose). There are linguistic cues in each statement that position it in a structural diagram from which an outline can be built (see Zolten & Phillips, chaps. 4, 5). The title of the presentation is: "The Composition, History, Uses, and Operation of the Grevitz." Because there is no Grevitz, there is no sociocultural bias in the exercise. We have used this exercise on more than one thousand freshman and sophomore students. The pedagogical purpose of the outline is to train the students to perform similar procedures on their own notes before putting them into an outline for a public speech.

This title specifies an outline with four main headings. The idea is initially to find four statements among the sixty-two that represent the most general statements of the four main headings, then group the remaining fifty-eight items under the appropriate headings in proper sequence. Once the statements are grouped, subheads become evident, generating another reordering. Statements that do not seem to fit are cast aside and later, checked once the related items are put in order. The result is the generation of an outline of a speech about the Grevitz, which sounds coherent when read aloud.

Students have been able to perform this task solo with about 95 percent accuracy. The mean time for solution is approximately three hours. We have not been able to find any common feature in the 5 percent that do not succeed. We assume this means there is sufficient logic in the statements for them to find the proper arrangement. To provide them with additional cues, we present them with a blank structural diagram of the composition. Their task is to place the numbers of the statements in the appropriate boxes. The boxes are labeled so that once they are filled in, they can be formed into a outline from which it is possible to present a speech.

Following are the sixty-two statements in the order in which they are presented

The Composition, History, Uses, and Operation of the Grevitz

1. Another use for the Grevitz is to put out forest fires.
2. The salt should be dropped from a height of six inches.
3. The Grevitz has a long and distinguished history.
4. The Blugars use the Grevitz to induce euphoria at spring orgies.
5. If the Grevitz shell wiggles in the water, the water is too hot.
6. The third step is to blow hard at the fire.
7. In 1955 the Wallonians contracted for Grevitz sales with the Common Market.
8. Still another use for Grevitzes is bifurcation of the ego.
9. Female Grevitzes are light purple.
10. The water used for soaking Grevitz shells should be lukewarm.
11. The first Grevitz cost 34,069 grozziks (14 cents American).
12. The Swiss use Grevitzes to induce translucability at chocolate euphoria rites.
13. Great care should be taken in removing the Grevitz shell.
14. Andreas Klorp marketed the first Grevitz at Krbitzke.
15. Grevitzes stimulate bifurcation at libidinous denouements.
16. The first step in operating a Grevitz is to remove the shell.
17. Grevitzes are composed of shell, body, and maffle.
18. There are four main uses for the Grevitz.
19. The Grevitz may be used in winter to eliminate earwigs.
20. When inserting the Grevitz, do not twist.
21. When the shell has been soaked, install Grevitz in the left ear.
22. The first step in firefighting is throw the Grevitz over your right ear.
23. Klorp perfected the Grevitz with the help of Denigram Geech.
24. It is easy to identify the composition and color of Grevitzes.
25. Grevitzes do an excellent job of bifurcation in plenifors libido.
26. When inserting the Grevitz, use a gentle pressure.
27. The body of the Grevitz lodges inside the shell.

28. Twisting may injure the ear.
29. Finster developed the Grevitz in his lab at Gezornemplatz.
30. The second step in using Grevitzes in firefighting is to stamp the ground.
31. The second step in operating the Grevitz is to soak the shell.
32. Shells are three times larger than body and maffle combined.
33. Geeks and other pagans use the Grevitz to induce euphoria at bar mitzvahs.
34. Use voodoo with your Grevitz to seduce earwig males.
35. Klorp reduced Grevitz cost to 4,000,577 grozziks. (11 cents)
36. The first Grevitz was developed by Sigwald Finster in 1801.
37. Twisting may break off the maffle.
38. A final use for the Grevitz is to eliminate earwigs.
39. To operate a Grevitz takes considerable skill.
40. Finster used a distillation process to produce the first Grevitz.
41. Water used to soak Grevitz shells should be lukewarm (85 degrees).
42. Male Grevitzes are bright purple.
43. Grevitz shells should not be discarded because they are delicious with Kaltmede.
44. Today the Grevitz accounts for 60% of the Wallonian economy.
45. Grevitzes can bifurcate the libido in cases of DTs.
46. Push on Grevitz with left elbow.
47. The Grevitz was perfected in 1906 by Andrejas Klorp.
48. The first use of the Grevitz is to induce euphoria.
49. Salt should be dropped at two grains per corner.
50. After the earwig has been seduced via voodoo, stamp on it with foot.
51. The maffle sticks out of the shell, 1/5 the length of the shell.
52. In 1951 Grevitzes we included in the free trade agreement with South Pludge.
53. Grevitz shells should not be discarded for they provide protection for fleebs.
54. From 1951 to the present, Grevitzes have sustained the Wallonian economy.
55. Other Grevitzes are mauve.
56. A pinch of salt should be dropped into Grevitz soaking water.
57. In 1962 the Wallonians enacted the Grevitz Protection Bill.
58. The salt should be dropped at 8 grains per second.
59. Use right index finger to guide insertion.
60. The temperature of water used to soak shells shold be tested with the elbow.
61. Grevitzes' colors range from bright to dull associated with gender.
62. After the shells have been removed they should not be discarded.

This is the blank structural form for the exercise.

At present, a computer program can sort the statements in the Grevitz problem into the proper order. This is done by finding, in each sentence, cues to its location in the diagram. The premise on which the search is based is that each sentence can be reduced to a prototype and its components found in a lexicon. It takes the computer considerably longer to do the task than it takes a human. However, the purpose of the program is not to devise a system to replace humans, but to use the program to understand human composition processes.

Based on the program, we offer the hypothesis that any set of human statements can be put in order, provided they are recast into prototypical statements each of which contains a cue to connect it with statements preceding and following. We argue that this is implied in grammar anyway. Our experiments with programming Burke's Pentad (Phillips & Erlwein, 1989) shows that while, at the moment, the technical act of programming an expert composition system is unmanageable, the logical connections are obvious and confirm the theory that discourse is composed of statements rationally connected according to a rule system members of a language group are familiar with. The Grevitz illustrates this proposition in its solutions, which looks like this:

Table I

24					I
17		A	61		B
32 (1)	27 (1)	51 (1)	42 (1)	9 (2)	55 (3)

Table II

3									II
36		A	47		B	54			C
29 (1)	11 (2)	40 (3)	35 (1)	14 (2)	23 (3)	52 (1)	7 (2)	57 (3)	44 (4)

Table III

18											III
48		A	1		B	8		C	38		D
33 (1)	12 (2)	4 (3)	22 (1)	30 (2)	6 (3)	45 (1)	15 (2)	25 (3)	19 (1)	34 (2)	50 (3)

Table IV

39												IV
16			31						21			C
(A)			(B)						(C)			
(1)	(2) 62		(1) 10			(2) 56			(1) 20		(2) 26	
13	a 43	b 53	a 5	a 60	a 41	a 58	a 2	a 49	a 28	b 37	a 46	b 59

Note how the boxes in the structures can be coordinated into a formal outline.

Outline of the Grevitz Composition

I. 24	II. 3	III. 18	IV. 39
A. 17	A. 36	A. 48	A. 16
1. 32	1. 29	1. 33	1. 13
2. 27	2. 11	2. 12	2. 62
3. 51	3. 40	3. 4	a. 43
B. 61	B. 47	B. 1	b. 53
1. 42	1. 35	1. 22	B. 31
2. 9	2. 14	2. 30	1. 10
3. 55	3. 23	3. 6	a. 5
	C. 54	C. 8	b. 60
	1. 52	1. 45	c. 41
	2. 7	2. 15	2. 56
	3. 57	3. 25	a. 58
	4. 44	D. 38	b. 2
		1. 19	c. 49
		2. 34	C. 21
		3. 50	1. 20
			a. 28
			b. 37
			2. 26
			a. 46
			b. 59

The sentences on the outline can be put together into the complete composition as follows:

The Composition, History, Uses, and Operation of the Grevitz

24. It is easy to identify the composition and color of Grevitzes
   17. Grevitzes are composed of shell, body, and maffle.
      32. Shells are three times larger than body and maffle combined.
      27. The body of the Grevitz lodges inside the shell.
      51. The maffle sticks out of the shell, 1/5 the length of the shell.
   61. Grevitz colors range from bright to dull, associated with gender.
      42. Male Grevitzes are bright purple.
      9. Female Grevitzes are light purple.
      55. Other Grevitzes are mauve.

3. The Grevitz has a long and distinguished history.
  36. The first Grevitz was introduced by Sigwald Finster in 1801.
    29. Finster developed the Grevitz in his lab at Gezornemplatz.
    11. The first Grevitz cost 34,069 grozziks (14 cents American).
    40. Finster used distillation process to produce the first Grevitz.
  47. The Grevitz was perfected in 1906 by Andrejas Klorp.
    35. Klorp reduced Grevitz cost to 4,000,577 grozziks (11 cents).
    14. Klorp marketed the first Grevitz at at Krbitzke.
    23. Klorp perfected the Grevitz with the help of Denigram Geech.
  54. From 1951 to the present, Grevitzes have sustained the Wallonian economy.
    52. In 1951 Grevitzes were included in the free trade agreement with South Pludge.
    7. In 1955 the Wallonians contracted for Grevitz sales with the Common Market.
    57. In 1962 the Wallonians enacted the Grevitz Protection Bill.
    44. Today, the Grevitz accounts for 60 percent of the Wallonian economy.
18. There are four main uses for the Grevitz.
  48. The first use of the Grevitz is to induce euphoria.
    33. Geeks and other pagans use the Grevitz to induce euphoria at bar mitzvahs.
    12. The Swiss use Grevitzes to induce transluctability at chocolate euphoria rites.
    4. The Blugars use Grevitzes to induce euphoria at spring orgies.
  1. Another use for the Grevitz is to put out forest fires.
    22. The first step in firefighting is throw the Grevitz over your right ear.
    30. The second step in using Grevitzes in firefighting is to stamp the ground.
    6. The third step is to blow hard at the fire.
  8. Still another use for Grevitzes is bifurcation of the ego.
    45. Grevitzes can bifurcate libido in cases of D.T.s
    15. Grevitzes stimulate bifurcation at libidinous denouements.
    25. Grevitzes do an excellent job of bifurcation in plenifors libido.
  38. A final use for the Grevitz is to eliminate earwigs.
    19. The Grevitz may be used in the winter to eliminate earwigs.
    34. Use voodoo with your Grevitz to seduce earwig males.
    50. After earwig has been seduced via voodoo, stamp on it with foot.
39. To operate a Grevitz takes considerable skill.
  16. The first step in operating a Grevitz is to remove the shell.
    13. Great care should be used in removing the shell.

62. After the shells are removed, they should not be discarded.
   43. Grevitz shells should not be discarded because they are delicious with Kaltmede.
   53. Grevitz shells should not be discarded because they provide protection for fleebs.
31. The second step in operating the Grevitz is to soak the shell.
   10. The water used for soaking Grevitzes should be lukewarm.
      5. If the Grevitz shell wiggles in the water, it is too hot.
      60. The temperature of the water used to soak shells should be tested with the elbow.
      41. Water used to soak Grevitz shells should be heated with propane.
   56. A pinch of salt should be dropped into Grevitz soaking water.
      58. The salt should be dropped into the water at 8 grains/sec.
      2. The salt should be dropped from a height of six inches.
      49. Salt should be dropped at two grains per corner.
21. When the shell has been soaked, insert Grevitz in left ear.
   20. When inserting the Grevitz, do not twist.
      28. Twisting may injure the ear.
      37. Twisting may break the maffle.
   26. When inserting use a gentle pressure.
      46. Push on Grevitz with left elbow.
      59. Use right index finger to guide insertion.

Notice the clear form of discourse as the structures combine. Take for example, Roman II. The organizing rubric is, "The Grevitz has a long and distinguished history." The cue word is "history." It implies a sequence of necessary and precedent items. The machine can prompt for the main headings. Statement 36 contains the cue word "1801." It also contains another cue, "first." The machine scans for both "second" and another date. It discovers several other dates. Statement 47 contains the cue "1906." Statement 54 contains 1951. So does 52. But 54 reveals a span "…1951 to present" and thus introduces another time period. Statement 52 then becomes the first of a series of necessary/precedent statements under 54. Statement 7 contains the next date, 1955; and 57 contains 1962. Now what of 54. The word "present" is a valid synonym for 1991 and thus it becomes the fourth unit under the heading. It may also become an organizing rubric for a classification structure dealing with the "state of Grevitzhood today" or the "present situation of Grevitzes." Should the speaker wish to do so, this could be divided into "present economic conditions affecting the Grevitz; present social conditions; present political conditions, etc." Each of the subunits, economic, social, political, could be further subdivided. Eventually, it is possible to divide down to the sentence level, should the composer of discourse desire to do so. The structure thus drives the formation of the outline.

Pedagogically speaking, this is important. Students are often bewildered by the notion of an outline. They are not usually aware of the conscious process of putting steps in order, and thus, they make errors that confuse the listener. By prompting the composer through sequential organization, they are constrained to get items in proper sequence.

Roman IV also determines a time structure. This time, however, the cue words refer to steps not events. We have "first" (16), "second" (30), and "has been" (21). The words "Another use for the Grevitz is to put out forest fires" (1) cue that this is the second, third, or fourth entry under 18, "four . . . uses." The cue words "first," "second," and so on, connected with "forest fires," place the sentences in proper order as a time structure subhead in a classification.

During the program, the logic is impeccable, as it organizes the sentences and establishes order. Humans are not quite as orderly, nor do we expect them to be. The human can get points out of order and thus confuse a reader or listener. The logic of the computer program illustrates a pedagogical goal, that is, to train humans to be as orderly as possible with their compositions.

The logical step after programming the Grevitz problem is to take a variety of outlines produced by humans, reduce the statements into a generic form similar to that used on the Grevitz problem and ascertain whether a computer can be trained to put them back together in coherent order. The Grevitz, after all, was a setup, carefully designed so it would accommodate to programming. Hypothetically, a human speaker could be trained to organize statements following the algorithms that guided the Grevitz program. For example, think of all the simple sentences that can be written to complete "I want to talk about dogs." I want to talk about . . .

> *The way dogs appear* could include a description of a prototypical dog or of various sorts of dogs. It could also involve any sensory description, including the way dogs bark or feel.
> *How dogs breed* refers to a process consisting of a series of steps connected in necessary and precedent order.
> *The uses of dogs* is a simple classification in which connections like "work dogs," "pet dogs," show dogs," and so on, can be connected as a set.

The effect of training on dogs calls for a more complex structure like cause/
effect (dogs can be trained by rewarding them when they are correct) or
(dogs can be trained according to the trainer's personality). Subsequent
propositions can be introduced by "because" or "for example," a provision of enthymemic and exemplar capability.

We must grow bigger and better dogs is an argument. A need must be
demonstrated for growing a bigger and better dog and a plan provided
through which the need can be met (without producing werewolves
or other undesirable "critters").

And so on. Each of the following topics can be similarly structured.

How dogs are trained
How dogs developed
What kinds of dogs there are
What people do with dogs
How dogs eat
What dogs eat
What dogs really are

This chapter opened with the question, What is teachable? Our
demonstration that composition is a process sufficiently orderly to be
amenable to computer programming demonstrates that potential speakers and writers can be taught rules of order to guide their efforts to
produce texts that can be understood by listeners and readers.

A PREAMBLE TO A PEDAGOGY

The effectiveness of the artificial intelligence program convinced us
that we could effectively teach students to structure social messages. The
general success of vocal trainers similarly led us to believe we could have
the same kind of effect in the classroom. Thus, disposition and delivery
became the main units of instruction in a pedagogy designed to improve
competence at social discourse. Our theory is based on the following
assumptions:

1. The speaker has decided on a topic. If the speaker has not selected
a subject, we assume we can motivate such selection or, *in extremis*,
assign a topic. In fact, the idea of assignment is quite appealing, since
most social discourse is "assigned" in the sense that it must conform to
the context in which the discourse is being carried on as well as be
responsive to what other people are saying.

2. Any topic can be phrased as a single simple sentence. Any com-

pound or complex sentence can be reduced. We can test the logic of our structuring by requiring the speaker to phrase the content in machine programmable statements. Later on, the speaker can rephrase to eliminate redundancy and take advantage of synonymy.

3. The importance of the topic is (for the nonce) irrelevant although it is possible to exhort students to read, listen, and discover ideas suitable for social discourse.

In the following chapter we will essay a theory of modification of social discourse based on rhetorical principles and tested through the logic of artificial intelligence.

7

A Theory of Performance Modification

BACKGROUND

Our purpose in this book is to justify a pedagogy capable of modifying the performance behavior of inept social communicators. We described the technology of the pedagogy in chapter 2. In the preceding chapter, we explained its contents. We will now consider the classical and contemporary theory on which a theory of performance modification is based. Our content was derived mainly from a consideration of the classical "Canons of Rhetoric." Documentation of the theory is based on contemporary accomplishments in artificial intelligence.

Some Definitions

We have defined "competence" as *"the demonstrated ability to . . ."* We regard a person as competent to do something if he or she has done it once before in ordinary circumstances. We define "pedagogy of social discourse" as *means and methods of enabling a person to display a new competency or perform an old one with improved skill.* When a person cannot do something or other, it is evidence of "incompetence."

We began our argument by asserting that shyness was a member of a class of deficits termed *rhetorical incompetence,* which we defined as *errors in social discourse that rendered the discourse insufficient to satisfy the speaker's exigence for a social situation.* Error is any act (of composition or delivery) that appears to contribute to insufficiency of the message. There may also be errors in thought, but these are not the province of the teacher of speech communication, for they can only be detected by inference from performance. The goal of instruction is *modification of performance* so that the speaker more closely satisfies the social exigence.

"Satisfy an exigence" implies a personal judgment of a social situation. Deciding what satisfies is much like what an optometrist does when refracting lenses. The optometrist finally is required to ask, "Does this one or this one seem better." With all his refined knowledge of lenses, the optometrist must rely on the patient to define the correct prescription. He may look for paradoxes and contradictions in what the patient says, but in the final analysis the judgment about satisfaction remains entirely with the patient. So in discourse, the final judgment of effectiveness remains with the speaker, although it can be negotiated with a teacher or critic.

Our theory also assumes that *the process of composition of discourse is consistent among humans regardless of type or situation; it is orderly, partially replicable, and amenable to errors many of which can be corrected*. Our formal pedagogy concentrates on errors in disposition and delivery. We have argued that this is most productive because both processes are orderly and sequential hence amenable to systematic modification. This makes them suitable for modification in the classroom rather than the clinic.

We assume that if we can find errors in either process, we can (1) call those errors to the student's attention and (2) provide ways and means of modifying behavior to correct the errors. We may also draw inferences about the causes of the errors in mental processing and make gratuitous comments about how that might be improved. The relationship required to carry this out is delicate and calls for sophisticated understanding of teaching methods. Our emphasis in this chapter is on the theory of-instruction. We will discuss the teaching itself in the following chapter.

Orderly procedure. For starters, we assume that despite a mythology about how social talk ought to be spontaneous the process is so complex that it must be controlled by the speaker. Although social discourse often appears disorderly, we ascribe problems in it to errors in organization or sequencing. Most irregularities can be explained by a calculus of extraction of orderly components, leaving the smallest possible residual unexplained. Our consideration of structure in the previous chapter led us to believe that the overt processes of composition can be simulated on a computer.[1] Thus, we commence with the argument that the composition of discourse proceeds through a limited set of steps and processes including (but not confined to):

> Exigence: Impressions are gained from a social situation from which a potential speaker concludes that some salubrious modification can be made through discourse.
> Audience Analysis: The purpose of the intervention is specified and targeted. An audience is chosen. The speaker then discovers relevant information about the audience as a guide to selection of ideas and topics about which to speak.
> Goal Setting: The goal of the intervention is specified. The speaker decides first on a desirable behavior to be evoked in the audience and then on personal behavior goals in the form of actions to be taken.
> Invention: A message or appeal is chosen. The speaker searches through memory and discovers relevant topics and ideas to be included in discourse. The search of memory includes a review of past experience, real and vicarious, to discover communication situations similar to the present one from which ideas about content and tactics can be extracted.

Each of the preceding steps is carried on in the speaker's mind. They are not amenable to direct intervention by a teacher or critic, although they can be influenced by exhortation, critique, and example. The student can report his or her thinking spontaneously or in response to questions. Once the speaker has spoken, a listener or critic can infer relationships between mental processing and external performance.

> Disposition/Structuring: We have discussed this step at length in the previous chapter. A structure is selected to accommodate the information and tactics that constitute the message. Topics and supports are arranged within the structure. This process can proceed to the sentence level. While it is not possible to control vocabulary, critique can be offered about the quality of vocabulary and suggestions made for vocabulary improvement. We include *style* in this step of the process.

1. See Phillips and Erlwein, 1989. In this article, a theoretical model of a composition system based on Kenneth Burke's Pentad is presented. The flow chart for the system is clear, and despite problems in implementation, there is no question about the fact that rhetorical composition is a logical process amenable to programming. While we may not yet know enough about human data processing to simulate it perfectly, nor have machinery sophisticated enough to accommodate to the programming if we could, the model is sufficient to permit us to proceed as if orderly procedure was a reasonable assumption. This, I believe, is "face validity."

Delivery: The speaker speaks. We have already discussed the fact that there are a great many effective systems for the training of delivery. We include in the delivery process the adaptation of delivery to information received from monitoring the audience.

Memory: This fuels the process. The speaker contains a memory (database) of past experiences and information with evaluations of the effectiveness of various ploys, strategies, tactics, clichés, and arguments. Each experience is stored in memory and has an effect (real or potential) on each subsequent experience. Instruction can include information and directives on how to process information and what is relevant to store and use.

Incompetent discourse. Here is a situation that can arise from a number of disorderly processes and conditions, some of which are amenable to modification through teaching, and some of which are not. Our concept of *pedagogical triage* impels us to argue that the teacher/critic should devote her/his efforts to the most manageable components.

Genetic Inheritance: This varies from speaker to speaker. This does not predestine a speaker to competence or incompetence, but if propensities are evident, compensations can be made. This is especially important with genuine speech defects for which a sophisticated technology of improvement exists.

Faulty Learning: This can affect any component of the process. Parental modeling and instruction, learning and schooling shape the process of thinking that underlies composition of discourse. Failure to provide training in the techniques of effective discourse also affects future attempts at speaking by the child.

Memory Problems: These are frequent and generally not amenable to pedagogical intervention. Memory may be defective; the speaker may not be adept with mnemonic systems, and most likely, the speaker simply may not have enough or proper information stored in memory. The task of feeding memory falls to the entire educational system, not to speak of the culture in general.

Problems in Invention: Although the discipline of rhetoric has claimed "invention" as its own for centuries, it is the common property of all disciplines. Potential errors in invention include ineffective retrieval of information, erroneous interpretation of events, biased evaluations, inadequate assessment of potential listeners, and inadequate analysis of the social scene in which discourse is to be presented. This may result in defective goal setting. Of all the processes associated with memory, the two most amenable to pedagogical modification are audience analysis and goal setting. These two processes can be made overt and students provided with formal heuristics for preparation coordinated with the process of organization. We understand that it is a general goal of education to teach students "how to think." We take no stand on the extent to which this is possible, but we argue that there is some evidence that people somehow learn how to modify the way they think. We prefer to believe that this is the result of effective instruction of some sort.

Problems in Composition: This represents the main thrust of our pedagogical theory. Errors in selection of structure and deployment of information can be corrected. The discipline of competitive forensics, for example, purports to teach its participants how to select and arrange effective argument. Composition processes like Toulminian argument claim to do the same. There is considerable experiential (but not experimental) evidence that composition can be improved via effective teaching.

Literacy: The work of E. D. Hirsch (1987) highlights the importance of literacy and especially shared literacy. Our ability to size up situations and select relevant topics and ideas depends on our literacy, which, itself, is a function of both formal instruction and life learning. The interventions required to modify literacy are far too extensive for the discipline of speech communication, but discourse represents a viable way to assess literacy level and thus provides a source of inferences about literacy that might function as useful advice to social performers. We consider the concept of "literacy" analogous to the canon of "style."

Mechanical Errors in Delivery of Discourse: These can be identified and remedied through directed exercises. This area of instruction has a documented track record of success.

Instruction proceeds (see chap. 2) through lecture, reading, performance and criticism, and directed activities. These are formal and can, theoretically, be justified by our experience with structuring. The principles of artificial intelligence helped us to construct an empirical model of the components of discourse that we can use as the basis for a formal pedagogy. We are not arguing that it is now possible (and it may never be) for a machine to compose discourse, but by acting *as if* it were possible we can develop a model that will enable us to identify errors and test pedagogical methods of correcting them.

It is important to repeat our starting premise; that deficiencies in social discourse are damaging to the individual. We used and continue to use shyness as our main example, but the reader must remember that we have not even begun a taxonomy of rhetorical incompetence. It could include shyness, garrulousness, poor timing, braggadocio, defective memory, lack of information, inability to intone, and so on. This is not the time or place to start such a taxonomy, but developing one will eventually be important. The irregularities and omissions we observe in orderly process will provide a basis for construction of our taxonomy.

A second important premise is that the metaphor of orderly procedure derived from the machine solution to the Grevitz problem supports the argument that pedagogical remedies can be made available in the form of a technology of social performance modification.

An Introduction to Silicon Consciousness

Those who study communication sometimes get carried away by the belief that it is inclusive of all human activity. The communication metaphor is used by a great many scientists. Cells "communicate" with each other through the endocrine system; neurons "communicate" via neurotransmitters. The whole theory of operant conditioning is based on a communication metaphor. We use the term to refer to the use of *symbols* and physical cues associated with them in speech and writing by humans to influence other humans. But the case, really, is that communication pervades all human activities. It is included, but it does not, itself, include. Thus, communication must always have content derived apart from the process of communicating. There is information and lore about communication, which, itself, is not part of the communication process. Traditional modes of instruction that are based on the belief that learning a vocabulary and theoretical formulations about a process confer skill at the process cannot be substantiated. One can learn *about* communication without learning to communicate, and one can learn communication skills without ever encountering communication theory or learning the names for the parts of the vocal mechanism.

The symbol. So far, we have not even attempted to define "symbol." Clearly, when a person is jabbed by a needle and says "ouch," communication has, in a metaphoric sense, taken place. The afferent system received a message (it was stimulated); the efferent system responded (as a reflex). This is a simple system, stimulus/response, which despite complexities and subtleties specifies one-to-one correspondence as a perfect response and permits a deficit analysis of deviations.

The formal symbol is defined (Random House, 1987, p. 1926) as "something used for or regarded as representing something else; a material object representing something, often something immaterial." This is a fascinating definition. It is the definition of an algorithm of contingency. If X is present, then we call it Y. The definition of symbol is a tautology based on a social agreement that definition is based on social agreement. But the fact of social agreement also implies one-to-one correspondence. With all possible errors that can arise in connotation and faulty learning for example, identification, interpretation, application, and eventual selection of the symbol—if the thing warrants the symbol, it ought to get it, and if it does not, then it is an error. There are blurs and fuzzy edges, but by and large, the word "symbol" is best exemplified by "let X equal its specified equivalent (definition)." X is something. It represents something else; whatever it is assigned to represent. The symbol does the work of an algorithm even though it is consensual and often imprecise and laden with connotation. While we recognize imprecision, when we respond to a symbol at all, we respond "as if" it was precise. In no way are we arguing for the Korzybskian illusion of a language based on mathematical certainty. On the other hand, the digital logic of neurons seems to support the contention that we behave toward symbols as if they were exact. At least the speaker believes it to be when he utters it and the listener believes it to be when she hears it. And vice versa.

A symbol is used (passive voice) by people, consistently for a purpose; to represent something material or immaterial, "the unknown quantity." The "meanings" of symbols are the result of consensus. They are learned through acculturation. Dictionaries record the agreements. The emotional impact or connotation of a symbol is derived or assigned by the individual from context and is not part of social lore.

That is what makes communication precarious. The tools are precise enough, but people tend to use them imprecisely. They often misunderstand what they and others create with them. This intriguing semantic potpourri suggests that there may be considerable benefit in considering symbolic communication as an algorithmic system. It is instructive to note that when we resort to such metaphors to describe human processes, we are imposing artificial order in the sense that artificial was used by Herbert Simon (1982) to refer to the imposition of artifice on the confusing semi-entropy of human behavior.

Artificial intelligence. Artifice creates an artificial intelligence out of natural human thinking.[2] Thinking is a multidimensioned, apparently disorderly process to which order must be applied to generate output.

2. We will, no doubt, repeat redundantly, over and over again, the doggerel that artificial intelligence is an appropriate antidote for natural stupidity.

Recent innovations in artificial intelligence have exposed new knotholes through which we can view human symbolic behavior. A computer presents a possible analogy to some processes of human thought. Think of a computer that could compose discourse. The computer is a silicon environment, not a feeling creature. Like the corporation, it has no legs to be broken nor soul to be damned. The only relevant analogy between the silicon mind and the carbon mind is that both can process data according to rules. And this may be a sufficient analogy to warrant the question, Would a computer modeling the logic of the human composition process help us understand the process?

However, if we could model a complete composition system on a computer, we might learn how an orderly machine followed human rules. If the human rules were illogical, the machine would produce disorder. This would provide a basis for critique of the human rules. One way to test the rationality of human rules is to put them into an "expert system" and require a human to follow the imposed order. We could ascribe the errors we observed to human failure to follow the system or to the system itself. Both human and system are correctable.

We do not imply that our machine needs to duplicate the human composition process. This would be impossible for a great many reasons. In a pair of articles in the January 1990 *Scientific American*, John Searle and Paul and Patricia Churchland summarize the arguments about artificial intelligence. They agree that at our present level of knowledge, we cannot teach computers to think, only to simulate. But, the Churchland's argue, when more is known about how the brain works, it may be possible to produce a functioning mind (Searle, 1990, pp. 26–31; Churchland & Churchland, 1990, pp. 32–39). We are not sufficiently arrogant to argue with these authorities. In fact, our use of artificial intelligence is for critical and diagnostic purposes. We are only testing an orderly process by means of an expert system. We do not call it thought.

What our machine must do is reflect back our own logic without emotional overtones and connotations so we can observe it. We must observe the human composition process so that we can employ a calculus to reduce it to algorithmic (simple) systems. We do not believe for a moment that it is possible, but like the Greek mathematicians used calculus to approximate the error of irregular shapes, we propose to make our calculus tell us all it can about the inherent order in the composition process. What do we need to know to accomplish this?

A Metaphor for Intelligence

Speech is an output of a complicated process carried out in the mind. Consider this metaphor! The mind is composed of an infinite number of planes, each of which contains information coded as edited memories of events, symbols, and notations on value. Each plane rotates on its own axis orthogonal to all other planes, but which together form a bounded space. Forget, for a moment, the paradox of an infinite number of planes in a bounded space. It is not crucial that a metaphor be logical, especially when we are not certain about what it represents anyway.

The information is processed chemically and electrically by the brain and coded into memories of experience, real and vicarious, coded in symbols and images together with values (or affects) assigned for some reason. There is no "firsthand experience" anywhere in this system. All firsthand experience is handled by reflexes. As Freud made clear, humans do not respond to events but to their memory of events, however accurate or inaccurate.

The symbols and images are literally coded and stored as configurations of neurons in a juxtaposition of on-off positions, but having said this, we must admit that neither we nor anyone else actually knows exactly what is stored. Neurons are not normally ambiguous. They either fire or not (although sometimes some fire more strongly than others). We will not rule out the possibility of the existence of partially fired neurons. Their effect would be to impose disorder in any system based on digital neurons. We assume that neurons are digital and their configurations are regular. We believe this both because we are told that it is so (Churchland, 1987) and by the fact that we can receive, store, and retrieve information in relatively regular fashion. We do not write our own storage code. It is written and hard-wired into us genetically, and we learn to use it. When we try to get a computer to simulate our processes, we act like Baron Frankenstein and code the monster. But code it we must, somehow, and on our terms but in its language.

Now we come to a pretty pass, a paradox. We want our computer to simulate a human process so we can observe it, but we are not sure of what the human process is. We believe it to be regular and amenable to digital coding. We can try a number of regular processes to observe the effects of regularity. When we discover error or discrepancy then we can inquire whether it is because we failed to program accurately or because there were irregularities in the human processes. If there are irregularities, we seek them in idiosyncratic human response and continue to regard the system as pristine.

The rotating planes are in constant motion, responding to information from both internal and external environments and also to information derived from the operation of the planes. When information comes in, it is recorded, sometimes on an existing plane and sometimes on a new one. The sphere has limitless capacity to create new planes (since their number is infinite *in potentia*). The more experience and the more processing, the more planes and the more information, and the more sensitive and subtle the classes. Sometimes a single bit of data is stored in so many places that it becomes a category in itself and generates a new plane.

Information comes through "mysterious" processes called sensing, including relatively uncontrollable processes like seeing, touching, tasting, hearing, and smelling as well as controlled processes like looking, reading, listening, sniffing, feeling, sampling, and so on. Furthermore, the system can also respond to itself, that is, through some "mysterious" process called thought, the mind can line up one or more planes and either modify their contents or create a new plane with a record of some conclusion drawn from scrutiny of their contents.

The motion of the planes can be represented by a number of controlled operations going on simultaneously. That is, a human can see, hear, smell, touch, taste, and process in a variety of combinations. A human can manipulate consciously movable parts like limbs, body, lips, and eyelids while processes on which the body depends are carried on autonomically: heartbeat, digestion, endocrine production, circulation of blood, breathing, and so on. The question is, with all this going on simultaneously, *What controls the output?*

It is important to note that information comes in not only from the external environments but also from what the body senses about itself. The human responds to both physiological and social environments, and all information is potentially available at any moment in any combination. We do not know the limits on how much can be sensed at one time, but we know it is virtually impossible to sense only one thing at a time.

We also have not developed the technical capacity for machine simulation of thought even in the restricted and modified silicon environment despite advances in parallel distributed processing (Rumelhart et al., 1987). We can, however, use artificial intelligence to separate processes and examine them a few at a time. Where linearity is important, our simulations can achieve considerable accuracy.

The act of communicating is linear. A person can only speak or write one word at a time. We might consider speaking and writing to be digital systems, while internal processes in mind/brain defy description. They may appear as Gestalts or analogic systems. Speaking and writing are done in finite time. Time, according to that redundant adage, is nature's way of making sure everything does not happen at once. The odd thing is that a great many things happen at once inside the brain, and thus, thought is not necessarily bounded by time. It can go on when it cares to and in its own fashion. Its conscious outputs, however, are controlled by time. To achieve communication output, mental processes must be integrated so that output is controlled, structured according to rules, made relevant to social situations, produced in intelligible form, and monitored.

If we can describe how humans order information prior to output, we can discover its basic structure and code it into the machine as a system. We can test the system and use the results to guide the performance of "human systems" on whose activity the machine system is based. We need not ask the computer to compose or utter sentences. Our actual simulation so far is restricted to structuring the message.

The Requirements for Teaching a Computer to Compose

The evidence of error. We have used the twenty centuries devoted to the development of rhetorical theory as sources for the headings we will use for the major components of the process of composition of social discourse. We have chosen the Canons as the basis of our working taxonomy of components because they are relatively discrete and invariant.

By way of review, a potential speaker assesses a social situation and decides that an intervention would be productive. Next he identifies the listener and specifies the nature of the intervention. Once this is done, the speaker selects a topic, locates the ideas necessary to develop it, and puts them in order. Then he can compose paragraphs and sentences and speak them. Up to the point of where words are spoken and written, the processes are mental and not amenable to direct intervention. Our goal is to find some way to help speakers impose coherent order on their ideas and speak them in a clear and interesting manner. A secondary goal is to assist the imposition of orderly procedure on the underlying mental processes.

The effectiveness of discourse is judged by its outcome on a variety of scales: true or false, effective or ineffective, pleasant or unpleasant, right or wrong, and so on. Speakers only have control over their own speech; thus anything speakers do to impede their own effectiveness can be considered erroneous and a legitimate goal for modification. In setting personal goals, a speaker may have a strategy for evoking a response from a listener, but the actual performance consists of tactical moves. The speaker must control those tactical moves, hypothesizing that if they are executed successfully, they have a reasonable chance to attain their strategic objectives.

We identify defects in delivery by listening. We can describe and classify mispronunciations, dialects, vocalized pauses, malapropisms, inappropriate inflections, misstatements, syntactical and grammatical errors, as well as vocal flaws in intensity and quality of sound production. Many of these errors can be corrected by training and exercise. We infer errors in mental processing from observed discourse. Heuristics can be provided to facilitate correction of these errors, but the effect of the heuristics is not amenable to empirical observation.

We can identify defects in disposition by observing inappropriate word selection and disorganized sequences of ideas. These errors can be corrected by training speakers to organize and sequence their ideas.

Sequencing steps. To teach a computer to make discourse requires a taxonomy of the steps of the composition process. Regardless of the number of simultaneous processes underlying it, actual discourse proceeds one step at a time. Though composition of discourse may appear irregular, its order is imposed by the fact that the complexity of the act requires integration of brain, lungs, vocal cords, mouth area, and resonators in such a way that multiple processes are integrated into a string of discourse. Even accompanying gestures and expressions are integrated as part of the composition processes. A person cannot say two words simultaneously or make two gestures at the same time with the same hand.

The Decision Process in Composition

The difference between a genius and a retarded person does not necessarily lie in brain capacity. We can assume that each of them has essentially the same almost-infinite capacity to process information. But the genius knows what and when to report and is capable of doing so. Otherwise, who would know he or she is a genius.

Who knows what great thoughts are thought by those who do not know that they are thinking great thoughts or, if they know, do not know when to report them or, if they know when to report, are unable to do so in a skillful and convincing manner. We are what we are largely because social rules herd us into slots based on our verbal output. The causal chain is clear and simple—great thoughts yield great utterances that, in turn, yield great reputations if, and only if, the utterances are consensually regarded as evidentiary of great thoughts. Thus, a main criterion for detecting error in discourse is a social judgment on its effectiveness. (Discourse is often judged to be erroneous, if it is delivered poorly.)

How do we decide what to say and when to say it? Presumably, we have a set of decision rules we use to search memory. Consensual validation and dual perspective lead us to infer that our ways of thinking are similar to those of others. Our ability to understand one another provides evidence of this "deep structure" notion of the basis of the communication process. Because we have common physiology we have common processing rules.

We can describe our common process of collecting and organizing information by extending the metaphor of the rotating planes. The potential speaker throws a "line" into the planes in order to attract information. This process is like the statistical operations in factor analysis. The fictitious line has a kind of adhesive that attracts relevant information. Relevant is defined tautologically as information attracted by the adhesive. In theory, it also repels irrelevant information. Errors occur from applying the wrong glue or in mistaken interpretation of things that cling to the line. There are serious questions about whether things just cling or whether there is effort exerted to make them cling and even about how the glue gets made. We continue to make metaphors about this process because we cannot yet observe it.

The decision to participate in a social situation is purposive. The speaker may have a need to impress someone, control some decision, obtain a response, or release some emotion. Once the speaker makes the decision to speak to a particular audience, she searches for topics and supports. Eventually she selects a limited amount of information to transmit, codes it, arranges it, and utters it in sequential fashion.

For example, in an ordinary social conversation, a question, "How do you like the food?" may evoke the response, "Delicious!" Underlying the response could be the speaker's wish to compliment the host, impress the person who asked the question, or observe the norms of social conversation regarding food evaluation. If the speaker took the time to prepare a public speech, conversation would probably end. Social responses appear spontaneous, but they are processed in a fashion similar to formal presentations. People set goals for social discourse, although the speed at which it is carried out obscures the formality of the process.

It is hard to believe there is no command center directing such a process. On the other hand, if we go too far with this metaphor we find ourselves trapped in homuncular theory. If we decide there is a little man inside the big man running the console, then we must inquire what governs the behavior of the little man. Is it a littler man? And so on, to infinity. If we reject homuncular theory we must either accept a universe of process or one controlled by God.

If we abjure the process explanation and rely on God, we must argue that we think because God made us able to think. Or, in the words of one machine scientist, "I think I think, therefore, I think." Furthermore, trying to teach a machine to think and compose discourse is like Baron Frankenstein building his monster. Lay off, lest ye be damned. Or it might be like the centipede, who, when asked what leg he starts out with, gets so caught up in contemplating the process is never able to walk (or speak) again!

The centipede is our model of the hazard of self-reflexiveness! There are a great many natural processes that work in a sort of entropic way, that is, they work and continue to work until they are interfered with. The centipede is not a terribly intelligent beast. An inquiry into the starting leg would be sufficient to paralyze it or at least alter the operation of its motion system. We are arguing that this is precisely the kind of intervention a human makes in himself during the composition process; only some are able to tolerate the shock of formal thinking. There is interference with natural processing to apply the artifice required to coordinate the parts of the body that produce the utterance.

We do not know *how* this goes on, but we know *that* it goes on and furthermore it goes on in a fashion sufficiently similar from person to person that it is possible to generate common codes and modes of understanding and response. And that is our argument for order. And it also stipulates the limit of the theory we are laying down here. We are not inquiring into why things happen. We are only asking which of it is sufficiently orderly and replicable to be useful in the building of a technology.

And so, with all due humility, we can say we will never "know" but we can know something. The question is, What can we find out by imposing orderly procedure on the discourse process just to see how it could work if it was an orderly process?

How Machines Think

Jackson (1985, p. 5) declares "intelligence is the ability to act rightly in a given situation." He also notes (p. 8) that introspection is the main source of information about intelligence used in artificial intelligence research. Thus, "smart machines" are the result of careful, introspective, self-analysis conducted by the machinemakers, largely because machines are not able to do careful, introspective analyses of themselves.

This is an important issue, probably the essence of the difference between human and machine intelligence. The machine cannot think about itself. It is not self-reflexive. Humans may name their machines, but the names confer only identity and not ego. That is why the machine is a proper place to test the vivacious force of composition logic. If a program based on observation of human processes is able to guide a human to produce a competent composition, we have the basis for a technology of performance modification *for humans*. Remember, our quest is to discover what can be modified in way to improve rhetorical competence—*in humans, not machines!*

The essence of learning from artificial intelligence is to describe the activities to be carried out *in the given case by a given machine*. The machine we really seek to explain is the human machine. If humans compose according to standard rules from an idiosyncratic repertoire of information, our computer could be programmed heuristically, equipped with an individual human as a data set, and authorized to direct humans in the composition of discourse. If the compositions done by various humans similarly directed were themselves similar in form then we could accept the hypothesis that composition of discourse can be algorithmic.

Now consider that the machines contain vicarious human intelligence in the form of programming. Humans do not program computers in a form indigenous to silicon intelligence. In fact, what intelligence exists inside a computer is human intelligence adapted to a digital environment. The versatility and complexity of the digital environment enable humans to simulate their own intelligence as they (humans) understand it. Thus, we argue that the human is a complex machine compelled to resort to simple systems in order to output information in the form of oral and written discourse. Symbols in the form of code can be installed in a computer sufficient to command the computer to act as if it were a competent (mistake-free) human and subject to its limitations, that is, having neither legs nor soul, it could supervise and direct the process in its human master.

To render the logic less vulnerable, we need not require our computer to use a database as such. Once we have mapped our algorithms and deployed our heuristics, we can confront a human with a sophisticated expert system to guide composition. The system uses a simulation of error-free human composition logic in the form of heuristic questions to guide a human through the logical system of composing. The errors we see produced by the human-as-database would be construed as modifiable human errors in the orderly and willful component of the composition process. We presume analogous errors could be identified *in vivo*, although we could not document errors in invention nor account for errors made because of interference of the subconscious. The program can be modified when we observe consistent errors made by humans following the system.

The Crucial Role of Error

It is easy to detect error in a computerized system. When a human interacts with a computer, he must do so on the computer's terms. When a human communicates with another human, it is equally important to remain within the respondent's capabilities. In any communication process there is regression to the least capable. That is, in natural social discourse, the person with a point to make is obligated to adapt the point to the level of comprehension and felicity of the least capable listener, carry the *onus probandi* as it were. Recall that we have argued that rhetoric is actually the constraints imposed by situation and audience. Rhetoric is not carried out to gratify personal whim but to accomplish human objectives.

A felicitous calculus a la Jeremy Bentham can be generated to describe the relationship between human and human or human and machine. The machine is only functional when it can accept commands. The machine cannot tolerate ambiguity. Thus, the human communicator must arrange subjects and predicates as perfectly logical commands and encode them in a language in which the machine is capable. Such a calculus might be useful in evaluating effectiveness of discourse *in vivo* as well.

Although a basic assumption of artificial intelligence is that a machine can do human tasks but not necessarily the way humans do them, the reality in discourse is that the best a machine can do is simulate operations humans are capable of performing. Extended mathematical operations, use of fractals and pixels and other machine functions may be beyond the manual dexterity or boredom tolerance of humans, but humans could do them with somewhat the same enthusiasm that the Children of Israel had when they built the pyramids. Robotics actually renders machines capable of doing more than humans can do (mechanically), albeit the things done are still intrinsically human tasks performed in a machine environment. Thus, the errors made by a machine performing a human task according to a model derived from human thought processes will be human errors.

AN ATTEMPT AT APPLICATION

Currently training in composition and performance of discourse tends to emphasize individual differences and proceed in clinical fashion. This is especially evident in the most popular area of pedagogy, public speaking. Despite the fact that textbooks appear to offer composition systems, instructors tend to resist formalization and allow a wide range of variation in both composition and presentation. But there is no evidence that this is righteous (in a police sense). It curries creativity and nurtures idiosyncrasy. It is questionable whether it improves the learner's effectiveness at social discourse.

Data on the relationships between pedagogical methods and improvement of performance are scarcer than hen's teeth. The connections simply have not been formally studied. The professional pedagogue rests her case on "gut level feelings that things work" mostly derived from personal experience or anecdotes of others. There is, however, no way to counter the impressive argument that students at schools that do not offer public speaking courses do quite well as public speakers. No one has had the courage to compare graduates of, say, Brown University, which has no required speech course and those of Penn State at which public speaking instruction is both endemic and epidemic.

The data on altering behaviors associated with shyness are somewhat more imposing (Oerkvitz, 1975). Success can legitimately be ascribed to methods rather than instructor charisma. The problem now is to integrate this premise with machine simulation to produce a prototypical expert system for training speakers-in-general in composition and performance of discourse.

An Attempt at Modeling

An attempt was made to program Kenneth Burke's Pentad. (Phillips & Erlwcin, 1989). The five components of the Pentad subsume the five classical canons. Thus, we reasoned, if we could simulate the whole process, we would have captured the canons in a set of algorithms and heuristics.

Heuristics are statements or questions designed to "point out, stimulate interest . . . as a means of furthering investigations" and "encouraging a person to learn, discover, understand, or solve problems on his or her own as by experimenting, evaluating possible answers or solutions." Heuristics are a way to impose order on " a trial-and-error method of problem solving when an algorithmic approach is impossible."

It is impossible to take a purely algorithmic approach to the process of composing human discourse except in a machine program. An algorithm is "a set of rules for solving a problem in a finite number of steps." We do not yet know enough about how humans compose competent discourse to be totally directive about how to do it. We can, however, use rule-appearing advisories, such as systems of outlining or documenting, and formalize them into algorithmic steps.

As we demonstrated in the preceding chapter, there are trainable processes that lie outside the speaker. The examination of the Pentad enables us to locate internal and external heuristics. *Internal processing can be criticized by inference. External processing can be modified by training.* This is the crucial consideration in a technology of teaching.

Agent. The heuristics of agency refer to data and how it is deployed. The standard questions about speech purpose, audience, and topics imply that the agent is actually a database for the composition process. Whatever heuristics are implied by the other components, the agent is the person who must respond. The thought processes underlying composition exist within the agent. They are directly modifiable to the extent that they can be observed. Theoretically, they can be observed via computer modeling, but the difference between carbon and silicon intelligence makes the analog dubious, at best.

Scene. The heuristics of scene refer to the nature of talk required by a social situation. Questions must be raised about past events, and successes and failures, leading to a choice of tactics with some reasonable probability of success. The data to which heuristic questions are applied are the social situation, especially the other people present.

The crucial component is the agent's impressions. He can be asked direct questions to prod the memory process. What memories does he have of previous associations in similar scenes? What memories does he have of these particular people? If the people are strangers, how does the speaker associate them with memories of real and vicarious experience? What transferences are operating? What stereotypes does the speaker assign to the other participants? What does the speaker think the listeners know or believe about him? About his ideas? What changes does the speaker want to make in the listeners? What reason does he have to believe that such changes are possible? What does the speaker think must be done to alter the way the listeners think, believe, or behave? What hypotheses can the speaker develop about how to change the audience? What hypotheses does the speaker have about his ability to bring about such changes? What constraints exist in the situation? What does the speaker believe he can and cannot do? Formalizing the process of self-inquiry places tangible data in front of both the speaker and the potential critic.

Purpose. The purpose is generated by the agent based on analysis of the scene. It is not an automatic process, although Bitzer's "rhetorical situation" could be interpreted to mean that the process is behavioral, that is, the scene contains an exigence to be discovered by the agent. It is quite the opposite.

The speaker encounters a scene that creates an impression of alternative futures in which she plays some role. She generates goals out of her own perceptions and desires. Heuristics are necessary to confine her to selecting attainable objectives. The crux of the analysis would be to distinguish what is possible from all of the desirable possibilities. This is done by making connections between possible speaker behaviors and desirable listener outcomes. It is a process of hypothesizing and thus amenable to a sort of scientific investigation.

It is interesting to speculate about how speakers actually select goals. Does the speaker actually know what she wants from the world in general and look for it in the case at hand? For example, "I want to take control," "I want them to adore me," "I want them to listen attentively," "I want them to hear and obey"? Or does the speaker encounter a situation and ask, "Hey, what can I get out of this?" Does the speaker seek a trigger to pull: "What must I do to get them to . . . ?" Does the speaker assess what is up for grabs in the scene? "I could take my turn to talk by telling them a story." Our hypothesis is that competent composition depends on localizing, that is, finding the probabilities in the given case and fitting them to some broader personal objective.

There are heuristics external to the speaker that she can apply. For example, she can seek to modify listeners' information, attitude, or behavior. This requires her to specify listener behaviors that would be signs that the objective was attained. It is not sufficient merely for her to satisfy her own ego demands. She may appeal to standards like desire for money and goods, safety, status and reputation, power, altruism and social interest, friendship and love, and sex; the urgency to affiliate; acting out hatred and hostility; envy, taking revenge, and sheer hedonism. But she must take care not to project too much of her own value structure on others. Her decision must be based on an assessment of what it is possible to get in the given situation. She must be aware of the best, worst, and ordinary in the given case.

Clearly the complexity of this process defies programming at the moment. But the logical process is clear enough to provide a basis for a heuristic technology to guide the analysis process. For example, each goal carries with it a burden of proof. Whatever appeal is selected constrains the choice of information and tactics. This can be done by providing examples, citations, generalizations, expositions, illustrations, narrations, and so forth, appropriately delivered.

A decision must also be made about the use of emotional proofs. There is a great deal of persuasive power in the use of force, bribery, cajolery, begging and wheedling and whining, extortion and blackmail, oaths, tortures, blind faith, and related suasions. There are also gray areas like sycophancy and "viewing with alarm." It is a matter of moral choice whether the speaker uses these devices. They may have deleterious social consequences, but they can also be very effective methods of goal seeking and there is a logic to their use. Their unplanned use often results in sociopathic behavior with unfortunate consequences (imprisonment or commitment, for example.) for the user, but more often, they injure the audience. Sometimes their use is only mildly counterproductive, like pitiable behavior in shy people. For the most part, however, fidelity to rhetorical schema means that any inartistic tactics deserve evaluation in terms of efficacy exactly the same as artistic appeals.

There is a real problem in programming inartistic proofs, since they are often nonverbal. What we would have to do is account for tactical plans. The paradox lies in the fact that we apply morality to the distinctions between artistic and inartistic proofs, and morality is not an attribute of a silicon environment. It is for this reason that any contemplated program must use a human database, that is, the program must draw on human experience in making choices of tactics.

Once the speaker has selected a purpose, he must engage in a formal memory search. In the last chapter, we demonstrated that the process of structuring constrained the use of memory by organizing the search. Structural requirements for effective composition demand the orderly extraction of examples, enthymemes, metaphors, analogies, citations, narrations, aphorisms, commands, and so on, as needed to make discourse interesting and credible to others. A theoretical formal search program can be generated out of the structural requirements to satisfy *onus probandi*. The result is the individual enters the rotating planes with some idea of what to seek and can eventually extract lines of text code to form into paragraphs and sentences.

Agency. Agency is a process that exists outside of the speaker. The substance of chapter 6 was a discussion of how the requirements of structuring provide an organizing rubric for information. The process must be formal; therefore, it is compatible with the formal heuristics of structuring.

The composing process requires the speaker to generate a topic or main idea, discover a structure in which to organize the topic, select and arrange information to support the ideas, adapt the information to the targeted listener, and find markers to indicate ways and means to start, finish, and make transitions between points. The concept, "residual message," provides a useful organizing rubric by specifying what the speaker wants his audience to remember and respond to. At this point we are well into the composition process. Ordinary assessment against logical and grammatical criteria is required. We are assuming here that it is possible for a human to take control of this process.

Act. The act is the performance. This includes the words and the accompanying gestures, intonations, inflections, and pauses. The agent is the actor, but as an actor, he is amenable to control by a critic, teacher, or coach. Criticism can focus on any or all aspects of delivery, but because delivery is a formal process amenable to empirical examination, it can be measured by equipment and studied in terms of probabilities. It is the eventual stimulus that motivates the listener to respond.

All of the processing contained in the preceding processes are irrelevant if the act of delivery is ineffective.

Though we would prefer to consider art invulnerable to digital control, delivery appears programmable. Theater directors have been doing it for centuries. An actor's performance consists of a series of manageable acts. Choreography, or even simple blocking, is sufficiently digital to indicate the potential of studying delivery in a behaviorist model. The formal systems of delivery training are uniformly successful in the act of training. It is carry-over that presents the major problem. Carry-over depends mostly on motivation, another abstraction that defies programming. Still, the evidence that delivery *can* be modified is overwhelming. We refer the reader to the works of Stern (1989), Lessac (1965), Linklater (1975), Black and Irwin (1969), and Boone (1988), among others, as examples of working systems for training vocal delivery.

Recent studies of performance of top athletes (reported in popular periodicals) emphasize the point that athletes do not think about what they are doing when they do it. They have, presumably, thought about it sufficiently to make it responsive enough to appear automatic. Kicking a field goal does not allow the kicker the luxury of counting steps or ruminating on charging linebackers. The plan must be operationalized in programmatic form.

Problems in Programming the Invention Process

Our first problem is that the only way we can understand the process of invention is by inference from performance. We do not have a direct and formal explanation of the process of thought. Therefore, we have no way to account for perceptions of exigence and selection of social goals other than the testimony of the speaker.

The second problem is that we cannot account, in advance, for the way a listener will respond to discourse. We can attempt to explain it only after we observe it. Therefore, we must operate from probabilities. The writing of sentences is, literally, a mathematical consideration. There are certain combinations of phonemes that are intelligible in a given language group. The person engaging in social discourse must take care to adhere to the rules for juxtaposition of words in that language group. Individual words may be intelligible, but when they are combined, they can become unintelligible if the rules are not followed.

It is not germane to this discussion to discover the source of the rules. We need not defend deep structures. In fact, once we have discovered what people do, we can impose order on discourse even if it means limiting ideas. We can subordinate ideas, make one idea conditional on another, exemplify, illustrate, show similarities and differences, exclude, and so on. Theoretically, there are algorithms that can take subject and predicate and form them into sentences, although program writers have not succeeded in working out the "bugs" associated with problems in idiom, synonymy, idiosyncrasy that characterize most languages. We do not propose to design a computer program to write sentences. We *do* propose to guide the composition process so that the sentences the speaker naturally produces assume a form in which they are intelligible and interesting to listeners. This process has been described in the preceding chapter.

Machine simulation of the process of invention and style seems impossible at the moment because of the complexity of databases. In our metaphor, we regard each speaker as a database. A human database is always incomplete. It contains some common data and some personal data. Sometimes, a search of a human database is fruitless; information must be sought outside. The human can also create fictions or lies.

Goals and appeals. Once the speaker is presented with alternatives, the criteria for selection are related to listener motivation. In humans, this process is still "mysterious," that is, we have evidence that it happens, but we do not know the algorithms by which the mind carries it out. The speaker must make the best guess possible of the listeners' needs and wants and synthesize them with his own in order to guide the goal-setting process in rational directions.

The possible goals and appeals appear to be limited. They arise out of a common literacy. Psychologists have studied them and generated some theoretical lists that could serve as heuristics. For example: survival, safety, acquisitiveness, pleasure, hedonism and sexual arousal, the general welfare. status, altruism, and so on.

The preceding list does not presume to be exhaustive. It is presented merely as a sample of the categories that could be included in a taxonomy of appeals should one want to attempt to write it. Selection of a given appeal suggests a proper structure, for example, "You should seek status because . . . " implies an argument; or "You may achieve safety by . . . " implies a set of directions. Once the choice has been made, the process can become external, formalized, and amenable to a technology of instruction.

Problems in audience analysis. There are some simple questions that must be raised about any audience.

—To whom do I want to speak? What does the listener know about me and my ideas? Why do I believe this? The questions obviate errors in her assumptions. The fact that people do not normally question the fidelity of their analogies is a source of error. We presume we have seen accurately and inferred appropriately. Heuristic questions constrain us to question these assumptions. The first heuristic is, "How do I know what I think I know." The others follow from that.
—What does the listener believe about me and my ideas? Why do I believe this?
—What attitude does the listener have toward what I want him/her/them to know, believe, feel, or do? Are they hostile (to what degree), favorable (to what degree) or neutral?
—What are the natural behaviors the listener uses to show approval and disapproval?

The answers to these questions are subjective. Sometimes they come from noetic revelation, transfer, and pressure from the unconscious. But, once answered, they can guide subsequent preparation. What is more important is that they give a cue to self-esteem.

Self-esteem is an ephemeral that cannot be managed with a program. A speaker must believe himself capable of speaking before he speaks. The question of how much of what kind of evidence a person needs before self-esteem is sufficient to support discourse is intriguing philosophically and defiant of any empirical measurement. Still, it is a consideration that must be taken, and which further impedes the possibility of programming the entire composition process.

THE MAJOR OPERATIONS

Exactly what would it take to program discourse? Given that most of it is impossible, an examination of the orderly and disorderly processes can provide genuine insight into the variables that affect competency. The quest for order is also a quest for the basis of the content of a pedagogy.

Sequencing the Steps

There is *a* sequence of operations. We do not know yet whether it is *the* sequence. While we respect the hard-wiring notions embodied in Chomsky's deep structures, it does not mean that all humans compose in the same fashion. On the other hand, the principle of dual perspective implies they are similar enough so we can presume consistency in both composition and understanding.

In a tentatively sequential order, here is what we think takes place, acknowledging at the outset that some processes are simultaneous.

1. Impressions from a social situation are processed.
2. A decision is made to intervene with discourse.
3. An audience is selected.
4. A purpose is defined.
5. Information is sought about the audience and situation.
6. The specific goal of the intervention is defined.
7. Criteria for identifying whether the goal is accomplished are specified.
8. The message or appeal is chosen.
9. Topics to support the message are discovered.
10. A main structure for the presentation is selected.
11. The content of the message is arranged in the structure.
12. Structuring continues down to the sentence level.
13. The utterance is delivered.
14. The result is monitored and analyzed and the process continues.

The programming possibilities. If we were to take a stab at programming invention, however, we could discover some of the logical sequences potentially amenable to instruction. For example, we could take some topical headings, say, from Aristotle's *Organon* and Roget's *Thesaurus* and use them as key words to help a potential speaker choose sayables. We could phrase them as heuristic questions to be applied to any issue. For example, we could apply them to "shyness:"

Essential Qualities: What must a person be or do in order to be shy? Does this person fit the category?

Description: What does a shy person look like, sound like, feel like, act like? Similarly, about any noun, we could ask: How tall, long, or wide is it? Is it rough or smooth? Creamy or lumpy? And so on.

Taxonomy: What categories of shyness are there? Are shy people neurotic? Are they inept? Are they lovable? What are the demographics of shyness?

We could continue the process by examining various properties of shyness (or anything else) such as economic value, strength, location, relationship, similarities and differences from whatever, the emotions it evokes, and so on. The speaker can use these questions and the resulting answers as a source of ideas (examples and enthymemes) to fit into the structure of his discourse.

It is clear how the process could be facilitated by machine programming. We are not controlling or training thinking, but we are helping the composition process by organizing the results of thinking. Robert Nisbet (1977) suggests that the process of thought could be guided by metaphors such as landscape, portrait, climate, mathematical formula, growth, absurdity, demonic, diorama, divinity, machine, loving, national state or formal organization, court, family, decay, vengeance, rejection/hatred/contempt, desire for extinction, repair, laboratory analysis, and so on. People relating in society can be portrayed as friend, lover, colleague, enemy, superordinate, subordinate, hero, significant other, conscience or superego, adviser, healer, nemesis, *Gegenspieler*, stranger, military formation, teammate, parent, pet, slave, and so on. The nuances of metaphoric topics play a major role in making a speaker's words acceptable to a listener. They too could function as heuristics in a machine program designed to facilitate composition.

Eventually a decision must be made on the utility of enthymemes and examples derived from metaphor. Metaphors are fictions and reifications; enthymemes and examples used in argument must be empirical. Confirmation is imperative in documenting credibility. Our intelligent machine, like its human analog, must face the issue of how to decide what kinds of statements are cogent. This is mainly a matter of criticism. A human makes such decisions by reviewing experience or out of habit or by instinct. A computer might review a database and form habits by playing probabilities, but instinct seems defiant of programming. It is at this essentially literary point in the invention of discourse that the prospect of machine programming of the entire process of composition breaks down.

This does not mean the process is disorderly, however. It merely means that the process is so complicated that even the humans that carry it out cannot explain it. It is not a simple matter of problem solving as in Dewey's *How We Think* (1935) or Perkins' *The Mind's Best Work* (1981). The description of the Grevitz exercise in chapter 6 indicates how difficult it is to understand the logic of the obvious. Rhetorical invention, or thought, for the moment has best remain the province of the philosopher and neurophysiologist.

The Formal Process

The penultimate step in the composition process is the forming of a structure. Theory of structuring conceives of discourse as teleological. The guiding rubric or purpose of discourse shapes the components of discourse. However, possible cognitive goals are limited by the available structures. Communication can only take place when the message sent is cognate to the message received. Thus, the social conventions about connection of ideas must be observed however uncreative they may seem.

The personal and interpersonal goals to be achieved through social discourse present another mystery, another component of the invention process. We intend, however, to demonstrate in the final chapter of this book that they too are amenable to order. But, once the goal is specified, the topic determined, ideas discovered, and adjustments to the audience made, the formal process of arrangement proceeds through a system of structuring and substructuring. This was the focus of the previous chapter and represents the component of the process of composition most amenable to formal instruction.

The important point to be made here is that when we proceed to form the structure, we make the move from the complex multidimensioned processing that characterizes invention or thought to the simple system of arranging ideas and uttering them that characterizes presentation.

However refined and sophisticated thinking might be, it can only be evaluated when it is communicated. In talk or on paper, this is one word after another. Paper words occupy space and visual attention and take time to read. Oral words occupy time and auditory attention and take time to hear. In both cases, they must be interpreted by the listener who must then make decisions about an answer. This returns the process, once again, to invention or thought. At this point, we discover that artificial intelligence could well be the antidote for natural stupidity.

Connections and Transitions

The final step in the composition process is to connect each outline point through the use of transitional terms. The process of structuring and deploying supports brings the speaker to phrasing. This is done initially by connecting the components of the structure with connective terms including but not confined to:

Linkers: And, but, or now, so
Subordinators: Because, since, although, if, as although, however, in
   order that, so that, after, before, once, since, until, when, whenever,
   while, whether, that
Correlators: Either . . . or, neither . . . nor, both . . . and, not only . . .
   but

Adders: Also, besides, furthermore, moreover, too, in fact, in addition,
    that is to say, to be sure
Distinction Markers: Anyway, however, nevertheless, on the contrary, on
    one hand . . . on the other
Illustrators: For example, for instance, namely, that is
Consequentials: Accordingly, for instance, namely, that is
Orienters: First/second/etc., further, later, then, to begin, in conclusion,
    finally

At this point the speaker must select specific words, a process usefully
described by linguists sufficiently so that modestly successful efforts have
been made efforts at machine composition of sentences.

AN INTERNAL SUMMARY

The fundamental premise of the theory: pedagogical effectiveness is
attained by guiding formal acts of composition. Effectiveness of social
discourse is measured by its influence on the events and people toward
which or whom it is directed. Evaluation is not simple, however, since
it includes observation of the effects of discourse on listeners followed
by the speaker's assessment of events. In no case can we assert that any
given modification has a particular impact.

Substantiation of the theory depends on simulation. We argue that
the process of composition has integrity apart from its existence in a
carbon intelligence, and that this integrity of process can be simulated
in a silicon intelligence in such a way that error can be detected. In
order to do the simulation, we must observe the composition process
carefully as it is conducted by humans. Furthermore, we cannot compro-
mise our program by making it entirely binary. We must, in fact, depend
on a cyborg, a human database inserted in the circuit of composition
heuristics and algorithms, to demonstrate in an observable milieu the
possible errors in the process. What we will do is discover the heuristics
of composition, confront our human database with them and direct a
composition, then analyze the final composition as we apply the algorithms of direct discourse.

We justify this process in biomedical research. Our initial purpose
in this book was to discuss how shy people can become more effective
communicators. We agonized about whether shyness was a pathology
or a critical state identifiable by a social label. We discovered it did not
matter. Whatever the etiology, shy people are ineffective communicators. We decided that our goal was to make them more effective. To

achieve this means that they must modify their behavior. Our question was to discover what modifications to make, to avoid the ambiguous and global advisories about internal processes and to concentrate on recommendation of acts that can be modified.

Like it or not, we now have a pathology. We may not meet the standards for the medical model, but we can use a model from medicine as a basis for justification of our theoretical quest. It is simply this: biomedical research is a life-and-death matter. If the researcher makes an error, the organism to which the error applies will very likely die. While inept speakers do not die because they attempt to follow inapposite advice, they are certainly injured. Our idea is to find a sufficient way to test our therapeutic propositions before they are applied, so we can at least meet the minimum criterion of administering no deadly medicines.

In biomedical research the idea is to find out how much of a substance will cure the disease without hurting the human being more than the disease itself. All drug interventions are dangerous and all have potential impact. Investigation of the effectiveness of drugs begins with consideration of theoretical impacts. These are modeled on the computer and those deemed promising are then tested on animals. The formal and specified procedures for working up a drug take years, and all safeguards must be honored. We have not been quite so careful in human interventions. For two millennia we have been trying to improve speaking performance by offering recommendations to students, and we have little information that consoles us with our success.

Our problem may well be that we have never applied orderly procedure to our quest. We are arguing here that by modeling the composition through artificial intelligence, we are offered at least one scientifically based way to test the efficacy of propositions about how communication behavior can be effectively modified. Unfortunately, we do not have the ability to test our methods on intermediate animals, since there is a definite scarcity of other speaking animals. On the other hand, if our theory is accurate, we can have more than a theoretical (or wishful thinking) belief that a method of intervention will be effective.

8

Reducing Reifications to Behaviors

THE PROBLEM OF DOING RESEARCH IN PEDAGOGY OF SOCIAL PERFORMANCE

It is difficult to test a pedagogical theory. The kind of control available to hard scientists is not available to those who measure behavior changes. Furthermore, human ecology, internal and external, provides a virtual infinity of potential influences on human behavior; and they interact. Thus, measurements of effectiveness must be relatively gross. On the other hand, they should be somewhat more scientific than the narratives of success swapped at fireside in the faculty club.

Measurements of effectiveness of teaching methodologies, to date, have been nothing more than defenses of the obvious. We model examinations after the New York Regents to measure subject-matter mastery and infer that teaching had something to do with success and failure. (We are becoming more aware, however, of the influence of social and economic factors.) The most widely used measures are popularity polls. We ask students to report what they think of this or that teacher, but this kind of measurement places emphasis on personality rather than methodology. For the most part, we rely on teacher reports of what they think worked.

We cannot do "double-blind" experiments in education or social science. Because instruction is mostly "delivered" by humans, we have a hard time holding independent variables constant across conditions.

Thus, when we define a particular methodology as a dependent variable, our measures are confounded by the power of teacher personality.

It seems obvious, of course, that teachers influence students, but it is not clear whether they actually "teach" them. It is more rational to regard teachers as "vectors," that is, means by which instruction is delivered.

In addition to all this, people have a right to be left alone. We cannot tamper with them as if they were laboratory animals. We can only teach those who come to be taught. This eliminates the possibility of random sampling in any kind of experiments. Our conclusions are necessarily confined only to our observations of the students who happen to be there.

The final problem in research in pedagogy of social communication is that it is mainly based on criticism. We may find it simple enough to detect what errors a student is making. It is considerably more complicated to find a way to get the student to accept his or her behavior as erroneous. And once teacher and student agree that a behavior must be modified, finding the proper technology of modification and implementing it is a very difficult task.

Problems Assessing the Effects of Criticism

In ordinary life, people learn through criticism. Parents and teachers correct childrens' behavior. Children learn whom to trust and believe and whom to ignore. Gratuitous criticism, in any case, is an invasion of privacy, but in reality, our response to anyone else represents gratuitous criticism. If people like us, they modify in accord with what they think we want (to the extent they can). If they do not like us, they get away from us. If they cannot get away (as from a mother or boss), they do their best to ignore us or give absolute minimum compliance (AMC for acronymophiles).

There is a natural tendency to hold parents responsible for the sins of their children. The implication is that those who offend were improperly trained in the home. Separating parental influence from influence of schools, peers, and unexpected events is a matter of argument, however. Furthermore, for criticism to be effective, it has to be accepted.

People have a right to take what criticism they like. On the other hand, they are required to take whatever social consequences attend upon their social incompetence. Teachers have no right to change per-

sonality, but they must teach students what they need to know to participate in the classroom; and sometimes this changes personality.

There are some genuine issues of privacy and civil liberties in the
formal teaching of writing and speaking. It is one thing to teach general
propositions about communication and associate them with the skills
generally required for survival in society. It is something else again to
require people to subject themselves involuntarily to what they might
see as remedial programs. We might consider even the most innocuous
course in public speaking as (in a sense) remedial, since all performance
instruction seeks to alter public performance behavior, hence social
appearance, hence social evaluation, hence personality.

We could, of course, operate in a Darwinian model and let those
who, somehow, learn to be skillful, win the rewards. Furthermore, it is
not necessary to compensate the inept. People have the right to choose
to fail. Moreover, it is impractical to try to modify the performance
behavior of an unwilling student.[1] The best that can be hoped for is a
kind of grudging compliance to the letter of the law like "Good Soldier
Schweik." In most cases the unwilling students does his best to ignore
instruction or forget it as soon as it is given. (A recent study of more
than a thousand public speaking students during the last week of the
course showed that 50 percent had not yet learned their instructor's
name.)

Given the constraining propositions that the instructional process
must be voluntary and is, by nature, clinical, we face the question of
whether we know anything about it. The lore, handed down from
generation to generation about how to teach public speaking and related
formal performance skills has little to offer to a pedagogy of performance
modification. There is no official "way to teach" public speaking. In
fact, most instructors devote themselves to teaching theory in the hope
it will enable students to modify themselves. This is not an altogether
bad choice. It does little harm, and it sometimes alerts students to
deficiencies. The problem comes when they inquire about what to do
about their perceived inadequacies, especially those perceived by others.

People are concerned about what people think of them. Therefore,
they are often responsive to programs that offer improvement. They are
wary, however, of instruction that requires them to make choices. They
seem drawn to formulary programs like Dale Carnegie or Toastmasters.

1. Murphy's Law on this matter goes as follows: Don't try to teach a pig to sing. In the
first place, it's impossible. In the second place, the pig don't like it.

Students prefer programs that offer them techniques for acquiring specific skills. (Our survey showed they preferred to learn about organization of ideas and techniques of delivery rather than theoretical matter.)

They also like courses that promise to help them manage their feelings. This complicates programs that seek to modify performance behavior. Our experience with the Penn State Reticence Program showed that it takes a lot of work to distract students from talking about how they feel. Even the most reticent can get eloquent when given free opportunity to discuss their feelings. (The whole profession of psychoanalysis is based on this proposition.) Given these barriers, how then can an instructional technology designed to modify performance behavior proceed?

SYSTEMATIC INVESTIGATION OF METHODS FOR TEACHING SOCIAL COMMUNICATION

To date, there has been little systematic study of pedagogical methods for teaching social discourse skills. Teachers are left pretty much to their own devices to decide which techniques to apply in the classroom. As a result, a great many presume to teach the whole Canon; they try to teach thinking and literacy as they emphasize originality in topic selection and creativity in approach.

Each teacher is his own scientist as he develops a repertoire of effective teaching devices. But it is hard to document the effectiveness of any given technique to outsiders. Testimonial, in fact, is the only available method.

Furthermore, many teaching techniques are effective only in the hands of the teacher who invented them. They depend on the power of the teacher's personality. Charismatic teaching characterizes most instruction in oral performance behavior. In fact, the typical speech teacher will document his success by claiming his students "like him." Most students express their satisfaction when they do their course evaluations, although it is questionable what they are actually evaluating. There have been no formal efforts to compare the actual speaking of students under Condition A versus Condition B. If would be very threatening, professionally, to have third-party experts evaluate comparatively the skills of various teachers students.

Effectiveness may, furthermore, be independent of satisfaction. The student who is satisfied with instruction may not have changed. In fact, there is the gnawing suspicion that students are most satisfied when instruction confirms their identity and their biases, and they are not required to change at all. They do cosmetic performances for the instructor confirming both their own and the instructor's identity. They may carry nothing out of the classroom into their lives.

Learning is not necessarily fun, although it can be gratifying. Modifying the communication habits that underlie human personality requires considerable time and energy. A person can claim to be improved when others take note of changes and adapt to them. It can produce an epiphany when the person who changed notices being noticed. It is spurious when the individual feels changed but continues to behave in the same way. It can produce despair when the individual becomes depressed by the fact that there has been no change.

The Scientific Method and Pedagogical Studies

Systematic study must necessarily focus on means and methods of modifying behavior. The purpose of any systematic research is to achieve prediction and control. The numeric metaphor that underlies the scientific method requires that the units of measure behave sufficiently like numbers to warrant extrapolation of conclusions about the behavior of numbers to the objects under investigation. Such precision is clearly not possible with social communication. Generalizations are hard to defend. Thus, individual teachers find it convenient to claim individual successes rather than defend any technology of instruction.

Pure science is based on models or paradigms. Applied science emphasizes reliable solutions to real problems. Social science produces advice about options or suggests alternative explanations. Philosophy provides rational and convincing explanations in the absence of scientific evidence. In any case, these forms of wisdom employ rhetoric to convince people of the purity and merit of their conclusions. They also employ metaphors to make the conclusions clear and persuasive to others.

The main problem in studying modification of performance behavior, however, is that the objects of study will not hold still. Humans have the power to control much of their own behavior, defying scientific explanation of it. Thus, we study the physiology of oral discourse scientifically, the process of relationships via social science, and the meaning of social behavior philosophically.

But, it is hard, when we study behavior modification, to pin down just what we can draw conclusions about. Our generalizations are always excessively broad, for example, if a person fears a communication situation, he or she may not perform well. Then again, he or she might, since we do not know precisely how expressions of fear relate to behavior or even whether expressions of fear are reliable indicators of whether a person is fearful. In fact, the word *fear* is not even a genuine noun. It is a descriptive label for a situational mental state.

Our generalizations, actually, function best when phrased as heuristics applied to the given case. For example, what role does fear play in this performer's case? What role does unfamiliarity play? How about motivation? Lack of experience? Each case of rhetorical incompetence contains its unique combination of influences and effects. It makes it hard enough to manage in a classroom let alone a laboratory.

What we learn from questionnaires is questionable. It is one thing to ask a person how he feels about a situation or what he believes he would do on a particular occasion. It is quite another thing to observe his behavior and draw inferences about what he might have been thinking. The verbal reports on the questionnaire can be quite misleading. They lack predictive power because we cannot see the behavior associated with the items on the scale. Thus, if we measure the effects of therapy by changes in scores on the tests, we do not know what we have changed besides the scores themselves. We must also concede the possibility that the tests may have an iatrogenic effect, suggesting possible feelings and behaviors to the subjects.

Consider the wide variations in conclusions drawn by people who have studied deficient socialization or shyness. McCroskey (1970, 1972, 1978, 1984; McCroskey & Richmond, 1982a, 1982b) asserts that anxiety in a given social situation can impede communication and thus, by removing anxiety, communication can be improved. My own arguments (Phillips, 1965, 1968, 1973, 1977, 1980, 1981, 1982, 1984, 1986a, 1986b; Phillips & Butt, 1967; Phillips & Metzger, 1973; Phillips & Sokoloff, 1976, 1979) claim that social reticence arises from lack of skill or perceived lack of skill. Shyness specialists like Buss (1986) and Zimbardo (1977, 1986) ascribe communication problems to some kind of personality disorder or problem with self-esteem, while Kagan (1986) ascribes the difficulty to genetic factors.

None of the assertions are true, none false, and furthermore, none can be demonstrated with scientific certainty. They can only be argued and applied in the given case. People who do not perform well socially probably lack some skills, are anxious about it, and may have personality problems because of it. They may have even been born with tendencies to withdraw from socialization. In fact, ascribing behavior to genetic influences is a kind of a cop-out. Regardless of what a person inherits, he is still required to function in a personal social milieu and thus will develop a personal repertoire of social behaviors. In any case, some change is possible.

Public-speaking training exemplifies the problem of identifying, classifying, and measuring communication incompetencies. A teacher can notice a defective outline or sloppy delivery. Ascribing a cause is somewhat more difficult. There is little or nothing that can be measured, no data about causal connections. The universals requisite for diagnosis and treatment in a medical sense are simply not present, nor are the clearly defined variables necessary to scientific investigation.

Systematic Study and the Clinical Model

Rejection of the medical model precludes formal scientific investigation. However, this does not mean we cannot examine incompetent social communication systematically. Indeed, many "findings" about shyness, for example, have come from the study of large numbers of people in consistent conditions. But there are real questions about the usefulness of the findings. What can a teacher do about loneliness or lack of self-esteem? Presence in a class makes it more difficult to be lonely; encouragement and praise for successes might help self-esteem, but neither condition is a legitimate objective for classroom instruction.

The idea of "knowing" the student is also intriguing. It would be useful to know how a student acts in natural conditions, but this would require a complex case history from each class member. Furthermore, all it could possibly do is give some insight into the causes of the problem. While it is interesting to speculate on causes, there is nothing that can be done about them in class either. A teacher cannot alter genetic programming or rerun the student through elementary school training. Thus, instruction must be essentially traditional, twenty or so students sitting in a classroom working through a common syllabus.

If, however, we want to operate clinically, which, incidentally, seems to be warranted by the rhetorical approach, we ought to look carefully at the basic clinical model. It is important to understand that clinical medicine is far from an exact science. Medical science produces information about events in the body from which generalizations can be made about what is "normal," but the clinical physician must concentrate on the specific patient, because human physiology varies widely and people react differently to the same pills. In the final crunch, knowledge of anatomy and physiology defines a range of possibilities, it constrains medical choices only by setting outer limits.

There are some intriguing subtleties in clinical medicine. Despite generalizations about blood pressure or any other body process, the doctor is dependent on the patient for reports about his or her reaction to the conditions that determine the illness. Diagnosis can rarely be made without some oral report. The physician depends on the patient to evaluate the effects of both pathology and treatment and to provide information that the doctor cannot obtain through the use of instruments and tests. Even machine tests like EKG or angiogram are open to interpretation and debate, despite their scientific appearance. Recommendations for treatment or surgery are, in the final crunch, judgment calls that, in the given case, are the reason for soliciting "second opinions."

The analogy to training people to be skillful communicators should be obvious. There are generalizations relevant to what a person must do to be effective. There are obvious constraints imposed by physical and intellectual capability. There are only a limited number of assignments, programs, and exercises that are demonstrably effective. Optimum instruction demands that the teacher make the best possible match between problems, remedies, and student capabilities.

Clinical psychiatry. Psychiatric problems are even more difficult to deal with because of imprecise language. Physicians can objectivize most of the nouns referring to pathological conditions. A psychiatrist often cannot. A problem like depression cannot be described objectively. The patient may talk about being "blue" or "having a downer," while the psychiatrist may use the somewhat more impressive "dysphoria," but in any case, the language is either a report of internal feelings not amenable to confirmation or the psychiatrist's informed *opinion* based on observation and patient report. Thesauruses give testimony to the indescribable quality of human sensations. We give names to what we feel, but we depend on dual perspective for our empathy. Sensations, says Wittgenstein, are nothing until we name them.

The words we use to name them are limited, but they can apply to a virtual infinity of sensations. Once a reference to a sensation becomes lingua franca it takes on the ability to confuse us. How does one distinguish between a person who is "having a downer" and one who is "blue"? The answer is by social consensus about linguistic denotation and connotation. The consensus, however, may have little to do with how the person feels.

The diagnosis of speaking problems is more like psychiatric than medical diagnosis. McCroskey (1986) defines communication apprehension as a "broadly based anxiety related to oral communication" measured by a twenty-four item scale. Phillips (1986) defines reticence as a condition that exists when "people avoid communication because they believe they will lose more by talking than by remaining silent." Buss (1986) describes shyness as "discomfort, inhibition, and awkwardness in social situations, especially with people who are not familiar" with the social situations. Each definition depends on personal reports and social judgments. There are no symptoms characteristic of each case, nor is there a common etiology. Thus, there is no available "treatment of record."

When we evaluate speaking, we rely on our experience, real and vicarious, which leads us to some kind of debatable judgment about whether something is wrong and if so what. Decisions on what to do about it are generally consensual between instructor/clinician and student/client.[2]

The biggest problem in modifying inept performance behavior is the student/client's preoccupation with feelings. We simply do not know how the client feels, even though she may tell us a lot about it. Some people enjoy talking about their emotions; others are Gary Cooper-like. But the only benefit from talking about feelings is the practice at talking. The teacher really does not have the time to sit and listen to a student talk about her anxieties and fears. We simply admit they exist, to some degree, for everyone.

Furthermore, this is not what we are out to modify. We are not practicing palliative teaching. Palliative medicine depends on client reports of "feeling better." But there is no point to palliation when our goal is to modify behavior. We believe on good authority that as the student becomes more skillful, they will feel less anxious and fearful. If fear and anxiety remain crippling for a few, there are clinical psychologists willing and able to work directly on the problem. The pedagogical

2. There is the apocryphal story about the three baseball umpires, the first of whom said, "I call 'em as I see 'em!" The second counters with, "I call 'em as they are!" The third smiles smugly and tops them all with, "they are nothing til I call 'em." There are some speech pathologies that "are" something. A cleft palate can be located and confirmed, and a stutter can be identified phonetically, although the severity is a matter of judgment. Problems like "poor organization," or "lack of vivacity" are about as precise as a morning-after-the-opening movie review.

imperative is to achieve consensus between teacher and student on precisely what behavior is inept and precisely what is to be changed. It is exactly what goes on in psychotherapy. In fact, group psychotherapy is firmly grounded in the premise that people with different problems may still be profitably treated together. Furthermore, the principle of the support group, especially for social pathologies, is also based on the premise of common treatment being effective even when people have problems that are quite different in etiology.

Operational definitions. Our epistemological propensities bias the way we label a condition. Those trained in communication apprehension or shyness will tend to talk about feelings. Those oriented toward psychology may refer to rearing; sociologists will emphasize peer influences. This kind of diagnosis does not provide sufficient data to support teaching, training, or therapy, but it does provide interesting debate topics. Only operational definitions based on observed behaviors can provide a useful basis for performance modification.

An operational definition for the process of modification is also necessary. We need to distinguish between teaching, therapy, and training. Teaching is required when cognitive restructuring is necessary. When a student does not understand a process or know the meaning of important words, for example, he does not know what an "exigence" is, the *teacher* provides simple explanations and examples.

When the student displays diagnosable pathologies, like stuttering or lisping, therapy is indicated. A *therapist* is most effective in problems of delivery that can be remedied through prosthesis, surgery, and various forms of physical manipulation and drill. It is also useful when anxiety is sufficiently pathological to qualify as a phobia or when there are personality or character problems that qualify for diagnosis under the specifications in *DSM/III*.

Most modification of speech performance behavior comes through training. Training is based on the joint judgment of a critic and trainee that a particular behavior requires modification. *Trainer* and trainee work together to generate a training plan or procedure that would include exercises and assignments and a mode of evaluating progress. Training takes place at regular intervals until both parties are satisfied that it has either effected the desired change, or that the change is impossible.

THE PERVASIVE PROBLEM OF REIFICATION

The biggest problem in management of incompetencies in social discourse lies in the language we use to talk about it. So much of the talk about talk is metaphoric and abstract, it is hard to find labels to identify performance deficiencies.

Metaphor and the Study of Social Communication Problems

Limits on conclusions. A good metaphormaker has considerable power in the social sciences. By discovering similarities in apparently dissimilar situations and applying a metaphor to identify them, a social scholar can take advantage of aggregated data and use it to support argument on behalf of a particular point of view. Communication apprehension, reticence, shyness, and rhetorical incompetence are useful metaphors. They can help us understand *possibilities* in the individual case. Often, the metaphors provide us with heuristics we can use to identify associated behaviors.

The words of Combs and Snygg (1959) bear repeating because they capture the essence of the problem of modifying human behavior when they declare, "Everything we do seems reasonable and necessary at the time we are doing it. When we look at other people from an external, objective point of view, their behavior may seem irrational because we do not experience things as they do." They go on to offer this caveat. "However capricious, irrelevant and irrational his behavior may appear to an outsider, from his point of view at that instant his behavior is purposeful, relevant, and pertinent to the situation as he understands it. How it appears to others has no bearing on . . . causes of . . . behavior." This suggests that it may be our fate to deal forever with the given case. We may not be able to draw conclusions about the causes of behaviors. If we find generalizations at all, we would hope they were about pedagogical tactics and their effect on particular behaviors.

Impressions. Those who study problems in social communication generally study abstract nouns and metaphor, as opposed to the behaviors to which those words and metaphors are applied. They do not study individual speech acts such as breathing, phonation, articulation, and resonance. In fact, those processes can be measured with considerable precision and when they are deviant, specific treatments are indicated. The distortion in sound production caused by defects in the oral cavity like cleft palate can be treated by prosthesis and breathing and articulation exercises. Even minimal distortions in sounds characteristic of regional dialect or foreign accents can be modified through formal exercise. It is possible to establish ranges of normality and deviations with considerable precision.

But social communication is considerably more than the processes by which it is produced. Even the substance of social communication, "symbols," "phonemes to which meaning has been attached," "thought units," "rhetoric," "persuasion," "organization," "argument," "supports," can be classified with fair reliability, as can labels attached to problems like "communication apprehension," "shyness," "reticence," and "rhetorical incompetency." The classifications, however, are always imprecise. Rhetorical competence means more than accurate and grammatical production of words and intelligible deployment. To be effective requires that the speaker make choices about both the form and content of discourse and execute it well. The complexity of the process drives us into the use of reifications, for there is no other way to discuss the issue.

While the names applied to speaking problems and other communication concepts appear to be nouns, they are actually labels for critical categories that act like adjectives. They may be names given to collective judgments or conceptual abstractions. But they do not refer consistently to the same activities. In order to understand them, one must discover their referents, which can vary in individual cases. Even the common term *audience*, for example, is an abstraction referring to a bit of behavior large numbers of people have when they listen to discourse. There is no agreement, however, about whether *audience* refers to the common behavior of a collectivity or the aggregate of behavior of individuals. Whom does a speaker address when he speaks to an audience? Is it everyone at once, the least common denominator of beliefs, knowledge, and behavior, or is it to individual people whose knowledge, beliefs, and behaviors are inferred from observation while the speech is going on.

One last example: to the ordinary person, "listening" refers not to a state of the nervous system of an organism receiving sound waves but to a process of receiving information from talk. The physical process is inferred, except for those who measure it. Those who measure the physical accoutrements of talk are not necessarily concerned with its content. Talk may be described in terms of sound waves, phonemes, or paragraphs, depending on whether the person doing so is a scientist or critic. To listener, talk is a stimulus that, in some fashion, puts information into line for processing. Listening appears as a concrete and describable process, and so it is to the scientist. But in its relevant form, it is a common term to describe many uncommon operations, unique to the individuals carrying them on. Thus, we have difficulty defining concepts like "rhetorical incompetence" because it is extraordinarily difficult to find out what is reasonable or normal.

Our problem is how to synthesize whatever generalizations we can get with the relevant data about the given case. We cannot escape our responsibility to base teaching and training on clinical data. In this sense, our attempts to modify performance behavior resemble therapy. We have the same burden as the internist or psychiatrist to take what we know about humans in general and apply it to a particular person. If we avoid the individual case, we can be trapped by our reifications. Our generalizations provide us with working heuristics; our reifications guide us to referents that will vary from case to case. They help us understand what to look for but they do not tell us what we will find. The decision about what is and what to do about it is, when the rubber hits the road, a contract between trainer and trainer, teacher and student, clinician and client, doctor and patient.

Normality. Teaching and training are mainly for normal people. People who do not fit within specified boundaries are regarded as abnormal, thus candidates for therapy or special education. The education process is laden with connotations and relatively devoid of objective specifications. It is hard to escape the easy tautology that anyone who does not respond normally is abnormal and therefore entitled to treatment as an exception. Educators escaped the trap by making a great to-do about individual differences. The catch is that despite individual differences, instruction is administered to groups (classes) in which it is impossible to deal with individual differences. For those who are so deviant that they do not fit into a normal aggregate, abnormal aggregates are created.

The notion of abnormality comes from the medical model, and it is a difficult concept with which to deal. The word *shy*, for example, has pejorative connotations. Shy people are not quite with it. They may be cute and cuddly and reassuring to have around because they do not interrupt, but they are regarded as lacking in some *je ne sais quoi*, which, in essence, makes them abnormal.

Normal people are normal because they act normally, and because they act normally, they are called "normal." It is a neat tautology. It can only be interfered with by altering the definition of the word. For example, people with normal temperature will, when checked, read 98.6 degrees on a standard fever thermometer. No one is particularly upset at 97.4 or 98.9, but when three digits appear on the upper end, or the lower end drops below 95, people who know are alarmed. A high temperature is rewarded with bed rest, aspirin, chicken soup, antibiotics, and attention, whichever apply in the given case. Low temperatures receive blankets and warming—or a diagnosis of death.

On the other hand, people whose weight lies outside the range specified for their height, by somebody empowered to judge, are not abnormal in the same sense as the febrile person. Their weight is penalized with high insurance rates and threats of early demise.

Note the difference between the two. High body temperature is clearly associated with an identifiable pathological state and thus an indicator of trouble. Heaviness (as opposed to gross obesity, that is, 20 percent more than optimal body weight) is associated with a judgment about the association of high weight with potential pathologies. It is also associated with a social judgment about its connection with unattractiveness.

Words like febrile and fat have different meanings despite the fact that they both start with f. A febrile person is measured and treated; a fat person is labeled and usually admonished. Genuine sickness is "normally" rewarded by treatment by a designated expert. Social abnormality, however, is usually punished by social rejection and contempt.

There are few aspects of communication that can be described as numerically normal or abnormal. Normality may refer to numeric central tendency, social norms, or aesthetic standards. The latter category is interesting, because one kind of abnormality (above standard) is rewarded and the other kind (below standard) is ignored. Vocal characteristics can be measured on an oscilloscope and various sounds associated with squiggles on paper. But the squiggles are not the abnormality. Someone must judge the voice and declare it to be abnormal. Then its physical characteristics can be studied. The judgment may be based on social norms. People prefer an anchorperson sound; literate and cultured specialists may judge the aesthetic characteristics of the sound.

Rhetorically incompetent people cannot perform some simple composition and delivery tasks as effectively as rhetorical competent people. It is a judgment call. In the final crunch, we draw the line of social competency so low that virtually everyone can be called normal, although most are not good enough. This is sufficient to justify teaching. We need not worry about the *kind* of people we are teaching, merely about the behaviors we wish to modify. We arbitrarily declare the competent people to be "normal" even though there may be less of them than incompetent people. In any case, the problem is to draw the line that distinguishes a normal from an abnormal person.

The notion of personality provides another example. It is often assessed by scores on standardized tests that, presumably, are associated with some kind of behavior. The social judgment of personality, however, is made by people who meet other people and decide what kind of people they are, based on the way they talk. These judgments are expressed in the form of adjectives like "shy," "assertive," "taciturn," "forceful," "effective," or "inept," which may not correlate with test scores at all. Most personality measures end up with the use of an adjective posing as a noun. "Depressed" becomes "depressive", for example. What is actually happening is that evaluators observe behavior and label it. The label represents a judgment but does not refer to the specifics of behavior that led to its assignment. Those details are filled in idiosyncratically by anyone who hears the label. Specialists then gather data about personality after the fact.

Classification of Rhetorical Incompetence

There are few available nouns with which to classify the kinds and qualities of human speech. In its physical dimensions, it can be categorized through the use of spectrographs, oscilloscopes, and similar instruments. The wavelengths of sound and their overtones can be measured precisely. However, its social qualities can only be expressed in reifications.

Problems in social communication can be divided roughly into three groups: mechanical etiology, social performance, and emotional context. Mechanical problems refer to the wide range of communication disorders associated with physical or physiological pathologies characterized by clear cut deviations from norms. These are mostly problems in sound production—disorders of vocal range, pitch, intensity, fluency, or articulation. These problems may or may not have an emotional context, but there is no presumption that altering the emotional context will, in any way, solve the problem. Solutions are imposed either through medical treatment, surgery, or formal behavior modification.

Problems in social performance largely stem from the way people are seen, and problems with emotional context come from the way people see themselves. Based on these perceptions, people develop habits, attitudes, and concerns about speaking that either impede the process, make the speaker self-conscious, or cause the speaker to avoid participation. Solutions to the problems are negotiated. The person with a problem defined as "rhetorical incompetency" decides its nature and treatment with a trainer or clinician.

Establishing norms for rhetorical competency is virtually impossible. In fact, it would be paradoxical to attempt generalizations about rhetorical situations, since rhetoric itself is directed toward the given case. Each problem must be diagnosed on its merits, and treatment must be within the constraints imposed not only by the situation but also by the personalities of the people involved. Heuristic guidelines can be generated, however, because there are only a limited number of ways people can display their incompetence. It is those few overt behaviors that attract the attention of the teacher.

When cases can be classified by situation, therapy is appropriate. People who have problems with parents or peers need psychological treatment. When people speak in disorganized fashion or too softly or in a monotone, they can be taught.

In chapter 7, we listed ten problems that might interfere with competency. Some can be managed in the classroom, some cannot.

Genetic flaws establish propensities that must be taken into account. They cannot be modified, however. When a speaker falls far enough outside the normal range, he or she may require special treatment.

Faulty learning can be compensated for. If a student has not learned to read or has a limited vocabulary, recommendations for remediation can be made. The speech teacher cannot take the time for remedial reading instruction or vocabulary building.

Defective memory must be taken into account but cannot be dealt with directly. The speech teacher can advise about what ought to be remembered and can train the student in the use of notes and various other memory props.

Ineffective retrieval refers to responding to inappropriate memories. The speech teacher can provide heuristics for retrieval but cannot interfere with it directly.

Erroneous interpretation of events is a matter for cognitive restructuring. The speech teacher can provide heuristics for analysis of social situations.

Poor choice of options can be remedied by training the student so that he or she has more options.

Inadequate analysis of the scene can be improved by advising the student about what to look for as people respond.

Ineffective deployment of information can be dealt with only partially. The teacher can do little about internal data processing but can be very explicit advising about the type of information needed.

Defective choice of structure represents a main focus for instruction. It was dealt with in detail in chapter 7.

Errors in the delivery of discourse are also a main focus for teaching. Severe errors are referred to specialists. The matter of word choice and composition are jointly dealt with in structuring and delivery.

In general, diagnosis and treatment of incompetencies would focus on issues like the following: What are the behaviors that indicate inability to identify exigences in this particular situation? What modifications in oral performance behavior might remove these symptoms? Which of these modifications is possible for the person being trained? The same kind of analysis could be applied to topic selection, invention, disposition, style, delivery memory, and use of feedback.

The process fits a simple problem-solving format. The specific problem is defined in terms of behaviors specific to the problem. Treatment is directed only at the behaviors defined. The exact mode of treatment is decided on by trainer and student, based on common understanding of the nature of the difficulty and the possible modes of repair. Incompetent social communicators are not abnormal. They merely need to modify the form and manner of their discourse.

Humans have an urgency to name, measure, and count, but they are relatively deficient at describing. By creating abstractions they can avoid dealing with details. But it is hard to work with abstractions. For example, trying to modify personality that is measured by test scores is like counting the angels on the head of a pin. When the great taxonomist Haeckel (Stone, 1971) went mad, he became a recluse for several years. When he emerged he had a book, *On the Anatomy of Angels*. The scientific world was excited: here was a man depressed for a decade now bringing a wonderful humorous book to his waiting public. Surprise! The book was not humorous. Haeckel had provided elaborate calculations of the bone structure of angels correlated with the nature of the atmosphere and had literally designed the optimum angel. Thus it is when we attempt to understand personality through the scientific method.

What we cannot do is modify what does not exist.

We can legislate, however. As it was necessary to create the fiction of the corporation in order to carry out certain economic operations, it is necessary to create personality types so they can be managed. *DSM/*

III (1982) associates various labels with undesirable social behaviors, provides a plan for diagnosis through consensus, and thus empowers a group of specialized healers to manage those whose social behavior appears problematic for themselves and for others.

Communication problems fall into the psychological purview only when they are bizarre, are so troubling to an individual that he or she seeks "help." Whether helpers do any good or not is another story. The results are judged subjectively, and most psychological healers try very hard to get off the hook by refusing to take responsibility for cures. They say the individual must make his own decisions and we can only guide and advise.

Rhetorical incompetence is a label assigned to a given person, by self or others, in a particular situation. It refers to behaviors that can be modified. In chapter 2 we presented a teaching plan directed at rhetorical incompetence. In the chapters to follow we will discuss the teacher and his or her behavior in implementing the plan.

9

The Instructional Model

Our artificial intelligence metaphor led us to conclude that instruction directed at improvement of social discourse must follow orderly procedure. This chapter and those that follow discuss orderly procedure in teaching students who are rhetorically incompetent. Our discussion of "rhetoritherapy" in chapter 2 describes a training procedure designed to implement the performance aspects of the "Canons of Rhetoric," especially disposition and delivery. The program has been demonstrably effective for most who experience it.

In simple terms, rhetoric is the act of controlling one's communication in order to accomplish some social purpose. An expert speaker or writer is a competent rhetor, *a person who is master of both situation and language.* In other words, in order to be an effective communicator in any situation, it is important to know *how to use* speaking and/or writing to influence people, as well as to be skillful in *the act* of speaking and/or writing. We have equated skill with orderly procedure. We have also excluded *knowing about* speaking and writing from the process on the grounds that there is no connection between knowing about something and knowing to use it effectively.

Our inquiry here is into the question *what must a teacher do to help a student become rhetorically competent?* That is, what must students know about the effect of communication on human beings? What must they believe about themselves and their ability to communicate? What must they be able to do to convince themselves and others that they are skillful?

This approach makes the acquisition of rhetorical competency a matter of behavior modification; the removal of disabling flaws requires altering behavior. The process need not necessarily be Skinnerian. A rhetorical approach to behavior modification rejects the notion of operant conditioning as a formula. In fact, Skinner (1971, 1974), in his latest books on behaviorism conceded that operant conditioning schedules must be adapted to motivations unique to the individual whose behavior is being modified. Despite its apparent rigidity, behavior modification can be carried out in a humanistic manner.

The real importance of following orderly procedure, however, is that is precludes charismatic control of the students by the teacher. Our goal in the Reticence Program was to devise a relatively teacher-free pedagogy, that is, a technology of instruction delivered by a teacher in which (within limits) teacher personality is not the greatest influence on the student. We want the student to go away remembering techniques, not the teacher's personality.[1] Rhetorical competency is contingent on ability to comply with a program of conditioning in such a way that it can be carried over to life events. Certainly this describes teaching at its best.

Few people are totally inept at social discourse. Most of us can manage the ordinary routines of daily life even when we do not do well at them. But we are often situationally incompetent. Each person has social situations with which he or she simply cannot cope. Whatever the case, our social transactions can be analyzed in rational terms by examining our social goals and discovering the role of discourse in accomplishing them. The speaker who attains something approximating what he or she sought can be classified "competent."

Because we have defined rhetorical competence to refer specifically to behaviors involved in structuring and delivering messages in social settings, we have surrendered direct responsibility for modifying inven-

1. The reader may feel we are fussing excessively on this point. After all, the "common wisdom" is that the teacher ought to exert a personal influence on the student. We do not deny that the teacher should be respected, but when students become excessively attached and ascribe their success to the teacher rather than their own efforts, there is little carry-over. Students learn to please the teacher rather than improve themselves. Our mission is to teach for carry-over. This means the student must be able to perform in the absence of the teacher, and even after he or she has forgotten the teacher's name.

tion. Our concern with structuring and delivery is justified through our experiments in artificial intelligence.

The basic therapeutic model we advocate is called "rhetoritherapy." The name was selected tongue-in-cheek, for rhetoritherapy is not therapeutic in the sense of medical practice or psychological counseling. Furthermore, it seeks to modify behavior without using the operant conditioning characteristic of behavior modification in clinical psychology. It is pedagogy based on simulation and criticism. It contains the word "therapeutic" because it is clinical in the sense of being directly applicable to the given case.

Conceptually, it is a simple process. Students are assigned to perform in an ordinary classroom the kinds of tasks they would do *in vivo*. Their performances are criticized and heuristics provided to use in subsequent performances. They are then given experiences that require them to carry over classroom skills to life situations. They are not expected to make personal discoveries; inductive teaching is not used. The direction of their performance behavior is driven by a general systems hypothesis that modification of a particular behavior will improve general performance skill.

Criticism-oriented training is based on the principle that any skill or art can be improved through guided performance and informed criticism. Unlike counseling, students are not required to involute, cathart, or disclose personal secrets. There is no effort made to teach students to manage emotion except when it is directly related to performance. Emotion is modified through accumulation by students of a repertoire of behavior that extends their competence to relevant life situations.

Rhetoritherapy requires teachers to convince their students that the system works. They do this by putting them into situations where it is bound to work and calling their attention to the fact it has worked.

The fact that students sometimes have a distorted view of the rhetorical process presents an important paradox. In order to motivate them to commit to modifying their performance behavior, it is necessary to use cognitive restructuring to modify their understanding of the communication process. They are told that their training will be mainly in the improvement of techniques to accomplish personal social goals. They are advised that they must make a contract about what behaviors they will want to change. Part of the contract is the willingness to listen to and apply their instructor's criticism. In essence, this is a therapeutic contract.

The process must take place in a classroom for two reasons. First, the classroom subverts the notion that rhetorical incompetence is any different in quality from ordinary incompetence encountered by a student in any course of study. Students take a class because they need to learn. The assumption that they need instruction is basic to any pedagogy. We ask students to take courses in math because they do not know algebra or calculus. We require them to take courses in written composition because we believe they lack writing skills. Speech performance training purports to remedy deficiencies in social performance behavior, and there is no reason to apologize for having them.

Second, since students are being trained in public behavior, they need a public setting in which to be trained. However, since they are often tense and uncertain in such settings, they need a protected environment. Careful classroom management enables them to take social risks in a setting where their chances of failure are almost zero. And because the classroom also provides peer support, it, in essence, becomes a real laboratory for practicing social technique.

MODIFICATION OF SOCIAL DISCOURSE AS THERAPY

A course of study in anything provides for presentation of some information accompanied by various exercises and activities designed (1) to test the students mastery of the information and (2) provide them with an application to apply it. The former requires general compliance, while the latter permits individual adaptation. For example, in a speech classroom, everyone learns to organize ideas, but each student applies what he has learned to a particular topic to be addressed under a specific set of circumstances. What makes instruction therapeutic is the application to the given case. This is particularly important in teaching oral performance because the cognitive information measured by testing is actually irrelevant if it cannot be used to facilitate performance modification of a salubrious kind.

But the application of training to the given case has consequences for the individual. When a person alters her communication behavior, people respond differently to her. Shy people have complained, for example, that as they become more fluent they need to seek new friends because their old companions were used to their silence. They clung to their shyness despite the fact that improvement was possible because they feared their friends would not accept their new personae. Once a person has been identified as a "good listener," it is hard to accommodate to his or her new verbal skills.

Since personality is literally measured via communication output, permanent changes in communication output mean a literal change in personality. This may not, of course, be reflected in questionnaires about behavior. Students in the Reticence Program often made major changes in their performance behavior without changing the way they responded to questions measuring their apprehension level. It is often hard to change communication behavior because people find it more convenient to stay with uncomfortable certainty than risk the ambiguity of changed responses.

Self-Esteem

If change is desired and desirable, how is it best made? The elusive concept "self-esteem" is central with those who seek to change social behavior. The prevailing psychological idea is to modify self-esteem under the assumption that behavior change will follow. This proposition makes some sense. In simple terms, any person who sets out to do anything at all, usually believes he can do it. Those who speak in social settings have some beliefs, justified or not, about their skills. Those who believe that they can and will affect events positively are said to have high self-esteem. Those who are dubious about whether they can exert an influence have low self-esteem.

As these lines are being written, a newscaster is reporting that the California Commission on Self-Esteem has brought in its report. After fourteen years of study, they discovered that poor students, criminals, and addicts have low self-esteem. The commission advocates that everyone cooperate in creating an environment that enhances everyone's self-esteem. This is sad—for self-esteem is not a condition to be tampered with in its own right. It is a reification that results from a confrontation with reality.

Self-esteem is nothing more than a metaphor for self-evaluation. A person decides how well or poorly she has done and decides whether it is worth trying again. Those who try a lot and succeed have high self-esteem. Those who have been objectively ineffective or who cannot convince themselves of success even when it happens are likely to be reluctant to participate.

But there is such a thing as spurious self-esteem. It is possible for people to convince themselves that they are more effective than they are and then blunder. Their motto: Mouth Open, Foot Forward. There are, also, people who understate their ability. These people are sometimes regarded as shy, but no one really worried much about Gary Cooper or John Wayne. There are some who "cry with a loaf of bread under their arm." They have a largeness of riches in their social repertoires but complain about their awkwardness in social situations. Philip Zimbardo (1977) expressed considerable concern about shy celebrities. We shed no tears for them. They earn their millions on the stage, and more th; n likely their awkwardness in social situations comes from their ar· ie̓ty that someone might get attention they believe is rightfully theirs. ⋃ur concern is not with celebrity but with people who have difficulty managing the ordinary social experiences of life.

Because there is no pathology associated with communication incompetence, it is easy for people to assume the label. A great many inept speakers label themselves as such because they would rather be sick than stupid. A person who is shy, for example, is entitled to special consideration and pity. On the other hand, a person who is inept must learn something. It is easy to be abject and therefore entitled to consolation from others. A great many of the shy people we dealt with in the Reticence Program were actually quite unpleasant as human beings. Their shyness was clearly a strategy, an inartistic proof, designed to help them get what they sought from others. It is reasonable to view any incompetence as an inartistic proof, because in contemporary society, most disabilities are rewarded in some way. We have created special education for those who cannot cope intellectually and community service for lawbreakers. Whether our social values are as distorted as they appear is a moot question. The point is, there are often payoffs for ineptitude.

The preceding cynical, though realistic, view of the way diagnostic labels are used as proofs offers yet another contradiction of the medical model. The focus of rhetoritherapy is on specific performance behaviors. It is directed only at people who really believe they have a behavior that requires modification. They must decide what needs to be changed and then examine themselves to see if there is a possibility that changes can be made. The teacher has an additional problem: how to induce the individual to recognize that changes have been made.

Thus, instruction/therapy must be directed both at modification of the objective record and at the individual's view of that record. This means that clients must be trained in two resources: communication skills and critical facility. They must learn to speak well, know when they speak well, and be able to explain what went wrong when they do not speak well.

The Therapeutic Alliance

The first step in treatment is the formation of a therapeutic alliance in the best Freudian sense. It means:

The client is willing to make changes.
The therapist and client can agree on what changes are to be made.
The therapist is capable of facilitating the changes.
The client is physically capable of making the changes.
The client is willing to pay the therapist's fee.

The therapeutic alliance is a defense against spurious change that takes place when a person equates a magic formula with anticipated results, for example, the "five easy methods to be popular" means a person *is* popular. This amulet theory of instruction works with people who are already capable but who refuse to admit it. They buy the amulet and give themselves permission to be as effective as they already are.

Formulary methodologies present real problems to those whose social ineptitude is real. It is easy to say, "Be outgoing." It is something else again to figure out precisely what to do to appear outgoing to others. Learning presentational skills is very much like learning to be an actor. Our acculturation firmly locks us into habitual behavior patterns. Changing them often requires formal direction.

The power of the fee. One reason why formulary training appears to work is that people have to pay for it. Once they pay, they are reluctant to admit they got a bad bargain. Thus, whether it worked or not, they will claim it did and thus offer testimonials to others to buy it. It is odd, however, that not one of the methods has produced a long term effects study to demonstrate that the method actually worked.[2] It is even more disheartening to note that formal academic training in communication skills suffers from the same knowledge gap. Evangelical zeal to convert the heathen is not a valid measure of the success of treatment. And high

2. A recent invitation to Dale Carnegie systems to cooperate in such an investigation was summarily rejected.

enrollments do not necessarily measure the effect of a course, only its popularity.

Students pay tuition and patients pay fees. According to Freud, treatment has no value unless it caused a bit of discomfort in the wallet of those receiving it. People with deficiencies in communication skills do not take kindly to eleemosynary offerings. They do not like being patronized ("Speak up, I'm listening") or ignored. Often, when formal training is offered in an educational setting, it appears remedial. Students may want the training, but do not want to admit they are candidates for remediation.

This creates an apparent paradox. Students would rather be sick than stupid, but in the final analysis, they would rather be neither. It is only when they discover they are impaired and know they need help that they begin to define themselves as "temporarily" defective. Thus, it is important to make it appear that everyone is entitled to training. The optimum is a curriculum that provides choices, so students can believe they are getting the training they can benefit from most.

Once students are in a training program, the grade takes the place of a fee. Many remedial programs have little impact because students are not evaluated on how well they have done. Altruistic clinical or remedial treatment has been generally irrelevant largely because people tend to believe that treatment that costs nothing is worth its price.

Clinic or classroom. Clinical training is very private. The only skills clients acquire are fluency with a particular psychotherapist. One of the reasons analysis is, according to Freud, often "interminable" is because analyst and analysand must learn to talk well with one another before the treatment can work. Once they have learned to do it, it is very hard to separate them.

The classroom, however, presents the problem of motivation. Most classrooms are ritualistic. Students do not expect to be tampered with. They read the material and take the tests and those for whom the material has no further meaning (that is, they are not headed for med school or contestant status on "Jeopardy") will quickly forget it. Tampering with something as vital as presentation style, however, is a direct assault on personality, and speech students intuitively notice it. The arrangements are quite convenient. They perform their assignments, being cute when they can, or witnessing for their brand of faith or complying in some way by reporting as they did in high school. The professor notes improvement (although they rarely are able to document it—the Rosenthal/Pygmalion

[Rosenthal & Jacobson, 1968] Theory says they will find it if they are looking for it) and grades accordingly, rarely rigorously. The course is cake, the influence is nil.

Neither students nor other humans will change their behavior unless they are properly motivated. The argument that a course is required is not sufficient to document its importance. Most course requirements are testimonials to the democratic system of logrolling and bargaining anyway. Thus, the Reticence experience taught us a great deal about teaching strategies. That is, if you assess an extra cost, make a student feel special, and allow him or her to define learning goals, you may motivate them to make some measurable changes. Given that we are teaching *only* structuring and delivery, it is fairly easy to document gain, and the follow-ups at least garner testimony that the students think they have acquired something permanent. For these reasons, we will use the Reticence Program experience as a basis for this disquisition on teaching speech performance.

Some axioms of instruction. First of all, the teacher only offers instruction he knows he can provide. We know we can teach almost anyone to eliminate "and uh" and "y'know" from their speech or write a coherent outline. We have no assurance that we can raise self-esteem or quell anxiety. Furthermore, speech teachers often make promises about thinking and literary style. The teacher who remains empirical and deals only with modifications that can be made and measured is generally more successful in the classroom.

Second, there is no reason to make the situation worse than it is by labeling the students. Concentration on skills eliminates global labels. After a while, students stop thinking of themselves as shy or incompetent and begin to concentrate on changing specific behaviors.

Third, it is important to keep psychodynamics under control. Humans love to "testify." The shy people, especially, reach a point where they want to "spill their guts." When this happens, it should take place in the teacher's office and not be part of the classroom process. Those who "tell all" should neither be rewarded nor punished for it. Classroom instructors generally do not have the expertise to handle catharsis. Thus they should not encourage it. On the other hand, they can use the catharsis to teach students about controlling their output. Unlimited catharsis is boring. Good audience analysis dictates that the student stops talking about himself and focuses on issues more interesting to the audience.

Fourth, the limits of treatment must be specified. The Reticence Program lists only those area for which there are training programs. Everything else is blocked out on the grounds that techniques are not available to manage the process. The syllabus is fleshed out by making rational agreements on learning contracts with the students.

Finally, the process must be time limited. In no way should the student be permitted to become dependent on the teacher or the training sessions. Since modification is designed for carry-over, trainees must be pushed into life situations as quickly as possible.

Even when students are committed, however, they may tend to resist instruction. Learning to identify resistance and deal with it is an important component of the process of retraining.

THERAPEUTIC RESISTANCE

Incompetent speakers resist training the same way students resistinstruction and patients resist therapy. It is not clear, however, what resisters are resisting. Some may be frightened by changes in their self-image. Others may recognize a need for changing behavior but feel that it is impossible for them. They may not want to risk another failure. Still others may feel a need to renege on the therapeutic alliance. Resistances can be acknowledged, but they must be dealt with tactically. The trainer usually has neither the time nor expertise to use psychoanalysis to discover the reasons for the resistances.

The main tactic in overcoming resistance is to provide a milieu in which resistance is consistently challenged. However, it is not productive to accuse the trainee of resistance. This places him or her in a defensive position. If, however, the therapeutic alliance rules out resistance at the outset, the resister must display considerable tenacity to continue it. The syllabus must be adhered to; performance required; practice supervised; no excuses accepted. The student must either perform, fail the course, or be dropped from treatment. The cost of failure in this milieu provides impetus for the trainee to overcome resistance. There are specific techniques that can be directed against the main resistances in the given case.

There are ten major patterns of resistance: denial, suspicion, rationalization, transference, refusal to participate, self-fulfilling prophecy, programmatic activity, fighting criticism, narcissism, and the display of nervous mannerisms.

Denial

Rhetorical competency cannot be gainsaid. It can be confirmed by others when they see it. Competent performance has an effect on others. People can hear it, pay attention to it, be moved or informed by it, learn from it; they respond to it in affirming and rewarding ways. It has discernible components: it is well organized, replete with interesting narratives and examples, phrased in attention-getting language, and delivered in a versatile and expressive voice.

A great many inept speakers deny their small gains when they make them. Sometimes their preoccupation with feelings blinds them to the fact that they have succeeded in some social task. It is more comfortable to retain the old feelings of persecution and rejection. To avoid acknowledging success they may deny what they feel, report it inaccurately, or most often purposely misunderstand it.

Our society does not encourage people to discuss their social successes. It is, however, de riguer to kvetch about failures. It is considered braggadocio to say "Wow, I really snowed that S.O.B.!" People do it, but it is not acceptable social behavior. By the same token, involuted dialogue about social failure, while boring and narcissistic, is normal. It represents a kind of exchange. "You tell me your misery and I'll tell you mine." This is the substance of TV talk shows and the basis of the twelve-step system in overcoming addiction. Admit to one's abject state and find God entitles you to comforting buddies who will stroke and cuddle you, and you will stay sober one day at a time. Unfortunately, inept speakers cannot get by with comfort for their misery. There is no obvious habit for them to kick. Acquisition of skill demands discipline, and discipline is a lonely process.

Incompetent speakers must deal with their feelings about themselves. They may flinch when a teacher/critic confronts them with information about their social performance, but they must deal with it. On the other hand, they will try to evade responsibility exactly as they do in social situations in which they are rejected or ignored.

Offering the student hard data about their success is the best way to overcome denial, but sometimes the urgency to deny is so strong, student speakers can snatch defeat from the jaws of victory. They may literally handicap themselves by refraining from repeating what they have already done successfully. It is tempting for teachers to try to respond to their students' miseries, but when they do, they divert themselves from the prime directive, that is, to help bring about the changes agreed on in the therapeutic alliance.[3]

Suspicion

The natural suspicion inept people have of skilled conversationalists carries over into their attitude toward learning communication skills. For some reason, they do not flinch at learning writing skills, but many seem to believe planning and rehearsal are equivalent to manipulation. The justification for the idea that social discourse should be prepared is drawn from the notion that speech is enlarged conversation. Students are willing to accept the idea that they need to gather materials and do an outline for a formal speech, but they seem hostile to the idea of developing a repertoire of conversational options requisite for skill at social discourse.

Because social discourse is a shared responsibility, incompetent speakers must learn to ascribe credit and blame properly. They often tend either to take full blame for conversational failure or blame the other people entirely. Their preference is to be suspicious of the motives of others; they believe skillful speakers take advantage of them, and thus they despair of ever learning to compete well. The idea of audience analysis is hard for them to grasp. Sometimes they seize on it uncritically and act as if all people of a particular type (women, old people, bosses) respond in the same way. The idea of observing their listeners carefully and adjusting to their responses seems almost too complicated for them to grasp.

Teaching and practicing basic rules of etiquette are effective ways to allay suspicions. For example, no one has an obligation to listen (only to be polite by acting as if they are listening), and those who wish to speak have the burden of gaining and holding attention until the other person commits to the process. As a corollary, students must learn that it is sometimes impossible to get attention. Listeners have the right to be preoccupied, interested in something else, or simply unwilling to get

3. An interesting side note grew out of the study of fifteen hundred public speaking students reported earlier. The students were asked to evaluate the importance of various components of the course. Virtually unanimously they approved speaking assignments, followed by criticism by the instructor. More than half, however, said that comments from their fellow students were not important, and they were almost in unanimous agreement that private contact with their instructor had little value. So much for the advantages of the clinical method.

involved, and when this is the case, nothing a speaker can do will be successful.

Suspicion of the process of social discourse stems from various myths students have about it. Many have learned that they must be "authentic" and "let it all hang out." The principles of sensitivity training seem to be particularly appealing to inept speakers largely because they tend to shift the blame for failure to the other person. Because they believe conversation will only work with people with common belief systems, they resist notions of taking personal responsibility for their own social behavior.

The aphorisms of the medical model also breed suspicion. When incompetent speakers discover they must change their behavior, they seem to assert they would rather be sick than stupid. They claim disability and seek special treatment. It is hard for anyone to admit to his own ineptitude; particularly hard for people who have used their ineptitude as a major personality defense. Throughout training, students will continue to attempt to "get referred" to someone who can solve their problems for them.

Rationalization

Inept speakers are often skillful at explaining their personal failures to themselves and others. They are surprisingly fluent with their counselors (although reticent with their physicians). It is hard to take rationalization away from them.

It is important for them to understand that they are allowed to *share* blame for failure. Social conversation requires two or more parties. One person has no right to take all the blame if it fails (although there are a few exceptional souls who can effectively kill any conversation regardless of how skillful the others are). The idea is to get the trainees to use their rationalizations as part of their analysis. By identifying the other person as reticent, boorish, or pushy, the student speaker can devise strategies for the next encounter. Teaching students to recognize the signs of gaucherie can help them choose targets for their social forays intelligently. There is no point to permitting them to dream the impossible dream and seek to achieve unattainable social goals. By learning to recognize snobs, clods, egomaniacs, and other socially insensitive people, students can be helped to make intelligent choices about whom to address and how. Furthermore, by learning to analyze outcomes, trainees can parcel out the blame appropriately. They can make rationalization work for themselves once they can explain what the other party did to interfere with their goal seeking.

Transference

Transference is the most dangerous of the resistances. Students often improve rapidly once they commit to training. Unfortunately, virtually all of them go through a period when they believe that their accomplishments are entirely due to their teacher. They admire their instructor so much, they seek ways to spend time with him. They want to report their successes and be congratulated; whimper about their failures and get their heads stroked. They want to be displayed on teacher's refrigerator. Once they discover their instructor is available to listen, they try to dump their autobiographies.

This attachment can be a heady brew for the instructor. There is a real temptation for him to capitalize on his charisma. It is especially important that the teacher avoid giving any impression of sexual accessibility or even interest. A dispassionate demeanor can be attained merely by concentrating on helping the student get through the syllabus.

Unfortunately, teachers are sometimes tempted to countertransfer; to regard their students as children or lovers. By avoiding personal material in class and controlling office conferences, the teacher can maintain the impression of detachment. This does not mean teachers cannot be interested. It is what they are interested in that is crucial. Attention must be focused on behavior as opposed to feelings about behavior. In no way can the teacher allow her attention to be diverted from the task of behavior modification. (She should keep a list of counseling center phone numbers available, just in case.)

The importance of avoiding countertransference cannot be overstated. It is easy for trainers to "fatten" their egos by accepting the dependency of recovering students. Success, after all, is exhilarating for teacher and students alike. By maintaining physical and emotional distance, the trainer can expedite the students' attempts at autonomy. The less teachers know about the personal and private lives of their students, the better. The training program and the trainer must be temporary interventions. Successful social discourse depends on the independent versatility of the individual. The salient goal of training programs must be productive autonomy.

Refusal to Participate

Incompetent speakers often claim they can speak well enough, if they want to, but they simply do not want to very often. Denial of personal ineffectiveness is quite logical. Public scores are not kept on social victories and losses. When people suffer a social failure, they need not face it but can walk away from it and deny that it happened. The explanation takes the form of a rationalization (see above), another form of resistance. And once having denied the problem, there is no longer a reason to try to solve it.

Shy students often resist participating at all. First sessions are markedly silent. Students file in and sit apart from one another. If the light is off, no one will turn it on. Most will avoid eye contact with the instructor in the hope that by avoiding the teacher's gaze they will not be asked to respond to questions. Instructors are hard-pressed to find techniques of involving trainees. They do not volunteer.

A more subtle resistance is when students claim: "I could have gotten the job, but I didn't really try for it"; "She would have accepted my invitation, but I didn't really offer it." Sometimes they use tentative language: "You may not want to consider me for the job because I really lack the qualifications"; or "You probably won't want to go with me." Often, they hang back and wait for the other person to make a request.

They resist in real life, also. At social gatherings, they may approach a conversation group, hang around the edges and say nothing. If they do not get engaged in the conversation, they can withdraw and tell themselves that they did not want to participate anyway.

The antidote to denial is pressure to participate. Teachers use goal setting as a tactical device that demands activity. Carry-over emphasizes ways to carry over tactics learned in the classroom. Students are told to avoid spontaneity, since unplanned situations provide a perfect excuse for nonparticipation. When a person is reluctant to participate in a classroom exercise, however, the grade provides a good rationalization for overcoming reluctance. They can say, "I really wouldn't do this, but I must in order to get the grade."

Initial engagement is most effectively done by direct questioning. Teachers must have a standard protocol, almost like an interview by a TV talk-show host. What is your name? Where are you from? What is your major? What do you hope to do when you graduate? What do you do for fun on the weekend? Each student is quizzed separately. The first interviewed may be monosyllabic in their responses. Near the end of the sequence, some begin to open up. Others may evade the issue with nonresponsive answers. The trainer adheres to the protocol, asking the same questions of each students. Observing that they have a common problem often provides students with motivation to respond.

Self-fulfilling Prophecy

Students will often express a "self-fulfilling prophecy" of ineptitude. Once students begin talking, they talk a lot about their problems as a justification for retaining them. They are quite capable of talking themselves into ineptitude. Often they seem to be upset when things go well. We have seen them stop in the middle of a successful effort, do a "double take," and then lapse back into their old style of speaking.

The most effective way to counter self-fulfilling prophecies is to compel students to predict a more successful outcome. Goal-setting procedures and rehearsal help to convince students that they are prepared for any contingency, and they can do what they plan to do. Sometimes it is useful to ask students to role-play ineffective behavior to show them they have command over it.

Programmatic Activity

One sign of rhetorical incompetency is a tendency to habituate phrases, clichés, monosyllabic responses, vocalized pauses, and banal utterances. Part of students' incompetency lies in their dullness. Many incompetent speakers just seem devoid of information. They have trouble adapting because they, literally, have nothing to say. It is almost as if they convinced themselves that since they cannot talk well, they need not have anything to talk about.

In ordinary conversation they use only familiar topics. They have phrases they repeat over and over redundantly. By mastering a few social routines, they convince themselves they have complied with the requirements of social situations and excuse themselves from broadening their repertoire. Teachers can deal with this problem by guiding them to select goals they would not otherwise seek. Broadening their repertoire makes it less necessary for them to rely on formulas.

Antipathy to Criticism

Students are usually very edgy about taking criticism, although, oddly enough, they are fairly facile at giving it. Ineffective communicators are usually very critical of fluent people. They accuse them of being shallow and inconsiderate. They demean "small talk" and argue that most people talk too much or wave their hands about or confuse the issue with facts. They regard fluent and effective speakers as "show-offs." On the other hand, they regard comments made about their own talk as personal attacks. Often, they will preempt criticism by criticizing themselves and challenging their teachers to do something about it. Each time the teacher offers them a technique or system, they respond with extended recitations of the ineffective remedies they have previously tried.

Criticism well administered is the lifeblood of teaching performance behavior. In the following chapter we will deal with it extensively.

Narcissism

It is amazing how narcissistic we all can be. We have learned to concentrate on ourselves because of the possibility of social failure. We seem to believe that other people pay a good deal more attention to us than is actually the case. In fact, we notice only a few details about the people around us. We are only concerned when we are engaged with them.

Rhetorically incompetent speakers are especially sensitive to what others think of them. They believe others evaluate them in advance and try to intimidate and suppress them. For the most part, they place themselves in an adversary relationship with their listeners. There is, in this sense, a kind of paranoia that can be both protective and destructive. Because inept communicators tend to be hypersensitive to social evaluation, they keep out of situations they cannot handle or resort to inartistic methods to take control of them. On the other hand, this protective quality also keeps them from making a legitimate effort to participate socially in order to achieve interpersonal goals.

In some, this generates an approach-avoidance paradox. When instruction starts, they are attracted to participation because they believe it could be helpful. On the other hand, once they become involved, their natural suspicion keeps them from seeing their own personal gain and prevents them from conceding that they have improved.

Nervous Mannerisms

Sometimes trainees solicit reassurance and pity. It is clear that some of their habitual behaviors are designed to gain them exemption from social responsibility. By demonstrating that they are manifestly unqualified to participate socially, they request that others excuse them from living up to social norms. Their behaviors persuade others to provide entitlements associated with their problem. Furthermore, they gain a modicum of attention by becoming the objects of sympathy or antipathy. In any case, they seek and often earn diminished responsibility. If they do not, they are ignored.

Instructors are cautioned about empathizing with students. It is important to understand why they behave as they do, but not to display any emotion about it. Unconditional positive regard is not useful, because giving it tends to excuse inept behavior. To be effective, instructors must be firmly unforgiving of inept behavior. The simple Skinnerian formula of rewarding competent performance and either ignoring or actually punishing inept performance seems to be the most useful pattern of instruction. The goal-setting system that is the center of instruction is built on the premise that people will habituate effective behaviors. The basic idea of instruction is to pressure the students into situations in which they must admit success and use each success as the basis for taking on a more complicated and demanding situation the next time.

DOING THE DOABLE

There are two possible ways to study rhetorical incompetence. One is to discover the cause of the social *Angst* that makes it so difficult for some people to communicate. This orientation presumes that we can know why people have problems. *We do not!* They may have problems because they chose to have them, because they cannot help it, or because they are told by someone else that what they do is a problem. We presume that rhetorically incompetent people are somehow misoriented to social events in such a way that it precludes competent performance. All of this gobbledygook must give way to simple tautology. People are called incompetent because their oral performance leads to inferences, by themselves or others, that they are incompetent.

Labeling Theory

The sociological approach called "labeling theory" (Warren, 1982) offers a practical way to understand incompetence. Let us start with the premise that people are called incompetent or come to think of themselves that way because of *something they do or think they do*. Either they decide they are doing something wrong, or another person told them so. Regardless of the source of the label, the behavior is what is important. If we wish to modify the label, we must change the behavior it refers to. Changing the label alone will not help. Calling "retarded" children "exceptional" does little or nothing to change the way they behave. However, if we change the way incompetent speakers speak, it reduces the odds that they will be labeled "incompetent." Teaching must focus on the answer to the question, *Which of the behaviors that led to the label can be effectively modified?*

A Technology of Performance Improvement

The quest for a technology of communication improvement starts with identification of what can be modified. We are constrained by process. The person who wants to be socially effective must respond to what is going on. There is little time to ruminate. Exigences must be addressed by action, that is, by the utterance of words. The main speaker's heuristic is, What is expected of me now? Whatever happens, it must happen fast. In essence, this means that whatever is taught must be simple, and those who learn should be able to habituate it.

The Work of Robert Mager. Mager's (Mager 1962, 1972; Mager & Beach, 1967; Mager & Pipe, 1970) advice on goal setting is based on an analysis of methods effective for training skilled laborers and technicians. He argues that behavior can only be modified if the trainee wishes to have it so.

Will, in any case, is an important component of both teaching and therapy. However, it is another one of those "silly putty" reifications. We do not know what it is "to will" to participate. We must presume that presence in a situation that promises modification accompanied by assent to assignments that purport to facilitate modification is a sign of "will" or commitment to the process.

The steps in composition of social discourse can be specified sequentially as performance goals. They can each be associated with a preparation and performance technology. The heuristics are a self-evident series of questions that require personal accounts:

> What did someone do or say that indicates I must say something?
> What am I required to do? What must I not do?
> What do I want to say?
> How must this be adjusted to meet the needs of my listener?
> In what sequence should I say it?
> What words should I use to say it?
> How shall I speak it and what gestures must accompany it?
> What are the implications of the responses made to it?

Together, these questions are subsumed in organization and delivery.

Because social discourse is so much like public speaking, each of the units of composition represents a legitimate area for criticism.

Goal setting for particular situations is a major consideration in the tactics of presentation. The structure of the presentation represents the strategy dictated by the goal (for example, I must appear friendly, conciliatory, loving, confrontive). Each component is a tactical maneuver that (1) must be appropriate in the situation and (2) must appeal to the listener. In unfamiliar social situations the speaker may use clichés associated with general norms until he discovers what the boundaries are.

When conversants are familiar with each other, it is possible for them to appeal mutually to specific needs and wants. Competent speakers give evidence that they can handle clichés and interpret signs to meet the exigences of the listeners. When speakers become preoccupied with their own behavior and ignore that of their respondents, they take the chance of making narcissistic mistakes. That is, when a speaker is distracted from attention to the listener because he is paying attention to himself, he runs the serious risk of losing the attention and goodwill of the listener.

But make no mistake about it, the critic is engaged in the task of modifying personality. Sullivanian theory regards personality as a set of expectations. A speaker must, initially, meet the expectations the respondent has for her. If expectations are to be changed it must be done over a period of time and by agreement. That is why it is so hard for people to alter the way they are seen. Often, even when they have changed a great deal, the people who know them do not notice. To notice a change means one must accommodate to it. Thus, effective interpersonal behavior requires negotiation of responses.

The individual's behavior in response to the expectations of others is referred to as "role." The speaker can play an accustomed or required role or try to establish a new role by winning acceptance for the behaviors associated with it. In formal situations people are expected to play roles as assigned. At work, salespeople must talk about merchandise, physicians must talk about health, mechanics must talk about auto parts. When inappropriate talk is introduced in these social situations, the conversation becomes awkward and the purpose subverted. The same is true when intimates alter behaviors to which their partners are accustomed. When a person seeks to alter his role, he must persuade his partner to accept changes in his behavior.

Social responses are also reactive. The manner of delivery sets the tone for response. When a speaker is excessively forceful, it may trigger antagonisms. When the speaker is deferential, it may cue the respondent to take control. We are authoritarian or submissive mostly because we have been trained to be so. Simple prudence dictates that authoritarians avoid each other. The submissives thus become clientele for those who seek to dominate.

While much of the preceding may seem obvious, the subtleties and possibilities for complications are enormous. People do not fit comfortably into slots. Sometimes it is necessary for them to manage several roles. Fellow workers can be friends; relatives can be neighbors, and so on. Thus, social conversation must include bargaining about the particulars of role-taking. It is out of this bargaining that relationships are built.

A technology of performance modification requires methods and devices to facilitate a speaker's understanding of the exigences and contingencies of social situations as well as its possibilities. This must be based on a heuristic repertoire. A speaker must be able to abstract from one situation to another, for to demand adjustment on an individual basis is to invite schizophrenia. People stand to gain or lose by the way they behave in a given social situation. The game is one of "entitlements," learning what is at stake and skillfully implementing whatever it takes to earn it.

Figuring Out What We Are Entitled To

We all have fantasies and dreams, some so vivid as to be facts in their own right. We rarely see what is; mostly, we see what we want to see. There is a peculiar phenomenon that can occur when people meet for the first time. We observe a new person and make a decision about how to respond. If the person makes an impact, we may fantasize situations involving them. When we encounter them the next time, we may act as if our fantasy had actually happened. If we fantasized intimacy, we might presume. If we fantasized hostility, we may antagonize.

One need not be a Freudian to understand that our social goals and behaviors are sometimes constrained by thoughts and ideas over which we do not have full control. We tend to transfer our feelings; to see bosses as fathers, mates as parents. Even if we accept the premise that all behavior is rational to the behaver at the time of behavior, it is not possible to give a complete account of the reasons for it. We can ask questions and get answers but there is no reason to believe people know the reasons for their behavior or would or could tell the truth about them, if they did.

Clearly, most of us want from others more than we can get, and we are accustomed to demanding, not bargaining. Our socialization as infants leads us to expect others will serve us. The way we live our lives pushes us into narcissism. "If I am not for myself, who will be for me," goes the proverb. But it continues, "if I am for myself alone, what am I?" And it concludes with, "and if not now, when?" The admonition seems to be an imperative to maintain conscious control of social rhetoric.

Furthermore, underlying our socialization is the assumption that things proceed according to some rational pattern, that is, that relationships are legalistic, rule dominated. But the very idea of a rule of law implies the existence of a system of rewards and punishments. If you are good all year, Santa comes, at least if your parents are in the higher socioeconomic brackets. Our neo-Calvinist psyches assure us that if we are rewarded, it is because we deserve it. Some, however, are crushed in the process, because they also learn the alternative, that is, if they are not rewarded, it is because they did not deserve it. A few fight back by trying to make themselves more virtuous. But when the football team prays that the Holy Mother of Victory blesses their endeavors, does that mean that the losers are damned?

There is a horrible logic in this outlook, for it assures that the rich will get richer and the poor poorer. Those who learn early on how to get what they want through the use of discourse forge straight ahead, usually at the expense of the less apt. The person with high self-esteem acts and succeeds and gets higher self-esteem. Those who do not succeed suffer from low self-esteem, which keeps them from risking and therefore from succeeding. For example, many of the shy people we have encountered were simply afraid to act socially because they knew "who they were." They believed they were entitled to be treated as shy people.

As every congressman knows, you cannot mess around with entitlements. Try reducing pensions or tightening the criteria for government largesse. We all want what we have coming (although sometimes we risk getting it "real hard"). The process of qualifying for real and imagined entitlements characterizes most adult discourse. What does a father, a boss, a mother, a lover, a child, a lawyer, a clerk, have coming? The speaker must assess the claims to entitlement and decide what to deliver.

This is where a cost-benefit analysis is necessary. Does the respondent want more than the speaker wishes to deliver? Is the speaker capable of delivering what the respondent wants? Decisions about whether to participate in social conversation are essentially economic. The actual participation succeeds only if the speaker is skillful. Thus, social competence depends both on the ability to analyze and the ability to perform.

The concept of entitlement is the simplest possible way of assessing performance. The critic merely asks, "What is the speaker after?" This opens a clear series of questions: "What is he doing to get it?" "How is the other person responding?" "What can the speaker do to bring the response more into line with his expectations?" The process is clouded by the fact that it is virtually impossible to measure the linear effect of one's behavior on outcome. On the other hand, a good critic can come up with defensible hypotheses and test them in the next experience. Gradually, by accretion, the speaker's repertoire grows.

The irrational belief in spontaneity interferes with the assessment of effectiveness of oral discourse. We argue that there must be a discoverable order in relationships. That, in fact, is the substance of the final chapter of this book. Our students must abandon their belief in "vibes" and accept the concept of orderly procedure. Otherwise, instruction simply does not work. Some ineffective speakers invest so much hope in the magic moment that they are distracted from doing anything for themselves. Since we are preoccupied with doing what *can* be done, we cannot afford to spend much time "dreaming the impossible dream." Most of our students are very much like Don Quixote or Candide when they arrive in class. We need to train them to be more like Mr. Spock, who really had very few relationship problems.

Getting What We Are Entitled To

The first task of a conversant is to decide what to seek; the second is to try to get it. This means making claims and offering demonstrations that will motivate the other party to comply. People expose their claims to entitlement as they specify their identity. I am new in town means I am entitled to special treatment in the form of information and guided tours. I worked hard on the project means I am entitled to a reward. I am your parent means I am entitled to your love. In essence, people offer their identity to document their claims. The entitlements are subsumed within the social norms. For example, if there is a law that says all veterans are entitled to pensions, then all that is required is documentation that an individual is a veteran. If the social norms say bosses must be obeyed, then occupying the appropriate position is sufficient to justify giving orders.

The situation is less obvious in voluntary relationships. To what is a friend entitled? If a person believes that friendship includes productive conversation, then the person who cannot converse well is not entitled to be a friend. Thus, regardless of feelings, the person who cannot deliver what the other believes is an appropriate entitlement, is not likely to qualify in the relationship.

It is unrealistic to believe, however, that assuming or claiming a role, is sufficient to guarantee the entitlements. Declarations of identity are valid only when ratified. The employer/employee relationship is a hard-core model. An individual is contracted to be the employee of another individual. He is compensated with so many dollars. In return, he has to spend a given number of hours doing the assigned tasks. If the tasks are not done, the employer can break the relationship. If the employee is not paid, he can sue. The employer has the burden of proof that the task was not done. The employee has the burden to show that it was.

In short, we argue for equity in our relationships. It does not matter whether they are formal or informal, the only way to get our share is to argue for it. If we resort to force, we are likely to shatter the relationship. If we are caught violating the rules, we are penalized for it. Equity is the theme underlying the whole business of making people more competent at social discourse. The reason we try to do it is to raise the odds that people will be able to get their fair share. This is obvious in formal relationships like governments and corporations.

What is the case, however, in a social relationship? It is characteristic of people to express confusion about the nature of friendship. Most people cannot specify a set of qualifications for their friends. They mainly respond to behaviors without a real plan. When two people are able to satisfy each other, they have a relationship. The exchange need not appear equitable to the outside observer. However, it must satisfy those involved. When the object of exchange is no longer valuable to one of the parties, the relationship may come apart. If the worker is unsatisfied with his job, he can quit and seek another. When a friend or lover is no longer satisfied with the exchange, the matter is much more complicated. To help understand these complications, we turn to the work of George C. Homans.

Communication as the Medium of Social Exchange

People can be pressured into relationships by inartistic means. They can be bribed or intimidated. Appeals to pity and duty can also work, but mutually gratifying relationships are usually the result of careful negotiation. In any case, the nature of the relationship can be understood by listening to the talk and observing what is being exchanged.

Social relationships are not machines guaranteed to work until the parts wear out. Sometimes sand gets into the crankcase. Sometimes one or both parties change their view of the entitlement rules. It happens. It is not possible to get another person to conform or comply automatically.

The simplest way to analyze relationships is to assume that people make decisions for some reason. Every request for an entitlement must be accompanied by an offer of some behavior that will comply with the listener's entitlement. Homans' (1975) behaviorist view is that it is possible to describe all human relationships as some form of exchange of goods, services, and sentiments. People make their own arrangements about equity. Thus, exchange need not be in kind. One person may give a great deal of service to another in exchange for demonstrations of appreciation and affection. That would appropriately describe a mother-child relationship. Formal relationships like salesperson and customer or physician and patient can be analyzed based on formal role descriptions. Private relationships develop an economy of exchange based on agreements made by the partners. To modify the arrangement requires modification of actions, that is, one individual could change the requests being made or change what is offered to the other. The ability to make these changes is essential to maintenance of relationships. Inept communicators, especially shy people, have inordinate difficulty managing such changes.

Homans' behavioral model of exchange is based on the premise that if an act has been rewarded in the past, it is likely to be rewarded if repeated. On the other hand, he points out, the nature of reward is variable. The more a person receives a particular kind of reward the less valuable it becomes. Thus, exchanges are often disrupted when one or both parties decide that proffered behaviors are no longer valuable.

Relationship partners must adapt mutually to changes in behavior both individual or collective as well as to environmental changes such as appearance of third parties. When one party in a relationship alters behavior, the other party is required to react. The reaction may range from panic and separation to submission. More often, the reaction is some kind of negotiated adjustment of behavior for mutual accommodation. When parties stay connected there is no way to escape modification. Thus, a dissatisfied employee may seek work elsewhere; a dissatisfied spouse may obtain a divorce. Otherwise, the single constant in relationship is change.

If skill at making changes is important, then a person who lacks skill is likely to resist change. Shy people cling tenaciously to their few relationships. They despair of making the accommodations necessary to form new ones. The axiom is that the person who has the least to lose by change has the most power in a relationship. The inept partner will give a great deal to sustain the status quo.

This places inept communicators (like shy people) at a distinct disadvantage, since one of their main problems is their difficulty in adapting to immediate social change. That is, perhaps, the reason why submissive people are so often poor communicators—or vice versa. Moreover, the uncertainty inherent in any social relationship demands continued connection through imposing order on the communication process. Skilled communicators have a distinct advantage in their relationships. It is easier for them to modify their own behavior; easier to argue against modification by the other person; and easier for them to make new relationships, should the relationship be terminated.

Mutual responses do not operate like servomechanisms. The "feedback" metaphor, which has permeated communication theory, is very dangerous. Feedback implies that a particular action will trigger an invariant reaction, somewhat like a furnace thermostat. Presumption may be in favor of relying on social norms, but it is important to be alert to the possibility of idiosyncrasy.

As usual, there is a paradox. What is a person to do? The obvious choice is to play the odds, do a sensible analysis of what has happened before and what usually happens in situations like this, and go with it. On the other hand, which odds do you play? When you are in a tense situation with your spouse, do you pull information from what you know about spouses in general or from what you know about the way men and women normally interact? Or do you pull information from your personal history with your spouse? Effectiveness in accommodating to change depends on a system of alternate scenarios acquired vicariously or by experience. Whatever the case, however, the speaker comes up with some sense of order and imposes to organize his or her discourse.

Private relationships are much more difficult to manage than public performances. Because the public speaker plays to the norms, his presentations can be scripted or formatted. In private relationships there is always someone else writing a share of the script. It is a grand improv. Because shy people have limited their repertoires and rely so heavily on predictability and certainty, they are materially hampered in their social dialogues. Consider this string of questions that might apply to any social experience.

Who is doing what? What impact does that have on you?
What opportunities do you have in this situation? With whom?
What do you have in mind for that person? Why do you have it in mind?
What do you want the other person to think, believe, or do?
Why do you think the other person might be willing to think, believe or do it?
What do you think the other person will want you to think, believe, or do in exchange?
Why do you think that person will want it?
What precedent can you offer for your analysis of this situation?
What similar situations have you observed that support your analysis of the situation?

Once the dialogue starts, these questions must be repeated after each response, for each response alters the situation. What do you do if the response is more than you expected? What if your comments are rejected? Effective speakers have a repertoire of adaptations they can make.

A Minor Paradox

The concept, "rhetorical competence," has three advantages. First, we can define it easily by evaluating and classifying overt behaviors. It is essentially empirically based and definable by estimating a deficit, for example, *rhetorical incompetence refers to the communication behaviors that account for the failure of an individual to accomplish a legitimate social goal.*

Second, we can allow for many causes of rhetorical incompetence, some of which can be modified and others not. We need not build a general nosology, since it does not fit the medical model. Nevertheless, we can create a taxonomy of counterproductive behaviors amenable to modification. Since evaluations of incompetence are based on observed behavior, modification of what is observed should lead to modification of evaluation.

Third, whatever the causes, there are only a limited number of overt impairments, the behavioral aspects of which can become the objects of pedagogical modification. The classical "Canons of Rhetoric" are useful as the headings for these impairments.

In the following chapter we will deal with the issue of criticism. We will try to demonstrate how the teacher of oral performance functions as a critic and offer some suggestions about how to make criticism effective. In the chapter to follow, we will deal with the issue of anxiety. People are concerned about social discourse. They fear it for a number of reasons. A great deal of research has been done to argue the case that anxiety, itself, is the general cause of incompetent social behavior. It is important to get a proper perspective on the role of anxiety so we can integrate pedagogies to deal with it.

10

Improving Performance through Criticism

In the previous chapters we have argued that the process of composition of social discourse must be orderly, and that the most effective approach to teaching it is through imposition of a formal technology of teaching that emphasized method and deemphasized the personal influence of the teacher. We used a computer model drawn from artificial intelligence to support our theory that communication performance can be improved by detecting and correcting errors in composition and delivery. We also noted that the other canons can be investigated and modified via inferences drawn from observed behavior.

In our explanation of the teaching process in the Penn State Reticence Program, we argued the case for ignoring emotion and concentrating on performance and criticism. The documented success of the program supports our argument. In this chapter we will explain how orderly criticism represents the teacher behavior most effective in modifying performance behavior. In the following chapter we will discuss what the teacher can do to prevent anxiety from interfering with the teaching process.

CRITICISM AND PERFORMANCE IMPROVEMENT

We learn at our parents' knee that criticism is effective. When we were children, criticism was used daily to teach us to brush our teeth or not to touch hot stoves. Parental criticism provides a model for school discipline. Our grades are a form of criticism, and later, our paychecks take the place of grades. Our friends criticize us by responding to our behavior. In fact, relationships can be described as mutual adaptations to criticism. Criticism is used by psychotherapists and physicians, football coaches and music teachers, art instructors and public-speaking teachers, and, of course, bosses, among others. Those who use it claim that it calls attention to flaws and defects and, when properly administered, provides remedies.

Criticism is commonly used to refer to particular kinds of acts by teachers directed toward improving student behavior. If we examine the definitions of "criticism" (Random House, 1987, p. 477). Here are the options:

> The act of passing judgment as to the merits of anything.
> The act of passing severe judgment; censure; fault finding.
> The act of analyzing or evaluating and judging the merit of a literary or artistic work, musical performance, art exhibit, dramatic production, etc.
> A critical comment, article, essay, or critique.
> Any of various methods of study texts or documents for the purpose of dating or reconstructing them.
> Investigation of a text or literary document.

Of the possibilities, only one actually refers to what teachers do: *censure, faultfinding.* Scholars are lured to practice each of the other forms for many reasons. It enables them to express their opinions; it gets them lines in print. But *censure and faultfinding* carry an obligation to administer correctives *exactly as in parental discipline.* In that sense, the orderly relationship between the student who wants to improve oral performance and his or her teacher is *parental.* The teacher passes *severe judgment* on what we do and tells us how to improve it.

Criticism in the form of faultfinding goes hand-in-hand with behavior modification. It doesn't help to offer a student a literary analysis of his oral performance; nor does training the student to perform literary critiques. It helps a great deal for a teacher to act like an *editor.* What an editor does for an author, a speech teacher does for a student speaker.

The Requirements of Faultfinding

Criticism is based on orderly procedure. We assume that the critic can identify an error and call it to a students attention. We also assume that the critic can propose a method that the student can use to correct the error. We thus assume that criticism, under certain circumstances, works; when critics know what they are doing and the person being criticized is willing to collaborate. We have also noted that the therapeutic alliance essential to performance modification entitles the teacher to be a critic and obligates the student to take the criticism offered.

The critic of oral performance focuses on errors in the presentation of discourse. Basically, these are flaws in organization and delivery. These would include (but not be confined to) obfuscating juxtaposition of ideas, poor documentation, faulty sentence structure and poor word choice, diction and related matters of delivery, use of body and facial expression, and suggestions about information that could be added, deleted, or corrected.[1]

The performance critic seeks incompetent behaviors and recommends ways to improve. The director of a play may seek to improve movement, intonation, lighting, costuming, and so on. Each time he points out a critical flaw, the actor or tech person is expected to remedy it. It makes life so much easier when the director can offer some alternatives.

Critics compare performance to standards derived from theory and experience. We have argued that pedagogy can also be based on standards derived from real or theoretical machine simulation. The inexorable logic of the computer applied to discourse makes errors obvious. The standard corrective would include ways and means of making the presentation sufficiently orderly to remove the error. The critic decides what an acceptable act should look like, compares the observed behavior to the standard, and offers the performer advice designed to adjust behavior until the results conform, in the critics eyes, to the standards set.

Labeling and Criticism

Labels assigned to performance imply particular types of errors. "Disorganized," for example, means the critic believes points are out of order. The student is entitled to ask, "What points are out of order?" The critic is obligated to reply. The axiom for this kind of criticism is, Do not point out an error unless you have a remedy.

1. This may appear to deal with invention. Actually, the recommendation of information to add or delete is relevant to the *onus probandi* imposed by whatever structure the speaker chooses. That is, the teacher does not try to make students more "creative" or "intellectual." He merely tries to help them fulfill the burden of proof they assume by the act of structuring.

Personality judgments like "shyness," for example, are used to describe social communication behavior that does not meet minimum standards of fluency and participation. Those who seek to modify human behavior generally must discover some stasis on which instruction or correction can hinge. The process of discovering stasis[2] takes place during the construction of the therapeutic contract. This may include negotiating what name to assign to an internal state and identifying what behaviors are associated with it; the effect it has on the student's life and its importance to the student as a goal to be accomplished.

That is, if a student describes his feelings as agitation and reports that he is bewildered by the necessity to organize information, the teacher may have to alter his understanding of the organization process (cognitive restructuring). The feeling of agitation may call for desensitization, or it may diminish once the student begins to acquire more skill. Her main effort must be directed at discovering what behaviors the student associates with the unpleasant feelings. Modification of these behaviors are the easiest goals to set because the student already has an emotional stake in the process. But, keep in mind *that it is not the teacher's purpose to alter the emotions.* The teacher (we hope) has the skill to modify the behaviors. It is presumed that alteration of the behaviors will change, consequentially, the way the student feels.

We have had few cases in the Reticence Program where anxiety made it impossible for the person to learn. In fact, a study of the effects of systematic desensitization carried out in the program demonstrated that systematic desensitization had no effect whatsoever (Kleinsasser, 1968). Serious cases in which shyness is a manifestation of a major personality disorder must be referred to the appropriate professionals. However, cases this severe rarely, if ever, appear in college speech classrooms. In the following chapter we will adjudicate communication apprehension to demonstrate that it is an ordinary emotion requiring no special treatment other than skills training.

Goal setting is a process by which trainer and trainee agree on what the trainee is to do to meet minimum standards for a particular

2. "Stasis" is an intriguing old concept. It refers to the central issue in the case. In a sense, the relationship between teacher and student is an argument. Teacher declares there is an impairment that must be remedied and offers a plan or procedure that, hypothetically, will make the desired change. The reason for changing is the crucial issue. Some students will respond to the teacher's influence; others will find a need in their own life. The effective teacher must appeal to the student's need. If the appeal is based on "do it for daddy," the change is usually temporary.

performance. It means assigning a label to the anticipated and desired outcome and associating particular behaviors with the label. To the extent the student finds the new label valuable, he will be motivated to attempt to perform them.

Setting the goals also specifies the role the trainer/critic is to play in the process. Each set of standards accepted by performer and critic is based on a view of the nature and purpose of relationships between human beings along with the moral values associated with those standards. Thus, modification of a reified state like "shyness" is based on moral judgments about what desirable behavior "ought" to be. The performer chooses to modify behavior if, and only if, he concurs for some reason with the critic's moral judgment or fears the consequences of the judgments of others.

Modification of Behavior

The process of modification is constrained by ability. Limits on performance are imposed by genetic inheritance and often by education and acculturation. But ability, itself, is a mystery. Because we cannot fathom the contents of a another person's mind (or even our own, for that matter), "ability" is a tautology. People are able to do what they have been observed to do. We also assume they are able to do what people like them have been observed to do. Each time people do something they have never done, they are deemed able to do it again; that is, it would not be unreasonable to expect him or her to do it again. Accordingly, we cannot presumptuously conclude that because people have not performed an act, they are not able to do it. If we assume that, we preclude training altogether. The trainer/critic must assume that a new behavior is possible if it is a norm to behave that way. The student has the burden of proof to show that the behavior is impossible. The teacher, for her part, generates teaching strategies from the assumption that the student is able to accommodate to training methods that have a reasonable probability of success.

Modifying human social behavior is a form of technology. While it cannot be predicted or controlled in a scientific sense, it proceeds based on hypothesis and test. While it may not be possible to devise universally effective pedagogies, there are enough alternatives to allow for a kind of "hacking" as we attempt to find modifications useful and appropriate in each given case. The procedures employed are selected based on precedent and vicarious learning. They are objectivized by observation and imitation. The person who seeks to change his behavior first practices the change and receives criticism on how closely it approximates the standard set. Each subsequent attempt should bring the student closer to his goal.

The process can become scientific when we formally seek generalizations that enable us to predict outcomes and control results. At the moment, the norm is to offer instruction and exercises *as if* we had the ability to predict and control, even though our confirming evidence is usually exemplary and anecdotal.

We must keep in mind that we are working with students in a classroom. However much we may prize the mystique of "individual differences" and "personal attention," the only utilitarian modus operandi is to consider the greatest good for the greatest number. Thus, assignments must be made for the class in common. Individualization takes place in the act of criticism wherein the teacher identifies different flaws for each person.[3]

Individualization cannot be rejected entirely, however. Social behavior is essentially rhetorical because individuals differ in what they seek, from whom, where and when, not to speak of differences in genetic inheritance, learning, experience, and acculturation. Thus, defective organization may be a legitimate label for a category of behavior problems, different ones of which can be found in different speakers.

The meanings of behavior differ as do evaluations. Common features can be isolated after the fact, but directives about what someone ought to do cannot be offered with any certainty of outcome. People label their own social performance, and they are labeled. Furthermore, they assign values to the labels. Thus, if a person is able to label his present performance with words of which he approves, he will defend the status quo regardless of how intensely the teacher/critic argues for modification. When the student agrees that his behavior has earned a denigrative label, he may choose to modify his behavior in order to modify the judgments made about it (and him).

There are two main ways students respond to denigration. Some

3. Generally, we recommend that criticism be administered in private. The norm in dealing with public speaking is to give criticism in public and even to allow classmates to participate. The latter process is actually like giving hunting licenses to blind people. We must assume that the teacher/critic is competent to identify flaws and talk about them. But if we are "passing severe judgment," censuring, and finding fault, the process ought to be one-to-one, in private, lest the student be pushed into a defensive posture and make public resistance to the embarrassment of criticism.

accept the label and proceed to behave in line with its predictions. Others use the label as a motivation to change. It is implied in the therapeutic alliance that the teacher *must* label behavior. She attempts to reinforce productive behavior by praising it. There is, however, no guarantee that praise will be sufficient reinforcement to sustain desirable activities. Anything she says that is negative may discourage the student despite previous praise. On the other hand, there are those students who respond best to extinguishing unproductive behavior based on punishment. Administration of criticism is where individualization becomes most important.

The contract between the teacher and student must make clear what form criticism will take, when and how it will be administered, and how the student is expected to respond to it. Whether the student responds constructively to the criticism depends on whether the teacher provides a viable alternative as well as whether the student is ready to make an effort to alter the disruptive behavior. The student may well be willing simply to put up with his own ineptitude. There is little the teacher can do about it. She can cajole, persuade, con, and threaten, but it is still the student's choice.

Teachers can spend a great deal of time trying to establish relationships with students. The purpose of the relationships, presumably, is to develop sufficient confidence on the part of the student to motivate change. More likely, it becomes a matter of transference and countertransference. Teachers can easily become charismatics. Students can learn to love and respect them. A warm teacher-student relationship, however, does not necessarily improve the odds that the student will make an effort to change. The experience in the Reticence Program demonstrated that time spent in cementing relationships with students generated little or no improved behavior. On the other hand, time spent rehearsing the student and demonstrating technique proved very profitable.

Thus, the labels become a very important part of pedagogy. Teachersmust seek precise labels for behavior, for a scientific pedagogy demands consistent identification of flaws so that common methods of modification can be developed. This can be done in a variety of ways. We can specify desirable behaviors, for example, via spectrographic analysis of the vocal qualities associated with social success (the definition of which also requires a taxonomy of situations and outcomes). There are already ways and means of modifying voices until they conform to specific standards and can be tested against objective criteria. While much of the process would be based on consensual standards, even those can be held constant with the proviso that anything consensually decided can be consensually revised.

SOCIAL BEHAVIOR AND THE CLASSICAL CONCEPTION OF CRITICISM

We have established that criticism only works when the student agrees to it. The process is most effective when the critic is prepared with recommendations for overcoming deficiencies. In fact, social exchange is a process of exchanging criticism; people change their behavior to obtain the approval of those they find important. Friends become friends because of the way they respond to each other. Each negative response suggests a behavior to be modified. Each person has the privilege of deciding how to negotiate behavior change. What is missing in friendships (and marriages) is the presence of a trainer who can provide the heuristics and algorithms of change. This is the role the teacher of performance behavior plays. The idealistic goal is to provide the student with enough experience so he can take over his own management.

Essentially, in social dialogue, each party evaluates the behavior of the other, decides whether it represents approval or disapproval, and chooses a response accordingly. To sustain a relationship we continue those behaviors that are rewarded and either discontinue or modify those that appear to evoke censure.

With this behavioristic model, social behavior can become very scientific. A speaker hypothesizes that a given action will evoke a desired response. He acts, examines the response, decides again, and then acts again, and so on. Competent speakers can, up to a point, control their own responses and predict with reasonable accuracy the responses of most others. Control means they can consciously select what actions to perform and then perform them as planned. Predict means they can anticipate the reactions of listeners with reasonable accuracy. It is the idea of conscious control that we try to teach to the inept speakers. When people are spontaneously responsive, they make errors, they insult others or confuse them. When people respond narcissistically for their own gratification, they can do considerable damage to others.

Quintilian believed that students should find models to imitate. This notion could easily become tedious if students took "imitation" in a literal sense like Rich Little. On the other hand, all of our communication skills are, initially, learned through imitation, first of our parents and teachers, then of our peers and heroes. The selection of what to imitate is important. It must be made with an eye toward feasibility. A five-foot, one-hundred-pound white woman will not become a Barbara Jordan, and a bulky man of Mediterranean ancestry will not become a Ronald Reagan. On the other hand, the small woman could copy Jordan's intensity, the bulky man could approximate Reagan's timing. It is here that criticism performs its most useful role by helping the performer select performable acts and guiding him or her in the performance.

What We Do Not Know about Criticism

We do not know precisely how criticism motivates behavior change, but we believe it does. The process seems similar to clinical treatment, but we know little about how that works either. Teachers of writing, art, drama, music, and speech use criticism to improve performance, with varying degrees of effectiveness. Medical and legal education follows a critical model. The apprenticeship of the intern and law clerk consists of practicing the profession under the scrutiny of a mentor who criticizes and advises. In essences, we are talking about *coaching*. In any athletic endeavor, the coach is empowered to criticize, correct, and drill the athlete in the "proper" procedure. In the final crunch, teaching performance skills becomes a matter of coaching.

We have not yet devised a way to measure, directly, the effect of criticism on behavior. We can argue, generally, that a critic can modify behavior, but we cannot take individual advisories and assess their impact. Occasionally, students will come back after a decade and recall some bit of wisdom they heard from their teacher's mouth and get very maudlin about how influential it was. These bits of sentiment are not to be trusted. It is sufficient merely to say criticism works in some cases.

Selecting a critic. We do not know how people select their critics, that is, why they will ignore what some people say, get defensive with others, and tumble head over heels to follow the advice of others. Some critics make them angry; some are regarded as irrelevant; some motivate them. We do not know how they choose which of the critic's words to take seriously. We know that when it works, the critic focuses the performer's attention on specific flaws. Sometimes the performer thinks up her own remedies; sometimes he looks to the critic for suggestions. The effective critic assumes status by agreement, somewhat like a voice or football coach. There is a presumption that the critic knows something the trainee does not know, to wit, how to modify the offending behavior. Advice is offered about the given case, but it is based on generalizations, and there is a presumption that behavior modifications can be generally applied. There is no reason to administer *ad hoc* criticism, since the event can never be repeated. Most critics base their recommendations on conventional wisdom, personal experience, or the social canons of good taste.

Training critics. We do not know how to train people to become good critics. There does not even appear to be a generally accepted definition of competent criticism. We seem to accept as a given that criticism will be taken, or tautologically, we assume that until it is taken it is not criticism.[4] In fact, there is an unfortunate tendency to ascribe failure to the willful rejection of criticism by the performer. "I told him what to do, why didn't he do it?" Rarely is the critic faulted for delivering criticism ineptly. He is usually faulted by the trainee for offering bad advice or for not offering a prescription for modification.

Some things we think we know. Criticism is most effective when performer and critic collaborate on identification of flaws and choice of remedies. Without agreement on the entitlement of criticism and its process, criticism is correction. In most composition courses, speaking and writing, instructors engage in correction simply because there has been no agreement between them and their students.

Elementary teachers know the form of compliance characteristic of correction. It is overt observance of the minute details of the regulations and total rejection once the student is outside the teacher's view. In the worst-case scenario, the performer merely rejects both criticism and critic.

The crucial issue is whether the performer is capable of following the teacher's directions. It is easy to administer moralistic correctives like "talk louder" or "use better evidence." It is something else again to provide heuristics and algorithms the student is able to use. The sad fact is that some inept performers *cannot* improve and they must learn to work easily with the status quo.

Rhetorical requirements in criticism. The critic who wishes to do something more than just damage the performer requires a rhetorical posture. He must accommodate his style to make it motivate the performer to comply. Some people respond to kindness, others to authority.

4. Herein lies the difference between criticism and nagging.

Some want rules, some advice. Others want gentle suggestions, while there are those who respond only to rigorous drill. Pedagogical criticism is more than just a process of noting flaws. In fact, effective criticism is forensic. The critic detects a need, devises a plan to meet it, and convinces the performer of the feasibility and desirability of the recommended modification.

The rub comes when the advice is wrong or the speaker cannot follow it. When this happens, confidence is breached, and the agreement is likely to be abrogated. That is why most formal criticism is greeted with resistance or apathy. Once the performer learns that the critic can make errors, it no longer seems sensible to attempt to follow the advice. The therapeutic alliance, so essential to successful psychotherapy, is an important feature in the successful operation of the critical process. When a performer plays the major role in deciding on what to modify and has some options in the approach, he assumes some responsibility for his own change.

Furthermore, when proposed remedies are not idiosyncratic, the teacher can document the argument that the they *ought to* work. If a particular technique has worked with most students in the past, it is reasonable to expect it to work again. One of the main problems with a private, clinical approach to criticism is that there is no peer support. The private relationship makes it impossible for the critic to argue a case for her recommendations.

CRITICISM AND THE CANONS

Most speech teachers use the canons as headings for their criticism. They may criticize selection and adaptation of topic (invention), organization of information (disposition), use of language (style), the act of speaking (delivery), and utilization of the repertoire (memory). The successful critic depends on a body of information drawn from real and vicarious experience as well as from "research." All the critic has is generalizations; what the performer needs is specific advice. The critic must guide the performer to appropriate application of the generalizations. The process is technological, that is, its goal is to make repairs in individuals in specific circumstances in such a way that the person criticized can adapt the advice to subsequent similar situations. Criticism that applies only to the past is only reprimand.

Criticism Based on Circumstance

There are some specific questions that apply to every social circumstance in which discourse plays a role. These define what the critic looks for.

Situation. What is the nature of this situation? The critic looks for flaws in assessment; that is, talking to strangers as if they were family, telling jokes at a funeral, or other obvious improprieties. To do an effective job requires the critic to know a good deal about social norms, phatic communication, and clichés and be able to demonstrate to the student when and how to use them.

Social situation. What is the relationship between the speaker and the other people present? The critic looks for presumptions like asking to borrow money too early or areas of omission like failing to introduce oneself to strangers. Again, the critic must rely on social etiquette for standards on which to base the criticism.

Goals. What are the speaker's personal goals, and which can legitimately be sought in this situation? Which are most likely to be accomplished? The critic looks for "go-with-the-flow" speech. The performer wants to arrange a date but does nothing to specify the goal, responding only to what the other person suggests or demands. The critic looks for lack of focus or commitment to a clearly defined objective. The critic can question the student about goals. Often, we discover, students are not able to articulate social goals either because they have none, or they have them but do not have conscious control over them, or because they think it is unethical to have social goals. The critic can provide the student with goal-setting formats to focus design of social goals.

Audience. To whom should the speaker appeal? Who would be the most likely person or persons to facilitate accomplishment of the goal? The speaker argues with the person who disagrees with him rather than appeal to the neutral listeners. The critic watches for alienating or irrelevant appeals, direct confrontation, or narcissistic demands. Speakers sometimes want to cathart, to express, to release emotions. Cognitive restructuring is necessary in these cases to advise the students that outbursts are generally counterproductive. The concept of audience analysis is very difficult to manage. Students must understand that while there are generalizations that can be made (for example, Catholics tend to oppose abortion; Jews probably won't eat pork in public; old people have aches and pains), they must be careful to avoid stereotyping and pay attention to behavior in context. There are, at present, few efficient formats for teaching audience analysis. Even the best instruction on this level is confined to cognitive advisories. By pushing students into using structural formats in composition, the critic can at least question the student about the intent of each component of the anticipated discourse.

In essence, this means writing alternative scripts for social situations using a best-, worst-, and most-likely-case scenario. This is provided for in the Penn State Reticence Syllabus (see chap. 2).

Exchange. Given what the critic know about people in general and the people present in particular, what can the speaker offer his or her listeners in exchange for their support? The critic looks for demands rather than inducements to exchange. The idea of exchange is probably the most irritating to the students. People do not like to think they must purchase the attention they seek. For some indefensible reason, they people "should like them for themselves." Consequently, inept speakers tend to demand attention and compliance and usually do not get it. When they discover that they are not getting what they want, they tend to withdraw. Cognitive restructuring can be used to sensitize students to the realities of social exchange. Rehearsal and role-play can be used to test their ability to appeal to others. The Dale Carnegie courses are particularly effective on this particular issue.

Constraints. What constraints are imposed by the norms of this situation? The speaker talks too little or too much, fails to acknowledge important people, or violates social taboos. The critic notes improprieties. The idea of propriety is very old and has dropped into disfavor in recent decades. However, the doctrine of propriety as enunciated by Longinus, and later as "taste" by Hugh Blair, is very important (Thonssen & Baird, 1948). Analysis of social situations constrains our behavior. Some things must be said to comply with the basic regulations for membership in a given social experience. The host must be acknowledged, the food praised, introductions performed in traditional ways (handshakes), and the proper small talk exchanged before moving on to more substantive and pleasant matters. However outmoded the concept may seem, the idea that etiquette was invented for the protection of social participants is very important. Also, etiquette is orderly. In the final chapter of this book we will offer several alternatives for imposing order on what appears to be chaotic social situations. Although compliance with social regulations is artificial, it provides a logic to which social participants can comply with reasonable expectations of salubrious outcomes.

The next question is, What shall the speaker say and how should he say it? At this point the critic plugs in on the canons for guidance.

Criticism Based on the Canons

Invention. Invention is the most difficult of the Canons to manage because all the critic can evaluate is the results of thinking (that is, the discourse itself). We pointed out earlier that invention is thinking, and that no discipline can claim thinking as its exclusive domain. The impossible dream of teaching students "how to think" might even be worth considering if only anyone knew how. On the other hand, critics of social communication usually have experience with the relationship between process and outcome and can offer students some sensible heuristic questions which may help them organize thought. By relying on the orderly procedure of structuring (chaps. 6 and 7), the critic can generate a format for retrieving and deploying ideas worthy of saying. The critic can seek evidence on which inferences about the invention process can be based. Does the content of the discourse give evidence that the speaker planned? This implies that a speaker must give a reason for speaking that appears rational to the critic in light of the situation in which discourse is to take place. Does the speaker seem realistic about identifying circumstances in which speaking is (1) desirable and (2) essential.

It is possible to get students to write coherent outlines and frequently they are able to say them intelligibly, but there is a real question about whether anything carries over. In the Reticence Program it became necessary to generate heuristic forms for virtually everything. It was not that the students were unable to think coherent thoughts, it was just that they did not appear to recognize them as such when they thought them.

Although, for example, setting goals appears to be a very simple concept, most students required formats to compel themselves to think rationally about them. If the speaker does not specify rational and realistic goals or demonstrate that she has adapted her ideas to potential listeners, training can be offered in orderly procedures for goal setting, topic selection, and adaptation might be the "treatment of record."

The critic can also look for content deficiencies. In any social conversation it is possible that a person has nothing to talk about but chooses to talk anyway. To create a pun, the critic looks for evidence of "go with the flow" while looking for "the goal with the flaw." A boring person may merely be socially inept because he requires instruction in matters other than performance. A great many speech teachers pick up this challenge. They urge students to read, watch television, and listen to others. The hypothesis appears reasonable; the more they read the more they have to talk about. In action, however, there does not seem to be much evidence that the natural aversion to learning characteristic of most students can be reversed by admonition.

Furthermore, intellectual content is not legitimate grist for the speech critic's mill. The analysis of deficiencies in invention starts with the assumption that the speaker has some reason for speaking and something to say. Certain competencies are fundamental to acquisition of communication skills: something to say and the mechanical equipment with which to say it. The speech critic can demand evidence and documentation, however. Once a student gets a speech structured, it is possible to guide research by pressuring for appropriate documentation.

Disposition. (See chaps. 6 and 7.) There are general rules and standards for intelligibility of discourse. Linguists have provided several models of intelligible sentence structures along with criteria for identifying ambiguous and unintelligible sentences. Aristotle's *Organon* (1853) provides a model for structures recapitulated in various forms like Toulmin's argument system, Venn Diagrams, and symbolic logic. Similar logical schema apply to the overall organization patterns of discourse. These include space, time, classification, analogy, comparison, metaphor, causal relationship, association, and argument, each of which is subject to a number of variations. The critic looks for lack of coherence as evidence of incompetence at disposition.

Can the speaker get ideas arranged in coherent fashion? Most texts devote considerable space to instruction in outlining; many teachers devote a great deal of criticism to it. However, there is very little direction given in how to translate the material on the outline to oral discourse. Furthermore, the problem of making social discourse coherent is not approached at all.

We assume intelligibility is necessary to accomplish speech goals, although we have little experimental evidence to confirm our assumption. In fact, various political successes and merchandising coups suggest that intelligibility is sometimes counterproductive. Actually, we know little more about the connection between arrangement and performance than Cicero and Quintilian told us. We assume there is a connection because when people are confused they say it is because they did not understand the sequence of ideas presented by the speaker. We judge the quality of a particular pattern of organization, and we infer that if it is modified in the proper direction, improved speech performance will result. The assumptions require confirmation in the given case. Thus, a great deal of criticism is devoted to modification of the arrangement of ideas.

On the other hand, there is a kind of mystical belief in the quality of note cards. Intercollegiate debaters carry around their little file boxes as though they contained the Holy Ark or at least a major memory chip. Many instructors in public speaking make a fetish out of requiring students to make note cards and hold them in their hands. All of this is part of the mythology of the virtues of the extemporaneous speech. Actually, very few public speeches in government and industry are extemporaneous any more. Teleprompters and ghostwritten scripts guide the presentations. Extemporaneity is important in social conversation, however. The question is, Do students learn much when they give extemporaneous public speeches that carry over into their social discourse? It is, of course, impossible to use note cards at a cocktail party or during a seduction.

Style. In the simplest sense, this refers to scripting and planning for performance. An actor is provided with words but must learn to deliver them well. A speaker must select his or her own words and learn to deliver them well. But there is no standard definition of "well." Some argue that there is an intrinsic quality of performance that can be assessed independent of an audience. Others say that impact on the audience is the relevant issue, and the influence of the components must be factored. Consider, for example, the simple case of a job interview. The interviewer has a set of questions (which imply that answers are forthcoming), but rarely does an interviewer have a formal set of standards by which to evaluate the answers. Each case is evaluated. But what is the basis for the evaluation? Suppose we had a standard for a good sensible answer, but suppose it was delivered badly. Or suppose an individual delivered a stupid answer well. What ought we teach an individual and in what proportion for what circumstance?

There are rules and they can be taught. As the schoolchild is taught written grammar, the speaker can be taught to select words and phrases and arrange them so they are suitable to a listening audience. The principles of structuring can be applied to paragraphs and sentences as well as to whole statements. It is important here to avoid the complexities of linguistics as they apply to word selection and sentence formation. Many artificial intelligence specialists have attempted to teach computers to compose and say sentences based on the probabilities inherent in various linguistic systems and theories. To date, this has been quite ineffective. Since our business is training student speakers to overcome their deficiencies, we urge teaching style as microstructuring, simply starting with the basic outline and working down to the sentence level.

At the very least, this kind of structuring can constrain students to be coherent. What apparently cannot be taught is how to be interesting. Vocabulary building does not help much. It would seem to be a cop-out to declare "they are what they are" but at the moment, we do not have any generally effective methodologies for helping students to become interesting.

Delivery. Delivery is the most obvious aspect of social discourse to criticize and relatively straightforward to modify. Students resist training in delivery on the grounds that it makes them seem artificial and insincere. It is easy to become preoccupied with modification of delivery. When this happens, training can become excessively mechanical. In fact, the experience of the elocutionists of the early twentieth century indicates that emphasis on vocal delivery may subvert training in the other canons.

On a primitive level, the critic can expect considerable success in modifying voice, diction, rate, and intensity. This is the basis of speech correction. The main problem here is that most speech teachers have never been really trained in the techniques of modification of delivery. Basic training in speech correction and theater speech would be a good place to start. If students are required to learn the International Phonetic Alphabet they acquire a common ground with their teacher-critic (assuming, of course, the teacher knows it).

It is very difficult, however, to connect delivery with personal psychology, mood, and sensation, as any good actor knows. Thus, delivery cannot be taught well without attention to content, organization, and style. Furthermore, acquiring versatility in adapting delivery to a variety of social situations is challenging even for the most skillful, so care must be taken to avoid acquisition of a standardized presentational format.

Memory. Can the speaker reasonably assess reactions to his or her presentation and draw from memory appropriate responses? This is the hardest of the Canons with which to deal. Experienced speakers claim it can only "develop" through practice or from careful artistic direction.

The operation of memory remains a relative mystery, however, and attempts at memory training have been simplistic at best and fraudulent in the extreme. Understanding the operation of the human data base presents a genuine scientific challenge to researchers. However, computer modeling can provide useful insights into processes and procedures for searching memory. It is sometimes productive to teach mnemonic devices or to train students to use general *topoi* as devices for searching memory (and libraries if necessary) for information to include in discourse. Propriety instructional programs like Dale Carnegie have gotten a bit of mileage out of teaching memory devices. These are helpful to students who want to remember carefully prepared speeches. They also seem to have some value at social gatherings where it is important to remember people's names. On the other hand, they appear to have very little value in helping students store information in a way that makes it easy to retrieve when needed. If it did, they would be getting better scores on multiple-choice tests.

Criticism Based on the Categories of Incompetence

The critic can seek specific failures in categories of incompetence.

Exigential incompetence. The speaker gives evidence of not being able to identify good reasons for speaking or appears to select reasons inappropriate to his or her personal goals. The critic pressures the student to provide a reason for speaking; to articulate a social goal to be accomplished through discourse.

Topical incompetence. The speaker cannot think up things to say, either says nothing, says inappropriate things, or repeats cliches. The critic can help the student acquire topics by exposing him or her to reading, viewing, and listening experiences and demonstrating how these can be used in conversation and formal discourse.

Invention incompetence. The speaker makes inappropriate appeals or present flawed, irrational, or ineffective argumentation. We use invention here to refer specifically to the process of retrieving (or gathering) information relevant to the speaker's goal or topic. It is the interface between the parallel distributed processing of mind and the linear programming of composition. We reassert the point that by focusing attention on disposition, the invention process can be guided by providing an organizing rubric for available information.

Disposition incompetence. The speaker appears incoherent or listeners appear to act as if she is incoherent. We have discussed this thoroughly in chapters 6 and 7 and offer the heuristics of structuring as the appropriate remedy.

Style incompetence. The speaker uses trite or obfuscated language, malapropisms, defective grammar, and/or incomprehensible syntax. Structuring is a useful way to manage style, as well. Problems in style can also be helped by guiding the student to vocabulary-building programs and providing models of excellent style as standards for imitation.

Delivery incompetence. The speaker is too loud or too soft; too rapid or too slow; hesitant; uses vocalized pauses; speaks in a monotone; speaks in an excessively loud or excessively soft voice. We repeat that the principles of speech correction and theatrical direction apply here.

Memory incompetence. The speaker does not seem to be able to apply past experience; cannot remember from time to time what worked and what did not. The person who invents an effective memory training system will make his million. The best the speech teacher can do is provide heuristic questions like, "what did you do before?" "What have you seen other people do?"

Feedback incompetence. The speaker ignores or responds inaccurately to listener responses. This is one of the hardest areas to teach. A good way to begin is to teach the student to notice responses. Most inept speakers simply do not observe their listener and consequently are unaware that feedback even exists.

Whichever taxonomy the critic employs, the subsequent process is experimental. Performer and critic agree on a specific course of action hypothesized to have a particular effect. The action is tried; the effect assessed and the next move specified. The axiom is, *A complete job of criticism includes identification of the defect, specification of the remedy, trial, and evaluation.* The process is repeated as necessary (batteries not included). *Cum rota viam tundit* (when the rubber hits the road), the stricture that the critic should not identify any problem for which she has no remedy severely limits what can be done in the classroom. Concentration on overt aspects of performance like composition and delivery appear to be the most productive.

RHETORICAL SENSITIVITY

Hart and Burks (1972; cf. Hart et al., 1980), in an attempt to synthesize rhetorical and social science approaches to communication, offered the concept "rhetorical sensitivity" as a basis for the criticism of discourse. The basic advisories offered by Hart and Burks center on adaptation and adjustment of speaker to listener. To the unschooled they may appear manipulative. Their authors claim they are rhetorical. In the Penn State Reticence Program, we have found them very useful as standards to which we can compare the adaptability of our students. With apologies to Hart and Burks, we present rhetorical sensitivity as we have adapted it to the pedagogical practice.

Components of Rhetorical Sensitivity

Hart and Burks defined a rhetorically sensitive person as one who can adapt to diverse social situations and perform reasonably well in most of them. The concept provides a good adjective with which to describe a socially competent person. Hart and his colleagues eventually designed a scale to measure rhetorical sensitivity, but the way they designed it, they used it to measure attitudes toward communication. Our concern in this book is with performance behavior. Therefore, we have interpreted the five qualities associated with rhetorical sensitivity as taxonomic critical categories into which various behaviors can be sorted. What we are able to include under each heading are the inferences about performance made as a result of observation of particular behaviors.

The rhetorically sensitive person (RSP) is able to change personality to meet a variety of social demands. Behaviorally, this means she can figure out what presentational style is most effective with a given listener and do a reasonable job of approximating that style. A competent speaker should be able to vary presentational tone, complexity and amount of information, and degree to which the listener is involved in direct response to what the listener says and does.

To accept this proposition means we cannot regard personality as a natural property (as in real self) but rather as a set of behaviors that present a Gestalt others will label. An RSP will have techniques to modify the way he looks to others. He will figure out how others want him to appear and adjust to it as best he can (without, of course, violating his ethical precepts).

The RSP avoids consistent or stylized behavior. This proposition appears corollary to the preceding. Effective communication is more than formulary. Though phatic communion can appear trite, it is a necessary preliminary to serious social contacts, each of which will require a responsive script for each encounter. Responsiveness means attention both to what is said and to the way it is said. If we communicate in order to make some kind of exchange, behavior must be responsive to the nature of the bargain being struck. What the listener responds can be understood only by interpreting the form, content, and manner of delivery of responses as well as the visible cues associated with performance. When behavior is excessively stylized and formulary, it interferes with the ability of people to interpret discourse and reduces the possibility of meaningful responses.

In short, stereotypical behavior is boring. The RSP has a sufficient repertoire of alternative behaviors that she will not bore even the people with whom she deals all the time. The notion of repertoire is important to the RSP. She is constantly alert to master new techniques of composition and presentation so that she has maximum control over the way she presents herself socially.

The RSP adapts and changes. Social communication is like a Markov Chain. Once the process starts there is no way to predict where it will go. Each verbal exchange is built from the contingencies of the dialogue that preceded it. An RSP has a goal in mind when a transaction begins but alters it realistically as the respondent provides more information. The speaker who continues speaking about a topic in which listeners are obviously uninterested gives evidence of deficiency in this quality.

The idea is to be responsive, not reactive. Inept speakers react consistently to all situations. When they are effective, it is quite by accident. The notion of constant change is important to the person who wants to acquire social skill.

The RSP can select usable information from available information. Clearly some people talk too much and some say too little. The RSP can select relevant sayables from a vast pool of possibilities. Time and tension interfere with a relaxed exploration for common interests. Aristotle identified what he called general and specific topics. The general topics were useful guides to questions that could be raised about what was relevant in any case. The specific topics were those ideas useful only in the case at hand. The RSP is able to synthesize the two for maximum adaptability.

Most of us are overloaded with information. We are often uncritical about what we use. The RSP is able to scan his own memory and knows where to go for more information. The selection process is always centered on accomplishing the goal and guided by the structure the RSP has designed for his presentation.

The RSP recognizes that there are alternative ways to present ideas. Speakers who have only one style are frustrated when they do not get the response they want. They do not know how to respond to the unexpected. A speaker must take into account the personal receptivity and ability of the listener. This includes understanding how familiar the listeners are with the topic and what biases they might have regarding it, their general level of literacy and their cognitive complexity. The idea of consciously analyzing listeners is alien to most people, yet it is the cornerstone of rhetorical effectiveness.

In short, the RSP will be able to argue, negotiate, cajole, plead, and threaten. She will be able to display gentleness when necessary and firmness when required. She will have an actor's repertoire and be able to play comedy and tragedy as well as perform in a musical review. The idea is "organized improv," for all social discourse is improvised. If it is done randomly, it is usually ineffective (unless it is funny). If it is controlled it is often highly effective.

Rhetorical Sensitivity and Rhetorical Competence

Rhetorical sensitivity is not necessarily synonymous with rhetorical competence. The problem with rhetorical sensitivity is that it functions as an adjective. That is, the judgments made about whether a person is rhetorically sensitive are global. They are made after the fact, and they take into account a Gestalt of behavior. Competency itself is made up of actions. A proper inquiry, therefore, might be, How should people act to earn the label "rhetorically sensitive"?

To answer this question requires consideration of specific characteristics of speech like structure of messages, choice of words, intonation patterns, and nonverbal cues. Information about content of discourse and its relevance to listeners is also important. The RSP must relate information to what others are saying in order to take full advantage of the social situation. We might also get information about the content of discourse; the topics discussed and their relationship to previous topics, the way the speaker refers to the listener, the kinds of arguments offered in support of assertions, emotional language used, and so on. We could make critical judgments about form and content including inferences about the nature of the composition process that underlies the discourse. But these judgments would be of the same quality as assessments of rhetorical sensitivity. In dealing with the concept "rhetorical competency," we must be very careful to concentrate on palpable and trainable aspects of oral social performance and be especially meticulous about distinguishing our evaluations from our observations.

The assessment of rhetorical competence depends primarily on the speaker's assessment of degree of success in a social situation. Did the unit of discourse approximately accomplish what the speaker set out to accomplish? If so, what were the observable components of that discourse? Given a number of people expressing satisfaction with the effects of their discourse displaying common features, to what extent are those features teachable? Rhetorical competence is a very practical concept synthesizing elements of performance with critical judgment and pedagogy.

Rhetorical sensitivity emphasizes the dialectical quality of social discourse. Talk is an exchange, even the formal talk made on the public platform. For talk to be effective, people have to be involved in it. Effective speakers can gain and hold attention and give it as well when others present their ideas. The only reliable evidence of rhetorical competency is observed performance. People who do not achieve reasonable social goals can be classified as problem communicators. Their behavior can be construed as a sign of incompetency. An examination of the potential deficiencies included in rhetorical incompetence will help us understand the skills essential to effective social discourse.

To Review

A rhetorically effective (competent) speaker is able to think up something to say that will make a difference in a social situation. He or she can put the ideas together in an intelligible pattern and select and arrange words to make the ideas intelligible to the listener. He or she can speak the words in such a way that they sustain attention and influence to listener. All of this is kept in a storehouse of ideas and experiences from which to choose ideas applicable to subsequent rhetorical situations. Finally, the rhetorically effective speaker is able to monitor his or her responses as well as those of the listener and adjust to them in process. Deficiencies in any of these areas are evidence of rhetorical incompetence.

"Rhetorical sensitivity" emphasizes the dialectical quality of social discourse. Talk is an exchange, even the formal talk made on the public platform. For talk to be effective, people have to be involved in it. RSPs can gain and hold attention, and give it as well, when others present their ideas. The only reliable evidence of rhetorical competency is observed performance. People who are observed failing at their attempts to accomplish social goals or those who regard themselves as failures can be classified rhetorically incompetent.

There is one last point to be considered in this discussion of pedagogy. It is the main impediment to participation in training, anxiety. Although there are many arguments about the role of anxiety in social ineptitude, for our purposes, the kind of anxiety we need to consider is the kind that keeps an inept speaker from seeking help. As we have noted earlier, we have found it to be very rare. However, most theorizing about incompetent speech performance has been done under the assumption that anxiety is the major cause. The influence of this variable is the topic of the following chapter.

Approaching the Social Milieu

Social communication occurs in context. In the final chapter we will offer some alternative ways of making the context appear orderly. It would materially help the instructional process if we could teach students to deal with the process of analysis of situation and audience. We need to answer questions like "What is there in social situations that make people fearful?" or "How can an individual extract relevant components from the incredible complexity of even the simplest appearing social situation?"

Taxonomy of behaviors. We have already indicated that one way to impose order over situations is to impose order through the creation of taxonomies. Throughout this book we have been advocating systematic methods of observation, evaluation, and training. Can we provide similar taxonomies for social situations?

Gist. We offered "gist" (Hirsch, 1987) as one way to simplify social complexity. To that end, we must understand the idiosyncratic view an individual has of the world. Hirsch argued that people do not learn through decoding specific symbols. Rather, he argues, they learn the gist of what is going on. Consequently, although each person will have a unique view of important aspects of relationship, one person's view will be sufficiently similar to another's so that it can be coded into common language and shared through discourse. While we have little or no control over internal processing (thinking), we can impose considerable control over output. By the same token, even though we cannot control individual social situations, we ought to be able to create models of understanding so we can share our perceptions and reach some common agreements.

Operation of information storage and retrieval. Our artificial intelligence metaphor instructs us that it is possible to impose order and create legitimate analogues to reality. Neurophysiologists are making great strides in identifying the standard processes of the operation of the brain. By following their work, we can become more and more precise in our machine simulation.

While general processes have localized effects, composition processes are sufficiently similar that we can exchange information. We know that individuals differ in the way they receive information. Some emphasize sight, others sound, and so on. Even so, when it is time to talk, everyone must follow the rules for producing talk; in writing, everyone must know the common symbols and connect them appropriately through common grammars. We can, at least, hypothesize that we can achieve similar community in social perceptions.

Physiological influences. The whole body plays a role in shaping social experience. As we examine the given case, that is, the behavior of an individual in a social milieu, we must keep in mind that his internal feelings exert some influence over his goal setting as well as his selection and execution of behavior.

Freud defined pleasure as the absence of pain. Humans are not usually aware of parts of their body unless those parts are malfunctioning. Malfunctions that call attention to themselves are important constraints on social behavior. We can apply these concepts to a defense of "dual perspective," that is, however different our feelings might be from those of anyone and everyone else, they are sufficiently similar that we can find words to express discomfort, pain, anxiety, fear, and so on.

Effects of learning and training. Essentially, hardwiring is important and the initial programming is crucial in shaping capabilities. We do not argue that early learning cannot be reversed, but what small humans learn about other humans and how they can be influenced exert considerable control over the choices they will eventually have to make about whether to participate and how to do it, if they choose to do it. Understanding what the individual has learned is important to consideration of how the components of the composition process work.

We can assume that we learn things in common about the social milieu. We learn about who is in charge, what followers must do, how to display loyalty, and how to rebel. They are common features of social experience regardless of where the experience takes place. Thus, we can assume everyone is taught something and everyone learns something about social experience. We can build on this premise to seek agreement on orderly procedure for understanding what is going on.

The infinite regress. We recognize the central paradox in taking a behaviorist position. Our argument is that while we accept the premise that all behavior is "caused," we do not reject the idea that a cause can be constructed in the mind of the individual. Our artificial intelligence analog necessarily omitted the possibility of self-generation of information. On the other hand, the possibility that humans choose from menus is a very important notion. We might not yet be able to account for behavior at the moment of choice, but it is obvious that a person can only choose from what is available.[5] That is, while we can map influences on choices, at some point, *within the socially interacting human* choices are made from a set of alternatives. We visualize some kind of grand multiple-choice design in which people confront choices of alternatives drawn from their own memory. Each human has unique sets of options from which to choose. The act of choice is partly independent, that is, it is constrained by what is possible but not restricted as reflex behavior. We allow for the existence of will, although we cannot explain it. *Thus, we account for will by willfully accounting for it.* We have examined options and rejected the pure behaviorist explanation because we know the contents of the black box are influential. We reject existential explanations because we understand the influence of indoctrination, acculturation, learning, conditioning, experience, and accident as constraining behaviors.

Our theory must account for willful behavior while accepting the possibility of behavior that is reflexive and actions taken for reasons not known to those who take them. Thus, we anticipate the unexpected. In fact, it becomes part of our rhetorical approach in which we train people to respond to alternative responses. In any given case, there is a "most likely" response and we seek it, but we equip our students with repertoires to enable them to react to alternatives.

5. Some years ago, a premed senior said farewell to this professor with the words, "I am now ready to solve all the problems of life, provided they are presented to me in multiple-choice form." This is not so farfetched. The metaphor of the planes allows for an infinity of menus from which choices can be made. It may well be that we can account for willful-appearing decisions merely by indicating that the permutations available in one mind are sufficiently different from those in another to preclude understanding the nature of the menus from which each must choose.

Evaluation of behavior. All of the preceding topics exert influence on evaluation. In the final analysis, what we try to do is ascertain how the speaker views the social situation so we can assess the effectiveness of the behaviors she chose in order to deal with it. We need to do this so we can assign blame to components in order to find the most effective pedagogy. If the causes of failure lie *entirely* in milieu, then it is pointless to blame the individual. It is, in short, hopeless to try to cope with the impossible. That is a project for clergymen and psychoanalysts. Our triage notion demands that we deal first with the simplest and most common problems and provide heuristics so that people can deal with their own exceptions.

Our theoretical posture now appears entirely behavioral, although not genuinely Skinnerian. We are concerned with what we see a person do and we measure competency by it. In considering its impact we can only take into account overt behavior or reports that can be verified through observation of overt behavior. Any pedagogics or therapies must be applied in such a way that they correct overt behavior and evaluated only to the extent that they are observed to modify the overt behavior of others in social situations.

We do not deny that emotions are influential, and we have provided a means for considering their impacts on individuals. We argue, however, that because their effects are idiosyncratic, our consideration of the given case will enable us to examine their effects on the individual without leading to generation of universal forms of clinical treatment.

11

Anxiety and Social Performance

Edelson (1988) points out that anxiety comes in two forms. First, anxiety can refer to feelings or impressions of states of affairs, real or anticipated. Second, it refers to responses to stress exciting the system to fight or flight. In the first case, anxiety is a person's evaluation that a state of affairs is dangerous. The individual may or may not be able to specify the nature of the danger. In the second case, an individual must deal with a specific situation and choose either to deal with it or avoid it. Both forms of anxiety are theoretically possible in shy or incompetent communicators.

The first form of anxiety may affect speakers' appraisal of a global situation, for example, the nature of an audience and impressions of harm that could come from unsuccessful performance. Most speakers feel a bit of this discomfort every time they speak. When the feelings are severe enough to paralyze the individual socially, he or she would be diagnosed as pathological and treated by a professional for some form of social phobia. Speech teachers rarely have to deal with this kind of person, although they often use the diagnosis as an excuse for their failures in teaching difficult students.

The second form may limit the ability of a speaker to respond to stimuli in a given social situation by blocking perceptions. But situational fears are rarely paralyzing. A person who is acutely aware of what is going on in an audience may occasionally be intimidated into silence, but mostly such a person responds awkwardly or out of synch. In either case, there are two variables with which a teacher can deal: (1) feelings about the situation and (2) performance in the situation. According to the common wisdom, anxiety or apprehension (intrinsic or situational) prevents a speaker from doing his or her best. Therefore, removal of the feeling will permit the speaker to do his or her best.

There is a tautological quality to this argument. People do not perform well because they are fearful, and they are fearful because they do not perform well. The question is where to make the pedagogical intervention. Programs designed to quell anxiety do not necessarily motivate people to engage socially, nor do they, in any way, improve social skills. We have observed several cases of persons who had been desensitized against social anxiety attempting social experiences and because they lacked the skills, they came away defeated, which started the anxiety process all over again.

Furthermore, we must be careful about how we react to what students report they feel. When students are allowed to ramble on about their social feelings, they are likely to say too much. When they are constrained in their reports by a questionnaire, what they tell us lacks detail. Thus, even though there may be a great deal of data about how students feel about speaking (and there is), the data does not have dimension. We simply do not know what each individual student means when they agree that they are apprehensive about a particular speaking situation.

However, training in skillful performance is possible in most cases regardless of how students feel. In fact, athletic coaches and theatre directors use this kind of tension to their advantage to motivate the gladiators and thespians to learn basic skills. People learn to respond to their tensions by involvement in practice or rehearsal. The more they practice, the more experience they acquire in dealing with their "fears." Thus, to call what they feel "anxiety" or "apprehension" does them a real disservice. The progress made by students in the Reticence Program demonstrates that guiding them to successful performance helps them acquire a repertoire of behaviors that enables them to deal more competently with their social environment. What they feel, at any given moment, becomes irrelevant once they have acquired performance skills.

People may choose social ineptitude, like shyness, as a defense against unpleasant feelings. They may also claim to be shy because their experi-

ence teaches them that they are ineffective. In either case, their feelings
are concomitants of their experience. We regard this as a critical element
in understanding communication competence.

Students can use their feelings as an excuse to evade training. Corporate structures, like universities, can require them to take training
whether they want it or not. Under those circumstances, their feelings
are irrelevant in all but the most extreme cases. Once they are in the
training program, as they acquire skills, their feelings become irrelevant.
People are entitled to feel as they choose, but in an academic setting
they are not allowed to use the way they feel as an excuse for avoiding
instruction.

We have already noted the behaviorist principles involved in the
Reticence Program. If a person gets good feelings from a performance,
it is a reward, and the person continues not only to perform but to
perform in the fashion that generated the good feelings. If a person gets
bad feelings, anxiety, disappointment, depression, frustration, boredom,
or whatever, from performance, they are punished, and as a result, they
may choose to avoid either performing again or using the style or
techniques that led to the bad feelings. The vector is important. It is
clear that modification of the feelings has little to do with the quality of
social performance. Altering the names we apply to the sensations we
feel has little to do with our skill at performing crucial acts, although
there are authorities who claim progress can be made by changing the
name of "communication apprehension" to "performance tension."

Most important, however, is to break the tautology. Even if a speaker
was genuinely anxious, it is questionable whether removing anxiety
about performance would alter performance. If the speaker was inept to
begin with, he would remain inept, although, presumably, he would
not worry about it as much. The best desensitization can do is make the
person more suitable to a training program focused on performance
behavior. In most cases, however, the first successful performance takes
the student through the steps of desensitization anyway.

Our theory of rhetorical competence requires us to emphasize observable behavior. In dealing with pedagogy or treatment, our focus must
be on those components of oral performance modification of which
would lead to alteration of overt oral behavior in particular rhetorical
situations. However, the scholarly literature in the field of speech communication is dominated by studies of "communication apprehension."
We must address this literature as well as the concept in order to complete

our theory of performance incompetence. In the following discussion we will use the word "anxiety" as synonymous with "apprehension."

THE RELATIONSHIP OF ANXIETY AND
SOCIAL PERFORMANCE

Throughout our Spock-like theory of communication competence, pedagogy has been stalked by personal emotion. We cannot deny that emotion exists. Despite the fact that our technology of teaching deemphasizes emotion, there is one emotion that must be dealt with directly. It is the passion of speech teachers to ascribe all forms of incompetence to communication apprehension. The concept has produced a mythology that has paralyzed the pedagogy of competent performance.

If we were playing "Jeopardy," the answers could be skills training, systematic desensitization, cognitive restructuring, improved competency, and psychotherapy. The question is quite simple: How do we treat communication apprehension? The reason we might want to treat it is because its authors and their followers regard it as harmful in its own right. Whether it is related to inept social performance is a question still unanswered. It is unanswered because those who study "communication apprehension" have failed to take into account the subjective nature of the phenomenon. They have also failed to explore the unique dynamics of anxiety in the given case.

Concern about the association of emotions with inept performance originated in the early years of speech as a discipline and crystallized in the study of stage fright (Clevenger, 1959). Somehow, scholars focused their interest on the nature of the affect rather than on the behavior associated with it. McCroskey (1970) seized the day in response to a report from the Ad Hoc Committee on Evaluation. The committee asked for a measurement scale that would identify anxiety or apprehension about speech performance. McCroskey gave them one. The original scale was designed to "measure" anxiety about public speaking, but it has subsequently been extended to group and interpersonal communication (with very little modification of the items).

McCroskey's scale purported to measure reports of perceptions of communication apprehension. He and his followers have, in essence, accepted as a premise that anxiety about speaking can be measured by a paper and pencil scale and that various forms of treatment or instruction can improve scores on the scale thus indicating reduction in anxiety about speaking (1984; McCroskey & Beatty, 1986; Richmond & Mc-Croskey, 1985).

They imply that anxiety about speaking has some effect on communication behavior. Anxiety is, thus, proffered as a cause of dis-eased (as opposed to diseased) communication however that may be defined and thus, measurement of it is *ipso facto* justified.

There is also a moral judgment implied here: it is pathological either to have such fears or to allow them to interfere with communication or both. The rationality of the apprehension is not in question. No one has inquired whether it is reasonable to be somewhat apprehensive about public appearances or social gatherings. No one has inquired whether it is normal, in the sense that normal means without pathology, nor has there been any attempt to investigate the specific case and ascertain whether or not people who report they are apprehensive (according to paper-and-pencil measures) have good and sufficient reasons for their apprehensions—or any reasons at all, for that matter. Finally, the only reported investigation into the individual nature of the apprehension was conducted under the rubric of the Reticence Program, where it became abundantly clear that virtually everyone will discuss feelings about performance, but there is no common language or frame of reference to suggest that there is a general kind of apprehension. The assumption in all paper-and-pencil measures is that apprehension is uniform in all cases and therefore amenable to measurement. Note should also be taken of the lack of tangibility of the paper-and-pencil measures. They have not been correlated with performance or physiological state, not to speak of referents and references. They are mostly short and unidimensional. Thus, it is not clear what they are measuring, if indeed, they measure anything at all.

A better question would be, Does emotion of any kind interferewith communication performance? The corollary question would be, If it does, in what situations and in what ways, for what persons? Emotion is not synonymous with anxiety or apprehension, however. Apathy might be an emotion that interferes with performance; so might anger, love, or envy. Furthermore, the work of Zimbardo and others indicates that some skilled public performers claim to be shy or anxious. We could inquire about whether the unidimensional measurement scales are capable of distinguishing between the apprehension felt by skilled performers and those who ostensibly avoid performance because of it. Finally, we have noted that shyness and anxiety are not synonymous.

Poor performers might be poor because they are apathetic about a given situation or about performance in general, or because they have not been trained. Furthermore, the nature of performance in a public-speaking situation might be sufficiently different from that in a group or social situations so that only a multidimensioned scale could pick it up. The PRCA is clearly unidimensional.

If anxiety is finally indicted as one of many causes of poor perfor-mance, it would be necessary to investigate whether the anxiety was fear of a particular situation or consequence, free-floating anxiety loosely associated with social appearance, neurotic anxiety about some harm that might befall the performer, or moral anxiety about some ludicrous or dangerous act the speaker might perform. In short, anxiety is not a simple concept, nor is its connection with performance of social dis-course a given. In this section we will explore the complex concept of anxiety in an attempt to assess its origins and speculate about the possible effects its various forms might have on social discourse.

AN ASSESSMENT OF THE PRCA

McCroskey and his associates have, of late, begun to conjecture about whether apprehension is "state" or "trait." These global reifications do not, however, bring us any closer to an understanding of the connection, if any, between the condition purportedly described by the scale and inept performance behaviors. In fact, those who use the PRCA as an ostensible behavioral major have abdicated from connecting with the internal dynamics of speakers.

The Freudian conception of anxiety (to be discussed later in this document) suggests that anxiety is *transitive*. This grammatical meta-phor implies that anxiety must have an object. There is anxiety "about . . ." something. The measurement devices used by McCroskey et al. focus on public speeches, group discussions, or social gatherings. These, however, are settings. They may be objects, but in their own right, they are not universally fear evoking. Somewhere in each anxious person, there is some image or impression that gives rise to anxiety in a purely reasonable and rational way. Combs and Snygg (1959, p. 22) argue:

> Everything we do seems reasonable and necessary at the time we are
> doing it. When we look at other people from an external, objective point
> of view, their behavior may seem irrational because we do not experience
> things as they do. . . . However capricious, irrelevant and irrational his

behavior may appear to an outsider, from his point of view at that instant his behavior is purposeful, relevant, and pertinent to the situation as he understands it. How it appears to others has no bearing on . . . causes of . . . behavior."

This point of view is corroborated by Boudon (1989). Boudon bases his argument on the work of Herbert Simon (p. 173), who is quoted as saying, "In a broad sense, rationality denotes a style of behavior that is appropriate to the achievement of given goals with the limits imposed by certain conditions and constraints." Simon identifies three variables that affect rationality: objective characteristics of the environment, perceived characteristics, or characteristics of the environment itself. The PRCA measures none of these variables. It only measures *reports* given by individuals, and even there, the reports are confined to the choices present on the scale itself.

The most potent argument for a connection between anxiety and performance lies in psychoanalytic analysis. An individual might be fearful about the environment. There may be enemies present in the room. They may be carrying knives. Or members of the audience might be carrying ripe fruit. On the other hand, the speaker may face memories, some frontal and some repressed, about past events in similar situations. Or the speaker may fear saying something gauche or stupid or inflammatory and be anxious about his individual ability to cope. Finally, there may be a free-floating anxiety about "people in general" that triggers a physiological reaction. In short, anxiety (apprehension) is a multidimensioned concept that cannot be reduced to a simple twenty-four items on a scale. In considering performance anxiety or communication apprehension, it is important to discover a connection between the anxiety and precedent events or conditions, for anxiety does not arise *ex nihilo* but is actually inherent in the human organism that suffers from it, a function of that organism's social history. Whatever exists inside the human interacts with environment, and the actual effect on behavior is constrained by the interaction of the individuals present in the speaking situation.

The arguments about the nature of the connection between apprehension and performance have been incomplete, less than convincing or worse begged the question. For example, Kelly (1982) and her collaborators argued the case that the apprehension-performance connection was spurious, while DeVito (1986, p. 16) begged the question by announcing that "communication apprehension is a decrease in the frequency, the strength, and the likelihood of engaging in communication transactions." McCroskey and associates are considerably more careful. They allege the connection and describe it globally (McCroskey, 1984, p. 33) and hedge their bets with statements like "there is no behavior that is predicted to be a universal product of varying levels of CA (communication apprehension) (McCroskey, 1984, p. 34). By implication, however, they seem to believe that apprehension is a uniform condition, and its effects can be measured quantitatively. However, a recent review (Allen, 1989) of 116 studies purporting to measure connection between anxiety and performance concludes that a great deal more research must be done to make such connections.

By and large, however, there is little evidence offered that self-reported reduction of apprehension is anything more than a change of scores on the scale. We do not know whether the people measured are actually better off. There may be something radically wrong with a person who does not acknowledge the threat inherent in a social situation. However, more to the point, the scores are simply *presumed* to represent a condition, the objective nature of which is not known. The assumption that anxiety or apprehension is *ipso facto* bad has never been documented. The content validity argued for such scales as PRCA (McCroskey, 1970) does not predict performance behavior.

In fact, Richmond and McCroskey (1985, p. 56) note in their explanation of the impact of communication apprehension on its victims that there is no *consistent* set of performance behaviors that can be ascribed to apprehension, shyness, or simple performance incompetence. This contradicts the implied message that reduction of anxiety as measured by reduced scores on the PRCA will bring about all manner of salubrious results. They argue that apprehension interferes with performance in *some* way. They explain in the final chapter of their book (Richmond & McCroskey, 1985, pp. 78) that the "basic theories about why people experience fear or anxiety about communication may be placed in three categories: (1) excessive activation, (2) inappropriate cognitive processing, and (3) inadequate communication skills. They offer systematic desensitization, cognitive restructuring, and skills training as potential remedies or pedagogies for dealing with the problem of *communication apprehension*. They do not deal with the problem of inadequate communication performance at all, although they imply that skills training improves performance and thus ameliorates anxiety or apprehension. More recently, scholars have focused attention on the concept of "competency" (Rubin, 1989) distracting attention temporarily from consideration of the relationship between apprehension/anxiety and performance of oral discourse.

APPREHENSION/ANXIETY AS A PSYCHOANALYTIC CONCEPT

The question of the relationship between anxiety and performance, thus, is still moot. The suggestion that there is a relationship is clearly psychoanalytic, however. Ascribing anxiety as a "cause" of avoidance of communication or social ineptitude is based on the psychoanalytic premise that our social behavior is influenced by our internal dynamics. The extent to which anxiety affects behavior is a legitimate matter for psychoanalysis. The standard definition (Edelson, 1988, p. 91) is "anxiety is a subject's appraisal of a state of affairs as dangerous." Note that there must be an object associated with anxiety. Psychoanalysts do not regard anxiety as a behavior, thus, approaching anxiety behaviorally fails to take into account the impact of anxiety as an emotion and as a major factor in the development of personality (Hyde, 1980, p. 140). In order to understand the phenomenological impact of anxiety, it is important to view it as a sensation to be named by the individual. It is inherently idiosyncratic and not amenable to any measurement beyond nominal. We can ask, "Do you feel anxious?" in certain situations or about certain people, but we cannot assume that any yes answers represent the same internal dynamic. Thus, it is possible that a great many people feel what high-communication apprehensives feel but choose to give it another name.

The communication apprehension model seems to be based on the notion that anxiety is a behavior to be reduced or eliminated by some methodology. DeVito (1986, pp. 16–17), for example, in what purports to be a "dictionary" of concepts in communication, imply declares that communication apprehension is fear of communicating, which leads to a "decrease in the frequency, the strength, and the likelihood of engaging in communication transactions." "Speakers" who suffer from it simply "avoid communication situations and, when forced to participate, participate as little as possible." The rest of the encyclopedic entry reiterates McCroskey's premises not as hypotheses but as generally accepted facts. It says nothing about communication behaviors, although McCroskey makes quite a point of this in most of his writing. If the only impact of communication apprehension is to reduce willingness to communicate, there is nothing to distinguish it, behaviorally, from the concept "unwillingness to communicate" conceptualized by Burgoon (1976). Furthermore, the concept of "will" is another occupant of the black box. It is not a behavior but an inference about the cause of a behavior. There may be a number of reasons why an individual chooses not to communicate besides unwillingness, for example, lack of opportunity, lack of energy, apathy, or simple inability to get a message together.

It is clear that most people feel something before they engage in discourse, formal or social. It is not clear what they feel or why they feel it. To assume that it is anxiety begs the question. Furthermore, anxiety as conceptualized by McCroskey and his followers is not compatible with the explanations given by psychiatrists, classical or contemporary. The fundamental definition offered by McCroskey (1984) as a "broadly based anxiety related to oral communication" fails to explain the nature of the relationship between the concept and behavior. "Related to" is not specific. In fact, the connection between communication apprehension and consequent communication behavior has been denied (Richmond & McCroskey, 1985, p. 87) with the statement "the course (in communication skills) had no effect on their (the students) level of apprehension or made it worse." Richmond and McCroskey (p. 85) also note that the main documented effect of eliminating apprehension is "reduced scores on the PRCA" or "reducing self-reported apprehension about communication" (p. 87).

If we are concerned, as professionals, with modification of performance behavior, the issue of anxiety or apprehension is relevant on two counts. First, we must consider the possibility that it causes some inept behavior in some people. Second, we must allow the possibility that it is an effect caused by inept performance of social communication or the reaction to it by others. Since the connection and/or its direction has not yet been definitively established, and since apprehension is clearly a psychoanalytic concept, exploration via classical psychoanalysis may be useful at this time to generate testable hypotheses about the connection between the two.

THE STANDARD DEFINITIONS OF ANXIETY

The *Random House Dictionary* (1987, p. 96) defines *anxiety* as "1. distress or uneasiness of mind caused by fear of danger or misfortune; . . . 3. *Psychiatry*. a state of apprehension or psychic tension occurring in some forms of mental disorder." *Apprehension* (p. 103) is defined as

Communication Incompetencies

"anticipation of adversity or misfortune; suspicion or fear of future trouble or evil." Both of these definitions objectivize the emotion, that is, the use of the terms demand identification of the feared object. What is the nature of the misfortune anticipated by a person who scores high on a communication apprehension test. The psychological definition refers to a "state" and *DSM/III* (1980, p. 228), the compendium of psychiatric disorders lists among "Anxiety Disorders" criteria for *social phobia*:

> A. A persistent, irrational fear of, and compellingdesire to avoid, a situation in which the individual is exposed to possible scrutiny by others and fears that he or she may act in a way that will be humiliating or embarrassing.
> B. Significant distress because of the disturbance and recognition by the individual that his or her fear is excessive or unreasonable.
> C. Not due to another mental disorder, such as Major Depression or Avoidant Personality Disorder.

There is, in this nosology, no reference to actual performance behaviors. However, it clearly identifies scrutiny or fear of humiliation as the source of the anxiety and also specifies that the individual recognizes that the fear is unreasonable. At the outset, it would seem sensible to attempt to explore further the self-reports of self-identified communication apprehension victims to see precisely what it is about social discourse that makes them anxious. If it is simply concern about the possibility of not doing well enough, we can hardly regard it as pathological. Actually that kind of response could be responded as appropriate motivation for learning.

Kuper (1985, pp. 34-35) ascribes anxiety to stress and notes that it is characterized not only by subjective feelings of apprehension but also by physiological manifestations such as increased heart rate, palpitations, tachycardia, sweating, muscle tension, irregular breathing, dry mouth, and possible vertigo, nausea, tremors and tics. Beatty's (1984) summary of the relationship between measured communication apprehension and physiological evidence shows limited and inconsistent connections. Kuper also notes (p. 35) that anxiety results from an appraisal of a situation based on the individual's skills, abilities, and past experience. Skills assessment has not, traditionally, been a component of paper-and-pencil assessments of communication apprehension. Furthermore, questions have not been raised about whether or not people who score high on communication apprehension employ the standard defense mechanisms associated with anxiety and applied when the individual does not feel capable of coping with a feared situation.

McCroskey and Beatty (1986, p. 279) are fairly inexplicit in their definition. They define apprehension as "a broadly based anxiety related to oral communication . . . an individual's level of fear or anxiety associated with either real or anticipated communication with another person or persons." They disconnect it from behavior by specifying that it is "a subjective, affective experience" and from shyness by defining shyness as a "predisposition to withdraw from or avoid communication with other people." Thus, they load the cards on behalf of a self-report measure, quite versatile in its ability to measure something or other consistently but incapable of defining either the source of apprehension or the verbal behavior connected with it. Furthermore, unlike the psychological specification, they ascribe it to both state and trait with a relatively fuzzy set of explanations. They allege it is "trait-like" (p. 281), a "relatively enduring personality-type orientation toward oral communication across a variety of contexts" that they claim are operationalized in PRCA-24. The problem seems to be that the PRCA-24 is administered at a particular time. Given the items on the scale, it is impossible to measure "enduring" characteristics. Furthermore, they also argue that it is situational and temporary and focused on communication with a given person or group. Apparently they are attempting a taxonomy of communication apprehension based on a two-way classification of state and trait. This is difficult to do with a scale that purportedly taps an attribute which ranges from 24 times 1 (the lowest score possible) to 24 times 5 (the highest possible score). An instrument like this cannot both classify types of an attribute and simultaneously regard the attribute as a unidimensional interval scale.

There are other flaws in the instrument as well. For example, items about public speaking are specific and refer to issues like "my body feels tense and rigid while giving a speech." Items are phrased as polar opposites, and so "relaxed" is offered as an antonym to "tense and rigid." Other specific public-speaking items are "I get so nervous I forget facts" and "My thoughts become confused and jumbled." Items referring to social conversation and group discussion are not specific. Other pairings are questionable, for example, tense and nervous versus calm, dislike versus comfortable, uncomfortable versus afraid to express myself. There is an item phrased "I dislike participating in group discussions." An item like this conveys no connotation of apprehension or anxiety. One can dislike something without being apprehensive about it.

Reliability and validity are also issues. Reliability can be calculated on a split-halves basis, but in this instrument opposites are next to each other in the scale. This is prejudicial because respondents will reference to the preceding item in order to maintain consistency. Thus, the charge can be leveled that the cards are stacked in favor of reliability. Finally, and most important, there is no effort made to validate the connection alleged between reports of apprehension, as measured by the scale, and actual performance. Validation could come from observation or verbal reports from speakers about particular situations. Consistently, those who argue for using PRCA as a measure of apprehension claim face validity for it. Face validity refers to a scale containing items representing the universe of constructs available. This is hardly the case on a 24-item scale. Thus, although it is almost heretical to do so, we question whether this scale measures anything at all. We charge that it does not measure apprehension. The authors claim it measures reports of apprehension, but these reports lie within such a limited range that the later broad claims made for the scale simply cannot be defended.

Furthermore, the definition of communication apprehension seems to diverge from traditional meanings of anxiety at this point in Mc-Croskey's theoretical development. Supporters of PRCA argue, for example, that skills training is not effective in reducing communication apprehension. Apparently, there is something to be gained simply from removing anxiety, although this is not specified. In fact, there is a peculiar restriction applied to the concept:

> The implications of conceptualizing CA as strictly an internally experienced phenomenon must be emphasized. Because CA is experienced only internally, the only potentially valid indicant of CA is the individual's report of that experience. Thus, self reports of individuals, whether obtained by paper-and-pencil measures or careful interviews, provide the only potentially valid measures of CA. (McCroskey & Beatty, 1986, pp. 286)

The PRCA is not a report of "experience," however. The items are global and refer to situations in general. Reports of experience would be responses to questions posed to individuals like "How did you feel when you gave that speech?"

They go on to rule out physiological measures, calling them "indirect evidence of CA and, thus . . . inherently inferior" (p. 286). Finally, they declare, "There is no behavior that is predicted to be a universal product of varying levels of CA" (p. 286). While they concede that some observable behaviors are likely to occur they emphasize that a person with high "trait-like" CA "may behave in a manner no different from anyone else." Kelly's work (1982b) seems to confirm this. Her report that untrained observers cannot distinguish between reticent and nonreticent students confirms McCroskey's assertions.

McCroskey and Beatty list three behaviors they claim are closely connected: avoidance of, withdrawal from, and disruption of communication and suggest that overcommunication might also be caused by CA. No behaviors are specified as sine qua non of any of the these conditions and thus, we have categories of behavior with no qualifications for membership. The connection between the gross categories of behavior is alleged but not documented.

There is also a paradox in their argument. In the first place, the introspection involved in this analysis appears very much like the philosophy underlying behaviorism as it emerged one hundred years ago. The emphasis was on examining behavior, not contemplating the mystic contents of the "black box." PRCA represents a black box. It has nothing to do with behavior at all. The value of subjective reports, however, is to provide cues to overt behavior. A physician, for example, takes reports of chest pains seriously and attempts a differential diagnosis by examining the patient for coronary artery blockage, transient ischemia, esophageal spasm, dyspnea, or any of the other conditions that might *cause* chest pain. The question of what *causes* people to report as they do on the PRCA is important, but it has not been investigated. Even more important is whether the items on the PRCA so limit what it is possible for people to report that it actually distracts investigators from exploring the range of empirical possibilities.

The Freudian implications are very important because a scale that purports to explore the effect of internal dynamics on performance behavior is actually investigating the Freudian notion that anxiety arises in ego as a defense against fears of potential destructive behavior arising in id or superego. McCroskey's explanation of etiology is also Freudian in context. The allegation that environmental influences in childhood are the main cause along with inconsistent reward and punishment and modeling are also Freudian (pp. 288–289). Only the reluctant suggestion of inadequate skills development (p. 289) diverges from a pure Freudian construct. They offer the proviso, however, that CA also affects public performers. They do not allow for the possibility that as people skilled in interpersonal communication may be inept on the platform, platform performers may be interpersonally inept. Interpersonal ineptitude, incidentally, does not necessarily come from anxiety. It might also come from a sociopathic personality or the behavior of a social marginal not skilled in the phatic communion of a specific social group.

The McCroskey view of anxiety is diametrically opposed to Skinner's. Skinner states (Skinner & Estes, 1972, p. 523), "Anxiety is . . . defined as an emotion state arising in response to some current stimulus which in the past has been followed by a disturbing stimulus . . . . The . . . anxiety state was extinguished when the tone was presented for a prolonged period without the terminating shock." This appears to indicate that Skinner believes that anxiety must be extinguished by experience. Skinner's definition of anxiety (p. 523) "anxiety has at least two defining characteristics: (1) it is an emotional state, somewhat resembling fear, and (2) the disturbing stimulus which is principally responsible does not precede or accompany the state but is 'anticipated' in the future." Although this is quite close to McCroskey's definition, Skinner's implication that behavioral manifestations must exist and be modified in order to quell anxiety provides another important area of investigation, that is, close examination of the actual performance behavior of communication apprehensives in specifically defined social situations in order to develop a taxonomy of behaviors associated with apprehension. These behaviors would represent targets for behavior modification in a Skinnerian model.

The assignment to write "Self-as-Communicator" papers in the Reticence Program provides a basis for analysis of the relationship between anxiety in its classical sense and behavior. Most students seem to report either neurotic anxiety or moral anxiety. Some are afraid of stimulating laughter and believe that others will dislike them because of what they say. Others express the belief that they will do something wrong when they speak. The most frequent error is that they will say something "dumb" or "stupid" or "ignorant." These expressions lie in the classical conception of anxiety and can only be derived from clinical data like interviews or the papers. Coles (1982, p. 257) suggests that the anxiety defenses enumerated by Sigmund Freud are behavioral responses in ego when anxiety suggests to ego that it may be overthrown. A careful examination of the Freudian theory of anxiety is important at this point so that we can understand (1) that anxiety is quite normal when people confront public speeches or unfamiliar social experiences, and (2) that very few people actually fall into a pathological range where the anxiety requires treatment in its own right.

THE CONTRIBUTION OF SIGMUND FREUD

Hall (1954, pp. 61–70) reviews Freud's conceptualization of anxiety by explaining that it exists in the normal personality as a warning to the ego that it is in jeopardy. Freud believed that anxiety represented a physiological excitation of the organism that had a special quality that distinguished it from tension, pain, or melancholy. He believed that it was a conscious state synonymous with fear resulting from one of three causes.

The cause of reality anxiety lies in the external world from a person or situation that poses direct harm. Freud believed this form of anxiety was acquired in infancy from early experiences of helplessness or fear of separation from the parent. With this kind of anxiety, the organism is tempted to fight or to flee. When one suffers from reality anxiety, action must be taken about a palpable situation. If the person feared aspects of the situation, he could flee (shyness) or take instruction or just do it. The anxiety could not be modified without challenging the situation in which it was nested. Most teaching of speech performance behavior must deal with this form of anxiety. Virtually all students experience some form of tension when they confront the prospect of speaking. The underlying premise of performance instruction is that by becoming familiar with the situation, students can be trained to master it.

Neurotic anxiety arises from instincts in the id. A person is afraid of being overwhelmed by an uncontrollable urge to commit some act or think some thought that will generate harm to himself. This form of anxiety can take three forms. Free-floating anxiety is a general fear that something nameless and dreadful will happen. Phobias are direct panic reactions to particular situations. The panic reaction occurs when a person does something totally out of character in response to anxiety in general. None of these apply directly to the speaking situation. Stage fright, a common reference to this kind of anxiety in the speech literature, simply does not exist in the psychiatric literature. Neither *DSM/ III* (1980) nor *The Comprehensive Textbook of Psychiatry IV* (1985) makes any reference to it.

Freud believed that anxiety was a component of personality and that people shaped their social choices in response to it. Personality, he argued, was formed by acquiring skill in dealing with frustration and anxieties. Personalities changed naturally, he noted, through maturation. Individuals grow physically through the oral, anal, and genital stages of development and acquire perception, memory, cognition, judgment, and the ability to think. Whatever stands in the way of accomplishing the pleasure principle impedes this growth, and most often, it is anxiety that administers the painful jolts that prevent humans from attempting to solve their own problems.

Many of the behavioral aspects of defenses against anxiety become intrinsic in the development of personality. Identification, for example, can be recognized by observing how people model their behavior after that of important others. The identification of narcissism is activated through the choice of associates whose behavior represents prized aspects of one's own personality. People will act like successful persons on the grounds that behavior is associated with success.

Sublimation is regarded as a rational defense against the pain of anxiety. The ability to rechannel energy from potentially dangerous id-level drives as well as from situations that induce anxiety is, according to Freud, the basis of artistic production. By training people to perform, energy devoted to anxiety is rechanneled to performance. In a Freudian model, anxiety would be reduced as the individual learns of his or her own ability to perform in the feared situation.

One of the major tasks imposed upon the ego is that of dealing with the threats and dangers that beset the person and arouse anxiety. The ego may try to master danger by adopting realistic problem-solving methods, or it may attempt to alleviate anxiety by using methods that deny, falsify, or distort reality and that impede the development of personality. The latter are called defense mechanisms. Defense mechanisms are irrational ways of dealing with anxiety because they distort, hide, or deny reality and hinder psychological development. People may repress ideas that they think will endanger themselves or others. They may also attribute the causes of anxiety to others. If a person feels anxious because they hate another, they may ascribe hatred to the other person to justify their own feelings and thus quell anxiety. Each of these defenses provides a justifiable excuse or alibi for behavior designed to escape from interpersonal anxiety. Oddly enough, the recommended therapy for high scores on the PRCA is desensitization designed to *reduce the scores*. The anxiety victim, thus, is enabled to claim an absence of anxiety without ever encountering the situation that presumably evoked it.

Moral anxiety also imposes controls over ego development. Fear of being punished by conscience, law, or the sanctions of valued others forces the individual into a number of counterproductive defensive postures. These basic Freudian postulates were the basis for the theories of interpersonal behavior offered by Alfred Adler and Harry Stack Sullivan. But Freud provided for his later critics a catalog of possible behaviors associated with anxiety as defenses

According to Hall (1952, pp. 73–122), Freud believed personality was formed by acquiring skill in dealing with anxieties. Maturation of perception, memory, learning, and judgment; physical growth, response to frustration in goal seeking; growth through oral, anal, and genital stages of development to a mature sexual adulthood all contributed to personality. Although Freud did not specify it, it appeared that the eventual objective of the organism was the formation of familial relationships.

Freud did not deal directly with language and communication. He apparently accepted it as a given, but clearly he believed that response to frustration accounted for much of interpersonal behavior, that is the communication and accompanying acting out that accompanied social living. Anxiety resulted, according to Freud, when goals were frustrated. This included unconscious and intolerable goals arising in id, socially unacceptable goals made taboo by superego, and the legitimate goals of living made difficult to attain because of personal inadequacies. In order to avoid or ameliorate the pain of anxiety, individuals developed defense mechanisms that could be described as behavior and talk. Talk was essential in psychoanalysis; in fact, it was known as the "talking cure."

Freud identified a number of methods of coping with anxiety arising in frustration of goal seeking, each of which could be described as a behavior including communication and action.

Identification, for example, referred to the incorporation of qualities of another person into one's own personality. This included narcissistic identification in which the individual found features in others that he or she prized in the self. Goal-oriented identification referred to adoption of the behavior of others more successful on the grounds that they would make one successful also. These patterns of incorporation could be described as imitation or modeling. Correlations could be made between the talk of individuals and their identification-objects.

Displacement and sublimation represented other forms of defense, regarded by the psychoanalysts as "legitimate" responses to goal frustration. Freud argued that legitimate tension that could not be directly resolved could be rechanneled to other useful productivity. This, in fact, was the way he accounted for artistic talent (energy from sex displaced to creativity). This raises the question about whether people with genuine anxiety about social discourse could channel the resulting energy into writing, painting, athletics, or other acceptable outlets. It also raises a question about whether sublimation and displacement could be used as the basis for training those whose communication anxiety actually disabled them at social speech.

The most important consideration in all of this is that it is essential for humans to engage satisfactorily in social discourse if they are to accomplish legitimate social objectives. To the extent that people are disabled at discourse, whether because of anxiety or lack of competence, identifying the exact nature of the disability is very important. The self-report of anxiety about types of social situations in no way describes actual behavior in specific situations. The ego defense mechanisms provide a basis for a taxonomy of disabilities at social communication.

Ego Defense Mechanisms

Hall (1954, p. 85) describes the defense mechanisms as follows: "One of the major tasks imposed upon the ego is that of dealing with the threats and dangers that beset the person and arouse anxiety. The ego may try to master danger by adopting realistic problem-solving methods, or it may attempt to alleviate anxiety by using methods that deny, falsify, or distort reality and that impede the development of personality. The latter are defense mechanisms." Defense mechanisms are irrational ways of dealing with anxiety because they distort, hide, or deny reality and hinder psychological development. The evidence of this is inept social communication. Repression, for example, represents a suppression of a primal instinct which has never been conscious, for example, the fear of incest or violence, as well as contemporary urgencies to have sex with forbidden persons or commit mayhem, on enemies. In order to avoid temptation and/or guilt, a great many people repress the images associated with the primal urge. The act of repression has ramifications, however. Often the result is psychosomatic exacerbation of symptoms of preexisting conditions (asthma, high blood pressure, arthritis, for example). Could repression also have consequences for social discourse? There may well be a great many people who suffer from anxiety about speaking who effectively suppress it. In the Penn State Reticence Program students are offered three options: public speaking emphasis, group discussion emphasis, and speech criticism emphasis. A great many people enrolled in the group discussion emphasis are inept speakers. While they do not generate high scores on the PRCA, they clearly seek to avoid communication. An effort to discover the extent to which they are repressing anxiety would be a useful way to compensate for some of the flaws in PRCA. The paradox in the paper and pencil test is that many of the people most likely to confirm the claims made for the test are able to hide from it through the mechanism of repression.

The use of projection as a defense mechanism is accomplished by attributing the cause of one's anxiety to the external world. The process is characteristic of a great many shy and reticent people who excuse their lack of participation or their social incompetence by talking about the insensitivity of others or complaining about how ridiculous it is to make small talk. These people could be investigated analytically to discover whether the rationalizations, excuses, and alibis they were using were based on projection as a defense against anxieties.

An intriguing notion is that people who avoid oral communication or do it poorly may actually be driven by reaction formation. In reaction formation, people may teach themselves to hate something they are strongly attracted to. McCroskey claimed (McCroskey & Beatty, 1986, p. 290) that many who show high communication apprehension scores actually are quite competent public performers. Zimbardo (1977) made quite a point about the movie stars and celebrities who complained of shyness. The phenomenon noted in the Reticence Program that students become very loquacious at about the seventh week of their training indicates that they may have suffered from paralysis because of contradictory drives, one toward speaking and the other toward avoiding it.

Fixation and regression might also account for various forms of social reticence or incompetency. Fixation, or remaining on a lower level of development is represented by a childish clinging to habits and practices of a younger age or by clutching at the security mechanisms associated with parents. The urgency many reticent speakers have to acquire formulas for social behavior may well be the ritualism often associated with this form of ego defense. Furthermore, a great many reticent speakers express hostility to "small talk." They claim that this kind of socialization is false and deceitful. Actually, they manifest behavior commonly associated with children who have not yet learned the social norms of adult socialization.

The Freudian explanation of anxiety contains potential for explaining phenomena like shyness and reticence and appropriately associating components of it to communication apprehension as measured by various scales. Hyde (1980, p. 140), however, argues that the "research movement of . . . scientific approach actually moves away " from an understanding of anxiety. In his discussion of the ontological basis of phenomenological anxiety, he urges concentration on actual speech behaviors in order to examine their possible role in causing or contributing to anxiety. Rather than ascribe inept behavior to anxiety, anxiety could be viewed as arising, in part, from the consequences of inept behavior. Hyde cites Heidegger, especially, as a basis for this argument. The reason is not incompatible with Freudian reasoning. Anxiety arises from somewhere, Freud argues. That somewhere could easily be inept socialization. In fact, various revisionists have responded to the Freudian constructs in precisely that way. Adler, Sullivan, and especially Horney have viewed anxiety as arising from incompetent social behavior.

INTERPERSONAL ANXIETY: ADLER, HORNEY, AND SULLIVAN

According to Ansbacher, Adler believed that anxiety was aggression turned upon the self (1936, p. 33). Anxiety both excites and enervates vasomotor systems. There should, in Adlerian terms, be physiological ramifications of anxiety. In fact, Adlerians claim that a feeling cannot be classified as "anxiety" unless there were demonstrable physiological symptoms. The connection between PRCA scores and physiology has been denied, however.

The social ramifications are quite obvious. The anxiety sufferer runs away from life (p. 276) and generates pretexts and excuses for avoiding what he or she does not like or feels they might fail at. This tends to embitter the sufferer and make him unsuited for human contact. People may avoid socialization because they fear that social defeats will prove them worthless in the eyes of others (pp. 303–305). The increased feelings of inferiority and insecurity intensify anxiety because the sufferer not only feels anxious about an impending social situation but also about the emotions generated in it. Adler ascribed the cause of social anxiety to pampering. The child who was helped too much or got too much too easily from parents may become anxious when placed on his own in society.

Karen Horney argued that anxiety was the one factor common to all neuroses (1937, p. 23). She argues (pp. 44ff.) that anxiety is always about a potential outcome from a social encounter, sometimes conscious, sometimes unconscious. We "go to any length to escape anxiety or to avoid feeling it" (p. 46). Because it arisessocially, from the fear of being isolated in a hostile world (p. 77), it can be ascribed to culture and upbringing. People displaytheir anxiety by the way they act about it. She identifies four defenses (pp. 50–53) people use against anxiety: rationalizing and explaining it, denying its existence, using alcohol and drugs to quell it, and avoiding situations that might trigger it. All of these have behavioral forms that can be examined in social situations.

Harry Stack Sullivan was the most comprehensive of the Freudian revisionists in his discussion of the social etiology and consequences of anxiety. Sullivan's work has been referred to as "the interpersonal psychiatry." In his system, anxiety is closely related to self-esteem. He describes it as the most awful emotion a person can suffer and asserts that to suffer anxiety is to experience loss of self-esteem (Mullahy, 1970, pp. 303–306).

Sullivan is quite direct in his assertion that anxiety is provoked in the social realm. People do not become disabled socially because they are anxious; they acquire anxiety because someone significant has disapproved of them or their behavior. In fact, the self comes into existence to evade anxiety; once anxiety sets in, the individuals become less alert to relevant factors in interpersonal situations. The relationship is circular, for once anxiety has set in, the refinement and precision of action related to resolution of interpersonal situations are sacrificed. Loss of self-esteem is synonymous with loss of self-confidence and if prolonged can lead to total demoralization of the individual.

The behavioral consequences are both obvious and dramatic. The anxious person cannot achieve intimacy with others, is often impotent or frigid, and may suffer psychosomatic ailments characterized by nausea and loss of appetite. Furthermore, the anxious person in generally unable to understand what is happening and consequently to learn behaviors that might ease the pain.

Sullivan distinguishes anxiety from fear by specifying that fear is an emotion aroused by novel situations, especially those that pose physical threats. Fear increases alertness and concentration and provides the energy necessary for the muscular action required to defend against the feared object. Even abnormal fears are not anxiety equivalents, for anxiety signals danger from within. Mullahy (1970) summed up these dynamics by pointing out that the self becomes organized and provides information to the organism. When the self sends erroneous information, that is, that specific situations are dangerous when they are not, fearfulness dominates the personality unable to get acquainted with reality. Reality takes on an ominous quality connected with anxiety.

Anxiety has its ramifications in personality, which Sullivan defines as what other people can see and hear when a person is with them (Chapman, 1976, p. 70). In essence, personality is regular behavior, the "enduring pattern" of behavior that characterizes a relationship. Sullivan argues that the defenses a person puts up against anxiety are reflected in social behavior. Anxiety always arises in interpersonal relationships (Mullahy, 1970, p. 367). Anxiety can arise in infancy; children can "catch" it from the mothering person. The initial onset of anxiety, in fact, is when the infant feels its relationship with the mothering person is in jeopardy. The infant behaves in ways calculated to alter the situation. We find this pattern: a person seeks to modify the social environment and develops feelings about the responses he or she receives. When interpersonal goal seeking is frustrated, the person can become anxious. This, in turn, interferes with the possibility of subsequent success at attaining interpersonal goals, which, in turn, affects choices made about whether and how to participate socially.

Chapman (1976, p. 80) argues that anxiety can be detected by self-report, interviewing, and observation of social behavior. Says Chapman (p. 84): "Anxiety (emotional discomfort) is caused by things that are going wrong, or have gone wrong, in an individual's relationships with other people, and especially the emotionally close people in his life. However, once anxiety appears it hinders a person's capacities to improve his interpersonal relationships; he is less able to solve problems that are producing or have produced his anxiety." Clearly Sullivan's theory argues for empirical investigation of connections between reported feelings of anxiety, observations of anxious behavior, and patterns of behavior, especially communication, in interpersonal relationships. The recommended therapy for anxiety-produced difficulties in interpersonal behavior consists of focusing the patient's attention on aspects of behavior that he or she has been previously unaware of and thus unable to resolve in a healthy way. This suggests the necessity of both cognitive restructuring and behavior modification. Quelling anxiety is insufficient to bring about changes in interpersonal behavior. In fact, without modifying behavior, anxiety will merely arise again as the individual continues to be unsuccessful at relationships.

Sullivan refers to the pattern of behavior manifested by anxious persons as "selective inattention" (Sullivan, 1964, p. 217), a process that consists of ignoring our own faults. It is especially important to note that anxiety is manifested not so much in feelings but in behaviors characterized by selective inattention (p. 219).

SUMMING UP THE ANXIETY ISSUE

There are four current approaches to the study of anxiety. The Freudian view focuses on anxiety as a feeling and regards it as sufficient to modify the feeling. However, Freud believed that a direct connection must be made between reported feelings of anxiety and actual behavior. Although it is implied in the Freudian view that modification of the feeling should result in modification of behavior, eventually experience is turned to as a method of testing the efficacy of therapy. Psychoanalysis does not remain entirely on the couch.

Behaviorists concentrate on overt behaviors under the assumption that anxiety is a response to the environment and modification of the environment is sufficient to modify the feelings. The neoanalysts believe in a circular connection. Anxiety arises in interpersonal relationships, and once it arises, it affects subsequent relationships. Thus, modification must be made of cognitive, behavioral *and* affective components of anxiety and behavior connected to it. Finally, the phenomenologists see anxiety as a phenomenon in its own right, a deep-seated discombobulation in the organism that, in essence, defies remedy.

Emphasis in the study of modification of speech performance behavior has, up to now, concentrated on one small aspect of the psychoanalytic point of view, the acquisition of information about self-reports of communication anxiety. While there are tacit assumptions made about the connection of these reports with communication behavior, they are not explicit. The most obvious second step is to take a Sullivanian, neoanalytic view and attempts to associate feelings about communication experience with communication itself. The process would be simple enough, indeed. It would consist of cataloguing and classifying communication behavior in fundamental social situations, somewhat like those suggested in rhetoritherapy (Phillips, 1977). The social situations include asking and answering questions, responses to simple interviews, fundamental socialization, and preparation and delivery of simple public speeches. The more complex forms of interpersonal communication including friendship formation and especially intimacy are, for the moment, ignored. By examining behaviors and associating them with explicit feelings about particular situations, insight can be gained into the possible direct relationship between anxiety and social communication including cause/effect relationships in both directions. To continue measuring apprehension with paper-and-pencil scales without making this association is a "searching after wind." We concede that people often report feeling anxious about social speech situations. There is now more to be learned.

At present, the terms "anxiety" and "apprehension" function as reifications, since they do not refer consistently to objective and measurable physiological conditions. Their existence as functions of scores on a paper-and-pencil test gives them identity without existence. To the psychiatrist and physician, however, anxiety is an objective condition, and it does not arise *ex nihilo*. By definition, it comes from somewhere. If we accept the consistent feature of all definitions of anxiety, we are confronted with the notion that anxiety has an antecedent. Thus:

If shyness is traceable to genetics, the anxiety associated with it would have to come from a propensity of the organism to respond negatively to human associations. The genetic result may well be an inbred aversion to particular types of contacts (as in a Jungian archetype), for example, to snakes or rats. Shyness in this mode would be classified as *trait*, and the associated fears would be considered *ingrained*.

If shyness is traceable to acculturation, there are a variety of possibilities. Consider *semantogenesis*: we are shy because we learned the word *shyness* and respond as we think shy people respond. Recent advances in *labeling theory* seem to support this possibility.

The process of contagion of anxiety documented by Liddell (1934, 1935) may also play a role. The parenting objects may have genetic involvement and transmit their fears and anxieties to offspring, much as Liddell's mothering sheep affected the lambs. Thus, anxiety could develop independent of any situation and develop eventually into a *free-floating anxiety*. Free-floating anxiety might result in a number of other ways, however, particularly out of a consistent string of social failures resulting in reduction of self-esteem and consequent avoidance of social engagements because of a fear of generating experiences that would further reduce self-esteem.

Acculturation may also include a form of *iatrogenesis*. That is, a person is told by some authority that a particular social encounter might be threatening. Much like the side effects of pharmacological treatment, a particular learning experience might carry with it situationally generated fears that are easily extended to subsequent experiences that appear similar. Fears generated this way would be *situational*, but sometimes so consistent that they would appear *traitlike*. We could go farther with this reasoning and even point to the possibility of *psychosomatic involvement*, that is, the fear associated with a particular social encounter might generate sporadically or consistently a potentially disabling physiological involvement. In Freudian terms, this could take the form of a *hysteria* in which a shy person converts social fear to physical symptom, which he or she uses to avoid social contact. Furthermore, doctors frequently report a phenomenon that affects them in medical school. When they read about symptoms of a particular disease or disorder, they begin to believe they have taken on those symptoms. It takes quite a while, they report, before it is possible to read about illness without becoming vicariously ill. Oddly enough, this condition has never been named, quite possibly because naming it might bring it into existence.

The vector could be reversed. Objectively speaking, people with various physiological impairments suffer concomitant disability in social encounters. Diseases that impair talk, for example, asthma, cerebral palsy, cleft palate, stuttering, and similar disorders, might appropriately set off an alarm system in the individual that could take the form of anxiety about an impending experience. Drugs could be another vector. The use of substances to alter mind and physiology is now commonplace. At one time, serious consideration was given to the use of drugs to overcome shyness. Certainly the use of alcohol and drugs to quell performance anxiety is not uncommon among amateur performers (and a few professionals as well). The tranquilizer is a standard psychiatric prescription for those who claim to feel tense in social situations.

We could complete our Freudian explanation by considering the possibility of recalled and repressed social trauma acting to generate the physiological tension associated with anxiety. Cathexis of repressed material may flood the individual at any moment, generating a flight or freeze reaction that, remembered on a subsequent occasion, may result in replication of the reaction.

State anxieties are from experiences that could arise from an individual traumatic event (discovery of an unzipped fly or showing slip while on the public platform), a vicarious conditioning (beware of the boss, Professor Dingle is a "bear"), and social mythology (you are supposed to be afraid when you are on the stage). Stage fright, in fact, refers initially to the tension most performers feel prior to performance. Those who are not trained to discharge it may be disabled by it. A series of disabilities might then lead to a personality involvement in which a state anxiety turned into a trait anxiety.

Contributing to this possibility is *defective training*. If a person is required to perform before learning techniques of performance, the resulting negative audience responses could, theoretically, condition fears that could become full-grown performance anxieties on subsequent occasions.

Thus, it would be facile to refer to "communication apprehension" as a cause of ineffective performance even if we had established the connection between anxiety and particular performance situations. The taxonomy remains to be developed, for without it, a mature pedagogy is impossible.

We have now placed communication incompetence in a socialsetting. It is observed in social settings. Its causes must be sought there as well. In the final chapter of this book we will examine the social milieu to see if we can discover regularities that might help us discover both etiology and effective modes of treatment.

12

The Milieu
of Incompetence:
A Quest for Order

Sound analysis of social settings is crucial to effective discourse. The teacher/trainer must employ cognitive restructuring to help the student make a practical orientation to the social milieu. Successful audience analysis, particularly, depends on how accurately the speaker assesses the social environment. It is important to make some kind of sense out of it, because each decision on a rhetorical tactic depends on a hypothesis about its impact on the social milieu.

Unfortunately, social settings often appear disorderly. Despiteobvious and apparent similarities among situations, each case has its unique twist, something that makes the situation different from all other situations. We argue that the only way to handle the potential confusion in social situations is to impose some kind of order. Indeed, the speaker depends on rational analysis of the social setting in order to set goals and devise strategies.

Order is imposed consciously or unconsciously. We believe that a speaker can be more effective if he is fully aware of the order he is imposing and in control of the inferences he makes about the social situation. Otherwise, he depends on random and opportunistic thought often reflected in clichés and prejudices for his information.

Social Settings and Communication

The purpose of this chapter is to introduce some alternative ways of finding order in social settings. We will offer some potentially useful models, most of which can be simulated on a computer. They are reifications, however. Thus, following Vaihinger's (1965) dictum, we pick what we like and act "as if" it is true.

Participants in communication evaluate each other based on what they exchange. Our analysis is based on four main sources of information. First are the clichés we have about personality. Personality designations are abstractions made up of various communication behaviors. The second source of information is vicarious learning corrected by experience. From this we get basic beliefs about human nature. Third, we rely on our previous experience in similar social situations as a source of precedents—tactics to try or avoid, depending on how successful they were previously. Fourth, we have some notions about our own capabilities, which constrain our selection of possible performance behaviors.

Actually, we do not react directly to social settings. We receive so much information that we must abstract it into some prototypical image to which we react. The minute we organize it, it becomes a fiction. The Freudian position is that we do not ever respond directly to situations. We take what we have in memory and react to it. The only time we interact directly with our environment is when we depend on reflex. When the impressions on which we base our actions are consistent with reality, we have a good chance of being socially effective.

The influences that shape our social attitudes include early learning and experience, parental influence and acculturation, schooling, archetypes (however implanted), religious beliefs and superstitions, traumas and catastrophes, real experiences, experiences with fiction, vicarious experiences, aphorisms and adages, passions, cravings, aptitudes, habits, compulsions, fears and repressions, hatreds, jealousies, and many forms of unconscious and subconscious influences including transference. When we choose to speak, we choose from this apparently disorderly database. Our object is to impose sufficient order to make it intelligible and useful.

Social Metaphors

Robert Nisbet (1977) argues that social science is based on metaphor. That is, in order to explain events, a social scientist must have a point of view. These positions are normally metaphoric. If you look at a social movement as a landscape you may see one pattern (for example, the city and the country reacted differently in the French Revolution). If you look at it as a drama you may see another (for example, several people were responsible for the political upheavals preceding the French Revolution). If you look at social life as a mechanism, then you must regard yourself as a moving part. And so on.

We engage in discourse to make our environment comfortable, and in order to do so we must have models that enable us to manage our own behavior. Continuing our computer analogy, we program our behavior based on some standard. We have our metaphors that come from the ways we learned to behave from our parents, teachers, and other relevant adults. Our goal is to get others to comply with what we want. It is impossible to step outside of this egocentric posture. We are social scientists writing our own theories of personal behavior.

Our situation is quite different from that of a physicist. A physicist is not a legislator seeking the greatest good for the greatest number. His metaphor is mathematical, totally governed by laws from which predictions can be made. When predictions do not come true, the physicist ascribes it to inadequate mathematics or sloppy experimentation. Biologists are somewhat less precise. Their models are built out of taxonomies. They name and classify things. When the unexpected happens, they create new names and new categories.

Neither of these models works for human interaction, although both can play some role. We communicate to achieve some goal, and we base our selection of what to say and how to say on our hypotheses about human behavior and social situations. But we also know that human behavior cannot be predicted like that of electrons or wheat seeds. The physicists and biologists sometimes have their problems, but most of the time they are quite secure in their predictions of what is likely to happen. Humans have the power to change and resist, and so our predictions are more about ball parks than bean pods. However, even though we are often constrained to work with metaphors and stereotypes, we cannot avoid the necessity of attempting to make predictions.

A SPATE OF METAPHORS

An Aristotelian Model

Aristotle's brilliant secret is that the topics, categories, common-places, the examples and enthymemes, are really locations available for storage of various types of information. If Aristotle had had a computer, he might have solved all our problems two thousand years ago. Aristotle's system is egocentric rather than sociocentric. It is subjective rather than objective. It appears to be based on the premise that even the most irregular-appearing personal systems can be spatial and chronological.

The Aristotelian heuristics provide humans with standard questions or *topoi* that apply to any issue or situation. These questions can be simultaneously or separately applied in parallel or discrete processes. Thus, a human can deal with heuristics of prestige applied in general while considering heuristics about safety in the given case. The complicated question that emerges might be, "Is it safe to seek to enhance my prestige in this situation?" or "Would my safety be jeopardized if I sought prestige and failed?" The combinations are virtually unlimited but they are orderly. In our attempt to simulate the Pentad (Phillips & Erlwein, 1989), we worked out a model for examining interactions between general and specific *topoi*.

The guiding premise in the search for topics is, *The purpose of discourse is personal gain.*[1] Each person has motives that drive his or her action in the social milieu. Kenneth Burke (1969a, 1969b) and Abraham Maslow (1954), among others, have suggested taxonomies of motives for human behavior. However, they are complex and not amenable to verification. Thus, we need to find simpler explanations based on behaviors. Homans (1975) provides such a model when he declared that the purpose of social relations is to get goods, services, or sentiments. Paramount in the category of services is information; with goods it is money, with sentiments it is love (or sex, if you are of the right age and physical condition).

Once we begin to generate subcategories, we can literally wallow in political and moral discussions. The point is, everyone wants something from everyone all the time. There is no other point to making discourse. With this deliciously egocentric starting premise, we can examine various models of discourse for ideas about how humans assess potential gain and loss in a social situation. The obvious questions for anyone in a social situation are, What do I want? From whom? What would I have to do to get it? Each of these questions can be broken down into

1. This proposition is clearly based on the Freudian Pleasure Principle, a simple minimax declaration about maximizing pleasure and minimizing pain. Freud defined "pleasure" as the absence of pain. Most of us would prefer a more positive definition of pleasure, and thus we usually reference it to goods, services, or sentiments exchanged.

subquestions. For example, the speaker must specify the goods, services, and sentiments she seeks. She must identify the people present and examine who might be able to provide them. Finally, she must examine her impression of their motives to figure out what she might offer in return.

The reader now has the option of engaging this text in an impassioned dialogue about altruism, the milk of human kindness, the essential goodness of human nature, and any number of other moral issues. We are, literally avoiding these questions; our quest is for possible ways to achieve an orderly analysis of human social behavior, not to create a moral tractate on the virtues of altruism.

Metaphors of Adhesion and Combat

The premise that communication is used for personal gain makes us harmonious with the principles of sociobiology (whether we like them or not). Once we fulfill the prime directive and work to preserve the species (usually by breeding), we select our own goals from stimulation, security, and status. There are a great many theories about how we go about doing this, many of them based on magic and wishful thinking.

While we acknowledge a debt to systems theory, symbolic interactionism, and rules theory[2] our primary debt is to Skinnerian behaviorism and some isomorphisms of rules theory. We will not argue that order actually exists in social interaction. We declare that in order to communicate, we must impose order on what we perceive.

This spares us from the more interpretive theories offered by authorities like Foucault (1972), Bateson (1987), or Harre (1986). We explored Kenneth Burke's Pentad (Phillips & Erlwein, 1989) as a model for machine simulation and discovered that despite the obfuscation of his theory by several generations of philosophers and rhetoricians, it is really quite a simple system in which the parts are named and their articulation clearly defined. Burkians would, no doubt, take exception to our belief that the Pentad is as close to a machine-friendly model as we could find. It is far more parsimonious and inclusive than any pure Aristotelian model, and it is amenable to replication and falsification, thus qualifying

2. We used as a basis for our theoretical taxonomy a most remarkable text. Stephen W. Littlejohn, *Theories of Human Communication*, 3rd ed. (Belmont, CA: Wadsworth Publishing, 1989). This up-to-date compendium accurately reviews most of the popular theories of human communication.

as appropriate for scientific investigation. Included in it are allusions to some of the more intriguing (and useful) metaphoric possibilities.

The adhesive metaphor. This moralistic metaphor is based on the belief that it is natural for people to get along with one another. This makes some sense, since as Becker (1962) tell us, we must get along sufficiently to raise our children to adulthood. But we do not have to like it.

The metaphor is based on the belief that clinging together is virtuous. "In union there is strength." Cohesion is defined as a virtuous goal, rather than a process, toward which human effort must be directed. Those who believe in it also believe that other folks are either righteous or can be taught to be. If they fight with us, it is because they are evil, and we, therefore, have the right to correct them.

The connection between beneficial social outcomes and cohesion has not been consistently demonstrated. For example, in democratic societies the adversarial process of parliamentary procedure is widely used, often with considerable effectiveness. Inherent in the adversary model is negotiation, another effective decision-making system. In fact, there are substantial arguments that too much consensus can be harmful as in groupthink (Janis, 1983).

More to the point, however, cohesion seems to be the antithesis of conviction. It is easiest to get consensus when participants in a social setting do not care much about the outcome. Thus, the only empirical way to measure cohesion is by the absence of competition.

The combat metaphor. Rhetoric is used for self-serving purposes. Sometimes individuals are best served when the general welfare is well served, but mainly humans try to get as much of their own way as possible. The hidden premise of the "given case" is that rhetoric is a way of maintaining an egocentric outlook in the face of sociocentric pressure. It could be defined as the process of using discourse to get your own way.

When everyone is self-seeking, some of them are bound to clash. In any kind of conflict, someone must win and someone must lose. This is something more than a zero-sum game, however, because people have the ability to interpret winning and losing as they see fit. Thus, they are capable of bargaining to mutual advantage, that is, a mutual win.

The combat metaphor appears useful for those who seek an orderly way to explain social interaction. For one thing, we can recognize conflict; we cannot always identify cohesion. We can argue that it is a desirable state of affairs, although conflict appears to be the normal state of affairs in human relations, with cohesion a special case of minimal conflict.

Our society certainly devotes considerable effort to managing and resolving conflict. Police, armies, legislatures, and courts function mainly as conflict resolution devices. We teach good manners and etiquette to prevent conflict, and we maintain rules in the form of constitutions because we also know that without them the winner in any conflict has the power to set the rules for subsequent conflicts.

But the position of the winner is precarious. Wyatt Earp continually had to use his gun to defend his reputation; the object of "king of the hill" is to push the king off the top. Laws and their enforcers defend those who cannot fight well. Governments and religions censure and punish violators. But the very institutions that exist to manage conflict are, themselves, the source of conflict. Even they must be curbed, usually by constitutions. In any society order must be imposed.

Realistically, the greatest good for the greatest number depends on a rule system that makes it impossible for one person or a group to control the whole society in their own interest. This model presumes that conflict is the natural state of human existence.

Nowhere is this more obvious than in social interaction. Families are often structured in authoritarian fashion. Children are natural anarchists who indulge themselves in sibling rivalry; they must be curbed by whatever rules the parents can impose. Since small children are rarely amenable to artistic rhetoric, some sort of inartistic strategy is required to keep them sufficiently submissive to permit the organization to function. Through familial rules of order, children learn how to deal with authority. Those who are alert recognize that by becoming part of the authority, they might be able to serve their own ends as well. For convenience, we teach our children to obey the laws of the state and the norms of courtesy. However, if we consider what it takes to hold a family together, we can get an insight into why it is so difficult to maintain order in the involuntary family called "the world."

In the final crunch, every human grouping, however large or small, must have a way of making laws, carrying them out, and resolving disputes that arise under them. Otherwise, we have anarchy, a situation controlled entirely by inartistic proofs. If we wish to be idealistic, we can argue that the best we can hope for is a set of rules that will allow artistic proofs to be deployed to resolve conflict.

Now, the question is how is authority established, defined, and imposed? In the first place, we cannot rule out the use of inartistic rhetoric, especially by established authority, to sustain itself in power. Artistic rhetoric is used to make necessary bargains inherent in governance. This is true among lovers, families, football teams, and nations.

But artistic rhetoric often fails to do the job. Lovers quarrel, couples divorce, crimes are committed, and there is civil disobedience and war. The tools of artistic rhetoric are effective in confrontations only when orderly procedure is enforced. Thus, the combat metaphor, by alerting us to the worst, allows us to impose orderly procedure on both formal and informal social relationships.

Cost-Benefit Analysis

Littlejohn (1989) asserts that social exchange theory and game theory explain relationships as a sequence of moves motivated by personal gain. This notion is entirely compatible with the combat metaphor. The process of simulation of social interaction is facilitated by assuming that each person acts in order to gain something from the social situation, especially from the other people in it.

By using Homans' (1975) model of relationship decisions based on cost-benefit analysis, cohesion and combat can be put in perspective and used simultaneously in a social model. "Cohesion" is an evaluation of a state of combat, a conclusion after the fact about humans who do not appear to be fighting with one another. Cohesion is, thus, a subhead of combat. Like "pleasure is the absence of pain," cohesion is the absence of combat.

The reasons for cohesion can be quite different, however. People may not be fighting because they have no stake in the situation; they may fear each other too much to risk fighting; or they may be exhausted. They may be apathetic, or they may be using "peace" as a proffered reward for compliance.

In an economic model, it is fairly easy to discover what is happening. Usually one person declares what should be done. The rest either agree or demur. Combat begins at the first demurrer.

We could inquire how the person who is making the decisions got herauthority. Is she the Earth Mother with the treasures of life to dispense? Was she elected or hired to make decisions? Has she beaten the others into submission? Or is she the only one who cares in a world of apathetics?

Interpersonal communication can be explained economically by seeking what gratifying behaviors one person is seeking from another. People reward each other for what they see as good behavior and punish behavior that makes them uncomfortable. Each of us has our own criteria, yet, there is reason to believe that there is some regularity in what people prefer. A glance at the periodicals that came in yesterday's mail is a case in point. In *Science News* (January 28, 1989, p. 59) there is a news report about the consistency of facial expressions across culture. People seem to feel and express similar emotions about similar social conditions. In the *Chronicle of Higher Education* (February 1, 1989, p. A44) the distinguished sociologist Amitai Etzioni criticizes what he calls the "me first model" of social science. He urges that it be replaced by an "I & we model." The fuzzy argument that follows reinforces the proposition that people are confined in their decision making to the information they possess. When they believe that their good is similar to the public good, they will appear altruistic. Otherwise, they will revert to natural narcissism and fight the public, sometimes even sacrificing their narcissistic tendencies to make deals with allies who will help them accomplish their personal goals.

While there are no universal propositions regarding what is rewarding and punishing, the cumulative commonplaces seem to indicate that people seek love, truth, beauty, status, not to speak of cash (and quite possibly revenge.) The speaker's quest is to read individual minds, guess what they are after, and offer it.

This means that the composition process must take into account that in any given audience (one or more) there are several motives to which appeals can be directed. Time usually restricts the number of appeals that can be made. It is confusing when too many appeals are made. The individual listener wants to believe the speaker is talking directly to him. So, competent discourse would appeal to the most probable motive. But how does the speaker discover what that is?

The answer may lie in consistencies among people. The reification "dual perspective" suggests that self-understanding can, on occasion, become general understanding, with a few Catch 22's. If the people have had similar experience and have generated similar values, or if they are disparate and have antagonistic values, predictions can be made.

The rhetorical *topoi* suggest heuristics for this analysis. What are the people seeking in this situation? Do they want money, power, or fame? Are they potential lovers or fighters? The answers to these questions create different scenarios. Composition of discourse requires rapid examination of the possible scenarios so that a performing script can be written.

But interpretation is always personalized. Humans use communication to help them minimize loss and maximize gain, where "the good life" is the maximum gain and death is the maximum loss. Death is an empirical state. "The good life" is a subjective matter. It is easy to find an antithesis to death. The antithesis to "a good life" is somewhat more obscure. Because "good" is individually defined, a dialectic of exchange is necessary.

In a world where supplies of everything are limited, we presume that one person's gain is another person's loss, and vice versa. Where the goal is status, for example, only one person can hold position number one. Where the goal is money or goods, winners take from a limited pool. Winners of any lottery get money. Losers get to throw away the tickets. When someone does something for you, it deprives them. If they pay you money, they expect goods or services (or possibly gratitude) in return. In social relations there must be a tender by the speaker to do something in exchange for the response sought from the listener. The speaker's reasonable goal is to present a quid pro quo of mutual gain via whatever exchange is proposed. Because we assign values variously, it is possible for both parties to gain from a negotiated exchange despite the fact that they were entirely egocentric in their goals. Thus, the combat metaphor allows for the maximum number of possible relationships in a simple enough model to simulate.

The biological imperative for social organization. The social enterprise theory of language (DeLaguna, 1963) argues that communication is a natural enterprise in which humans engage because their survival depends on it. It seems reasonable. Ethologists (Ardrey, 1970) claim that all humans seek survival, security, stimulation, and status (territory), not necessarily in that order. Ernest Becker (1962) argues that the human species uses speech to accomplish its biologically constrained goals. Becker further argues that it is essential for humans to form social units to protect fragile neonates until they reach functional autonomy. Humans are essentially frail; they cannot outrun fast rabbits or even block hungry hogs from their troughs. People, like many other vulnerable creatures, must pool their efforts to protect themselves, but cohesion is not a requirement of organization.

Order is. In fact, there is often considerable combat present in our biology that is used to define social order. In fact, the process of socializing requires humans to impose order on their natural tendency for gratification. Though they would like to appear spontaneous, disdainful of order, they cannot function without it. They demonstrate their respect for order and their understanding of its necessity in preserving security by their orderly performance reflected in conformity with norms and good manners.

The pleasure principle. The possibility that more than one person can be gratified in a social situation exists because of the "pleasure principle." Freud defined "pleasure" as the absence of pain. This is a useful model. Freud assumed that pain is objective and pleasure is not. Essentially, the Freudian model is based on the difference between words that have referents and those that must be interpreted. It is the difference between sensation and the interpretation of sensation. This is the sense in which people define social situations and what they get out of them. People are rewarded, if they think they are or claim to be. Timothy Leary, before he rotted his mind with drugs, made this clear in *Interpersonal Diagnosis of Personality* (1957) in which he defines compatible personality types, showing how they can gratify each other. Thus, the reason people engage in combat is to get what they want. If they cannot take it, they bargain for it. Discourse is the method they use.

Equity as a way to evaluate social behavior. We used the classical "Canons of Rhetoric" as a basis for our teaching method. They can also be used to explain social behavior. For example, the divisions of discourse into forensic, deliberative, and epideictic speaking fit a cohesion/ combat/ exchange model of social behavior. Forensic speaking is a combative method for resolving questions of guilt or innocence. Deliberative speaking has decision as its end product and thus often includes conflict as a means of making decisions. Epideictic speaking is evaluative and permits both benign and hostile assessments of people and events. Any evaluative process is dialectical. If it is evaluated good on a quality, its counterpart must be bad. These divisions can be used to sort out the purposes of discourse. Their value can be assessed by evaluating the extent to which they contribute to the desired end of "equity."

Equity is an evaluation of the state of affairs that has been attained by interaction. It is not a state of being, consequently it, too, is a reification. Conditions are called "equitable" when participants have gotten a relatively satisfactory share (by their own accounts) of what they were seeking in an interaction. A set of rules within an organization is regarded as equitable by those who are rewarded and as inequitable by those who are not. The haves and the have-nots are dialectically related. The haves seek to retain what they have and get more; the have-nots seek to reverse the positions. The process is the substance of social relationship. Participants compete within the rules for the rewards the rules provide. They can step outside the rules to get what they want, but they risk punishment if their efforts fail. In any case, they may try to change the rules to make them more favorable to personal attainment. This is the substance of democratic politics; each faction contends for a "piece of the pie" because the rules permit it. In totalitarian states, some people are authorized to seek their goals within the system, others are disqualified from seeking any goals at all. Those disqualified may resign themselves to trying to survive, seek another system in which the terms of combat appear more equitable, withdraw in despair or start a revolution. The combat metaphor makes regularity possible.

OPERATIONAL REGULARITIES IN HUMAN SOCIAL UNITS

All human social units are organized. Even the most casual friendship has rules. The rules are similar regardless of the size and complexity of the social unit. A government may appear more complex than a friendship, but the principles of governance remain constant.

Indigenous Processes and Qualities of Organizations

Organizations preserve themselves by finding ways to limit mortal combat. Uncontrolled combat can destroy the system, as divorces destroy families, strikes and lockouts destroy industry, and wars destroy societies. In order to prevent head-to-head combat from destroying the organization, participants learn to communicate artistically. This may take the form of bargaining or political campaigning. The goal is resolution. It is sometimes accomplished by consensus, sometimes by decree, and sometimes by one side defeating the other. Resolution is the proclamation of who won and who lost or which way things are going to be done in the future.

Any human social unit can be an arena in which some people engage in combat often while others watch. Combat preoccupies the participants and often amuses the spectators. A great deal of contemporary recreation is designed around various forms of combat, for example, chess matches, beauty contests, elections, sports, sibling rivalry, marriage, tenure and promotion committees, and selection of articles for publication in journals. There is, apparently, no limit to the issues about which people can fight. However, fighting follows a common pattern regardless of who is engaged in it or what it is about.

Fights can go on so long as they do not jeopardize the organization, which, as a matter of fact, is the *raison d'etre* for the fights. The organization, through its rules, makes it possible for fights to take place. The rules also provide the means of resolution. This proceeds through a series of social exchanges in which maintenance of the organization and equity for the membership are guiding principles. The process follows a common pattern:

1. Someone discovers that something must be done.
2. Someone suggests a way to do it and someone disagrees.
3. A procedure is established to carry on the combat. It may be a meeting, a committee, or the boss may decide.
4. Some say this and some say that. If "this" is chosen, then "that" is ruled out. Or both sides may agree to "thisandthat."
5. If no agreement is possible, the "law" is invoked. A vote may be taken, the boss may decide.
6. Once the decision is made, some means is devised for carrying it out; which could start the process all over again.

The reason a person decides to engage in combat is entirely egocentric. When members are asked to support the organization, they are, in essence, asked to protect their own nest. Thus, to discover what motivates a person to support the organization, it is only necessary to find out what the organization gives in exchange for support. In some cases it may be protection; or money, fame, security, or fear of punishment; or all of the above. The reason for supporting a company is money. The reason for patriotism is survival. The reason for family loyalty is security. When a member can no longer find rewards in the organization, he usually goes elsewhere, unless the organization has him imprisoned.

Thus, though members of an organization are expected to help attain its objectives, they also must be allowed to seek their own objectives within the organization. People who seek power in an organization usually have to promise various kinds of rewards to the members, citizens, or inmates.

The dramatis personae appear in roles specified by labels that provide job descriptions for the players, for example, mother, boss, employee, son, citizen. In a friendship or family, roles are defined by habit or tradition and ratified by the players. In a business they are the contracts of employment. In a nation they are the laws.

The available rewards (among others) are security, regular contact, some form of affection, and, occasionally, sex. In a political unit the roles are defined by laws, some of which prescribe activities (paying taxes, stopping for red lights) and proscribe others (murder, public lewdness). Penalties are provided for infractions, and an elaborate system is generated to detect and deal with violators. In a corporation the roles are defined by supervisory direction or formal job descriptions; the tangible rewards are pay, power, benefits, and perks.

Infractions in a baseball game are called by the umpire. In a nation the police and courts perform that function. In a corporation supervisors are authorized to identify and punish infractions, sometimes by reprimand, sometimes by termination of employment. In a family "father knows best" or some such rule prevails. In friendships each partner has control because if things do not go well, he or she can defect. In religions, so long as the authority of the clergy is honored, there is a process for identifying sin and gaining absolution.

In most cases, those who violate the rules suffer punishment. Sometimes, however, the rule violator is so strong and his behavior so compelling that he attracts others and succeeds in forming a new organization with new rules. The value of inartistic proofs is enhanced by the notion that cheaters sometimes win. There are few bloodless coups. Revolutions do not proceed on reason.

Social Control

However irrational it may appear at times, government is a logical process. Every social aggregate contains the commonplaces of government. There is a way to make decisions, a means of carrying them out, and some process for conducting and resolving disputes. There is always something to be gained or lost in and by the process.

Individual differences notwithstanding, the process of government proceeds by law from general to specific. A law is a generalization to be applied to a given case. The law is based on social commonplaces. For example, people prefer candy in their Christmas stockings except for anthracologists who would rejoice to find just the right lump of coal. Democratic governments would permit the peccadillo. Authoritarian governments would punish it. There would be no question, however, that note must be taken of exceptions.

Every social unit requires governance. Edmund Burke said "government is a contrivance of human wisdom to provide for human wants. The notion of "contrivance" implies that governance is a form of artificial intelligence imposed on human behavior to curb the quest for narcissistic gratification. It also implies that it is sometimes in the interest of the individual to form alliances, political parties, or friendships so that two or more people can make common cause. These common enterprises are generally temporary. Either people remain affiliated with them until they achieve their goals, or they change them so that new goals can be sought. A student stays in med school until the degree is earned; today Dartmouth Med, tomorrow the AMA!

Governance is imposed over people by people empowered by people, and it is a feature of every human grouping. People who are committed to remain together must find ways to simulate governmental features. Father may not know best or mama may not be the queen of the house, whatever, there is some form of legislation, execution, and adjudication in any and every family. Sometimes the kids take over; sometimes the lunatics take over the asylum. The outcome of control in any system of government is relative advantage or disadvantage to particular individuals, disparate equity. As we examine any social unit, we discover in some form, certain constants imposed by governance. We can examine units of discourse to see what aspect of governance it serves.

Making decisions or laws. Laws can be enacted inartistically by a dictator with a gun. They can be also be legislated. In small social units, consensus is possible. (Consensus is defined as an informal unanimous vote. This may happen because no one cares enough to disagree or because everyone fears disagreement.) In formal organizations there are written documents that specify the rule for making laws. Friendships and families run on an oral tradition.

Carrying out decisions through distribution of assignment. In formal organizations this is carried out through bureaucracy usually supported by some kind of police force. In totalitarian societies the work can be imposed on slaves or serfs; in democracies citizens can be persuaded, hired, or drafted. In the corporation individuals can be paid to comply, threatened with punishment, or exhorted to do their share for the good of the order. Friendships and families are similar to larger organizations. Families and friendships can be understood through this government metaphor. A father can be a dictator; the kids can be rebels, with or without a cause. Occasionally, a family or friendship achieves the sophistication of corporate decision making. On the other hand, it is very easy for families and friendships to disintegrate over issues of authority.

Adjudicating disputes in law or equity. In corporate organizations adjudication can be done through bureaucratic regulation, collective bargaining, or administrative fiat. Governments have law enforcement agencies and judicial systems. Families and friendships usually do not have formal judicial systems. In some, personal or parental authority can be identified. In others, if disputes are resolved at all, it is by brute force, rarely by agreement. Some families and friendships are anarchic, but they dissolve quickly when confronted with a dispute that cannot be resolved.

Currency of exchange. There must be reasons for belonging to an organization. These reasons can be found in the goods, services, and sentiments people bargain for. Trades are made, though not necessarily quid pro quo.

People may form alliances to bargain collectively or they may lobby individually. Alliances, however, are customarily temporary. Available rewards change consonant with the behaviorist principle that rewards will reinforce the behavior they seek until the rewards are in oversupply,[3] in which event, individuals change the rewards they seek as well as the behaviors they use to seek them. The same principle essentially holds true for punishments. Shifting values provide the dissonance necessary to discombobulate homeostasis and sustain imbalance, thus providing perpetual stimulation, ergo, motivation for combat.

Other variables. Organizations also acquire traditions, precedents, histories, norms, manners, and mores. These become a kind of literature and form the basis of entertainments that keep members' minds off inequities. Individuals get preoccupied with who gets what, and little jealousies can spin into highly distracting (or entertaining) feuds.

Gossip and the struggle for perks can be very engaging. When people cannot do much about the main business, they can distract themselves with combat over irrelevancies. Freud noted a tendency for people to develop personalized avocations in order to distract themselves from their main preoccupation and indulge themselves in self-reward. These

3. This is so with everything but money. There is never enough of that.

activities can keep people from paying attention to the main troubles (*panem et circensis*).

But all of the trivia is part of the competition. We can understand the motives for speech by examining the combats in which the individual is engaged. By using the simple question, "What game is this person trying to win?" we can guide and advise the choice of goals and supports and guide composition and delivery. We can focus on the primary issue of narcissism.

It is almost axiomatic that goods, services, and sentiments offered as rewards have no value unless others seek them. As W. S. Gilbert pointed out, "when everybody's somebody, no one's anybody" (*Gondoliers*, act 2).

The prime directive is that the organization must survive. In order to get people to work for the organization or the "common good," they must be convinced they will benefit from it. If members do not work for the common good, the organization disintegrates and people no longer have an arena in which to seek their rewards. That, in itself, is a reason for people to work for the common good. When the shop is padlocked, there is no pay. When an organization goes belly-up, its members quickly scurry to new organizations or they form new ones.

This view of organizations is based on the premise that resources (goods, money, and time) are in limited supply and not available to everyone. For anything to be valuable, its supply must be limited. Disproportion in supply denies some people the opportunity to get what they want. Sentiments, goods, and services are valuable only to the extent that they are scarce. Thus, ordinary dust has little value because it is generally available, while gold dust is valuable because it is difficult to find. Sentiments may be boundless, but the time in which they can be bestowed is quite limited. Thus, competition for attention precedes competition for affection. Scarcity economy confers value in predictable ways. In a corporate organization there are a limited number of influential and responsible positions. Their occupants earn the most money. In families love may be boundless, but it cannot be bestowed simultaneously, thus, attention is a measure of affection.

The predictable role of discourse. Oral and written discourse are artistic methods used by those with relatively less control over economic resources to achieve their pleasure principle, which includes convincing fellow creatures, especially superordinates that the rules entitle them to rewards while convincing their competitors that what they have is not worth taking. Resources are needed for this kind of competition, and thus resources become objectives of negotiation and combat. This translates into "only the washed deserve soap."

Most people subscribe to this Calvinist ideology. People believe they get what they deserve (real hard or not). The notion that "we who have" are entitled to what we have, and furthermore to what we can get, represents a main topic of discourse as social competition and exchange.

Those with power have inartistic means constantly at their disposal. They usually employ artistic rhetoric to make force seem palatable, but by and large, people seek power because with it they can get more of what they want while giving up less. The boss need not seek affection from the employees in order to get service when she has the power to fire them without notice.

Heuristics of Social Analysis

The implications of this kind of analysis should be obvious by now. Hypothesis: Lack of knowledge of operations and orderly procedures contributes to incompetent behavior. In the cognitive restructuring component of instruction, the speech teacher can guide the student to an understand of orderly procedure in social life. *Keep this is mind: we do not proclaim any of the metaphors we discussed here to be THE order of things in the social world. Our argument is simply that in order to talk with the social world, the speaker must impose SOME order.* To test this theory, we can hypothesize about the following:

Who has a stake and what are their qualifications, abilities, and entitlements? There is a dramatis personae for each situation. In a family, it would be mother, father, children; in a friendship, Sue and Sally, Bill and Bernie; in a work setting, the employees and the bosses; in a community, the factions and their representatives; in a governmental unit, the political parties and the citizens. The stake for each individual is the motive to which the speaker appeals. Discovering the stake enables a potential speaker to identify who might be influenced, in what way, with what appeals.

What is the nature of the situation? How are laws passed, executed, and adjudicated? What are each person's rights, duties, obligations, privileges, and what is prohibited. What are the consequences of violations?

What is being exchanged? A simple model of goods, services, and

sentiments is sufficient, although sentiments would require come interpretation. We could specify the goals available to humans (as general
topoi) as well as goals specific to the situations. In essence we are asking
what can people fight about.

What tactics are being employed? How do they work? The potential
speaker can assess probabilities by examining tactics compatible with the
norm.

*Who wins and who loses? If there is no clear-cut victory, how is the
issue resolved?* The appropriate audience for the tactics of discourse is
the party (or parties) who make the relevant decisions. It is probably
counterproductive to start out seeking a mutual win. This is an acceptable outcome after the confrontation.

Reality check. Wishful thinking is a major source of error. When
people believe they are entitled to sentiment for which there is no rule
or to charity when there is no money, they make mistakes in their
discourse. Those who believe people *ought* to do what is right, fair, and
moral often deceive themselves. That does not mean that people never
are nice to one another. It just means that "niceness" is one possibility.

That is why consensual validation is so important in composition of
discourse. The major question is "does anyone else see it this way?" We
may not be able to get confirmation, but corroboration of our ability
and our entitlement is always useful. The issue of personal entitlement
is very important. Entitlements provide the rules and regulations for the
rewards any organization can dispense.

NARCISSISM AND ENTITLEMENT

The easiest way to understand individual goal seeking is to stipulate
that egocentrism is dominant in personal decision making. Whatever
we do (however altruistic it may appear),[4] it is directed at serving our
own interests. What we say comes out of our memory and is controlled
by our brain. We are, thus, necessarily egocentric. We cannot think in
any other terms than our own.

Narcissism is the extreme of egocentrism; it is egocentric solipsism
devoid of even the semblance of rhetorical sensitivity. Narcissists are not
necessarily ineffective, however. They are often exceptional in their
ability to deploy inartistic proofs.

4. Sociobiologists make the claim that altruism is part of the programming for survival
of the species. It is an interesting notion and very useful in an orderly view of social
relations. See Wilson, 1978.

There is no way to escape narcissism. When we humans face trouble, we become narcissistic by the very nature of our being. Alfred Adler (1964) deals with narcissism by pointing out that sanity depends on being able to function in the social interest. That means, in essence, success in social relationships depends on a degree of skill at suppressing narcissistic urgency enough to recognize that one can benefit from the common good as well as be injured by seeking personal gain at the expense of others. On the other hand, no one can deny that getting something for nothing feels pretty good, and once a person becomes skillful at it, the processes are easy to habituate. Reward for successful behavior is, after all, a powerful way of learning. To facilitate rhetorical competence would, thus, require finding ways by which the incompetent could discover that rewards could be attained by effective participation.

This raises a powerful moral issue. We have consistently made the point that rhetoric is a neutral process. It can be used by anyone regardless of purpose or the value assigned to the outcome. It is always a means; never an end. Why should it matter if narcissists use it?

We argue that it is a matter of effectiveness. Narcissism interferes with the outcome of the greatest good for the greatest number. That is, rhetoric is more effective when it takes into account the goals sought by others. Inartistic rhetoric harms those on whom it is imposed, and its benefits to the user are usually short-lived. We can argue the benefits of a democratic orientation on the grounds that consideration for the goals of others provides a more general distribution of equity, thus benefit for all.

Thus, narcissism, which can be viewed as a moral evil, can also beseen as economically inefficient. It results, at best, in temporary gains, and it places the common good in jeopardy. We, therefore, regard it as a cause of rhetorical incompetence. To the extent it plays a role in composition, it distracts the speaker from audience analysis and precludes adaptation. Narcissists deny the possibility of attaining either utopian goal: "from each according to his ability and to each according to his need" or the "greatest good for the greatest number." The narcissistic component of human behavior thus motivates the quest for aggrandizement at the expense of others and disrupts the harmonious operation of social activity.

Narcissism is characterized (in *DSM/III*) by a sense of self-importance or uniqueness; fantasies of power, brilliance, and ideal love; exhibitionism; indifference to others; entitlement and expectation of special privilege; annoyance when people do not do what is wanted; exploitiveness; disregard for the rights of others; lack of empathy.

Apply dual perspective: we all have these feelings, although we might sometimes feel guilty about them. In nonmedical terms, narcissism is a *demand for special treatment made by a person who claimed to be entitled because of special personal qualities or membership in a special group.* In high school, we called narcissists "stuck up" or "ego trippers." In humanistic psychology they are called "actualized." Synonyms for narcissism run the gamut from the relatively neutral "high self esteem" to the virtuous "autonomous" to the invidious "vain." On the other hand, the incompetent often claim consideration because of their ineptitude. Narcissism is behavior that calls attention to itself because of its basis in special entitlements.

Diminished responsibility. This is an inherently narcissistic appeal. It does little good for the people who grant it. It may serve some eleemosynary purposes, assuage guilt, and quell moral anxieties but mostly it is a useful artistic ploy to claim membership in an entitled group when one lacks the qualifications or to argue that because of one's special condition, a new entitled group must be created. "Just make an exception this one time."

Narcissism appears to be the counterpart of "rhetorical sensitivity." A narcissistic speaker may appeal to others but does so without regard to their sensibilities. The narcissists aim to accomplish their ends without exchange, as opposed to theoretically "rhetorically sensitive" persons who, presumably, considers the other person in making requests. In any case, the narcissist demands compliance from the other without exchange.

The Prototypical Narcissist

Oscar Wilde's Remarkable Rocket is the prototypical narcissist.

> "I was saying," continued the Rocket, "I was saying. What was I saying?"
>
> "You were talking about yourself," replied the Roman Candle.
>
> "Of course; I knew I was discussing some interesting subject when I was so rudely interrupted. I hate rudeness and bad manners of every kind, for I am extremely sensitive. No one in the whole world is so sensitive as I am, I am quite sure of that."
>
> "What is a sensitive person?" said the Cracker to the Roman Candle.
>
> "A person who, because he has corns himself, always treads on other

people's toes," answered the Roman Candle . . . and the Cracker nearly exploded with laughter.

"Pray, what are you laughing at?" inquired the Rocket; "I am not laughing."

"I am laughing because I am happy," replied the Cracker.

"That is a very selfish reason," said the Rocket angrily. "What right have you to be happy? You should be thinking about others. In fact, you should be thinking about me. I am always thinking about myself, and I expect everybody to do the same. That is what is called sympathy. It is a beautiful virtue, and I possess it in a high degree."

Later on, the Rocket, having fizzled, failed, and been forgotten, finds himself in a swamp talking with a frog. The conversation goes like this:

". . . Well, good-bye; I have enjoyed our conversation very much . . ."

"Conversation, indeed!" said the Rocket. "You have talked the whole time yourself. That is not conversation."

"Somebody must listen," answered the Frog, "and I like to do all the talking myself. It saves time, and prevents arguments."

"But I like arguments," said the Rocket.

"I hope not," said the Frog complacently. "Arguments are extremely vulgar, for everybody in good society holds exactly the same opinions."

"You are a very irritating person," said the Rocket, "and very ill-bred. I hate people who talk about themselves, as you do, when one wants to talk about oneself as I do. It is what I call selfish ness [sic], and selfish ness [sic] is a most detestable thing, especially to any one of my temperament, for I am well known for my sympathetic nature. In fact, you should take example by me; you could not possibly have a better model."

Narcissistic discourse offers no exchange. The politician must promise the voters that they will benefit from his election. The merchant offers goods for money. Narcissists demand attention to self or condition because of self or condition. They attempt to persuade others that they are entitled. The effective narcissist must learn ways to make claims and demands while appearing to offer quid pro quo to satisfy the claims of others. Narcissists may seem to bargain, but they do not deliver unless it is convenient or they cannot escape it. When sentiments are involved, the narcissists exchange appearances, and since sentiments are intangible and we respond to our impressions rather than realities, we are easily taken in. The appearances are often as good as the realities and need not be judged further.

Consider some of the characteristics of narcissists' speaking. They often speak as if no reply is necessary; silence in the other is interpreted as assent. They alter the meaning of acts by changing labels, so that evil acts can be made good merely by changing their names. They place themselves in special categories (victim, cripple, deprived child, genius, hero) in order to make special claims. In addition, they often claim charismatic qualities by alleging they have special messages from authorities (God or the devil) or knowledge no one else has. Sometimes they claim special self-knowledge and present themselves as special because they are "actualized." Most important, they do not accommodate their rhetorical tactics to the understanding and values of listeners.

Narcissistic rhetoric can, on occasion, be very effective especially when the label they claim entitles them to a particular form of compliance by their listener. Labeling, operates like a cumulative commonplace. The label contains information about how to qualify for entitlements. For example, the label "mentally ill," implies certain kinds of restrictions and treatments. The label "criminal," means punishment and rehabilitation. The label "lover" means intimate access; the label "leader" means that others follow orders, and so on. We learn about social roles and positions in political and business hierarchies in the form of job descriptions associated with labels. The label directs the behavior of the person labeled as well as the behavior of listeners who accept the label.

Usually, those who offer a label as a claim to an entitlement can justify it. Where the entitlement is defined by law, for example, all that is required is to demonstrate qualification. For example, people over sixty-five show a birth certificate to claim social security. Where the entitlement is defined by social custom, negotiation is required. Narcissists declare their own qualifications and demand that they be accepted.

Above all, there is the issue of excuse making. Harry Stack Sullivan (Perry, 1982) once noted that remorse was a painless way of gaining exemption. "I'm sorry," makes the malefactor feel better, but it does not repair the damage. Narcissists are especially free with remorse and appeals for forgiveness, especially the childish, "I won't do it again," which, in adult form becomes, "Yes, I've learned from my mistakes." This all culminates in the demand for "unconditional positive regard." The Rogerian idealism gave license to some very exploitive demands, especially in interpersonal relationships.

Freak labeling. Claiming personal privilege because of exceptionality is widespread. For example, Nietzsche argued that there were "special people," *Uebermenschen*, who are entitled to take what they want. The law entitles the insane to exemption and special treatment.

The story of the "Elephant Man" illustrates how the "freak" label entitles the bearer to special privilege. A deformed person should be studied. The person who does the study is entitled to special honor. Because of the special honor, the scholar is obligated to provide special service to the freak. Those who are diagnosed as "mentally ill" are accorded special consideration by law and social convention. So are "leaders," "gifted children," "exceptional children," "creative thinkers," and so on. Contemporary medicine makes illness a persuasive process. The list goes on and on.

The line between personal necessity and narcissistic claiming isalso very thin. Consider, for example, the problems created by "mainstreaming" the mentally ill. Enrollment in regular school confers the label, "student." It was quite logical when parents of exceptional students began to demand diplomas, as if the diploma would make the child a student. The Wizard of Oz showed his understanding of entitlement and labeling when he offered the Tin Man a watch, gave a medal to the Cowardly Lion, and presented the Scarecrow with his diploma. The Wizard did not have empathy, but he understood the process of freak making and entitlement.

Biblical-type claims. Exceptionality is often claimed on the authority of vocabulary. Dictionaries, for example, function as "bibles" when they associate rewards with category memberships. On a very simple level, for example, philologists can thwart solecists by demanding compliance with the rulebooks of which they are custodians. Parents claim authority over children because of the definition of the word "parent." A job description becomes a legal enactment. When the law is universal, it is biblical. Bibles spell out payoffs and punishments. There are ways to earn the Kingdom of Heaven and ways to be damned. The specifications of the relationship between God and believers are spelled out, sheep and shepherd, for example. Sheep are entitled to grass. Shepherds are entitled to advise sheep. If God demands belief, to the narcissist that means assertion of belief is *prima facie* evidence of belief, thus the self-proclaimed "believer" is entitled to what believers are entitled to. The Bible, in short, is a manual about prediction and control. Through it, *people can discover what they are entitled to and how to demand it.*

Political claims. Americans are not quite so respectful of political claims. The two-party system and belief in government by laws instead of men make it difficult to discover values by examining memberships. Most Americans cannot understand how Marxists use their politics to justify their claims to exceptionality. But Marxism, in every sense, offers a mystical message. Membership in the party indicates belief in the system and entitles one to the payoffs. Political narcissism in the form of terrorism permits the perpetration of horrible acts with no guilt because one is *entitled* to do so because of membership. It is essentially the model Hitler developed in *Mein Kampf* now preempted by various Muslim factions to entitle themselves to acts of terrorism. The Charles Manson family and the Jonestown massacre are contemporary examples of political claims by narcissists resulting in obscene actions. The death sentence imposed on Salmon Rushdie is an example of the outlandish extent to which political narcissists will carry their demands for exceptionality.

Political and religious constructs are not natural—that is why they are called "constructs"). They are belief systems *construct*ed to define who has to do what to get what. Religious entitlement may include eternal life and perhaps authority to judge others—censor the adult bookstore down the block and persecute those who do not belong to the order.

Political entitlements are a bit more tangible. They include pensions, welfare, pork barrels, grants, other payoffs to special categories of people. The political process is made up of self-defined groups each trying to persuade politicians to entitle them. They do this by arguing they are already entitled because of the category they fit in. The argument is not about the entitlement but about whether the arguer qualifies for membership. Law specifies the entitlements associated with the categories.

When a law is being considered, the stasis is on the biblical quality of the words relating to categories. Once a law is passed, however, one need only qualify in the category. Thus, any member of a group that has negotiated itself a label or persuaded the others to accept the label can claim whatever the label entitles one to.

In nonlegal, for example, religious categories, it is necessary to make the system of rewards and punishments lawlike. This is done by referring to tradition and larding it over with ritual and usage. Protestants have an "ethic," subscription to which entitles them to earthly rewards. Catholics earn their place in heaven by observing religious formalities. Jews claim entitlement both on the grounds of the Holocaust and on their ability to keep meat and milk separated. Arabs gain the Kingdom of Heaven because of their willingness to make infidels suffer; Hindus because of their respect for cows. Blacks use history to support their claims; the entitlements come as compensation for slavery. Poor people claim it because they are needy ("and the greatest . . . is charity"). And so on.

There is diminished responsibility in politics, too. People claim it because of adversity. There is flood relief, subsidies for crop failure, support for second-rate regional theater, unemployment compensation, Medicare and Social Security, food banks and free cheese, and so on. These comments should not be construed as opposition to provision for the genuinely needy. However, we cannot provide for the needy without specifying how they qualify for entitlements. Consider the facility with which the model can be used to understand the claims and counterclaims made in interpersonal relationship.

The democratic political process is designed to function in a society without majority in which the issue of entitlement is in doubt. Thus, groups must use rhetoric to become entitled. They need to exchange with each other to become entitled. Once entitled, however, give-backs are hard to come by. When a political claim is confirmed, those who benefit want only to fill out the papers (social security). Once justified rhetorically, any entitlement can become narcissistic.

Analysis of Entitlement and Narcissism

Exclusiveness entitles. As the Rocket said,

> "I see you belong to the lower orders," thus explaining the frog's lack of insight. "I am not going to stop talking . . . merely because he pays no attention. I like hearing myself talk. It is one of my greatest pleasures. I often have long conversations all by myself, and I am so clever that sometimes I don't understand a single word of what I am saying." The dragonfly answered, "Then you should certainly lecture on philosophy."

But the Rocket knew that personal support and justification comes with the *"belief that everyone believes the same thing"* [italics mine].

> "Everybody in good society holds exactly the same opinions . . ." and to avoid knowing one's associates too closely for fear of threat to the common belief system through individual diversity. "I dare say . . . I should not be his friend at all. It is a very dangerous thing to know one's friends."

"Common sense, indeed!" said the Rocket indignantly; "you forget that I am very uncommon, and very remarkable. Why, anybody can have common sense, provided that they have no imagination. But I have imagination, for I never think of things as they really are; I always think of them as being quite different . . . there is evidently no one here who can at all appreciate an emotional nature. Fortunately for myself, I don't care. The only thing that sustains one through life is the consciousness of the immense inferiority of everybody else, and this is a feeling I have always cultivated."

Any orderly system of composition must include a routine for analyzing interpersonal social behavior. We have offered narcissism and entitlement as a basis for this analysis. Once the analysis is made, its constituent statements can be used as criteria for adjusting discourse to meet the speaker's egocentric goals. We can now describe the steps in the narcissistic process.

A person learns to be a narcissist by learning the basic algorithm of entitlement: those who qualify are entitled. The benefits can be discovered in laws or social norms. The next step is to find out how other people who have won the entitlement have gone about it, and perfect the technique. In essence, the entitlement seeker fills out the forms and then chooses from the menu (personal salvation, spiritual peace, happiness, good sex, cars and stereos, attractive companions, peak experiences, affluence, charm, sex appeal, happy kids, beautiful/handsome spouse, and a place to park in all crowded cities (not necessarily in that order).

Discourse seeks to persuade other people to believe the seeker fits the label. Once this is done, the entitlements should be automatic and if they are not, the seekers can claim "foul." Very often, however, the narcissist seeks only to persuade himself. Other people are merely reflectors.

The narcissist avoids the uncertainty of persuasion by stacking the performance deck so however the listener responds, it confirms the speaker. For example, the claim to special identity of the born again Christian is either confirmed, rejected, or ignored. Those who confirm are brothers. Those who reject are infidels. Those who ignore are ignored back. Since infidels are those who reject authentic claims, rejection becomes confirmation. Ignoring is accepted as affirmation since, to the narcissist, nondenial is affirmation.

The narcissistic system is available to competent speakers. Aristotle noted that speakers use ethos as a primary means of persuasion. Convincing the listener of who you are is an important element in getting him to concede to you what you want. Thus, the line between narcissism and competency is very thin.

Competent processing is based on a series of heuristics. The speaker asks, "Who must I be in order to get what I want?" Once this question is answered, the speaker must discover who has the authority to confirm the identity. This defines the audience; the goal is the payoff. Tactics and arguments answer the question, "What must I do and say, where and when, to qualify?" The final problem is to figure out whether you won or lost. If the payoff is immediate, there is no problem. When you apply for tax refund, for example, it should come within a specified time period. When you apply for the undying loyalty of a friend or spouse, the payoff is sometimes indeterminate and, in fact, must eventually be defined by the speaker.

Consider, that for a doctor, licensing is evidence of the entitlement to behave as a doctor. To act as a doctor before the license is a violation of the law. But how does a person seeking to be "beautiful" know she is getting what she earns? And lurking in the background is the intriguing questions, "what are the penalties, if I don't do it well enough?"

The practical reality of assessing effectiveness is that what a speaker is really doing is managing impression. The speaker has no control over anything in the situation other than his own actions. The reaction of listeners is not linear. Thus, the only way to evaluate success is for the speaker to *compare what she got with what was available*. Realistic goalsetting remains the matrix for effective discourse. You cannot get what the listener cannot give.

The aspirant to an entitlement, whether competent or narcissistic, goes through four processes before the decision about effectiveness can be made.

Identity. The narcissist may operate much like the Remarkable Rocket who was prepared to dominate the wedding celebration of the King's Son. The Rocket fizzled because he shed self-pitying tears on himself, was thrown out. He is found by two small boys who ask, "Look at this old stick; I wonder how it came here." The Rocket is astounded at being called an "old stick," decides they meant "gold stick," and is satisfied. The boys throw the Rocket on the fire (not knowing it is a rocket). They go to sleep, the rocket fires and flies to the sky. "Now I am going off . . . I know I shall go much higher than the moon, much higher than the sun," but no one saw him. Now, really a stick, he falls to earth and hits a goose, who remarks, "Good Heavens . . . It is going to rain sticks." " 'I knew I should create a great sensation,' gasped the Rocket and he went out." The fact that the boys did not confirm his identity notwithstanding, the Rocket found a way to sustain his claim. The competent speaker prepares a formal plan by which identity can be claimed. Included in that plan is verifiable confirmation.

Confirmation. Entitlement claims often consist of excuses (I wasn't myself today), complaints (people like me suffer from discrimination), remorse (I feel so bad about what I did), and demanding (it's my turn). There is a social convention that automatically allows these claims.

Identity is genuinely established by confirmation. A competent speaker tries to give a listener a good reason for confirming identity. The narcissist merely wants a reflection. To the narcissist, everyone else is a reflecting pool. What the narcissist does is "inartistic," for it offers no pretense of proof. It is somewhat like the actor in a bad play depending on the identification in the program rather than on his performance to create his character.

Linguistic acculturation. When confirmation depends on group membership, it is important to learn to talk like other members of the group. It is easy for prospective members of groups to listen to members and imitate their language. The language of altruism, victimization, and artistry is also easy to learn. In these cases, the *word is the thing*.

Furthermore, linguistic acculturation is part of growing up. Children learn to be sons and daughters, students, and friends by learning the language of family, school, playground, and street. They learn to fit into social groupings, political/religious organizations, and occupations partly by learning the language. But language alone is not enough to qualify for adulthood. There must also be competent action, which usually includes recognition of the needs of others and development of equitable exchanges with them. Narcissists do nothing more than learn the language so they can fit into the group that approves it.

Therapy eligibility. Ineffective people are penalized. Those not competent on the job get fired. Inadequate mates get divorced. Those who cannot keep friends are lonely. Failures often get depressed. Once depressed, they qualify as sick. Those who lose their jobs draw unemployment compensation for a time. Depressed people earn treatment. Inept narcissists must be prepared for this final game in order to hedge their bets. Munchausen syndrome is the final narcissistic inartistry. He may actually have to get sick to gain the entitlement. There is no better way to get the full attention of society than to assassinate a major public official. There is a trial, incarceration, press releases, appeals, and eventually a public execution with a maximum of pomp and ceremony.

The final payoff in our society is obtained through loss. It is so important for everyone to fit somewhere that the losers also have their niche. Prisoners are to be pitied and rehabilitated. If poverty (or poor upbringing) drives a man to crime, he has a second chance. He can find God, go on the lecture circuit, or fit into prison society and have movies made about him. If he is driven to drink, he has many public, private, and religious organizations at his disposal. If he is poor, he can throw himself on the mercy of the system. Even those who die are entitled to be mourned. It is sad to contemplate the plight of the person who has no disability and must blame himself when he fails.

Part of therapeutic entitlement is being humble about it. Old people who act like they deserve their Social Security benefits are a real drag. Haven't they read in the magazines about how people can have good sex well into their eighties?

There is a Calvinist aura around narcissism. Success is the evidence of election. Outsiders are important because they define insiders. Minorities would not be minorities and would be entitled to nothing, if majorities did not make them what they are. The narcissist needs rejection as well as acceptance to authenticate the claim.

Those who model on the popular culture can see themselves as exclusive. They are the only ones who finished all the exercises, tried all the recipes, went to all the EST classes, or learned how to assert like no one has ever asserted. Those who pay the rent, drive about, and dress right because they cannot afford not to are justified in believing they are special. All they need do is look around and see the excluded of society: the old; the poor; the handicapped; the tacky; the middle class; the peasants; the great unwashed; the anti-intellectual, blue-collar, beer-drinking, polka-dancing, bowling-shirt-wearing denizens of the union hall who are unemployed because SONY does make a better stereo, and Mazda a better car, and if the unemployed were any good, it would not have been that way and the Japanese would have been out of work.

THE FINALE

This book started as an essay on shyness. Shyness is a disease, a pathology, a social strategy, a personality type, a set of ineffective communication behaviors, among other things. It is caused by genetic flaws, defective learning, situational intimidation, apprehension and fear, among other things. Shy people suffer in some form, among other things. Shy people suffer in some *je ne sais quoi* fashion. They need treatment, instruction, admonition, and kindness. Unfortunately, their plight is not unusual. Our twenty-five-year study of shyness convinced us that a great many people have serious problems with social communication.

We decided, after considerable exploration, and many years of treating the condition, that shyness is but one of many forms of disabling ineffective communication. The label chosen for disabling ineffective communication is "rhetorical incompetence." This is a useful label because it is based on errors made in the communication process. While we may not be able to describe the qualifications of a person who is rhetorically competent, we can point to specific reasons why individuals failed to accomplish rhetorical goals. These reasons can be specified and identified as components in the process of composition of rhetorical discourse.

The advantage of this kind of analysis is that we can avoid the fuzzy, obscure, subconscious, mysterious, and unique and concentrate on general rules. We have enough substantiation of similarity among human beings both in the lives they live in the social world and in the processes they carry on in their minds. Thus, we can presume that their communication behavior is governed by algorithms and heuristics. Consequently, we propose a theory of therapy, instruction, or treatment based on the premise that what we are doing is correcting errors in the composition process. It is based on the theory that even when order is not apparent, in social life or in discourse, it must be imposed in a socially consensual way.

We can discover how to do this by observing the composition process, logging its regularities and programming them into an expert system to be administered on a computer to a human-cyborg acting as database. The human is paced through the rule bound processes of composition and errors corrected. What seems irregular and hard to understand can be managed by finding some sort of order into which it can be sorted. We have offered some possibilities in this chapter.

We do not have an infallible system. There are individualdifferences. What we have is a calculus of probabilities in which our orderly interventions can be assessed for their effectiveness, modified accordingly, and used only when it appears their advantage will outweigh the undesirable concomitants.

It is a theory that must be defended by testing hypothesis. But the prognosis is good; the equipment is ready; the programs are written. Time to turn on the switch!

And back to our shy people with whom we started. They, and those others whose communication skills do not meet their needs, require answers. Teachers and therapists have been offering them answers for centuries. Most of the answers are entirely unsatisfactory, not necessarily because they were wrong but because the people who needed the answers were afraid to accept them. The unmanageable variable in the process is human will. There is no change without the will to change. We do not understand what will is. We do not understand why some people will commit to a tedious course of action in order to "improve," while others simply wander about hoping for the best. For the moment, we will leave these answers to the psychologists.

Analysis of the social milieu demands the consideration of personal motives. The impelling logic of the combat metaphor combined with the perception that people are essentially egocentric provides an orderly way to analyze situations. Teachers of speech are not obligated to restructure sociological ideas and ideals, but it is helpful in guiding students to selection of achievable goals to provide them with realistic and useful models of social interaction which they can use to guide their choices.

The enterprise of this book has been to justify orderly procedure in the diagnosis and treatment of communication problems. We have conceded that there are mysteries that cannot presently be accounted for, but we have argued that if we analyze and teach in a systematic and orderly way we will solve the greater number of problems. We also argued that the most of the mysteries will be resolved eventually. In our lifetime, schizophrenia has been removed from the list of communication problems and placed in the category of chemical disturbances of the brain. Within the last week, a popular science magazine headlined the news that researchers in Texas have claimed that stuttering is not a learning disorder but a disturbance in transmission of messages from Wernicke's area to Broca's area.

And so we program our computer and get to work. As more order is discovered, we can program it and use our findings to make the humans we teach a little less incompetent at performing their rhetorical tasks.

Appendix

Bibliography

Index

Appendix:

Perspectives on Communication Competence

By Rebecca B. Rubin

BACKGROUND OF THE CONCEPT

Although interest in communication competence dates to the ancient Greeks (Rosenfield & Mader, 1984; Spitzberg & Cupach, 1984), there is as much or more interest in the construct today. Current writings on cultural literacy (Hirsch, 1988) point to effective communication as an outcome of (*a*) cultural knowledge and (*b*) skillful use of schemata that guide our interactions with others. Ten years earlier, Wiemann (1978, p. 311) urged increased attention to communication literacy, "the ability to enact all possible behaviors a person needs in order to respond appropriately to communication tasks at hand." Wiemann's definition, influenced by scholars in related disciplines, later grew into our current conception of communication competence.

Writers about communication competence from outside the communication discipline had very narrow and discipline-specific views of competence. In psychology, communication competence referred to social adjustment (Foote & Cottrell, 1955). In organizational management it referred to human relations skills necessary for the management of interpersonal relationships (Argyris, 1962). In linguistics, communi-

Reprinted, with changes, from *Speech Communication: Essays to Commemorate the 7th Anniversary of the Speech Communication Association*, edited by Gerald M. Phillips and Julia T. Wood (Carbondale: Southern Illinois University Press, 1990). Copyright 1990 by the Speech Communication Association.

cation competence was an innate language structure (Chomsky, 1965) that contains elements of appropriateness and success (Hymes, 1971). And, in sociology communication competence was linked to the development of the self-concept and social competence (Goffman, 1963; Mead, 1934).

Communication scholars have taken a more general stance and viewed communication competence as knowledge about appropriate and effective communication behaviors, development of a repertoire of skills that encompass both appropriate and effective means of communicating, and motivation to behave in ways that are viewed as both appropriate and effective by interactants. As Professor Phillips indicates in this book, if we view competence as perfection, few, if any, people would achieve communication competence. Most scholars, therefore, view communication competence as an ideal state, one to which people should strive.

Communication research has consistently revealed that people can be severely affected by a lack of communication skill. One study estimates that about 25 percent of the general population has substandard communication skills (Vangelisti, Daly, & Mead, in press). A similar study, reporting that over 30 percent of college students cannot give adequate directions or that almost 50 percent cannot describe a point of view that differs from their own, emphasizes that communication training is sorely needed in our society (Rubin, 1982). And, as Professor Phillips explains here, communication apprehension or shyness can be debilitating in everyday life (see also McCroskey, 1977a; Powers & Smythe, 1980).

My goal here is to provide an overview of the major perspectives that have guided communication scholars in their examination of communication competence. Because of space restrictions, this review will not discuss the intricacies of particular studies but will explain the broad issues and areas of consensus found in our research investigations and programs. Then, I will examine major issues in theory and measurement that relate to these perspectives.

Communication competence has been studied from a variety of perspectives. I have classified these into three main types based on common theoretical bonds—cognitive, social/interpersonal, and communication skills.

Writers employing a cognitive perspective view communication competence as a psychological or mental process, either innate or developed, that guides behavior. Linguists (Chomsky, 1965; Habermas, 1970), for instance, judge utterances on their competence (grammatical structure) or performance (acceptability). They focus on the innate system of grammar and rules by which people master language and generate sentences. Chomsky defined linguistic competence as knowledge of what is acceptable (a system of grammatical rules based on an innate language apparatus) and performance as the use of language in social interaction.

According to Chomsky, all potential sentences available to a speaker are within the speaker's domain, given a set of generative rules that allow for novel utterances. Linguists were not interested in language variation owing to culture or other regional features.

Several cognitive theorists have disagreed with this view. Hymes (1971), for instance, agreed with the acceptability notion and argued that community norms determine acceptability of linguistic performance, but believed that this definition lacked an essential element—success. Krauss and Glucksberg (1969) argued that communication competence should be distinguished from linguistic competence because children learn grammatical rules by age three, show adult-level linguistic performance by age seven or eight, but do not use cognitive and role-taking skills until much later.

More recent cognitive views focus on congruence of mental images. Powers and Lowry (1984) defined communication competence as basic communication fidelity, a congruence of cognitions that takes place after communication has occurred. This definition of communication competence is concerned not with social appropriateness or accuracy of the communicator but only with congruence of constructs created in the minds of the participants. Theorists who focus on the coordinated management of meaning would also argue that construct congruence is important for competent communication (Pearce, 1976).

Developmental theorists work mainly from a cognitive perspective. As Cronkhite (1984) noted, they formerly examined how children acquire language (Bloom, 1978; Ervin-Tripp & Mitchell-Kernan, 1977), but lately they have addressed questions of how children develop social skills needed for peer interaction (for example,Van Hoeven, 1985). Constructivists, for example, point to the importance of cognitive development and construct congruence in children's abilities to understand the perspectives of their peers (Clark & Delia, 1977; Delia & Clark, 1977).

Haslett (1984) also examined the development of communication in children and identified four distinct competence areas: understanding the value of communication, using conventional signs, appreciation of dialogue requirements, and development of conversational styles. The study also focused on how mothers facilitate competence in their children by interpreting what they say, serving as models, extending children's communication, providing interaction opportunities, and demonstrating activities. This points to a more social notion of the communication competence development.

Social or interpersonal competence stems from a sociological view of an individual's interpersonal interaction and describes the process by which people acquire prosocial behaviors and use them to manage interactions. This line of inquiry appears rooted in dramaturgical theory, which argues that people are actors who play roles during interaction with others. G. H. Mead (1934) viewed role-taking (the ability to take another's perspective) as the constituent element within communication competence, and Goffman (1963, 1967) focused on the development of "face and line" in everyday social, symbolic interaction.

Wiemann (1977) interpreted Goffman's basic views that social rules guide interactions to mean that people must achieve their goals without losing face or breaking the rules governing the situation. Cegala's (1981) work on interaction involvement was also built on these principles; he viewed competence as behavior focused on the other during the interaction. Similarly, Redmond's (1985) work on empathy concluded that other-focused behavior is the essential ingredient in communication competence.

Bochner (1984) referred to social or interpersonal skills as bonding competence. He cited Bochner and Kelly's (1974) treatise on interpersonal communication competence, Hart and Burk's (1972) research on rhetorical sensitivity, Argyle's (1972) work on nonverbal communication, and Wiemann's (1977) study of verbal/nonverbal interpersonal communication as evidence that social skills are important; people must be able to diagnose the situation and plan how to achieve an objective, then achieve the objective through strategic verbal and nonverbal communication.

Relational competence research is an extension of this line of inquiry. It concentrates on adult-adult interactions and the social skills needed for relationship development. Spitzberg and Hecht (1984), for example, developed a model of relational communication based on four components: motivation, knowledge, skill, and relational outcomes.

Reardon (1987) was able to distinguish between cognitive social skills (empathy, social perspective taking, cognitive complexity, sensitivity, situational knowledge, and self-monitoring) and behavioral social skills (interaction involvement, interaction management, behavioral flexibility, listening, social style, and monitoring one's own anxiety). With this model, Reardon suggested that both the cognitive and the social or interpersonal perspectives have sufficient research support. Some communication researchers, however, have adopted a third approach, one that identifies context-specific cognitive and social communication skills.

Communication skills theorists extended their focus beyond broad interpersonal or social contexts and concentrated more on skills specific to a particular context or situation. They identified behaviors that are seen as competent by communication recipients in interpersonal, group, organization, media, and intercultural contexts.

In the interpersonal context, research has examined relational impressions formed by interactants and the interpersonal, prosocial skills that comprise interpersonal competence. Researchers such as Bochner and Kelly (1974) identified empathy, descriptiveness, owning feelings, self-disclosure, and behavioral flexibility as components of interpersonal competence. Other researchers have developed similar schemata and add to this list qualities such as social relaxation, assertiveness, interaction management, altercentrism, expressiveness, supportiveness, behavioral flexibility, immediacy, and control (Argyris, 1962; Duran, 1983; Foote & Cottrell, 1955; Wiemann, 1977).

In group communication, Hirokawa and Pace (1983) looked at the effectiveness of groups in relation to behaviors used by group members and the accuracy of the final decision. Effective groups had members who rigorously evaluated the validity of the group's opinions and alternative courses of action, based decisions on accurate facts and inferences, and had a facilitative leader. Bradley (1980) examined the importance to group members of leaders' task-related knowledge levels (competence). Group members acted toward competent leaders with less dominance, more reasonableness, and less hostility; the highly competent leader was more persuasive.

In organizational settings, researchers have looked at both the communication skills of workers and the rules by which they come to understand their roles in the organization. Research consistently points to three general skill areas necessary in organizations: listening (understanding directions, distinguishing facts from opinions), speaking (using appropriate words, pronunciation, and grammar), and human relations (cooperating, resolving conflict, perspective taking, acting friendly) (DiSalvo, 1980; Monge, Bachman, Dillard, & Bisenberg, 1982; Muchmore & Galvin, 1983; Wheeless & Berryman-Fink, 1985).

Specific organizational communication skills such as advising, persuading, instructing (DiSalvo, Larsen, & Seiler, 1976), business writing, telephone communication, interviewing (Staley & Shockley-Zalabak, 1985), and cognitive differentiation (Sypher, 1984) are also identified in the literature. Rules-perspective research distinguished between regulative and constitutive rules used to manage communication in the organizational context (Harris & Cronen, 1979). Wellmon (1988) found the most common rules focused on listening, acting in a friendly manner, good leadership, providing feedback, and using empathic interaction skills. Other studies have examined communication competence of specific organizational individuals. For instance, research has suggested the following:

1. Mediators need to use structuring mediation strategies and reframe the disputant's utterances (Donohue, Allen, & Burrell, 1988).

2. Health-care professionals need interpersonal communication skills to build relationships and listen effectively (DiSalvo, Larsen, & Backus, 1986; Morse & Piland, 1981).

3. Teachers must motivate students, give constructive feedback, be supportive, and establish good rapport with students and coworkers (Swinton & Bassett, 1981), be dramatic, impression-leaving, relaxed, open, and friendly (McLaughlin & Erickson, 1981; Rubin & Feezel, 1986), and give effective feedback, explain lessons clearly, question effectively, adapt to the audience, and direct others effectively (Cooper, 1986; McCaleb, 1984, 1987; Rubin & Feezel, 1986).

4. Elementary-school children must be able to control others, share feelings, inform, ritualize, and imagine (Allen & Wood, 1978). 5. College students must have both a knowledge of communication principles (Levison, 1976) and ability to listen effectively, use nonverbal codes, evaluate oral messages, express and organize ideas, and take the perspective of others (Bassett, Whittington, & Staton-Spicer, 1978; Rubin, 1982).

Media or television literacy focuses on critical viewing skills, critical televiewing, and television receivership skills. Anderson (1983) developed a receivership skills project to teach children to interpret and critically understand both their own motives for viewing and the content of the material viewed, and develop strategies to manage viewing amounts and program choices. Lloyd-Kolkin (1981) also identified basic television critical viewing abilities: evaluating and managing one's own television viewing behavior, questioning the reality of programs, recognizing arguments used on television, counterarguing, and recognizing the effect of TV on one's own life.

In cross-cultural settings, interpersonal concepts are stretched across cultures to include elements such as interaction posture, empathy, interaction management, role-oriented behavior, and display of respect (Ruben & Kealey, 1979). Viewing competence as culture-specific, Cooley and Roach (1984) argued that consideration of an individual's cultural background is necessary to assess competence. Context-specific knowledge is instrumental in impressions of communication competence that people form (Pavitt & Haight, 1986). Yet Chen (1988) found support for a culture-general interpretation: basic communication skills were central to intercultural communication competence for sojourners from a large variety of cultures; interaction involvement, social adjustment, self-consciousness, and self-disclosure were also important.

These three perspectives represent different philosophic positions. The cognitivists (especially the structural sociolinguists) viewed language ability as innate and did not include the social (that is, appropriateness) nature of communication as an important element. Support for the cognitive view is much more limited than that for the social or communication skills approach. The prevailing developmental view is influenced by the social skills approach; children are seen as perspective takers who develop these social skills as they mature.

The social skills theorists focused mainly on interpersonal relationship skills and the process of taking others' perspectives for increased understanding. This view significantly influenced communication research on interpersonal competence but lacks a practical or training orientation.

The communication skills movement, because of its focus on skill enhancement through instruction, provides instructional guidelines for each of the many skills comprising competence. Some have argued that these skills are much too specific and that the whole impression is more than a sum of the parts. Others have contended that the social skills approach is impractical because instruction cannot change empathy and other personality predispositions.

Thus, there is support for both the social and the communication skills approaches; that is, only two of the three perspectives have figured prominently in competence research. Given this, it is appropriate to urge future researchers to use either of the two empirically supported theoretical positions to guide their work and to focus attention in particular on research designed to clarify the relative explanatory power of the two alternatives that have survived initial tests of validity.

CURRENT UNDERSTANDINGS ABOUT COMMUNICATION COMPETENCE

There appears to be a consensus on four major premises: (*a*) communication competence is an impression or judgment formed about behavior; (*b*) competence entails both appropriateness and effectiveness; (*c*) people develop a repertoire of skills, a body of knowledge, and motivation to use both; and (*d*) skill can be improved through education. These tenets and research supporting each will be examined in this section.

Impression or Judgment

Communication competence is best conceived as an impression or attribution formed about others (Phillips, 1984; Rubin, 1985; Spitzberg & Cupach, 1984). Just as with source credibility, communication competence is attributed to a communicator on the basis of those behaviors perceived and judged by others. Several research studies have taken this other-rated approach (rather than using self-report instruments) when examining communication effectiveness (Brandt, 1979; Freimuth, 1976; Rubin, 1985). Some have compared behaviors with impressions. Street, Brady, and Lee (1984), for example, found that males who spoke faster were evaluated as more socially attractive and competent than those who spoke slower, and females who spoke faster were rated as more competent.

Roloff and Kellermann (1984) also viewed competence as an evaluative judgment of a person's behavior rather than an individual's conception of his or her own skills or traits. They argued that people perceive and evaluate others' communication within the relationship on the basis of both verbal and nonverbal behaviors exhibited in the situation. Interactants have their own standards of performance for use in the evaluation, so different raters may reach different conclusions.

Pavitt and Haight (1985) have detailed the process by which these observations are made. Somewhat like the early philosophers' approach to communication competence as eloquence, Pavitt and Haight argued that past researchers have assumed that people use an "ideal communicator" image to judge another's competence and have relied on the premise that there is only one such image. They argued that there are general prototypes, skill-related prototypes, and logically superordinate prototypes. Which prototype is used depends on what the person is looking for. A follow-up study confirmed that people use an "average person" prototype to form impressions of others (Pavitt & Haight, 1986).

Cooley and Roach (1984), however, argued that "competence itself is neither perceivable nor measurable; it can only be inferred" (p. 15). Phillips (1984) agreed that competence was an inference about a behavior, not the behavior itself. His discussion of labeling theory highlights his position that competence is an inference made about artifacts of speakers; the inference should not be made about the speaker him/herself. Labeling theory research suggests that the label can have a profound effect on the one who is labeled—he or she begins to act in ways consistent with the label and thus makes the prophecy self-fulfilling. So, past controversy that centered on whether competence itself can or should be perceived has resulted in an understanding that communication competence is mainly this perception or judgment and does not exist apart from it.

Appropriateness and Effectiveness

From the early classical views on propriety (Longinus) and taste (Blair) to neo-Aristotelian views on effectiveness as a criterion for discourse (Rosenfield & Mader, 1984), virtually every definition of communication competence includes the mandate that communication be both appropriate and effective. Appropriate behaviors are those that others judge to be consistent with the rules of a particular society, and effective behaviors are those that ensure the accomplishment of a communication goal (Bochner & Kelly, 1974; Phillips, 1984; Wiemann, 1978).

Various communication theories see appropriateness as central to the communication process. For example, in coordinated management of meaning (Pearce, 1976), communicators must invoke the use of social rules to manage meanings created between them. Harris and Cronen (1979) examined these rules in an organization and identified strategic competence as a way of cooperating with others and tactical competence as a way of attaining goals; competence, then, is knowledge of appropriate rules and the skill to accomplish goals while using these rules with others. In constructivism, the concepts of listener-adapted messages and perspective taking focus on the need to use socially appropriate communication.

Modern opinions also concur that communication must be effective to be competent. Bochner and Kelly (1974) viewed communication competence as a combination of appropriateness and effectiveness, and Hale's (1980) study of communication competence emphasized only the effectiveness of communication. McCroskey's (1982) essay, however, argued that effectiveness is an unreliable estimate of competence; he reasoned that it was more important for people to be able to communicate in a certain way than to actually do it. He favored a definition more closely tied to the demonstration of knowledge of the appropriate communication behavior without mandating effectiveness. One respondent to McCroskey (Backlund, 1982) agreed with this distinction and described how competence and effectiveness differ in cognitive, psychomotor, and affective domains. Another respondent (Spitzberg, 1983) argued that both appropriateness and effectiveness are necessary for competent communication.

Early distinctions between competence (appropriateness) and effectiveness (goal accomplishment) seem to have faded. Most researchers today agree that both elements must be present. Both appropriateness and effectiveness are context-specific, but effectiveness involves more— the accomplishment of objectives. Spitzberg and Cupach (1984) saw appropriateness as existing if social sanctions are invoked when norms or rules are violated and effectiveness as existing if goals or objectives are achieved. Current interpersonal communication texts adopt these definitions (DeVito, 1989; Reardon, 1987; Rubin & Nevins, 1988).

Both appropriateness and effectiveness are taken into account when a communicator adapts to the situation; this combination of behaviors is sometimes termed "behavioral flexibility" (Bochner & Kelly, 1974; Duran, 1983). Duran and Zakahi (1984) viewed competence as adaptability, the ability to perceive interpersonal relationships and adjust one's own goals and behaviors to the other's. This strategy assumes a repertoire from which to draw behaviors and the ability to perceive others accurately.

Skill, Knowledge, and Motivation

Humanistic and social science research alike have acknowledged a trilogy of domains: psychomotor, cognitive, and affective. For example, persuasion research has long understood that there is a difference between behavior change, change in knowledge, and attitude change. Also, education consistently distinguishes among teaching a student to do something well, learning how to do it, and liking it. Translated to the communication competence area, skill, knowledge, and motivation are distinct elements of communication competence.

Communication competence involves developing both a repertoire of skills and a body of knowledge (McCroskey, 1982). The idea of a repertoire of skills has strong theoretical support. For example, Goodall (1982) defined communication competence as a repertoire of skills or strategies used to understand and respond in interactions. Ammon (1981) distinguished skill (knowing how) from knowledge (knowing about); he saw linguistic competence as a structural representation of linguistic knowledge rules, and communication competence as both skill and knowledge. Ammon thought skills were necessary for communication performance, but not sufficient to explain variance in performance (that is, knowledge has some effect). As Wiemann (1978) suggested, "It is not enough "to know" what is appropriate behavior, but the student must also "know how" to perform that behavior. In other words, neither cognitive nor performance knowledge alone is sufficient for literate behavior" (p. 314). Wiemann and Backlund (1980) identified the rift between cognitive (Chomsky, 1965) and behavioral (Bochner & Kelly, 1974) definitions and argued for a dual approach. People need both knowledge of rules and skilled, appropriate performance.

There is consensus that competence requires performance. Spitzberg (1983) argued that you cannot tell whether a student has knowledge unless there is performance (either on a test or in a behavior), so knowledge and skill are intricately entwined in communication competence through performance. Likewise, Duran (1982) and Cegala (1981) took the stance that effectiveness and performance are integral components of communication competence. Cooley and Roach (1984) also accepted the view that communication competence has both behavioral and cognitive components. Hirsch (1988, p. 62) adhered to the cognitive view that "expert performance depends on the quick deployment of schemata" that are models of operating according to well-known patterns of behavior and their variations. For example, when people listen, they use short-term memory for generating meaning for themselves and long-term memory for later recall. The cognitive schemata used in communicating with others are highly developed methods of speaking, knowledge of subject matter, and enough flexibility to share strategies with others and change strategies when necessary. According to Hirsch, "literate adults have internalized these shared schemata and have made them second nature" (p. 68).

Reardon's (1987) typology of communication behaviors incorporates this view. Spontaneous behaviors are unplanned, subconscious, and unmonitored; emotional reactions such as sadness and anger are spontaneous. Scripted behaviors are culture-specific; when the behavior is learned, planning and monitoring occur and become automatic with increased practice. Contrived behaviors involve conscious planning and monitoring; they are reasoned behaviors. Instruction is focused on turning effective and appropriate behaviors into scripted or automatic.

Skill, then, is a matter of judgment (choosing correctly from a repertoire), and knowledge is a matter of inference (making connections among bits of information learned about situations and communication). One without the other does not lead to competence; both require some type of behavior to be assessed. Rubin (1985) found a strong relationship between knowledge and skill in her communication competence research and recommended that both be taught in communication classes.

Some scholars include motivation as a third element in conceptions of competence. Spitzberg and Hecht (1984) developed a model that tested the hypothesis that communication satisfaction is derived from an individual's conversational knowledge, skill, and motivation. They found that skill and motivation were strong predictors of communication satisfaction; conversational knowledge was minimally related. Motivation was also identified by Rubin (1983) as the third dimension of competence, and evidence suggested that motivation is highly influential in judgments of communication skill (Rubin, Graham, & Mignerey, 1988).

Research has presented mixed evidence for the existence of motivation (see Rubin & Feezel, 1986), but skill and knowledge seem to persist as strong components of communication competence (Rubin, 1985). However, if motivation is defined as communication apprehension or interaction involvement, then there is considerable evidence that motivation is also a component and may underlie enactment of knowledge and skill (Cegala, 1984; McCroskey, 1977a; Rubin, 1985).

Communicators must build and consult behavioral repertoires to act in knowledgeable and skillful ways (Rubin, 1983). Allen and Wood (1978) expanded upon Connolly and Bruner's (1974) definition of competence and developed a model in which competence consisted of (1) developing a repertoire of communication acts, (2) selecting from that repertoire the most appropriate communication acts according to criteria, (3) implementing these choices effectively through verbal and nonverbal means, and (4) evaluating these communication attempts according to elements of appropriateness and effectiveness (Allen & Wood, p. 289). Training, Allen, and Wood (1978) argued, should focus on these four components. Skill instruction should be coupled with selection strategies for criteria development, practice, and evaluation. "Theoretically, then, the communicatively competent individual is the product of a learning environment which permits the development of appropriate behavioral and cognitive skills, shapes a positive affect for communication, and provides opportunities for use and reinforcement of those abilities. One of our functions as communication professionals is to foster the creation of such environments" (McCroskey, 1984, p. 267).

ISSUES IN COMMUNICATION COMPETENCE RESEARCH

There are three issues that deserve extended dialogue in future communication competence research. The first focuses on which theoretical orientation can best explain communication competence. The second raises the question of which form of measurement is most appropriate. And the third centers on whether communication competence is a state or a trait.

Theory

Which theory or theories best explain communication competence? Kerlinger (1986) explained that theories must specify relations among variables, explain which variables are related to others, and allow for prediction by means of a set of testable hypotheses. Cooley and Roach (1984) translated these basic principles for communication competence. They stated that a theory of competence must be explicit, empirically relevant, abstract, and logically rigorous, and that it take into account the effect of culture on behavior and specify the relationship between competence and performance. One model that partially satisfies these criteria is Parks' (1985) model of interpersonal competence. Parks identified a hierarchy of nine control levels and used these to rate degrees of competence. Levels 1 through 4 deal with psychomotor competence, or sensory and motor control. To be competent at this level, people must be able to control speech muscles, sense environmental events and control reactions to them, control combinations of muscles, and to execute these organized combinations of actions.

Most current definitions of communication competence assume level 5 competence (sequence control)—the ability to put together actions to achieve goals in the stream of interaction. This includes the more molecular aspects of communication competence: formation of phrases; ability to discriminate between verbal and nonverbal actions; and communication, timing, and interaction management strategies. Level 6, relationship control, concerns the behaviors necessary to establish satisfying interactions with others—abilities to create and understand interaction rules, constructions, perspectives, and causes of behavior. Level 7, program control, involves skills such as role-taking and behavioral flexibility. Incompetent communication is that which is damaging to one's self-esteem and physical health, is socially inappropriate, or is violent. Competence requires both cognition, behavior, and evaluation: "To be competent, therefore, we must not only "know" and "know how," we must also "do" and "know that we did" (Parks, 1985, p. 174). Levels 8 and 9 focus specifically on abilities to understand and use basic principles and to consult idealized self-concepts when devising and adjusting goals.

Parks' (1985) model is attractive because it helps us understand the relationship of motor and linguistic skills to more modern conceptions of communication competence. In fact, all the perspectives outlined earlier are understandable in the model. It is also appealing because it identifies the individual as the locus of control, it reposes responsibility for actions in the communicator, and it merges the cognitive and behavioral perspectives. Future research must focus on aspects (such as culture) that impinge on a person's degree of control and explain how self-concepts influence behavior. We would expect persons with a greater degree of control to be better able to adjust images for self-perceived judgments of communication competence, for example.

Another theory, especially useful in understanding how to improve communication competence, is repetition theory (McGuire, 1985). This behavioristic learning-theory approach (applied to communication competence) would view competence as a repertoire of behaviors that work as created rewards (stimuli) to produce a response (repeated behavior). Through repetition of behavior in similar situations, a person is gratified, especially if the behavior is rewarded. A student, for example, would receive gratification by positive reactions from friends to behaviors developed in an interpersonal skills class. Once in the repertoire, these interpersonal skills would be used time and time again, as long as they produced gratification. Through this repetition of behaviors, repertoires or styles are created. The larger the repertoire, the more flexible one can be.

Repetition theory is useful because it helps us understand the logical processes involving communication competence and the relationship between knowledge and skill. It also explains the effect of culture and how socialization affects behavior. However, propositions and hypotheses need to be developed and tested before we can adopt repetition theory for communication competence. For example, with repetition theory we would expect that (*a*) the more different situations an individual experiences, the higher the level of perceived communication competence; (*b*) the greater the rewards accrued for appropriate or effective behavior (see McCroskey's [1982] "chicken leg" argument), the greater the communication competence; (*c*) people will be more motivated to repeat competent behaviors that are rewarded (this will have a profound effect on communication apprehension and reticence training programs); and (*d*) an increase in knowledge of appropriate and effective behaviors will result in an increase in skill. These expectations lead the way for future research on communication competence. Both control theory and repetition theory provide many promising avenues for research.

Measurement

Because of the close relationship between the definition of competence and how it is measured, the measurement technique decidedly helps to define the construct theoretically and operationally. A self-report instrument such as the interaction involvement scale (Cegala, 1981), for example, focuses on an individual's own assessment of how actively perceptive, responsive, and attentive he or she felt in the conversation. Competence, here, is a self-report of one's awareness of being involved; the theoretical base emerges as a cognitive element of competence because of the nature of reported affect or feeling called for by the scale. A knowledge test, however, might tap knowledge of basic speech principles and feelings toward the communication process (Levison, 1976). Additional self-report instruments examine self-reports of appropriateness and effectiveness (Duran, 1983; Rubin, 1985). Recent evidence suggests that self-reports are invalid when used to assess skill, possibly because people are not sufficiently aware of their own behaviors or the effects of these behaviors on others (Cupach & Spitzberg, 1983; Rubin & Graham, 1988; Rubin et al., 1988).

In contrast are behavioral measures of competence in which an individual communicates while being rated on standard criteria by either a trained observer (Rubin, 1982, 1985) or a participant (Spitzberg & Hecht, 1984). These techniques are based on a communication skills approach to competence both theoretically and operationally. For the observer to render a judgment, the skills must first be identified precisely, and the observer must then evaluate an individual's competence employing criteria specified for each of the skills. Behavioral measure researchers agree that self-report measures provide unreliable and possibly invalid indicators of communication competence, but they disagree about who should make the judgment. Those who use trained raters would ask, How reliable are the judgments of inexperienced and untrained interactants? Those who use interactants would wonder, How valid are raters not involved in the communication interaction?

State or Trait?

The state-or-trait debate has received extensive treatment elsewhere (Andersen, 1987). The basic issue, stated in communication competence terms, is, Is competence a disposition or cross-situational tendency, or is it an event or state that changes with the situation and can be altered by instruction? Many measures of communication competence assume a cross-situational tendency (for example, McCroskey's early work on communication apprehension, 1977b), but others argue that a situation-specific measure is mandated (Phillips, 1984; Rubin, 1982). This controversial issue is made even more prominent by the measures created to assess communication competence.

State measurement focuses on a particular context, place, or time. For example, Monge et al. (1982) and Rubin (1982, 1985) created instruments to measure organization communication competence and communication competence in educational settings, respectively. The instruments identify communication skills specific to the situation, and raters assess communicators on these skills.

Trait measurement examines personality or predisposition factors that influence communication and, therefore, perceptions of competence. For example, Hart and Burks (1972) proposed that some people are more rhetorically sensitive than others, and those people exhibit more flexibility and appropriateness in their behavior. Hart, Carlson, and Eadie (1980) developed a scale to test this, one that taps attitudes toward change, not behaviors. Later, Eadie and Paulson (1984) found that there were differences among the rhetorically sensitive, the inflexible "noble selves," and too-flexible "rhetorical reflectors." Noble selves scored higher on impression leaving and dominance, and lower on friendliness, than the other two groups. The rhetorically sensitive and rhetorical reflectors differed in perceived competence and style.

The question remains, Is there an element of cross-situational competence, or is the context highly influential in a person's ability to communicate? Cupach and Spitzberg (1983) and Pavitt and Haight (1986) found evidence supporting the situational view. Rubin (1985) also found evidence that we need to examine communication competence in context. However, traits also exist; both rhetorical sensitivity and communication apprehension exhibit cross-situational consistency. Spitzberg and Cupach (1984) argued that traits (cognitive complexity, rhetorical sensitivity) can contribute to situational competence, although the evidence to support this claim is sketchy (Rubin & Henzl, 1984). Andersen (1987) also suggested that we stop examining traits isolated from other variables and look at these cross-situational and consistent traits (for example, communication apprehension) in relation to states, situations, feelings, and the like. Research continues to point to a need to use both state and trait measures to examine communication competence until we have a firm understanding of which measures assess traits and which estimate state-influenced behaviors. In fact, an interactional research strategy would allow researchers to discern intersecting qualities of states and traits.

Here we see directions for future communication competence research. We must further refine and test promising theories to determine the extent to which the theories allow us to predict changes in and the effects of communication competence. We must develop valid and reliable measurement instruments that adhere to the conceptual basis of communication competence. And we must examine the impact of the context on communication behavior.

Bibliography

This bibliography is in two sections. The first section is an alphabetical listing of all references cited in the text. The second section, which is subdivided and annotated, is an enumeration of works that have influenced this book.

References Cited

Ad Hoc Committee. (1969). Research note. *Spectra 5*, 3–4.

Adler, A. (1964). *Social interest: A challenge to mankind*. New York: Capricorn Books.

Adler, A. (1969). *The science of living*. New York: Doubleday Anchor.

Allen, M. (1989). A comparison of self-report, observer, and physiological assessments of public-speaking anxiety reduction techniques using metanalysis. *Communication Studies, 40* (2), 127–139.

Allen, R. R., & Wood, B. S. (1978). Beyond reading and writing to communication competence. *Communication Education, 27*, 286–292.

American Psychiatric Association. (1980). *Diagnostic and statistical manual of mental disorders* (3rd ed.). Washington, DC: Author.

Ammon, P. (1981). Communication skills and communicative competence: A neo-Piagetian process-structural view. In W. P. Dickson (Ed.), *Children's oral communication skills* skills (pp. 13–33). New York: Academic Press.

Anderson, J. A. (1983). Television literacy and the critical viewer. In J. Bryant & D. R. Anderson (Eds.), *Children's understanding of television: Research on attention and comprehension* (pp. 297–330). New York: Academic Press.

306

Andersen, P. A. (1987). The trait debate: A critical examination of the individual differences paradigm in interpersonal communication. In B. Dervin & M. J. Voight (Eds.), *Progress in communication sciences* (Vol. 8, pp. 47–82). Norwood, NJ: Ablex.

Ansbacher, H. L., & Ansbacher, R. B. (1936). *The individual psychology of Alfred Adler: a systematic presentation in selections from his writings.* Harper Colophon Books.

Ardrey, R. (1970). *The social contract.* New York: Atheneum.

Argyle, M. (1972). *The psychology of interpersonal behavior* (2nd ed.). Baltimore: Penguin.

Argyris, C. (1962). *Interpersonal competence and organizational effectiveness.* Homewood, IL: Irwin-Dorsey.

Aristotle. (1853). *The Organon.* London: H. G. Bohn.

Aryes, J. A., & Hopf, T. S. (1987). *Visualization, systematic desensitization, and rational emotive therapy: A comparative evaluation.* Paper presented at the annual meeting of the Speech Communication Association, Boston, MA.

Backlund, P. (1982). A response to communication competence and performance: A research and pedagogical perspective, by James C. McCrosky. *Communication Education, 31*, 365–366.

Bassett, R. E., Whittington, N., & Staton-Spicer, A. (1978). The basics in speaking and listening for high school graduates: What should be assessed? *Communication Education, 27*, 293–303.

Bateson, G. (1987). *Steps to an ecology of mind, collected essays in anthropology, psychiatry, evolution, and epistemology.* Northvale, NJ: Aronson.

Beck, A. T. (1976). *Cognitive therapy and the emotional disorders.* New York: International Universities Press.

Becker, E. (1962). *The birth and death of meaning.* New York: Free Press.

Begnal, C. F. (1985). *A comparison of reticent and nonreticent women's communication about friendships and relationships.* Unpublished doctoral dissertation, The Pennsylvania State University.

Bitzer, L. F. (1968). The rhetorical situation. *Philosophy and Rhetoric, 1* (1), 165–168.

Black, J. W., & Irwin, R. B. (1969). *Voice and diction, phonation and phonology.* Columbus, OH: C. E. Merrill.

Blair, H. (1970). *Lectures on rhetoric and belle lettres.* New York: Garland Publishing.

Bloom, L. (Ed.). (1978). *Readings in language development.* New York: Wiley.

Bochner, A. P. (1984). The functions of human communication in interpersonal bonding. In C. C. Arnold & J. W. Bowers (Eds.), *Handbook of rhetorical and communication theory* (pp. 544–621). Boston: Allyn & Bacon.

Bochner, A. P., & Kelly, C. W. (1974). Interpersonal competence: Rationale, philosophy, and implementation of a conceptual framework. *Speech Teacher,* 23, 279–301.

Boone, D. R. (1987). *Human communication and its disorders.* Englewood Cliffs, NJ: Prentice Hall.

Boone, D. R. (1988). *The voice and voice therapy.* Englewood Cliffs, NJ: Prentice Hall.

Boudon, R. (1989). Subjective rationality and the explanation of social behavior. *Rationality and Society,* 1(2), 175–196.

Bradley, P. H. (1980). Sex, competence and opinion deviation: An expectation states approach. *Communication Monographs,* 47, 101–110.

Brandt, D. R. (1974). On linking social performance with social competence: Some relations between communicative style and attributions of interpersonal attractiveness and effectiveness. *Human Communication Research,* 5, 223–237.

Burgoon, J. K. (1976). The unwillingness-to-communicate scale. *Communication Monographs,* 43, 60–69.

Burke, K. (1969a). *A grammar of motives.* Berkeley: University of California Press.

Burke, K. (1969b). *A rhetoric of motives.* Berkeley: University of California Press.

Buss, A. H. (1986). A theory of shyness. In W. H. Jones, J. M. Cheek, & S. R. Briggs (Eds.), *Shyness: Perspectives on research and treatment* (pp. 39–46). New York: Plenum Press.

Carnegie, D. (1964). *How to win friends and influence people.* New York: Simon & Schuster.

Cegala, D. J. (1981). Interaction involvement: A cognitive dimension of communicative competence. *Communication Education,* 30, 109–121.

Cegala, D. J. (1984). Affective and cognitive manifestations of interaction involvement during unstructured and competitive interactions. *Communication Monographs,* 51, 320–338.

Chapman, A. H. (1976). *Harry Stack Sullivan: The man and his work.* New York: G. P. Putnam's Sons.

Chen, G. M. (1988). Dimensions of intercultural communication competence (Doctoral dissertation, Kent State University, 1987). *Dissertation Abstracts International,* 48, 2192A.

Chomsky, N. (1965). *Aspects of the theory of syntax.* Cambridge: MIT Press.

Chomsky, N. (1975). *Reflections on language.* New York: Random House.

Churchland, P. S. (1986). *Neurophilosophy: Toward a unified science of the mind/brain.* Cambridge: MIT Press.

Churchland, P. M., & Churchland, P. S. (1990). Could a machine think. *Scientific American,* 262(1), 31–39.

Clark, R. A., & Delia, J. G. (1977). Cognitive complexity, social perspective-taking, and functional persuasive skills in second-to ninth-grade children. *Human Communication Research,* 3, 128–134.

Clevenger, Jr., T. (1959). A synthesis of experimental research in stage fright. *Quarterly Journal of Speech, 2,* 134–145.

Cohen, H. (1980). Teaching reticent students in a required course. *Communication Education, 29,* 222–228.

Coles, E. M. (1982). *Clinical psychopathology.* London: Routledge & Kegan Paul.

Combs, A. W., & Snygg, D. (1959). *Individual behavior: A perceptual approach to behavior.* New York: Harper & Brothers.

Connolly, K. J., & Bruner, J. S. (1974). *The growth of competence.* New York: Academic Press.

Cooley, R. E., & Roach, D. A. (1984). A conceptual framework. In R. N. Bostrom (Ed.), *Competence in communication: A multidisciplinary approach* (pp. 11–32). Beverly Hills, CA: Sage.

Cooper, L. (1932). *The rhetoric of Aristotle.* New York: Appleton-Century-Crofts.

Cooper, P. J. (1986). *Communication competencies for teachers: A CAT subcommittee report.* Annandale, VA: Speech Communication Association. (ERIC Document Reproduction Service No. SP 028 649).

Corsini, R. J. (Ed.). (1984). *Encyclopedia of Psychology.* 4 vols. New York: John Wiley & Sons.

Cronkhite, G. (1984). Perception and meaning. In C. C. Arnold & J. W. Bowers (Eds.), *Handbook of rhetorical and communication theory* (pp. 51–229). Boston: Allyn & Bacon.

Cupach, W. R., & Spitzberg, B. H. (1983). Trait versus state: A comparison of dispositional and situational measures of interpersonal communication competence. *Western Journal of Speech Communication, 47,* 364–379.

De Laguna, G. M. (1963). *Speech: Its function and development.* Bloomington: Indiana University Press.

Delia, J. G., & Clark, R. A. (1977). Cognitive complexity, social perception, and the development of listener-adapted communication in six-, eight-, ten-, and twelve-year old boys. *Communication Monographs, 44,* 326–345.

DeVito, J. A. (1986). *The communication handbook: A dictionary.* New York: Harper & Row.

DeVito, J. A . (1989). *The interpersonal communication book* (5th ed.). New York: Harper & Row.

Dewey, J. (1933). *How we think, a restatement of the relation of reflective thinking to the educative process.* Boston: D. C. Heath.

DiSalvo, V. S. (1980). A summary of current research identifying communication skills in various organizational contexts. *Communication Education, 35,* 231–242.

DiSalvo, V., Larsen, D. C., & Backus, D. K. (1986). The health care communicator: An identification of skills and problems. *Communication Education. 35,* 231–242.

DiSalvo, V., Larsen, D. C., & Seiler, W. J. (1976). Communication skills needed by persons in business organizations. *Communication Education, 25,* 269–275.

Domenig, K. (1978). *An examination of self-reports of reticent and non-reticent students before and after instruction.* Unpublished master's thesis, The Pennsylvania State University.

Donohue, W. A., Allen, M., & Burrell, N. (1988). Mediator communicative competence. *Communication Monographs, 55,* 104–119.

Duran, R. L. (1982). [Forum response]. *Communication Education, 31,* 246.

Duran, R. L. (1983). Communicative adaptability: A measure of social communicative competence. *Communication Quarterly, 31,* 320–326.

Duran, R. L., & Zakahi, W. R. (1984). Competence or style: What's in a name. *Communication Research Reports, 1,* 42–47.

Eadie, W. F., & Paulson, J. W. (1984). Communicator attitudes, communicator style, and communication competence. *Western Journal of Speech Communication, 48,* 390–407.

Eccles, J., & Robinson, D. N. (1984). *The wonder of being human: Our brain and our mind.* New York: Free Press.

Edelson, M. (1988). *Psychoanalysis: A theory in crisis.* Chicago: University of Chicago Press.

Ellis, A. (1989). *Inside rational-emotive therapy.* San Diego: Academic Press.

Ervin-Tripp, S., & Mitchell-Kernan, C. (Eds.). (1977). *Child discourse.* New York: Academic Press.

Flexner, S. G. (1987). *The Random House dictionary of the English language* (2nd ed.). New York: Random House.

Foote, N. N., & Cottrell, L. S., Jr. (1959). *Identity and interpersonal competence.* Chicago: University of Chicago Press.

Foucault, M. (1972). *The archaeology of knowledge.* New York: Pantheon.

Freimuth, V. S. (1976). The effects of communication apprehension on communication effectiveness. *Human Communication Research, 2,* 289–298.

Fremouw, W. J. (1984). Cognitive-behavioral therapies for modification of communication apprehension. In J. A. Daly & J. C. McCroskey (Eds.), *Avoiding communication: Shyness, reticence, and communication apprehension* (pp. 209–215). Beverly Hills, CA: Sage.

Fremouw, W., & Scott, M. (1979). Cognitive restructuring: An alternative method for the treatment of communicatation apprehension. *Communication Education, 28,* 129–133.

Freud, S. (1975). *Beyond the pleasure principle.* New York: Norton.

Gardner, J. W. (1983). *Imitation of model speakers of speech in their own milieu, a descriptive study.* Unpublished doctoral dissertation, The Pennsylvania State University.

Bibliography   311

Gazzinaga, M. (1985). *The social brain: discovering the networks of the mind.* New York: Basic Books.

Gilkinson, H. (1942). Social fears as reported by students in college speech classes. *Speech Monographs, 9,* 141–160.

Gilligan, C. (1982). *In a different voice: psychological theory and women's development.* Cambridge: Harvard University Press.

Goffman, E. (1959). *Presentation of self in everyday life.* Garden City, NY: Doubleday Anchor.

Goffman, E. (1963). *Behavior in public places.* New York: Free Press.

Goffman, E. (1967). *Interaction ritual.* Garden City, NY: Anchor.

Goldenseon, R. M. (Ed.) (1970). *The encyclopedia of human behavior, psychology, psychiatry, and mental health.* Garden City, NY: Doubleday.

Golding, W. (1959). *Lord of the flies.* New York: Capricorn Books.

Goodall, H. L. (1982). Organizational communication competence: The development of an industrial simulation to teach adaptive skills. *Communication Quaterly, 30,* 282–295.

Habermas, J. (1970). Toward a theory of communicative competence. In H. P. Dreitzel (Ed.), *Recent sociology no. 2: Patterns of communicative behavior* (pp. 114–148). New York: Macmillan.

Haiman, F. S. (1951). *Group leadership and democratic action.* Boston: Houghton Mifflin.

Hale, C. L. (1980). Cognitive complexity-simplicity as a determinant of communication effectiveness. *Communication Monographs, 47,* 304–311.

Hall, C. S. (1954). *A primer of Freudian psychology.* New York: World Publishing.

Harre, R. (1986). *The social construction of emotions.* Oxford: B. Blackwell.

Harris, L., & Cronen, V. E. (1979). A rules-based model for the analysis and evaluation of organizational communication. *Communication Quarterly, 27,* 12–28.

Harrison's. (1987). *Principles of internal medicine.* Eugene Braunwald et al. (Eds). New York: McGraw-Hill.

Hart, R. P., & Burks, D. M. (1972). Rhetorical sensitivity and social interaction. *Speech Monographs, 39,* 75–91.

Hart, R. P., Carlson, R. E., & Eadie, W. F. (1980). Attitudes toward communication and the assessment of rhetorical sensitivity. *Communication Monographs, 47,* 1–22.

Haslett, B. (1984). Acquiring conversational competence. *Western Journal of Speech Communication, 48,* 107–124.

Hirokawa, R. Y., & Pace, R. (1983). A descriptive investigation of the possible communication-based reasons for effective and ineffective group decision making. *Communication Monographs, 50,* 363–379.

Hirsch, E. D., Jr. (1987). *Cultural literacy: What every American needs to know.* Boston: Houghton Mifflin.

Hoffmann, J., & Sprague, J. (1982). A survey of reticence and communication apprehension treatment programs at U.S. colleges and universities. *Communication Education, 31,* 185–193.

Homans, G. C. (1974). *Social behavior: Its elementary forms.* New York: Harcourt Brace Jovanovich.

Hopf, T. S. (1970). Reticence and the oral interpretation teacher. *Speech Teacher. 19,* (4), 268–271.

Horney, K. (1937). *The neurotic personality of our time.* Cleveland: W. W. Norton.

Hyde, M. J. (1980). The experience of anxiety: A phenomenological investigation. *Quarterly Journal of Speech, 66(2),* 140–154.

Hymes, D. (1971). Competence and performance in linguistic theory. In R. Huxley & E. Ingram (Eds.), *Language acquisition: Models and methods* (pp. 3–26). New York: Academic Press.

Jackson, P. C., Jr. (1985). *Introduction to artificial intelligence.* New York: Dover Publications.

Janis, I. L. (1983). *Groupthink, psychological studies of policy decisions and fiascoes.* Boston: Houghton, Mifflin.

Kagan, J., & Reznick, J. S. (1986). Shyness and temperament. In W. H. Jones, J. M. Cheek, & S. R. Briggs (Eds.), *Shyness: Perspectives on research and treatment* (pp. 81–90). New York: Plenum Press.

Kaplan, H. I., & Sadock, B. J. (Eds.). (1985). *Comprehensive textbook of psychiatry* (4th ed.). Baltimore, MD: Williams & Wilkins.

Kelly, L. (1982a). *Observers' comparisons of the interpersonal communication skills of students who self-selected a special speech course and students who self-selected a regular speech course.* Doctoral dissertation, The Pennsylvania State University.

Kelly, L. (1982b). A rose by any other name is still a rose: A comparative analysis of reticence, communication apprehension, unwillingness to communicate and shyness. *Human Communication Research, 2(8),* 99–113.

Kelly, L., & Duran, R. L. (1988). *Rhetoritherapy revisited: An empirical examination of its effectiveness as a treatment for communication-related problems.* Paper presented at the annual meeting of the Speech Communication Association, New Orleans.

Kelly, L., Phillips, G. M., & McKinney, B. (1982). Reprise: Farewell reticence, goodbye apprehension! Building a practical nosology of speech communication problems. *Communication Education, 3,(31),* 211–222.

Kelly, L., & Watson, A. K. (1986). *Speaking with confidence and skill.* New York: Harper & Row.

Kerlinger, F. N. (1986). *Foundations of behavioral research* (3rd ed.). New York: Holt, Rinehart & Winston.

Kleinsasser, D. (1968). *The reduction of performance anxiety as a function of desensitization, pre-therapy vicarious learning, and vicarious learning alone.* Unpublished doctoral dissertation, The Pennsylvania State University.

Kohlberg, L. (1981). *Essays on moral development.* San Francisco: Harper & Row.

Korzybski, A. (1962). *Science and sanity, an introduction to non-Aristotelian systems and general semantics* (4th ed.). Lakeville, CT: International non-Aristotelian Library.

Krauss, R. M., & Glucksberg, S. (1969). The development of communication: Competence as a function of age. *Child Development, 40,* 255–266.

Kuper, A. & J. (1985). *The social science encyclopedia.* London: Routledge and Kegan Paul.

Lasch, C. (1978). *The culture of narcissism.* New York: W. W. Norton.

Leary, T. F. (1957). *Interpersonal diagnosis of personality, a functional theory and methodology for personality evaluation.* New York: Ronald Press.

Lessac, A. (1965). *The use and training of the human voice, a new approach to the bio-dynamics of voice and speech.* New York: Self-Published.

Levison, G. K. (1976). The basic speech communication course: Establishing minimal oral competencies and exemption procedures. *Communication Education, 25,* 222–230.

Liddel, H. S. (1934). *The comparative physiology of the conditioned motor reflex.* Baltimore: Johns Hopkins.

Linklater, K. (1975). *Freeing the natural voice.* New York: Drama Book Specialists.

Littlejohn, S. W. (1989). *Theories of human communication* (3rd ed.). Belmont, CA: Wadsworth Publishing.

Lloyd-Kolkin, D. (1981). The critical television viewing project for high school students. In M. E. Ploghoft & J. A. Anderson (Eds.), *Education for the television age* (pp. 91–97). Athens, OH: Ohio University Cooperative Center for Social Science Education.

McBurney, J. H., & Hance, K. G. (1939). *The principles and methods of discussion.* New York: Harper & Brothers.

McCaleb, J. (1984). Selecting a measure of oral communication as a predictor of teaching performance. *Journal of Teacher Education, 35*(5), 33–38.

McCaleb, J. L. (1987). A review of communication competencies used in statewide assessments. In J. L. McCaleb (Ed.), *How do teachers communicate? A review and critique of assessment practices* (Teacher Education Monograph No. 7, pp. 7–28). Washington, DC: ERIC Clearinghouse on Teacher Education.

McCroskey, J. C. (1970). Measures of communication-bound anxiety. *Speech Monographs*, 37, 269–277.

McCroskey, J. C. (1972). The implementation of a large-scale program of systematic desensitization for communication apprehension. *Speech Teacher*, 21, 255–264.

McCroskey, J. C. (1977). Oral communication apprehension: A summary of recent theory and research. *Human Communication Research*, 4, 78–96.

McCroskey, J. C. (1978). Validity of the PRCA as an index of oral communication apprehension. *Communication Monographs*, 45, 192–203.

McCroskey, J. C. (1982a). Communication competence and performance: A research and pedagogical perspective. *Communication Education*, 31, 1–7.

McCroskey, J. C. (1982b). Oral communication apprehension: A reconceptualization. In M. Burgoon (Ed.), *Communication Yearbook 6* (pp. 136–170). Beverly Hills, CA: Sage.

McCroskey, J. C. (1984). The communication apprehension perspective. In J. A. Daly & J. C. McCroskey (Eds.), *Avoiding communication: Shyness, reticence, and communication apprehension* (pp. 13–38). Beverly Hills, CA: Sage.

McCroskey, J. C. (1984). Communication competence: The elusive construct. In R. N. Bostrom (Ed.), *Competence in communication: A multidisciplinary approach* (pp. 259–268). Beverly Hills, CA: Sage.

McCroskey, J. C., & Daly, J. A. (1986). Oral communication apprehension. In W. J. Jones, J. M. Cheek, & S. R. Briggs (Eds.), *Shyness: Perspectives on research and treatment* (pp. 279–94). New York: Plenum Press.

McCroskey, J. C., & Richmond, V. P. (1982a). Communication apprehension and shyness: Conceptual and operational distinctions. *Central States Speech Journal*, 33, 458–468.

McCroskey, J. C., & Richmond, V. P. (1982b). *The quiet ones: Communication apprehension and shyness* (2nd ed.). Dubuque, IA: Gorsuch-Scarisbrick.

McGuinness, B. (1988). *Wittgenstein, a life*. London: Duckworth.

McGuire, W. J. (1985). Attitudes and attitude change. In G. Lindzey & E. Aronson (Eds.), *Handbook of social psychology* (Vol. 2, pp. 233–346). New York: Random House.

McLaughlin, M. L., & Erickson, K. V. (1981). A multidimensional scaling analysis of the "ideal interpersonal communication instructor." *Communication Education*, 30, 393–398.

Mager, R. F. (1962). *Preparing instructional objectives*. Belmont, CA: Fearon Publishers.

Mager, R. F. (1968). *Developing attitudes toward learning*. Belmont, CA: Fearon Publishers.

Mager, R. F. (1972). *Goal analysis*. Belmont, CA: Fearon Publishers.

Mager, R. F., & Beach, K. M., Jr. (1967). *Developing vocational objectives*. Belmont, CA: Fearon Publishers.

Mager, R. F., & Pipe, P. (1970). *Analyzing performance problems or you really ought to wanna'*. Belmont, CA: Fearon Publishers.

Maslow, A. (1954). *Motivation and personality*. New York: Harper & Row.

Masserman, J. H. (1964). *Behavior and neurosis, an experimental psychoanalytic approach to psychobiological principles*. New York: Hafner Publishing.

Mead G. H. (1934). *Mind, self & society from the standpoint of a social behaviorist*. Chicago: University of Chicago Press.

Merloo, J. (1964). *Unobtrusive communication*. The Hague: Van Gorcum.

Metzger, N. J. (1974). *The effects of a rhetorical method of instruction on a selected population of reticent speakers*. Unpublished doctoral dissertation, The Pennsylvania State University.

Monge, P. R., Bachman, S. G., Dillard, J. P., & Eisenberg, E. M.(1982). Communicator competence in the workplace: Model testing and scale development. *Communication Yearbook*, 5, 505–527.

Morse, B. W., & Piland, R. N. (1981). An assessment of communication competencies needed by intermediate-level health care providers: A study of nurse-patient, nurse-doctor, nurse-nurse communication relationships. *Journal of Applied Communication Research*, 9, 30–41.

Muchmore, J., & Galvin, K. (1983). A report of the task force on career competencies in oral communication skills for community college students seeking immediate entry into the work force. *Communication Education*, 32, 207–220.

Muir, F. L. (1964). *Case studies of selected examples of reticence and fluency*. Unpublished master's thesis, Washington State University.

Mullahy, P. (1970). *Psychoanalysis and interpersonal psychiatry: The contributions of Harry Stack Sullivan*. New York: Science House.

Nisbet, R. A. (1976). *Sociology as an art form*. New York: Oxford University Press.

Oerkvitz, S. (1975). *Reports of continuing effects of instruction in a specially designed speech course for reticent students*. Unpublished master's thesis, The Pennsylvania State University.

Owen, O. F. (Ed.). (1842). *The organon or logical treatises of Aristotle*. London: Henry C. Bohn.

Parks, M. R. (1985). Interpersonal communication and the quest for personal competence. In M. L. Knapp & G. R. Miller (Eds.), *Handbook of interpersonal communication* (pp. 171–201). Beverly Hills, CA: Sage.

Paul, G. L. (1966). *Insight versus desensitization in psychotherapy*. Stanford, CA: Stanford University Press.

Pavitt, C., & Haight, L. (1985). The "competent communicator" as a cognitive prototype. *Human Communication Research*, 12, 225–241.

Pavitt, C., & Haight, L. (1986). Implicit theories of communicative competence: Situational and competence level differences in judgments of prototype and target. *Communication Monographs*, 53, 221–235.

Pearce, W. B. (1976). The coordinated management of meaning: A rules-based theory of interpersonal communication. In G. R. Miller (Ed.), *Explorations in interpersonal communication* (pp. 17–35). Beverly Hills, CA: Sage.

Perkins, D. N. (1981). *The mind's best work.* Cambridge: Harvard University Press.

Perry, H. S. (1982). *Psychiatrist of America: The life of Harry Stack Sullivan.* Cambridge: Belknap Press.

Perry, L. A. M. (1985). *Communicating culture, oral histories of ten middle-management women.* Unpublished doctoral dissertation, The Pennsylvania State University.

Phillips, G. M. (1965). The problem of reticence. *Pennsylvania Speech Annual,* 22, 22–38.

Phillips, G. M. (1968). Reticence: Pathology of the normal speaker. *Speech Monographs, 1 (35),* 39–49.

Phillips, G. M. (1973). *Communication and the Small Group.* New York: Bobbs, Merrill.

Phillips, G. M. (1973). The reticent speaker: Etiology and treatment. *Journal of Communication Disorders,* 6, 210–218.

Phillips, G. M. (1977). Rhetoritherapy versus the medical model: Dealing with reticence. *Communication Education. 1* (26), 34–43.

Phillips, G. M. (1978). Rhetoric and the proper study of mankind. *Communication Education,* 17, 3.

Phillips, G. M. (Ed.). (1980). The practical teacher's symposium on shyness, communication apprehension, reticence, and a variety of other common problems. *Communication Education,* 29, 213–263.

Phillips, G. M. (1981). Freak repair. *Speech Communication Association of Pennsylvania Annual.*

Phillips, G. M. (1981). *Help for shy people.* Englewood Cliffs, NJ: Prentice Hall.

Phillips, G. M. (1981). Science and the study of human communication: An inquiry from the other side of the two cultures. *Human Communication Research,* 7, 361–370.

Phillips, G. M. (Ed.). (1982). Symposium. *Communication Education.* 31(3).

Phillips, G. M. (1984). A competent view of "competence." *Communication Education, 1* 33(1), 25–36.

Phillips, G. M. (1984). Reticence: A perspective on social withdrawal, In J. A. Daly & J. C. McCroskey (Eds.), *Avoiding communication: Shyness, reticence, and communication apprehension* (pp. 51–66). Beverly Hills, CA: Sage.

Phillips, G. M. (1985). The rhetoric of the remarkable rocket. *Speech Communication Association of Pennsylvania,* 7.

Phillips, G. M. (1986a). Rhetoritherapy: The principles of rhetoric in training shy people in speech effectiveness. In W. H. Jones, J. M. Cheek, & S. R. Briggs (Eds.), *Shyness: Perspectives on research and treatment* (pp. 357–374). New York: Plenum Press.

Phillips, G. M. (1986b). Treatment/training of speaking problems: A study in reification. *Communication Quarterly, 34,* 4.

Phillips, G. M., & Butt, D. (1967). Reticence revisited. *Pennsylvania Speech Annual, 15.*

Phillips, G. M., & Erlwein, B. J. (1989). Composition on the computer: Expert systems and artificial intelligence. *Communication Quarterly, 36,* 1. Phillips, G. M., & Jones, J. A. (1988). *Communicating with your doctor: Rx for good medical care.* Carbondale: Southern Illinois University Press.

Phillips, G. M., & Metzger, N. (1973). The reticent syndrome: Some theoretical considerations about etiology and treatment. *Speech Monographs, 40,* 220–230.

Phillips, G. M., & Sokoloff, K. A. (1976). A refinement of the concept of "reticence." *Journal of Communication Disorders, 9,* 4.

Phillips, G. M., & Sokoloff, K. A. (1979). An end to anxiety: Treating speech problems with rhetoritherapy. *Journal of Communication Disorders, 12,* 385–397.

Phillips, G. M., & Zolten, J. J. (1976). *Structuring speech.* Indianapolis, IN: Bobbs-Merrill.

Pilkonis, P. A. (1986). Short-term group psychotherapy for shyness. In W. H. Jones, J. M. Cheek, & S. R. Briggs (Eds.), *Shyness: Perspectives on research and treatment* (pp. 375–385). New York: Plenum Press.

Powell, B. (1981). *Overcoming shyness: Practical scripts for everyday encounters.* New York: McGraw-Hill.

Powers, W. G., & Lowry, D. N. (1984). Basic communication fidelity: A fundamental approach. In R. N. Bostrom (Ed.), *Competence in communication: A multidisciplinary approach* (pp. 57–71). Beverly Hills, CA: Sage.

Powers, W. G., & Smythe, M. J. (1980). Communication apprehension and achievement in a performance-oriented basic communication course. *Human Communication Research, 6,* 146–152.

Quintilian, M. F. (1987). *Quintilian on the teaching of speaking and writing, translations from books one, two, and ten of the institutia oratoria by James J. Murphy.* Carbondale: Southern Illinois University Press.

Random House (1987). *The Random House dictionary of the English language.* S. B. Flexner (Ed.). New York: Random House.

Reardon, K. K. (1987). *Interpersonal communication: Where minds meet.* Belmont, CA: Wadsworth.

Redmond, M. V. (1985). The relationship between perceived communication competence and perceived empathy. *Communication Monographs, 52,* 377–382.

Rekart, D., & Begnal, C. (1989). Accoustic characteristics of reticent speech. *Journal of Voice*, 3(4), 324–336.

Richmond, V. P., & McCroskey, J. C. (1985). *Communication apprehension, avoidance, and effectiveness*. Scottsdale: Gorsuch, Scarisbrick.

Riesman, D. (1950). *The lonely crowd*. New Haven: Yale University Press.

Roloff, M. E., & Kellermann, K. (1984). Judgments of interpersonal competency: How you know, what you know, and who you know. In R. N. Bostrom (Ed.), *Competence in communication: A multidisciplinary approach* (pp. 175–218). Beverly Hills, CA: Sage.

Rosenfield, L. W., & Mader, T. F. (1984). The functions of human communication in pleasing. In C. C. Arnold & J. W. Bowers (Eds.), *Handbook of rhetorical and communication theory* (pp. 475–543). Boston: Allyn & Bacon.

Rosenthal, R., & Jacobson, L., (1968). *Pygmalion in the Classroom, teacher expectation and pupils' intellectual development*. New York: Holt, Rinehart & Winston.

Ruben, B. D., & Kealey, D. J. (1979). Behavioral assessment of communication competency and the prediction of cross-cultural adaptation. *International Journal of Intercultural Relations*, 3, 15–47.

Rubin, R. B. (1982). Assessing speaking and listening competence at the college level: The communication competencey assessment instrument. *Communication Education*, 31, 19–32.

Rubin, R. B. (1983). Conclusions. In R. B. Rubin (Ed.), *Improving speaking and listening skills* (pp. 95–100). San Francisco:Jossey-Bass.

Rubin, R. B. (1985). The validity of the communication competency assessment instrument. *Communication Monographs*, 52, 173–185.

Rubin, R. B. (1990). Communication competence. In G. M. Phillips & Wood, J. T., *Speech communication: Essays to commemorate the 75th anniversary of the Speech Communication Association.* (pp. 94–129). Carbondale: Southern Illinois University Press.

Rubin, R. B., & Feezel, J. D. (1986). Elements of teacher communication competence. *Communication Education*, 35, 254–268.

Rubin, R. B., & Graham, E. E. (1988). Communication correlates of college success: An exploratory investigation. *Communication Education*, 37, 14–27.

Rubin, R. B., Graham, E. E., & Mignerey, J. (1988, November). *A longitudinal study of college students' communication competence*. Paper presented at the meeting of the Speech Communication Association, New Orleans.

Rubin, R. B., & Henzl, S. A. (1984). Cognitive complexity, communication competence and verbal ability. *Communication Quarterly*, 32, 263–270.

Rubin, R. B., & Nevins, R. A. (1988). *The road trip: An interpersonal adventure.* Prospect Heights, IL: Waveland.

Rumelhart, D. E., McClelland, J. L., & the PDP Research Group. (1987). *Parallel distributed processing*. Cambridge: MIT Press.

Searle, J. R. (1990). Is the brain's mind a computer? *Scientific American* 262 (1). 26–31.

Simon, H. A. (1982). *The science of the artificial.* Cambridge: MIT Press.

Skinner, B. F. (1971). *Beyond freedom and dignity.* New York: Alfred A. Knopf.

Skinner, B. F. (1974). *About behaviorism.* New York: Alfred Knopf.

Skinner, B. F., & Estes, W. K. (1972). Some quantitative properties of anxiety. In B. F. Skinner, *Cumulative Record.* New York: Appleton-Century-Crofts. Snyder, C. R., & Smith, T. W. (1986). On being "shy like a fox": A self-handicapping analysis. In W. H. Jones, J. M. Cheek, & S. R. Briggs (Eds.), *Shyness: Perspectives on research and treatment* (pp. 161–172). New York: Plenum Press.

Sondel, B. (1958). *The humanity of words.* New York: World Publishing Co.

Sours, D. B. (1979). *Comparison of judgements by placement interviewers and instructors about the severity of reticence in students enrolled in a special section of the basic speech course.* Unpublished master's thesis, The Pennsylvania State University.

Spitzberg, B. H. (1983). Communication competence as knowledge, skill, and impression. *Communication Education, 32,* 323–329.

Spitzberg, B. H., & Cupach, W. R. (1984). *Interpersonal communication competence.* Beverly Hills, CA: Sage.

Spitzberg, B. H., & Hecht, M. L. (1984). A component model of relational competence. *Human Communication Research, 10,* 575–599.

Staley, C. C., & Shockley-Zalabak, P. (1985). Identifying communication competencies for the undergraduate organizational communication series. *Communication Education, 34,* 156–161.

Stanislavski, C. (1989). *An actor prepares.* New York: Routledge.

Stanislavski, C. (1989). *Building a character.* New York: Routledge.

Stanislavski, C. (1989). *Creating a role.* New York: Routledge.

Starkweather, C. W. (1983). *Speech and language: Principles and processes of behavior change.* Englewood Cliffs, NJ: Prentice-Hall.

Stern, D. A. (1982). *The voice and diction tapes* [Cassette Recording]. Hollywood: DAS.

Stern, D. A. (1983). *Acting with an accent* [Cassette Recording]. Hollywood: DAS, Inc.

Stone, I. (1971). *The passions of the mind.* Garden City, NY: Doubleday.

Street, R. L., Brady, R. M., & Lee, R. (1984). Evaluative responses to communicators: The effects of speech rate, sex, and interaction context. *Western Journal of Speech Communication, 48,* 14–27.

Sullivan, H. S. (1953). *Conceptions of modern psychiatry.* New York: W. W. Norton.

Sullivan, H. S. (1953). *The interpersonal theory of psychiatry.* New York: W. W. Norton.

Sullivan, H. S. (1956). *Clinical studies in psychiatry.* New York: W. W. Norton.

Sullivan, H. S. (1962). *Schizophrenia as a human process*. New York: W. W. Norton.

Sullivan, H. S. (1970). *The psychiatric interview*. New York: W. W. Norton.

Sullivan, H. S. (1971). *The fusion of psychiatry and social science*. New York: W. W. Norton.

Sullivan, H. S. (1972). *Personal psychopathology*. New York: W. W.Norton.

Swinton, M. M., & Bassett, R. E. (1981). Teachers' perceptions of competencies needed for effective speech communication and drama instruction. *Communication Education, 30,* 146–155.

Sypher, B. D. (1984). The importance of social cognitive abilities in organizations. In R. N. Bostrom (Ed.), *Competence in communication: A multidisciplinary approach* (pp. 103–127). Beverly Hills, CA: Sage.

Thonssen, L., & Baird, A. C. (1948). *Speech criticism: The development of standards for rhetorical appraisal*. New York: Ronald Press.

Vaihinger, H. (1935). *The philosophy of 'as if', a system of the theoretical, practical, and religious fictions of mankind*. New York: Barnes & Noble.

Van Dijk, T. A., & Kintsch, W. (1985). *Strategies of discourse comprehension*. Orlando: Academic Press.

Vangelisti, A., Daly, J., & Mead, N. (in press). Correlates of speaking skills in the United States: A national assessment. *Communication Education.*

Van Hoeven, S. A. (1985). What we know about the development of communication competence. *Central States Speech Journal, 36,*33–38.

Van Riper, C., & Emerick, L. (1984). *Speech correction: An introduction to speech pathology and audiology*. Englewood Cliffs, NJ: Prentice Hall.

Warren, C. A. B. (1982). *The court of last resort: Mental illness and the law*. Chicago: University of Chicago Press.

Walzlawick, P., Beavin, J., & Jackson, D. D. (1967). *Pragmatics of human communication: A study of interactional patterns, pathologies, and paradoxes*. New York: W. W. Norton.

Weed, L. L. (1975). *Your health care and how to manage it*. Burlington, VT: PROMIS Laboratory.

Wellmon, T. A. (1988). Conceptualizing organizational communication competence: A rules-based perspective. *Management Communication Quarterly, 1,* 515–534.

Wheeless, V. E., & Berryman-Fink, C. (1985). Perceptions of women managers and their communicator competencies. *Communication Quarterly, 33,* 137–148.

Wiemann, J. M. (1977). Explication and test of a model of communicative competence. *Human Communication Research, 3,* 195–213.

Wiemann, J. M. (1978). Needed research and training in speaking and listening literacy. *Communication Education, 27,* 310–315.

Wiemann, J. M., & Backlund, P. (1980). Current theory and research in communicative competence. *Review of Educational Research, 50,* 185–199.

Wilde, O. (1918). *Fairy Tales and Poems.* New York: Boni & Liveright.

Wilson, E. O. (1978). *On human nature.* Cambridge: Harvard University Press.

Winans. J. A. (1931). *A first course in public speaking.* New York: Century.

Winans, J. A. (1938). *Speech making.* New York: D. Appleton Century.

Young, K. S. (1989). *The use of audience analysis by instructors and students in a basic public speaking course.* Unpublished master's thesis. The Pennsylvania State University.

Zimbardo, P. (1977). *Shyness: What it is and what to do about it.* Reading, MA: Addison-Wesley.

Zimbardo, P. (1986). The Stanford shyness project. In W. H. Jones, J. M. Cheek, & S. R. Briggs (Eds.), *Shyness: Perspectives on research and treatment* (pp. 17–25). New York: Plenum Press.

Zolten, J. J. (1982). *The use of premeditated humor in interpersonal relationships.* Unpublished doctoral dissertation. The Pennsylvania State University.

Zolten, J. J., & Phillips, G. M. (1985). *Speaking to an audience:* A *practical method of preparing and performing.* New York: Bobbs-Merrill.

WORKS THAT INFLUENCED THIS BOOK

Over a forty-year career, it becomes hard to remember what you read and when. I have the strong suspicion that there is little that is original in this book. What is new is the way the parts are put together. Following is an enumeration of the parts that have been most influential. These are books, all well worth reading, not cited in the references above, but very important in the completion of this work. I have offered brief comments on their content.

Artificial Intelligence and Cognitive Psychology

Braitenberg, V. (1984). *Vehicles: experiments in synthetic psychology.* Cambridge: MIT Press. An imaginative exposition of cybernetic systems.

Chomsky, N. (1975). *Reflection on language.* New York: Random House. This is probably the simplest and most readable of Chomsky's works. It should be required reading for those who want a contemporary view of language and communication.

Fearnside, W. W., & Holther, W. B. (1959). *Fallacy: The counterpart of argument.* Englewood Cliffs, NJ: Prentice Hall. A thorough survey of the semantic and syntactic fallacies of reasoning presented in simple fashion with illustrations.

Gardner, H. (1985). *The mind's new science: A history of the cognitive revolution.* New York: Basic Books. A synthesis of psycholinguistics, cognitive psychology, and artificial intelligence to provide an overview of the latest "new" discipline.

Graubard, S. (Ed.) (1988). *Daedalus: Artificial intelligence, 117* (1). A thorough compendium of the latest thought in AI featuring most of the distinguished authorities.

Haugeland, J. (Ed.) (1981). *Mind design: philosophy, psychology, artificial Intelligence.* Cambridge: MIT Press. An early survey of AI including some seminal theoretical works.

Hiltz, R. S., & Turoff, M. (1978). *The network nation.* Reading, MA: Addison-Wesley. A preliminary discussion of computerized communication networks.

Jackson, P. C., Jr. (1985). *Introduction to artificial intelligence.* New York: Dover Publications. A useful introductory text in AI.

Kluwe, R. H., & Spada H. (Eds.) 1980. *Developmental models of thinking.* New York: Academic Press. Prototypical models for simulating mental processing.

McDonald, J. (1950). *Strategy in poker, business, and war.* New York: W. W. Norton. An introduction to zero-sum games theory.

Macnamara J. (1982). *Names for things: A study of human learning.* Cambridge: MIT Press. A robust and readable introduction to linguistics as interpreted by cognitive science.

Minsky, M. (1986). *The society of mind.* New York: Simon and Schuster. A compelling primer of the fundamental logic of AI. This book is the starting point for anyone who wants to learn about artificial intelligence.

Orenstein, R. E. (1977). *The psychology of consciousness.* New York: Harcourt Brace Jovanovich. A foreshadowing of cognitive science.

Penfield, W. (1975). *The mystery of the mind.* Princeton: PrincetonUniversity Press, 1975. An attempt to synthesize the concepts of mind and brain.

Penfield, W., & Roberts, L. (1959). *Speech and brain mechanisms.* Princeton: Princeton University Press. The seminal work on neuroscience.

Rapoport, A. (1966). *Two-person game theory: The essential ideas.* Ann Arbor: University of Michigan Press. The basic introduction to the theory.

Searle, J. (1984). *Minds, brains, and science.* Cambridge: Harvard University Press. Searle opposes AI and offers good reasons.

Scher, J. (ed.) (1966). *Theories of the mind.* New York: Free Press. Although nearly twenty-five years old, this is the most thorough compendium of philosophical and scientific ideas about how the mind works. It contains the works of most major contributors.

Toffler, A. (1970). *Future shock.* New York: Random House. This is not quite a cognitive science book but its ideas have become the substance of much of the cognitive science text.

The Works of Ernest Becker

Becker is an unsung hero-philosopher who deals dramatically and incisively with the human condition. See the following:

(1962). *The birth and death of meaning.*. New York: Free Press.
(1964). *The revolution in psychiatry.* New York: Free Press.
(1968). *The structure of evil.* New York: Free Press.
(1973). *The denial of death.* New York: Free Press.
(1975). *Escape from evil.* New York: Free Press.

The Works of Sigmund Freud

The works of Sigmund Freud are collected and published in English in L. Strachey (Ed.), *The Complete Psychological Works: Standard Edition*, 24 vols. (London: Hogarth Press, 1953–1974). Strachey was chosen by Freud as his English translator. While there is some argument about the image of Freud presented by this edition, most available volumes of Freud's writings and criticisms thereof are extracted from, or based on, the *Standard Edition*. Recently, new Freudian papers have been released and are published under the authorization of Freud's estate. Working with the *Standard Edition* is materially simplified with the use of Carrie Lee Rothgeb (Ed.), *Abstracts of the Standard Edition of the Complete Psychological Works of Sigmund Freud* (New York: International Universities Press, 1973). I used the following extensively in this work: *Essays on Infant Sexuality, Psychopathology of Everyday Life, The Interpretation of Dream, Analysis Terminable and Interminable, Beyond the Pleasure Principle, Civilization and Its Discontents, and Jokes and the Unconscious.*

Clark, R. W. (1980). *Freud: The man and the cause.* New York: Random House. A readable and simple biography emphasizing the location of Freud's work in contemporary thought.

Gay, P. (1988). *Freud: A life for our time.* New York: W. W. Norton. The latest and most definitive biography.

Jones, E. (1953, 1955, 1957). *The life and work of Sigmund Freud.* 3 vols. New York: Basic Books. This is the authorized biography of Freud done by a disciple. It displays Freud as his followers want him to be seen.

Stone, I. (1971). *The passions of the mind.* Garden City, NY: Doubleday. Although a novel and very easy to read, this book is quite accurate as it describes the basic premises of Freudian theory. I have cited the story of Haeckel above from this book.

Sulloway, F. J. (1979). *Freud: Biologist of the mind.* New York: Basic Books. This is an important biography because it emphasizes the medical and physiological aspects of Freud's work.

Important Literary Works

Albee, E. (1974). *Who's afraid of Virginia Woolf?* New York: Pocket Books. This portrait of a perfect marriage is a fine illustration of combat theory.

van Bertelanffy, L. (1968). *General system theory.* New York: George Braziller. This is the seminal work on systems that exerted a powerful influence on the study of organizations.

Bracken, P. (1964). *I try to behave myself.* Greenwich, CT: Fawcett Crest Books. Ms. Bracken's book on etiquette illustrates the operation of rules in socialization.

Dickson, P. (1978). *The official rules.* New York: Dell Publishing.

Dickson, P. (1980). *The official explanations.* New York: Delacorte Press. These two works represent the largest collection of Murphy's Laws available. They are indispensible for anyone seeking logic in the way social life is lived. One needs to keep tabs on Dixon. He has recently updated his work on Murphy's Laws and currently runs the Center for Codification of the Laws Governing Human Existence in his basement in Garrett Park, MD.

Elliot, B., & Goulding, R. (1975). *Write if you get work: The best of Bob and Ray.* New York: Random House. Bob and Ray are able to put almost everything into perspective. This book has important information about cranberries and Komodo Dragons.

Fairlie, H. (1978). *The seven deadly sins today.* Notre Dame: University of Notre Dame Press. A survey of the dark side of human nature.

Farber, L. H. (1976). *Lying, despair, jealousy, envy, sex, suicide, drugs, and the good life.* New York: Basic Books. Another survery of the dark side of human nature. It is only coincidental that they are adjacent to one another.

Gilbert, W. S. (1980). *The Bab ballads.* Cambridge: Belknap Press. Whatever the topic, Gilbert had something to say about it.

Graves, R. (1982). *King Jesus.* New York: Straus, Giroux. This novel is an excellent exercise in alternative explanations.

Green, M. (1962). *Treasury of Gilbert and Sullivan: The complete librettos of twelve operas.* New York: Simon & Schuster. For my money, there is nothing like a G & S opera to make the natural order and its absurdities perfectly clear.

Hampden-Turner, C. (1981). *Maps of the mind: charts and concepts of the mind and its labyrinths.* New York: Macmillan. Written by a British polymath, this book is a splendid exercise in reduction of complex philosophies to simple systems. I have used this book as a text in epistemology since it was published.

Heller, A. (1982). *A theory of history.* Boston: Routledge & Kegan Paul. A defense of historical methodology.

Kwant, R. (1967). *Critique: Its nature and function.* Pittsburgh: Duquesne University Press. The most concise explanation of literary criticism.

Mencken, H. L. (1982). *The American scene.* New York: Vintage Books. An inspiration to cynics.

Parrington, V. L. (1930). *Main currents in American thought.* New York: Harcourt Brace. A survey of the history of American Ideas.

Potter, S. (1970). *The complete upmanship.* New York: Holt, Rinehart & Winston. A humorous (but accurate) picture of systematic combat among civilized people.

Solomon, R. C. (1976). *The passions: The myth and nature of human emotion.* Notre Dame: University of Notre Dame Press. An attempt at a formal taxonomy of emotional reifications.

Turnbull, C. (1972). *The mountain people.* New York: Simon & Schuster. A sombre presentation of the death of a society in confrontation with a hostile ecology.

Psychiatry

Chein, I. (1972). *The science of behavior and the image of man.* New York: Basic Books. A behaviorist answer to Freudian psychology.

Ellenberger, H. (1970). *The discovery of the unconscious: The history and evolution of dynamic psychiatry.* New York: Basic Books. A detailed standard history of psychiatry; especially strong on mapping influences of one authority on another.

Feldman, S. (1959). *Mannerisms of speech and gestures in everyday life.* New York: International Universities Press. Feldman, a main-line Freudian, classifies ordinary clichés and ascribes purposes to them.

Horney, K. (1937). *The neurotic personality of our time.* New York: W. W. Norton. Although an old work, it is an excellent and contemporary statement regarding the orderly process of neurosis.

Ichheiser, G. (1970). *Appearances and realities: Misunderstandings in human relations.* San Francisco: Jossey-Bass. Ichheiser makes the case that humans respond not to real events but to their memories and impressions of them.

Maliver, B. L. (1971). *The encounter game.* New York: Stein & Day. In essence, an exposé of encounter groups, especially on their deleterious impact on individual behavior because of inability to generalize results.

McKinnon, R. A., & Michels, R. (1971). *The psychiatric interview in clinical practice.* Philadelphia: W. B. Saunders. The standard manual on taking the psychiatric history.

Rabkin, R. (1970). *Inner and outer space.* New York: W. W. Norton. The relationship between external stimuli and internal scripts.

Schafer, R. A. (1976). *A new language for psychoanalysis.* New Haven: Yale University Press. A British taxonomy of psychoanalytic concepts.

Sheehan, S. (1983). *Is there no place on earth for me?* New York: Vintage Books. A novel-type view of the problems society has in dealing with those who do not fit.

Szasz, T. (1961). *The myth of mental illness.* New York: Harper-Hoeber. Szasz shocked the medical world when he presented this argument against the entitlement of diminished responsibility.

Torrey, E. F. (1972). *The mind game: Witchdoctors and psychiatrists.* New York: Emerson Hall. An analogy between civilized and uncivilized therapeutic practices.

Science

Bernal, J. D. (1954). *Science in history.* Cambridge: MIT Press. This four-volume work by a British Marxist-scientist develops the orderly trends in the maturation of science with special emphasis on economic motives.

Davies, P. (1982). *Other worlds: space, superspace, and the quantum universe.* New York: Simon & Schuster. A clean and simple introduction to modern physics.

Eckstein, G. (1970). *The body has a head.* New York: Harper & Row. A classic poetic work on physiology.

Edwards, A. L. (1957). *Techniques of attitude scale construction.* New York: Appleton-Century-Crofts. Still useful for its simple explanations of scaling methods.

Gleick, J. (1987). *Chaos: Making a new science.* New York: Viking. A mind-boggling exposition of an alternative to order.

Gould, S. J. (1989). *Wonderful life: The Burgess shale and the nature of history.* New York: W. W. Norton. The principles of paleontology offered as a challenge to social science.

Gregory, R. L. (Ed.). *The Oxford companion to the mind.* Oxford: Oxford University Press. An up-to-date compendium of mind/brain information.

Kuhn, T. S. (1970). *The structure of scientific revolutions.* Chicago: University of Chicago Press. Kuhn describes the process of change in scientific thought, demonstrating how shifts in paradigms open new and orderly lines of research.

Medawar, P. (1982). *Plato's "Republic."* Oxford: Oxford University Press. A scientist/humanist examines and criticizes human thought.

Thompson, G. (1960). *The factorial analysis of human ability.* Boston: Houghton Mifflin. Thompson book is the seminal work on factor analysis and highly important in understanding the mathematical metaphor for human behavior.

Trefil, J. S. (1980). *From atoms to quarks: An introduction to the strange world of particle physics.* New York: Charles Scribner's Sons. A layperson's presentation of the complexities of hard science.

Weed, L. L. (1975). *Your health care and how to manage it.* Burlington, VT: PROMIS Laboratory. Weed is the master diagnostician. This book describes his system for making and interpreting medical notes.

Wert, J. E., Neidt, C. O., & Ahmann, J. S. (1954). *Statistical methods in educational and psychological research.* New York: Appleton-Century-Crofts. An out-of-print old friend.

Shyness and Communication Apprehension

Bryngelson, B. (1966). *Clinical group therapy for problem people*. Minneapolis: T. S. Denison. Bryngelson was a speech pathologist who did pioneer work in the treatment of stage fright and stuttering.

Carnegie, D. (1964). *How to win friends and influence people*. New York: Simon & Schuster. The Dale Carnegie system has been very effective for several decades in instilling confidence in speakers. This is the best-selling book that sums up the system.

Daly, J. A., & McCroskey, J. C. (Eds.). *Avoiding communication: shyness, reticence, and communication apprehension*. Beverly Hills, CA: Sage. This book sums up the research done mainly in the field of speech communication on communication apprehension and shyness.

Jones, W. J., Cheek, J. M., & Briggs, S. R. (1986). *Shyness: Perspectives on research and treatment*. New York: Plenum Press. This book sums up the research on shyness done mainly in the field of psychology.

Kelly, L., & Watson, A. K. (1986). *Speaking with confidence and skill*. New York: Harper & Row. A simple textbook for overcoming shyness written from a performance point of view.

Social Psychology, Psychology, and Sociology

Bales, R. F. (1979). *SYMLOG: A system for the multiple level observation of groups*. New York: Free Press. A good illustration of how orderly procedure can be applied to the disorderly process of describing how people associate with one another.

Carson, R. C. (1969). *Interaction concepts of personality*. Chicago: Aldine Publishing. A good survey of symbolic interactionism with emphasis on the work of H. S. Sullivan and G. H. Mead.

Davis, M. S. (1973). *Intimate relations*. New York: Free Press. A basic work on interpersonal interaction.

Gould, S. J. (1981). *The mismeasure of man*. New York: W. W. Norton. This is an excellent work on possible errors in drawing inferences and making generalizations.

Haley, J. (1963). *Strategies of psychotherapy*. New York: Grune & Stratton. This book is unapologetically antipsychoanalysis. It is a compendium of strategies and tactics for modifying behavior based on the hypnotic theories of Milton Erickson. It is especially strong in its explanation of paradox.

Hebb, D. O. (1966). *A textbook of psychology*. Philadelphia: W. B. Saunders. Generations of college students were reared on this text.

Hunter, F. (1963). *Community power structures: A study of decision makers*. Garden City, NY: Doubleday Anchor. Hunter was the pioneer in mapping the use of power in community decision making.

Kleinman, A. (1988). *The illness narratives: suffering, healing, and the human condition*. New York: Basic Books. A remarkable work on taxonomy making orderly distinctions between abstract human conditions.

Kruskal, W. H. (Ed.). *The social sciences: Their nature and uses*. Chicago: University of Chicago Press. A series of articles on the weaknesses of social science and the fragility of social research.

Milgram, S. (1977). *The individual in a social world*. Reading, MA: Addison-Wesley. The kind of psychological findings humanists do not like to read.

Sartori, G. (Ed.). *Social science concepts: A systematic analysis*. Beverly Hills, CA: Sage. An excellent illustration of the logic of taxonomy.

Schoeck, H. (1966). *Envy: A theory of social behavior*. New York: Harcourt Brace & World. Discusses the role of the dark side in human motivation.

Speech Communication and Rhetoric

Arnold, C. C., & Bowers, J. W. (1984). *Handbook of rhetorical and communication theory*. Boston: Allyn & Bacon. A summary of current research in the discipline.

Benson, T. W. (1985). *Speech communication in the twentieth century*. Boston: Allyn & Bacon. Another compendium of current research in the discipline.

Esenwein, J. B., & Carnagey, D. (1915). *The art of public speaking*. Springfield, MA: Home Correspondence School. For those who may not recognize the spelling, this is Dale Carnegie's original book. It demonstrates that the field wasn't founded yesterday.

Foss, S. K., Foss, K. A., & Trapp, R. (1985). *Contemporary perspectives on rhetoric*. Prospect Heights, IL: Waveland Press. Good summaries of current rhetorical ideas, especially Kenneth Burke.

Fry, D. (1977). *Homo loquens: Man, the talking animal*. London: Cambridge University Press. A good and thorough simple introduction to linguistics.

Goodall, H. L., Jr., (1989). *Small group communication in oganizations* (2nd ed). Dubuque, IA: William C. Brown. A text on orderly procedure in group communication.

Goodall, H. L., Jr., (1989). *Casing a promised land*. Carbondale: Southern Illinois University Press. An introduction to a new way of looking at communication.

Hauser, G. A. (1986). *Introduction to rhetorical theory*. New York: Harper & Row. A survey of ancient and contemporary rhetorical theory with thorough documentation.

Hayakawa, S. I. (1972). *Language in thought and action*. New York: Harcourt Brace Jovanovich. A simple and practicaly application of general semantics.

Mulgrave, D. (1957). *Speech: A handbook of voice training, diction, and public speaking*. New York: Barnes & Noble. Unapologetic techniques for training speech delivery.

Murray, E. (1937). *The speech personality*. Chicago: J. B. Lippincott. An early work integrating social psychology and speech composition.

Wilson, J. F., & Arnold, C. C. (1983). *Public speaking as a liberal art* (5th ed). Boston: Allyn & Bacon. The prototypical (and one of the best) speech text.

Wilden, A. (1987). *The rules are no game: The strategy of communication*. London: Routledge & Kegan Paul. A stirring statement of the unspeakable: humans in a state of war.

Wood, J. T. (1982). *Human communciation: A symbolic interactionist perspective*. New York: Holt, Rinehart & Winston. An important text based on symbolic interactionism.

My Own Relevant Publications Not Cited Above

Phillips, G. M. (1965). PERT: Logical adjunct to the discussion process. *Journal of communication, 15*(2). The first appearance of the Standard Agenda for group decision making.

Phillips, G. M. (1966). *Communication and the small group*. New York: Bobbs-Merrill. In this book I introduced standard agenda as a teaching device.

Phillips, G. M. (1975). Introduction to the Og principle of research. In K. Johnson (Ed.), *Research designs in general semantics*. Dallas: Gordon & Breach. Some speculations on the relevance and accuracy of statistically based research in communication.

Phillips, G. M. (1976). Rhetoric and its alternatives for the study of interpersonal communication. *Communication quarterly, 24*(1). A synthesis of rhetoric theory with the intimate questions indigenous to interpersonal communication.

Phillips, G. M. (1978). Rhetoric and the proper study of mankind. *Communication Education 27*(3). A continuation of the notion that rhetorical criticism can be applied to social discourse.

Phillips, G. M. (1981a). Science and the study of human communication. *Human Communication Research, 7*(4). A mature statement of some of the hazards of behaviorism applied to social discourse.

Phillips, G. M. (1981). *Communicating in organizations*. New York: Macmillan. Introduction of formal structuring systems for analyzing organizational communication.

Phillips, G. M. (1984). *Support your cause and win*. Columbia: University of South Carolina Press. Application of rules of order to political campaigns.

Phillips, G. M. (1986). Men talking to men about their relationships. *American behavioral scientist, 29*(3). An example of the effectiveness of oral history as a research technique.

Goodall, H. L., Jr., & Phillips, G. M. (1984). *Making it in any organization*. Englewood Cliffs, NJ: Prentice Hall/Spectrum. Formalities of individual survival in the organizational milieu.

Phillips, G. M., & Eisenstein, L. (1985) *Adult problem solving*. Dubuque, IA: Kendall-Hunt. Application of standard agenda to problems of midlife crisis.

Phillips, G. M., & Erickson, E. C. (1970). *Interpersonal dynamics in the small group*. New York: Random House. Development of the standard agenda in a sociological mode.

Phillips, G. M., & Goodall, H. L., Jr. (1981). Assumption of the Burden: science or criticism. *Communication quarterly, 29*(4). Adjudication of the relationship between behavioral research and rhetorical criticism.

Phillips, G. M., & Goodall, H. L., Jr. (1983). *Loving and living.*. Englewood Cliffs, NJ: Prentice-Hall/Spectrum. Especially strong discussion of the formalities of interpersonal conflict.

Phillips, G. M., Metzger, N. J., & Butt, D. (1975). *Communication in education*. New York: Holt, Rinehart & Winston. A first: introduction of a list of competencies in oral communication.

Phillips, G. M., & Santoro, G. M. (1988). The use of computer-mediated communication in training students in group problem-solving and decision-making techniques. *American journal of distance education, 2*(1). A summary of an innovative method of teaching group discussion.

Phillips, G. M., Wood, J. T., & Pedersen, D. J. (1979). *Group discussion: A practical guide for participants and leaders*. Boston: Houghton, Mifflin. Development of communication behaviors associated with the steps of standard agenda for group discussion.

Phillips, G. M., & Wood, J. T. (1983). *Communication and human relationships*. New York: Macmillan. Orderly systems in interpersonal relationships.

Wyatt, N. J., & Phillips, G. M. (1988). *Studying organizational communication*. Norwood, NJ: Ablex. The heuristics of organizational research.

Index

Act, 146–147
Actuarial projection structure, 110
Agent (Agency), 143, 146
Algorithm of contingency, 131–132
American English: training systems in speaking, 93
Analogy structure, 109
Anthracologist, 268
Anxiety: absence of, 6; causes of, 243–244; Freudian conception of, 233–234, 242–243; interpersonal, 248–251; McCroskey view of, 242; methods of coping with, 245–248; moral judgment implied, 232; in personality, 250–251; as a psychoanalytic concept, 236–237; psychological manifestations of, 238–239; and shyness, 5; about social contact, 7; and social performance, 228–254; standard

definition, 236, 237–243; state, 253–254;
Apprehension and performance, 234–235
Argument structure, 111–113; cohortative tense, 113
Aristotle, 67, 74, 87
Artificial intelligence, 82, 96, 132–133, 140–141, 154, 225–226; basic assumption of, 142; structural fundamentals, 113–115
Artistic proofs, 73, 74, 262
Attention, 72
Audience, 166, 212
Audience analysis, 28, 85, 87, 128; problems in, 148–149

Beck, Aaron, 13
Behavior modification, 95, 159, 205–208
Biomedical research, 153–154

Structure (structuring), 28, 128;
available for discourse, 101–105;
basic, 104–105, 106; formal
process, 151–152; fundamentals
of, 105–124; general principles,
105–106; interpersonal goals,
152; mathematical set, 104;
message, 101; number of, 104; of
outlines, 102; principles of, 217;
programming, 98–105
Structure structure, 108–109
Style, 70, 79–80, 216–217; errors
in, 92; incompetence, 219
Sublimation, 244, 245
Sullivan, Harry Stack, 249–251
Sullivanian theory, 192
Superego, 15
Suspicion, 184–185
Symbols: defined, 131
Symmetrical relationships, 10
Systematic desensitization, 18, 204,
244

Tactical processing, 77–78
Taste, 297
Taxonomy structure, 107

Teaching. *See* Pedagogy
Textbooks on speaking, 61
Therapeutic alliance, 179–182, 207,
211
Therapeutic resistance, 182–190
Therapy eligibility, 283–284
Time structure, 109
Topical incompetence, 218
Topoi, 100, 258
Transference, 186
Trivium, 97

Unwillingness to communicate, 237

Van Riper, Charles, 36
Values, measurement of, 53
Visualization, 18
Voice: quality of, 59; vocal
variation, 60

Warren, Carol, 9
Wernicke's area, 100
Will, 71, 191, 227
Winans, James, 67

Zero-sum game, 260

Gerald M. Phillips received the B.A., M.A., and Ph.D. degrees from Western Reserve University (now Case-Western Reserve) in Cleveland, Ohio. He taught at the North Dakota Agricultural College and Washington State University before coming to The Pennsylvania State University, where he is a professor of speech communication. He recently celebrated his twenty-fifth anniversary at PSU. Since 1965, he has been director of the Penn State Reticence Program, a course directed at shy students. He has served in various editorial capacities with journals and publishing companies and is active in the American Civil Liberties Union. His claim to fame is that he has four grown children, all married, all working, all living away from home, and all of whom pick up the check about 50 percent of the time